BATH

The

ENIGMA

Second Edition

A History of Bath Rugby Club

1865 – 2020

By Harry W. Barstow

Paperback ISBN 978-1-78705-938-2
ePub ISBN 978-1-78705-939-9
PDF ISBN 978-1-78705-940-5

Published in the UK by MX Publishing
335 Princess Park Manor, Royal Drive, London, N11 3GX
www.mx-publishing.co.uk [UK]
www.mxpublishing.com [USA]

Cover Artwork compiled by Brian Belanger

featuring Bath players Jonathan Joseph (with ball), Thomas, Louw and Garvey

This book is dedicated to my family

for their wonderful support and patience during the time I have researched and written the 2nd edition of 'Bath the Enigma,' namely: **Kathryn** (my wife) for her computer skills that put mine to utter shame, her creative ideas and artistic input, and our two sons, **Adam** and **Thomas**.

ACKNOWLEDGEMENTS:

My sincere thanks to the following:

Anne Buchanan: Bath Library, the Podium;

Bath Chronicle (and sister papers): archives in Bath Library;

Ben Hartley: Bath Combination;

Bob Ascott: Photography; and assistant **Alan Grebby;** (www.rugbyrec.co.uk)

Derek Carter: Photography;

(the late) **Geoff Pillinger**:   Head of Bath Past Players' research team;

Kathryn Barstow: Computer advice/**Adam and Thomas Barstow**: photography

Kevin Lawrence: Chairman, Bath Rugby Supporters' club; (www.allez-bath.co.uk)

Mark Hoskins: (Hon) historian, Bristol RFC.;

Patrick Casey: Rugby historian, and author of 'For College, Club and Country,' (Clifton RFC).;

(The late) **Reg Monk:** photography;

'World Rugby Museum, Twickenham': www.rfu.com/museum (Tel: 020 8892 8877)

Cheltenham College: (Christine Leighton, archives);

Clifton College, (archives)

Edinburgh Academy (archives);

Kingswood School, Bath, (David Brown, archives);

Marlborough College, (Terry Rogers, archives); and Monkton Combe School, Bath, (archives

Foreword

It was back in 2015 when Harry Barstow asked me to write a Foreword for his first book. I am very pleased to say that he has written a second volume and he has asked me again to pen a few words.

This book takes us up to the present and is again full of rugby lore, facts and figures and interesting data.

But it is still the same Bath club, steeped in friendliness and intimacy that makes the Rec. a special place to be. Bath is a small city and it is easy to make acquaintances, even now with the fan base spread wider, that same atmosphere abounds..

Well done, Harry, for all your hard work and painstaking research.

Happy reading.

Radley Wheeler
aka "Mayor of Frome"

Front Cover: (courtesy of Getty Images) Josh Bayliss storms in for crucial try in Bath's last match win 30-24 vs Northampton. 12 June 2021.

Contents

Chapter 1. The Beginning …………………………………..………….. page 1

Chapter 2. Within the Rugby Triangle (1840's onwards)..................... page 4

Chapter 3. A Georgian to a Rugby City (Mid to later 19th Century)………page 9

Chapter 4. Bath, Bristol and Somerset, a special relationship. (latter 19th Century)...page 14

Chapter 5. No alternative – Separate ways…………………………….page 19

Chapter 6. New home, new challenge. (1890's onwards)………….…...page 21

Chapter 7. A New Century beckons.(The early 1900's)……………...….page 26

Chapter 8. In the midst of Winter. (1900's continued)...………….…......page 30

Chapter 9. Winter turns to Spring (1908 – 14)…………………...….….page 34

Chapter 10. The summer that never came.(1914)…………………..…....page 42

Chapter 11. A time of quiet reflection. (1914 – 18)………………..…....page 44

Chapter 12. The Greatest day in History. (11th Nov 1918)……………......page 48

Chapter 13. The Restoration (1919 – 20)……………………...….……page 50

Chapter 14. 1922-23 …..When Bath came of age…………………....….page 55

Chapter 15. A challenging mid-twenties..page 61

Chapter 16. The 1920's – A Landmark decade? …………………….….page 65

Chapter 17. A Country within a Country. (1930-35)……………....….…page 68

Chapter 18. A seemingly impossible challenge. (1935-39)…………..…...page 78

Chapter 19. In the lap of the Gods. (1939-45)………………………...….page 85

Chapter 20. Bath (1945-50) - Rugby Yeomen…………………....….…page 90

Chapter 21. Great days. (1950-55) ……………………………...….……page 97

Chapter 22. Era of uncertainty. (1955-60) …………………….....….page 106

Chapter 23. The Ultimate Challenge (1960-66) ……………...……….page 111

Chapter 24. The Enlightenment. (1966-69)……………………..…………page 118

Chapter 25. Mixed signals. (1969-75) …………………………………..page 126

Chapter 26. Age of Promise. (1975-80)…………………..……………..page 138

Chapter 27. Countdown to the season that changed everything. (1980-83)...page 149

Chapter 28. The year of Destiny. (1983-84) ……………..……………..…page 155

Chapter 29. Excalibur! (1984-86) ……………………..…………...…..…page 165

Chapter 30. A bolt of lightning. (1987-90) …………………...…………page 178

Chapter 31. To play with one heartbeat. (1990-94)………..…...…………page 188

Chapter 32. The Burial of the Hatchet. (1994-96) …………….…..……...page 205

Chapter 33. Triumph amid The Maelstrom (1996-2000) ……………........page 216

Chapter 34. The Fateful Hour. (2000-03) …………….…..………………page 222

Chapter 35. Walking the tight-rope. (2003-10) ………..…..…………….page 228

Chapter 36. So nearly the dream Anniversary. (2010-15) …………........page 244

Chapter 37. The Enigma (2015-2020). ………………………….….. page 255

       Review post 2019-20 Season…………………..…………….page 262

Chronology. ....page 263

Bibliography………………………………………………….…..page 279

Tables /Results etc…………………………………………………..page 281

Chapter 1. 'THE BEGINNING.'

It is a near certainty that playing with footballs (doubtless of various descriptions) reaches back into distant millennia, though no universal sets of rules or established governing bodies existed. Organised sport after all was somewhat limited in ancient times, albeit not forgetting chariot racing (the Romans' answer to stock car racing), and medieval jousting that would never in a million years have gained a licence from today's Health & Safety inspectorate. But cricket was already evident in 18th century England; and come the 19th century sport really 'took off,' not least thanks to developments at Cambridge University and Rugby School respectively. Initially, these two institutions attempted to consolidate football under one guiding set of rules. However, by the end of the 1830's (if not before) Cambridge undergraduates realised that consolidation might be impossible to achieve. For while Old Rugbeians argued that handling was legitimate, others (Old Etonians for example) begged to differ, and the result of this impasse was a divide, each side now embarking upon their own chosen course and culminating in 1863 with the publication by Cambridge University of the codified Association Football rules. The football world (literally the world) was now to adopt these very same rules globally, and thus football separated into two distinct forms, namely football (soccer) and football (rugby). The Rugby School version however had yet to be consolidated into anything other than a somewhat vague format of guidelines (and that's putting it mildly), and this remained the case until the rules (laws) were standardized in 1871.

But although we know, thanks to the Cambridge codification, the origins of 'modern' football (soccer), do we know with any accuracy the origins of 'modern' football (rugby)? Possibly 'yes,' although one should treat the scarce available evidence with caution because 'hard' (corroborated) proof is lacking. Nonetheless Matthew Bloxham, a former Rugby pupil from 1813-20, submitted an article to **The Meteor (the Rugby School magazine)** in October 1876, stating that he had learned from a source, regrettably unnamed, that the change from a kicking game to a handling game had "*…. originated with a town boy and a foundationer of the name of Ellis, William Webb Ellis.*" He would further add: "that [in 1823] one William Webb Ellis, whilst playing football, "*caught the ball in his arms. This being so, according to the then rules, he ought to have retired back as far as he pleased, without parting with the ball, for the combatants on the opposite side could only advance to the spot where he had caught the ball, and were unable to rush forward till he had either punted it or had placed it for someone else to kick, for it was by means of these placed kicks that most of the goals were in those days kicked, but*

1

the moment the ball touched the ground, the opposite side might rush on." Matthew Bloxham continues: "*Ellis for the first time, disregarded this rule, and on catching the ball, instead of retiring backwards, rushed forwards with ball in his hands towards the opposite goal, with what result as to the game I know not, neither do I know how this infringement of a well-known rule was followed up, or when it became, as it is now, a standing rule.*" So perhaps we never will now know 'how the infringement was followed up or when it became a fixed rule.' Yet interestingly, it seems that it was (is) a common misunderstanding to assume that it was forbidden to 'handle' the ball at Rugby School during this era. Instead, it was forbidden **'to run forwards with the ball in hand,'** not the same thing. Equally it is a misunderstanding to assume that Rugby School immediately prepared a set of rules and duly announced to a startled world their discovery of a new form of football to be known as rugby football; because the Webb Ellis story is merely a report of a pupil who (true or otherwise) reportedly broke the rules as then practiced on the football fields at Rugby. Nor did Rugby School codify its own version of football until 1845.

William Webb Ellis Photograph, courtesy of *Thomas J. Barstow*

Today alongside the school one can see the imposing statue of William Webb Ellis that commemorates this very event with the now legendary words: "*This stone commemorates the exploit of Will Webb Ellis who with a fine disregard for the rules of football as played in his time first took the ball in his arms and ran with it thus originating the distinctive feature of the rugby game A.D. 1823.*" Yet not everyone accepts the above exploits as valid. After all, Matthew Bloxham had actually left Rugby School three years prior to this particular game that has passed into folklore. But his brother John was a contemporary of Webb Ellis, and furthermore one is entitled to ask: "*why would Matthew Bloxham anyway wish to write a fiction?*" Yes, it appears that his account was not substantiated by other sources. But if inaccurate, then Bloxham himself would have risked almost certain ridicule. None came it seems. Indeed, if his comments had raised doubts then one would have expected that his contemporaries (surely the best jury in this matter) would have stated them openly. But, apparently, they didn't. Moreover, Webb Ellis was not a name plucked from an obscure archive at Rugby.

On the contrary, records tell us that he was a bright young pupil destined to gain a scholarship to Oxford. He was moreover a capable sportsman and a very good cricketer, playing for Oxford v Cambridge in the 1827 Varsity match. So, it is at least a possibility that **1823** might just be **'that year'** when handling the ball and running simultaneously towards the opposition laid the foundations of the game we know today. If so, then it was well timed, an era no less when Britain and Europe would experience a renaissance since that epic moment in 1815 when Waterloo had concluded some 20 years of European conflict. Now, the Industrial Revolution moved into over-drive, alongside a sporting revolution. Moreover, exactly twenty years since a youthful Webb Ellis reportedly broke those presumed rules of football, a rugby football club was founded in London, namely Guys Hospital in 1843. Initially playing on the open spaces of Blackheath near Greenwich, it was their early endeavours that perhaps inspired some of those who would later establish another club, one which took its name from that same venue.... Blackheath.

Now, it is sometimes claimed that Blackheath were the first 'open' club in the game's history, and they became known as 'The Club' precisely because in contrast to Guys, they were open to all-comers. And yet, the Liverpool club would dispute this, claiming that their formation on the 19th December 1857 got them across the 'start-line' just ahead of Blackheath (founded in 1858). **The Rugby Football Union** itself was formed six years later, the twenty-one founder members attending their inaugural meeting at London's Pall Mall Restaurant, Regents Street in *1871*; and included among those members would be the Harlequins, Richmond, Blackheath and Guys Hospital, all of them rugby families destined to adorn the pages of an illustrious rugby history. Others however, for instance Queens House (Greenwich) and the once famed Old Boys club, namely the Marlborough Nomads, would pass into the pages of that same history. Meanwhile, it was in 1871 that the first standardised laws for Rugby football were finalised; and at Raeburn Place, Edinburgh, the first rugby international was played (between Scotland versus England), with the hosts winning by one goal and one try against England's single try. Then, one year onwards in 1872 at Menton in the south of France, the days of one William Webb Ellis would end, having devoted his life to service with the Church. Yet it seems that we can only guess if he ever played in any official game of rugby football, or ever expressed an interest in its later developments, a perplexing fact for those seeking to establish the accuracy or otherwise of that oft-quoted report of a one-time pupil who *"first took the ball in his arms and ran with it."* But......someone it seems claimed to have witnessed such a game, and noted too the part played by a certain player. That player (as quoted by M.H. Bloxham) was indeed **William Webb Ellis**....and who are we from this distant point in history to dismiss outright such a report of a possibly pressed-ganged participant, maybe clueless as to what on earth he was supposed to do, who then ran with the ball (at that time in the wrong direction). And, rightly or otherwise we revere this young schoolboy. Indeed, the rugby World Cup is named in his honour as the Webb Ellis Cup. And his name will surely live-on wherever the sport is played.... forever!

Chapter 2. WITHIN THE RUGBY TRIANGLE. (The 1840''s onwards)

Bath Football Club, founded in 1865, is thought to be the first open club in the West Country, although the circumstances surrounding club's formation are not exactly clear. While it is known that the Clifton club (founded 1872) was formed by ex-pupils of Clifton College, is it possible that another rugby playing school (or schools) directly influenced those who the founded the Bath club? The answer is 'no,' since Kingswood, almost certainly the city's first rugby-playing school did not introduce the game until 1868-69 (see: *History of Kingswood School, p. 265).* But though it is probable that Bath would follow Kingswood's later progress (and vice versa) it is possible that certain sporting enthusiasts in the city (see Chapter 3) were already aware of rugby developments at Marlborough College. There is no certainty here, though 'invaluable' details of the formative years of the rugby-game are recorded in their college archives. Situated twenty-five miles east of Bath and founded in 1843, Marlborough ranks among the great influences in the game's early development, and it was partly thanks to the arrival *"of [Mr] Cotton as Master in 1852, bringing with him the traditions of the Rugby Bigside ...."* that rugby would gain a strong foothold at the College. The early format would doubtless have been a culture-shock to the uninitiated (see: *A History of Marlborough College, 1843-93, Ch. XXV),* not least the sight of that curious rugby ball, of which one had already been displayed at the Great Exhibition (Crystal Palace) in 1851. Meanwhile rugby posts now existed, the art of drop-kicking encouraged, and each team could comprise some forty or even fifty players, though none enjoying rights of protection from the Geneva Convention, and *"when a player was collared he was supposed to be bound to have the ball down, but not infrequently he had to be 'scragged' into submission...."* And if that doesn't sound bad enough, there was the infamous 'grovel,' and the name says it all, whereby the ball and its carrier could be held up over the line to secure (or not to secure) a touchdown.

Not surprisingly it would have been a rarity to see anything approaching a swift passing movement, and the rules were, to put it mildly…. liberal. Admittedly 'hacking' over a player (hooking the instep of an opponent's leg) was frowned upon at Marlborough, though not at some schools. But good old scragging was allowed, so too tripping a running player. Thus, initially this was a sort of hybrid game, part soccer, part rugby and part chaotic. But did Marlborough's law-abiding majority really enjoy this form of 'recreation? For the bigger guys the answer was a probable *"you bet."* Less certain is how the smaller guys felt. After all, initially *"anybody who cared to put in an appearance was welcome to play, but* [hardly surprisingly] *no more than thirty or forty pupils out of the entire School availed themselves of the doubtful privilege."* In house-matches a team could be sixty strong and one tactic was to grab the unfortunate smaller guys in order to be *"thrown on to the top of the 'squash' to bring it down."* However, the decision of Mr Tomkinson (the Bursar) to permit beer for capped players doubtless provided a rocket-booster to recruitment, and the College would later move to the forefront of rugby development. And there was much to develop, including methods of scoring. For instance, in the formative years the chief aim in rugby was to kick goals, and under Marlborough rules these could be gained by a place kick or a drop goal. In fact, until 1869, Marlborough allowed a goal to be scored from a punt. The scrums, known then as scrimmages, consisted of players standing upright, while tries initially counted for nothing at Marlborough, nor it seems, anywhere else. Although the first ever recorded inter-school (rugby) match had already been held in Scotland on 13th February 1858

The Marlborough XX 1867.
Acknowledgements to Marlborough College

between Merchiston Castle versus the High School, it is thought that the **Marlborough v Clifton College** game (20th November 1864, Mr T. Rogers, Marlborough archivist) is generally regarded as the **first inter-school rugby game in England.** The delay in commencing inter-school competition is hardly surprising however, for there were no cars or coaches available. Furthermore, at an isolated Marlborough College there were no other established clubs or rugby playing schools in the neighbourhood either. But, when the railway began to connect the Nation ('thank you' Mr Brunel and friends) it seems probable that it was the train that enabled Clifton to reach Marlborough via the Swindon junction, while horse-carriages would presumably have then brought the team to their destination; and if it was cold on that winter's journey across the Wiltshire Downs, then no matter, because on the rugby field the temperature was about to get decidedly hot.

However, Clifton College, founded in 1862, were a team of barely two years rugby experience and, there was another difficulty during this era regarding different interpretations of the rules: Marlborough had always permitted both tripping and scragging. Clifton went one better. They permitted tripping, scragging and…. Hacking! And this was just asking for trouble! The two teams that day were twenty strong and Marlborough were captained by J.A. Boyle, described as a 'fast runner and a sure place-kicker,' and moreover rated a brilliant "drop" (i.e.: a drop goal specialist). Meanwhile the match soon got somewhat heated, not least as Clifton, having agreed beforehand to refrain from their own practice of hacking, nonetheless found it increasingly hard to resist the temptation to do so. Marlborough's reaction was predictable. They too began hacking. Things then deteriorated further and skipper Boyle was heard to shout a request to a member of staff (one Dr Bradley): *I think we'd better stop the game, sir, hadn't we?"* But Dr Bradley would have none of it, and his 'Nelsonian' response said it all: *"No, no! They'll think we're afraid of them. Win the game first, and then talk about stopping if you like!"*

Well J.A. Boyle did just that, and with time fast running out, he dropped a 'beauty' plumb between the Clifton goal-posts.' But, the friendliest of occasions this was not. Indeed, Marlborough's own post-match report included the observation that *".... the harmony of the game was rather spoilt by differences as to rules and the rather eccentric notions on hacking that the Cliftonians seemed to have."* But as always, there are two sides to a rugby tale, and not surprisingly Clifton's C.B.L. Tylecote (see: a History of Clifton College, pp. 272-3) saw things differently: *"I was one of the Clifton football team that went to play against Marlborough. What a match it was! You could hardly call it football!! I was playing full-back, and being pretty quick on my feet in those days, got off pretty cheaply."* He was obviously one of the lucky ones, because by all account's others were somewhat less fortunate. Furthermore, such was the angst aroused during this inaugural 'clash' that these two great rugby schools would not resume fixtures until 1891. But if the tactics that day in 1864 were somewhat basic, so too was their rugby kit, with trousers (casuals) simply tucked into socks, while shorts (and initially they would be knee-length) were not common until the 1890's. Boots would be stud-less, with bars (usually two) instead of studs; and while changing-rooms would often be arranged by clubs with a local pub or inn, schools would utilise their own facilities. Indeed, in these formative years it was sometimes the schools who were the teachers and the clubs their pupils and, when in 1872 the Clifton club was founded, they announced that they would play *"as at Clifton College,"* although they stipulated that it would not follow the practice of tripping or hacking!

Meanwhile, until the late 1870's the backs were primarily a defence line, and little else. They were positioned behind the forwards, often only four in number, and consisting of two half-backs (i.e.: half-way back behind the forwards) and two other backs who were positioned well back in defence (i.e.: full-backs). It was during the 1860's however that Marlborough (and probably other teams) were already experimenting with another back player who was positioned between the half-backs and the full-backs; in other words, positioned three-quarters back behind the forwards and hence the origin of the 'three-quarter' terminology. Even so, for some years this lone three-quarter-back was simply an extra tackler. Indeed, not until the 1870's and the perception of those such as Sydney Morse of Marlborough (later Marlborough Nomads & England) did this attitude change, when Morse concluded that a three-quarter-back could also fulfil an attack role. But these were still 'early days' and would remain so at Marlborough until the captaincy of the legendary England international Harry Vassall in the late 1870's. Vassall's days at Marlborough, followed by his inspirational leadership at Oxford University in the early 1880's would help transform rugby football from the negative to the positive and from defence to attack, not least due *"to the plan of systematic combination among the forwards which he evolved."*

As for the all-important question of scoring, confusion reigned well beyond 1871 when the RFU had established the official laws of rugby football, and this partly explains why games were not infrequently recorded with two quite different results that depended entirely upon whose scoring method one was utilising. Indeed, Marlborough were but one school/club who during the 1860's had devised their own scoring system, their rules reading thus: *"3 Rogues (touchdown by defence behind their own goal line) =1 touchdown. 4 touchdowns = 1 goal. 3 goals = a game was won."* Nor was it unknown for the method of scoring to depend upon negotiations between the two captains prior to the game, nor uncommon therefore to see a result given not in points actually scored, but rather by the way scores were made. Hence the **first ever rugby international** (Scotland v England, 1871, (in Edinburgh) was scored as follows: *"Scotland won by 1 goal, 1 try as against 1 try by England."* Meanwhile in 1873 the Anglo-Scottish momentum continued with the first game between Carlisle and Scottish Border club Langholm, an encounter that both clubs claim (with perhaps a touch of poetic licence) as the first ever 'international' club fixture.

Meanwhile, to the north of Bath lay Cheltenham College, who alongside Marlborough and Clifton now completed a geographical West Country triangle of three inspirational centres of rugby. Founded in 1841, Cheltenham College had adopted the rugby game as early as 1844 thanks partly to the influence of Charles Acton (later Ball-Acton) from Rugby school. However, as was invariably the case during this period, the rugby played in Cheltenham's early days had little resemblance to the game the college would later help to inspire. Indeed, one chastened pupil described it thus: *"….as merely a rush in which someone is sure to go down and perhaps get well kicked before he gets up again;"* good training for one **Francis D'Aguilla** on later serving as a major (Royal Engineers) in the Afghan War of 1878-80, but not before gaining the distinction as **Bath's first international** when capped for a victorious England in their second encounter against Scotland at the Kennington Oval in February 1872. Moreover, the D'Aguila name lived on through his brother J.D'Aguila, who captained both Bath and Somerset from the late 1870's to the mid-1880's, and J.B.S. D'Aguila (a son) who would later play for both

Bath and Somerset in the 1890's.

The Cheltenham College name would live on too, and when Francis D'Aguila ran out with England at the Oval, so too did fellow Cheltonians William Pinching (England) and likewise Renny Tailyour and W. Brown for Scotland. Capable therefore of producing no less than four internationals in a single international match, it is hardly surprising that the College's sphere of influence would extend far beyond the Cotswolds. In fact, it would extend as far as Cardiff who, on their formation in 1872 chose initially to adopt the Cheltenham College rules. This link then continued for a number of years and it was in season 1883-4 that Cardiff, on a visit to the College, reportedly fielded the game's **first four three-quarter system** into their back division.

As for the Cheltenham College rules, there were in addition those originating at Clifton and Marlborough, and probably one will never know just how many variations did exist until the official RFU laws were finally accepted as uniform throughout the game. Indeed, at Cheltenham one player claimed that he had played under seven (yes, seven!) different sets of rules during his playing career, and Wiveliscombe in West Somerset (once a formidable side) were another club who had produced their own version in 1872, albeit the **RFU had already issued their formalized laws of rugby in 1871**. But in an era when communications were not exactly 21st century, it would take at least a decade before the official laws had fully percolated down to the far corners of the game itself. Indeed, not until 1880 did Cheltenham College itself fully adopt those same RFU laws formulated in 1871. Rule variations notwithstanding, the rugby trio of Clifton, Cheltenham and Marlborough proved worthy disciples of Rugby School. Clifton produced three England 'captains' in E.K. Scott (1948), P.D. Young (1955) and D.G. Perry (1965), and a stream of internationals (for England, Wales, Ireland and Scotland) have flowed from the ranks of Cheltenham College, while Marlborough's influence reached not only westwards, but equally to London with the formation of their remarkable Old Boys club, namely the Marlborough Nomads (London based and among the original members of the RFU), who from their formation in 1868 to their sad disbandment in 1911 competed at the highest levels of the game. As for internationals, Old Marlburians seemed to run off a conveyor belt, with some twenty-nine players for England even before the 1914-18 War. It is no mere coincidence therefore, that within the influence of this 'Rugby Triangle' a group of formidable clubs would emerge, namely Bath, Bristol, Gloucester (and not forgetting the Cheltenham club), and whose collective genesis in all probability was partly influenced by a trio of famous rugby schools, namely Marlborough, Clifton and Cheltenham.

Chapter 3. A GEORGIAN TO A RUGBY CITY. (The mid to later 19th century)

When (1836 to 1841) Isambard Brunel was constructing a two-mile railway tunnel under North Wiltshire's towering Box Hill, he could hardly have guessed who one of the beneficiaries might be. But once this railway link from London's Paddington to the far corners of the West Country was completed, it proved a Godsend to a string of rugby clubs, among them Bath, a club which (see Bath Football Club, Centenary book, 1865-1965, p.17): *"was formed by a few enthusiastic men of the city."* Among these enthusiasts was Mr T.Gandy (later a chairman of the club), Mr Walter Sants and Mr Martin Wood, while later (1882-3) Major-General C. Fitzroy Mundy would be the club's first President. Moreover, the club is generally recognised as the first rugby club in the South West, and as was common practice in the 19th century they described themselves as 'football clubs.' The Bath Centenary book (p. 17) suggests that *"there is no doubt that [the game] originally came to Bath through the colleges in the city."* But did they? Because unfortunately no dates are given to establish this claim, and a number of local rugby schools folded prior to or during the Great War. Moreover, their relevant records are scarce at best or no longer exist; although it is certain that Bath College fielded a full XV by 1878 (see: Bath College Register, 1878-1908, p.123, at Bath Records Office, the Guildhall, Bath). However, it is possible that these *'few founding enthusiasts'* were aware of the rugby developments within the Marlborough-Clifton-Cheltenham Triangle.

And we do know from the **Kingswood School** archives (History of Kingswood School, p.265) that in the late 1860's when former pupil Frederick Robert Wilton (by now a Cambridge graduate) returned, he *"introduced a new code of football rules, drawn up by the masters for the use of the school. This would be 1868 or 1869. The rules were quite impracticable, and were soon withdrawn; then we fell into a kind of spurious Rugby, which served its purpose fairly well."* So, here we have written confirmation of actual dates **(1868-69) when the game was introduced at a Bath School**. And interestingly, Kingswood played a Bath XV on the Rec on 26th October 1977 (Bath winning 30-7) to commemorate their *rugby centenary*, unaware that the celebrations were staged almost a decade too late. **Bath however, celebrating their own centenary in 1865,** had commenced the game some three seasons prior to Kingswood, and so it seems likely that they, *not the colleges,* founded the game in the city.

Furthermore, it was to the club's good fortune that during the winter months they had access to the broad expanses at North Parade, and the Centenary Book (p.18) refers to an 1871 report in Keene's Bath Journal of *"an interesting [rugby] match that was played on the North Parade Ground"* between Bath and Bedminster, with the opposition captain kicking the game's one and only goal. It was a certain W.G. Grace, the same 'WG' who would pass into cricketing legend. But Bath did not stay North Parade. Indeed, they proceeded to make a 'grand tour' of the city with venues including the Lambridge Meadows, Claverton Down, the Kensington Meadows, next a possible short stay at the Taylor's Field along the Warminster Road, followed by arrival at Henrietta Park. And interestingly a letter (Bath & Wilts Chronicle & Herald, 6 Sep.1930) from club enthusiast

Frank Melluish refers to most of these venues when describing his first visits some *"48 years ago"* to watch Bath, a club which he says: *"played first at Lambridge, then Kensington Meadows, then in Henrietta Park, later on the Rec [far side of the ground] and now on the present side by the river."* His reference to the move to Henrietta Park is significant, since it was there that fortune smiled with the availability of the Pulteney Meadows. Now Pulteney Meadows was to be the 'Big One,' but not before the club considered adding something extra to the club's name, apparently a fashionable practice at this time. Hence initially Bath were known as the Bath Zoaves (famed French-trained Algerian troops). But this name didn't really 'catch on.' So, they had another try, namely the Bath Rovers. This too hit the buffers. Bath Wanderers didn't fare much better either. So, they settled for Bath once again save for the addition of 'Bath Rugby' come the professional era.

Naturally, there could be no rugby without fixtures, and the following Bath list for season 1880-81 and possibly the first complete list on the club records, states who they were now playing (see: Centenary book, p. 19):

1880/1881.

October	30th	Great Western FC at Bath.
November	3rd …	Wells FC at Bath.
"	6th …	Devizes FC at Bath.
"	13th…	Rockleaze FC at Bath.
"	17th……..	Competitive College – College Ground.
"	20th…..	Bath College – College Ground.
"	24th….	Weston super Mare at Bath.
"	27th…	Competitive College – College Ground.
December	4th…	Swindon Rangers FC at Bath.
"	11th…	Bristol Grammar School at Bath.
"	15th…	Wells FC at Wells.
"	18th…	Westbury Park FC at Bath.
January	1st	.. Rockleaze FC at Bristol.
"	8th	… Clifton FC at Bath.
"	15th	…Devizes FC at Devizes.
"	22nd	Clifton FC at Redland.
"	26th	…Bristol Medical School at Bath.
"	29th	…Swindon Rangers at Swindon.
February	12th	….Great Western FC at Swindon.
"	26th	….Weston super Mare at Weston super Mare.
March	5th	. ….Westbury Park FC at Clifton.

Later, Clifton and Gloucester featured among Bath's fixtures of the 1880's, and as early as **1872 when Francis D'Aguila's had won his debut cap for England** (see also Ch. 2) a young forward by the name of Herbert Fuller had joined the club. Albeit a mere nineteen years of age, Bath awarded him the club captaincy. It proved a wise decision, for Fuller (at times a Clifton player too) was both gifted and a born leader. He won six Blues at Cambridge, and then between1882-84 six caps for England, proving again that Bath could provide players of international class. True others, Blackheath for example,

The England XX that beat Scotland at the Kennington Oval (5 Feb 1872) One player and his signature is absent from the Photograph. D'Aguila (circled) was Bath's first International player.
Photograph by kind permission of the World Museum of Rugby, Twickenham.

produced many more internationals in those early years. But Bath had demonstrated that they too could produce players of top quality.

Furthermore, in addition to Bath's international contingent (eg: D'Aguila) there was a growing momentum for rugby among local schools in the city, including **Monkton Combe,** who switched from soccer to rugby in 1878 (see: A goodly heritage, A History of Monkton School, 1868-1967, p. 34). This local rugby parish duly extended to the

Competitive College, Grosvenor School, the Hermitage School, and Bath College, each privately run; though as mentioned none sadly surviving beyond the Great War. Meanwhile Bath Grammar School (later King Edward's) was competing against the likes of Kingswood by 1882, and not surprisingly the Bath club wanted a slice of this local action for a potentially invaluable source of future players. Indeed, Monkton Combe had barely got their rugby posts up before Bath arranged a friendly against these newcomers, winning (rather embarrassing if they had lost) by 2 goals and 1 try to nil.

It was hardly surprising therefore that **local school's rugby** would extend further afield, and the 1888-9 fixtures of Kingswood reflected this expansion (see: History of Kingswood School, p.221):

Hermitage:	Won 2 goals 2 tries to nil;
Bristol G.S.:	Won 2 tries to nil;
Monkton Combe:	Won 1 goal to nil;
Old Boys:	Won 2 tries to 1 try;
Hermitage:	Lost 1 goal to 4 tries;
Monkton Combe:	Lost to 2 goals;
Wycliffe College:	Lost 1 goal to 4 goals 2 tries;
Bristol G.S.:	Draw 2 tries each;
Wycliffe College:	Lost to 3 goals 1 try.

Prior Park College and Beechen Cliff would be among others to later join this rugby family, and it was inevitable therefore that the rugby DNA of this Georgian city would be further enhanced as a result of this expansion, producing (among other players) the Timmins brothers of Bath College, of whom forward T.B. Timmins would later captain Bath from 1903-1906, while England Trialist centre James Timmins would step into the Bath team in the late 1890's to play for the club and Somerset with distinction for more than a decade (see: Bath College Register, 1878-1908, Bath Records Office, Guildhall, Bath). Then there was winger Vincent Coates (Monkton Combe and later Haileybury & ISC) who would one day accompany Timmins in the same Bath team, and who was set to achieve great things.

'But what of a club-house,' one asks, the 'home from home' where rivalry on the pitch is (fingers crossed) transformed into friendship off it.' And the answer is that for many years the club did not have one. So, they improvised, and included among their 1890's favourites was the Christopher Hotel, and also the Angel Hotel in Westgate Street; while from 1914 onwards the Red House was utilised until the opening of the Club House on the Rec in 1954. Even so, for Bath to evolve fully into a rugby city there remained one not immediately obvious piece of the jig-saw to be put into place; though by the early 1880's put in place it certainly was with the arrival on the rugby scene of Walcot, or to be more precise.... the Victoria club. Not for the first time, few if any in Bath would have foreseen the significance when in 1882 a newly formed club-side appeared along the Upper Bristol Road at Victoria Park; and since the Park was the venue for home matches,

Victoria was the name the club adopted. It was not the only such club in and around the city formed during this era. But Victoria, later re-named Walcot Victoria in 1893 and finally to Walcot in 1895 were to be the first of a remarkable family of 'Junior' clubs destined to underpin rugby in the city, and who would form themselves into a thriving **Bath Combination** in season 1901-2. With this Combination and numerous schools adopting the game, the rugby foundations of the city were now effectively complete; and at its centre was a Bath club that, with Soane (first capped for England in 1893) already boasted three internationals to its credit. Thus, did this Georgian city become a Rugby city too. And none too soon either. For during this era the wider game was undergoing far-reaching changes. Hence a further question now required answers: 'could Bath show that they too had the capability to successfully adapt to the ever-growing competition now set to confront them?'

Chapter 4. BATH, BRISTOL AND SOMERSET–A SPECIAL RELATIONSHIP, (latter 19th century).

As Bath stepped into the 1880's they were by now part a rugby family that had rapidly undergone many changes. By the late 1870's the game had already discarded 20-a-side rugby for the 15-a-side game; the Home Internationals now included Ireland and Wales, joining in 1875 and 1881 respectively; and at the club level Blackheath had risen to the forefront of the game, and one distant day a 'son' of this same London club would arrive at Bath and set this West Country family on the road to greatness: his name.... Peter Sibley! And, during the latter 19th century it was men such as Harry Vassall who transformed the game (see Ch. 2), the Old Marlburian whose captaincy of Oxford University in the early 1880's helped transform the forward tactics of rugby. Meanwhile his native county of Somerset (for whom he played) featured another highlight of the 1880's, namely the emerging popularity of county rugby. Then....in 1888 another outstanding West Country club was founded, namely Bristol, resulting in a rivalry with near neighbours Bath that would prove to be perhaps unique in English rugby. Bristol in fact could hardly have timed their arrival better, as this same 1880's era would witness (inter alia) the **development of the four-man three-quarter line,** with two centres and two wings. Officially, this story begins with Cardiff. But it is possible that it began with a somewhat less known club, namely Wiveliscombe in west Somerset, where among its 19th century inhabitants lived the sports-worshipping Hancock family. By trade they were brewers, a family of ten sons (two thirds of a rugby team) of whom seven would progress to play for Somerset. And of these, Froude Hancock (a giant of his day) would play for England; while Frank (moving to the family's business branch in Cardiff) would later grace the Welsh team as a back, or to be precise, a three-quarter back.

Here, one is indebted to the former Vice Presidents of Wiveliscombe R.F.C., namely Mr & Mrs Ted and Margaret Baker, and to Mr D.E. Davies (author of 'Cardiff Rugby Club, history & statistics 1876-1975') who, writing of the 1883-4 season, refers to 'the Cardiff club when short of a three-quarter to go to Cheltenham College.... secured the services of F.E. Hancock, recently arrived from Wiveliscombe. Two tries were scored that day, both by Hancock, and Cardiff realised immediately that here was a special talent in their midst. However, this presented the selectors with a headache for Cardiff's next (and more demanding) encounter at formidable Gloucester. The Welsh club were reluctant to drop the talented Hancock but, with their three regular backs available again, and with a surplus of riches at their disposal, Cardiff opted for the unorthodox. Thus, the team-sheet was duly produced, and there was something unusual about the line-up, because instead of nine forwards, there were eight. Instead of six backs, there were seven. And, instead of three names in the three-quarter backs, there were four, namely: W. B. Norton, Tom Williams, A.J. Stuart ....and F. Hancock.' Thus, did Cardiff meet Gloucester on 23rd February 1884, and though no scores were recorded, those present would doubtless have realised that the potential for 'open' play could be transformed as a result of the four three-quarters positioned between two half-backs and a full-back in a back division increased to seven; with virtually half a team operating in open play outside the scrum. The fact that a club such as Cardiff had adopted this format partly explains why this new concept caught the attention of others, and come season 1888-9 the Welsh national side also adopted the formation, likewise Somerset in season 1890/1 and by each of the Home Unions by the mid-1890's. And Bath? Well, the later match programme of Sat. 29 Feb.1936 (Bath v Bristol 100th match anniversary game) states that Bath first played with four three-quarters in 1888, in fact their first ever game against Bristol, and no more appropriate occasion could have been chosen. For the tale of Bath and Bristol is itself a history in its own right, and one in which coincidence would play a mysterious role in the decades that followed.

This inaugural game (according to the above 100th match anniversary programme) was played on Bath's Kensington Meadows on 27th October 1888, and Bristol, though recently founded, were nonetheless not newcomers to rugby. For they were an amalgamation, one led by the Carlton club, who had convinced rivals Redland Park that combining forces was essential if they were ever to rival the then formidable Clifton on equal terms. Westbury Park too were invited to join, but declined. However, the newly formed Bristol was to exert so strong a pull on local players that Westbury Park would fold as a direct result of their own players switching to the Bristol club. And talk about jumping in at the deep end, because Cardiff were among Bristol's first opponents and the West Country club lost heavily. But, their first game against Bath (according to the afore-mentioned programme) finished with a draw at three minors each. Ah, but if only the accounts of early rugby history were that simple. Because, as Bristol RFC archivist Mark Hoskins explains, details are complicated somewhat by Bristol records indicating that the inaugural game of 27th October 1888 was played, not at Bath, but at Bristol's County ground, Bath winning 3-5; while the records further report that a return match was played on 2nd February 1889 at Bath's Kensington Meadows, the Bathonians winning again by five points to nil. However, there are possible explanations for such discrepancies. First, in those formative years it was not unknown for different clubs to play by marginally different rules, and/or to apply somewhat different methods of scoring. Secondly, during these same early years, contemporaneous notes of rugby matches were not always produced, press reporting (assuming there was any) was often vague, so much could depend on memory. And memory is not always a reliable source of facts.

Yet the most significant outcome to emerge from the commencement of Bath v Bristol encounters was the forging of a Special Relationship of friendship, despite an intense rivalry. Furthermore, the impressively high standards soon to be set by Bristol would test Bath to the very limits of their resources and capabilities. Indeed, the sheer scale of the challenge was shown clearly enough some forty-eight years later at the time of the 100th official game between the two clubs. For while eleven matches had been drawn, Bristol had already won 71 encounters and Bath a mere 17. Indeed, it seemed at one stage that this domination might last forever! But, it was to Bath's credit that save for one exception that would be revealed on the occasion of that same 100th game (see Ch.18), they never

15

allowed themselves to become resentful of Bristol's undoubted achievements. Instead, they would draw inspiration from them, and it was precisely this attitude that many decades later would yield the richest of dividends. Meanwhile prior to the formation of Bristol, there was already the aforementioned Clifton club to think about, who in their first full season played Bath twice and comfortably beat Bath twice. Now, the Cliftonians (founded in 1873) shared many similarities with Bath, not least by their respective localities set amid the charms of Georgian splendour. Yet there existed one crucial difference, for while Bath were sufficiently close to Bristol to be a rival club, they were far enough away 'not' to be in contention for players. This contrasted dramatically with the challenge facing Clifton. They were certainly close enough to be rivals, but anything 'but' far enough away to avoid competition for that most essential of commodities......players! Hence Clifton, who in their first season had already produced a full England international in James Bush and another by the late 1880's in Hiatt Cowles Baker, found themselves in direct competition with Bristol. Bath fortunately were to be spared this drawback. And fortune smiled again during the 1880's when Bath discovered the potential of one Frank Soane, then a mere fifteen years of age who at school played soccer. He also played rugby. And play rugby he 'sure could!'

A forward, he grew strong and powerful. They called him 'Buster' for the simple reason he tackled so hard, and by season 1888-9 he was good enough (along with Bath three-quarter C.J.B Moneypenny) to gain selection for Somerset (at Wellington) against the first ever touring side from the Dominions, namely the **New Zealand Maoris.** Somerset went down by 4-17 (old scoring format). But this was hardly a disgrace against such formidable opponents. Then, by season 1892-3 Soane gained selection for England, and following his debut against Scotland would then gain three further caps. He was now Bath's third international. Much liked, Soane was a warrior on the rugby field, yet a gentleman off it. Indeed, he and his brother ran a music business in Old Bond Street. He was elected Bath captain from 1890-1898, 'walked' effortlessly into the Somerset side on numerous occasions and led the county from 1896-9.

So, how did his club face the challenges of the rugby transformation that occurred during the last twenty years of that extraordinary Victorian age? After all, the likes of Bristol, Gloucester and Cardiff were surging ahead; so too Blackheath, Richmond, Harlequins and others in the South East; nor forgetting the likes of Northampton and Leicester in the Midlands. Meanwhile up North dramatic developments were set to happen. But for Bath arguably the best guide to their abilities was provided by the level of recognition from their parent county, namely Somerset, not least because county rugby expanded so rapidly in the latter years of the 19th century and because county selectors generally provided an independent and unbiased opinion.

Somerset in fact fielded county teams from **as early as season 1875/6** and played their first ever match at Taunton against Devon, the Devonians winning narrowly (see: Seventy Years of Somerset Rugby, 1875-1945, p.4), with the game described thus: *"a very different affair to the one we now know. The teams usually changed at a pub, under* *crude conditions and walked to the ground. The maul in goal was still in being, the referee carried a flag, and was assisted by two Umpires - the fore-runners of the modern touch judge - heeling back was almost unknown, and the main idea was for the forwards to carry the ball on by sheer weight and strength, leaving the outsides to snap a scoring chance, generally from a pass by the half-backs."* But remember, this was still mid-

Herbert Fuller

1870's rugby. At the administration level too, Somerset affairs remained somewhat 'ad hoc,' until that is, the 6th September 1882 when a meeting was held at the Clarence Hotel in Bridgwater and the Somerset Rugby Union was officially formed. So, a new chapter had begun. The previous colours of yellow and black were cast aside. In their place the newly formed Union adopted the colours of the Somerset Cricket club, namely crimson, white and black. The results too were encouragingly good in that same 1882/3 season, Somerset winning all their inter-county games, victory against Devon (by a goal to nil) being the first. The peerless Vassall played in the Devon game, likewise Bath's 2nd England international Herbert Fuller, and for the newly formed Somerset Rugby Union this first season was a promising start.

Moreover, although the **official County Championship was not launched until 1890,** the county game was already arousing considerable enthusiasm, not least in the West Country, as typified by a reported "five thousand crowd at a drawn Gloucestershire v Somerset encounter played on the spa at Gloucester" (Bath Chronicle, 28 Dec. 1882).

Somerset furthermore enjoyed the good fortune of possessing a number of established clubs from whom to select county teams, and whose collective ability was shown by their first ever Northern tour when facing Lancashire and Yorkshire in season 1886/7. With Yorkshire soon proving themselves the best county side in England and Lancashire not far behind, it was the latter who would provide the first hurdle to face the following **Somerset line-up**: *S.M.J. Woods (Bridgwater) at full-back; B.W. L. Ashford, H.V.Merry (Wellington), S.C.Smith, captain (Weston super Mare) threequarters; F.H. Fox (Wellington) and F.C.Duckworth (Weston super Mare) half-backs; P.F. Hancock, E. Hancock, A.A.Glass (Wiveliscombe), W.H. Manfield (Yeovil), R.M.P. Parsons (Crewkerne), A.A.Hammil (Bridgwater), J.R. Walter (Wellington), H.Paterson, H.T. Gilmore (Weston super. Mare) forwards.*

Few if any of those attending this game in Manchester would have seen Somerset in action. But they would doubtless have learned that the Cider Men knew a thing or two about rugby. Somerset did hold the Lancastrians, beating them by a dropped goal and two tries to the Northerners' three tries; and assisting Somerset were no less than three England internationals, namely fullback S.M.J. Woods, F.H.Fox at half-back and the immensely strong forward Froude Hancock. Yorkshire at Wakefield was to prove just too much however, the result going to the hosts by way of three tries to one. But during this period that was the outcome for virtually all opponents stepping into white rose territory, such was their domination. Yet Somerset had shown that they too were no push-overs; and if any gap existed between county rugby in the West Country and the North, then it was a narrow one. Doubtless it was a disappointment for Bath that none of their players had been selected for that Northern tour of 1886/7. However, during this period it was the likes of Weston super Mare and Wellington who ranked among the strongest clubs in the county. Wiveliscombe too, thanks not least to the remarkable Hancock rugby dynasty, proved to be another valuable source of talent. Nonetheless, a glance at the successful Somerset season of 1896/7, a decade after that first northern tour, showed just how far Bath had progressed up the learning curve. This team (now fielding seven backs) had a distinctive Bath look about it, with no less than five players for Somerset in a 25-3 win, against fast-improving Devon: **Somerset:** *H.T.Gamlin (Wellington) fullback; R. Forrest (Taunton), W.F. Long (Bath), J.McTier (Bath), C.J.Sealey (Bridgwater Albion), three quarters; J.Merry (Wellington), C.G.Vincent (Bath) half-backs; F.Soane (Bath), E.T.Gilmore, T.P Gilmore (Weston super Mare), P.J.Ebdon (Wellington), G.Bradshaw (Bridgwater), H.B.Mole (Castle Cary), L.C.Powys (Yeovil), J.B.S D'Aguila (Bath), forwards.*

Thus, by the mid-1890's Bath had both survived and adapted to a number of challenges and changes confronting all clubs during this pioneering era, imperative in fact if one nurtured ambitions to achieve status as a first-class club. So, the signs appeared to be promising, and although Bath were not leading the pack, they arguably ranked among the pack that was doing the leading. Indeed, three Bath players had won caps for England, while Somerset selectors were taking far more interest too, and not least in the county performances of T.N. Parham, whose Bath rugby career extended from the 1880's into the 1890's and who was rated by many of his contemporaries as the best Bath half-back of the 19th century. That Parham was an 'outside' duly raised an important question, namely: 'could Bath now continue to produce the quality of backs that would be virtually essential to any club with ambitions of first-class status in the post 1900's rugby game?' Meanwhile their rivals Bristol were already proving to be such a club!

Chapter 5. NO ALTERNATIVE – SEPARATE WAYS.

As rugby advanced into the 1890's it might have appeared that 'all was well.' The club game was expanding, and in inter-County rugby, not least in the West, was attracting increasingly large support. Yet it was this same success that was producing a new and perhaps unexpected problem, one highlighted (among others) by the following encounter between rivals Leeds and Halifax. The venue was Headingley. The attendance (Peter Jackson, Daily Mail, 1ˢᵗ Sep. 2001) was…. *"27,654."* For an inter-club game to attract such crowds would even now raise eyebrows. But in northern parts during those latter years of the 19th century, such crowds raised some fundamental questions too. Indeed, amid the smoke-filled chimneys and down the deep, dark mines, where money was scarce and work was hard, northern rugby followers were speaking ever more frequently of one particular topic, namely *'Broken Time.'* Or as one would describe it nowadays, **'part-time professionalism,'** an arrangement that would allow for reimbursement of those wages lost owing to rugby commitments.

It was a forceful argument, one coinciding with the same issue being discussed in football circles, and as it happens in cricket; two other fast-growing sports whose moves to accommodate professionalism (semi or otherwise) seemed effortlessly simple by comparison with the RFU (Rugby Football Union) who viewed matters very differently, nothing less in fact than a determination to ensure the continuation of a totally amateur game. Indeed, the issue of 'broken time' reached *"boiling point at the RFU's AGM [1893],"* where a Mr. Hornby (in fact a true amateur) referred to an element of hypocrisy in this debate and reportedly argued for 'broken time' because some *"so-called amateur sides ask for large guarantees* [when playing away], *publish no balance sheets and distribute expenses far larger than paid to a professional player."* That was probably not an exaggeration either! Meanwhile, Yorkshire representatives further complained that 'although there are more clubs in the North of England than in the South, more Southerners than Northerners sit on the RFU committee;' *(*see: Rugby Chronology, Museum of Rugby, Twickenham; now World Rugby Museum).

As for a compromise…. there would be no compromise! Indeed the 'Great Schism.' as it became known *"was now to take on its own unstoppable momentum."* Initially (see again: Museum of Rugby) 'twenty clubs from Lancashire, Yorkshire and Cheshire met at the George Hotel, Huddersfield and decided to turn professional, forming their own governing body in 1895, namely the Northern Union (later known as Rugby League from 1922).' It was a bold decision, and the 'Divide' when it came was as sad as it was courageous. Because the rugby family was now divided, two different pathways would now be trod, and the siblings would not meet again for a long, long time. Yet, each code (Union and League) would now have the freedom to decide their own destiny.

This separation inevitably depleted the ranks within the rugby union game, and particularly so in the North. Yorkshire, the first ever winners of the County Championship in 1889, would triumph a further six times until relinquishing the title to

Kent in 1897. But by then the inroads of professionalism had taken their toll, and not for another thirty years would the Tykes, in 1926, triumph again in County rugby. Unlike Wales, who in the late 1890's would already experience the loss (among others) of the brilliant James brothers to the professional game, the South West had remained less affected by the dramatic events that had taken place in the North. But not entirely so, and in the following decade, Bath too would discover that they were within range of those northern scouts, who on occasions would take more than just a passing interest in what the West Country had to offer; and though Salford failed to tempt Bath's powerful forward Billy Thomas into professional ranks with a signing-on fee of £500 (big money then) plus bonuses for wins and further bonuses for tries scored, Oldham during this same period did succeed in tempting Bath's Tom White to 'go north' in 1909. A versatile player, his ability won him international honours in his newly adopted code.

Bert Comm .... The fullback went North with Woodward and Haines in the 1920's.

Acknowledgements: Bath Chronicle

Soon afterwards Bath utility back Vickie Alcott signed professional with Hull Kingston Rovers; likewise promising young forward Riley West (no relation to Tom West who had earlier joined Rochdale Hornets), and J. Robinson went North too. Commenting on this movement into professional ranks the Bath Daily Chronicle (Football Talk, 14th Apr. 1910) wrote of 'a Bath and Somerset flavour in the Oldham v Rochdale Hornets game of 2nd April, where Tom West ran home 2 tries for Hornets and Tom White scored another for Oldham.' It was therefore fortunate that Bath's recovery at this time from an earlier slump in the 1900's was not adversely affected by this loss of talent. Nor, again surprisingly, was Bath's surge during the 1920's adversely affected by the loss to professional ranks of Albert Woodward, Bert Comm and Ted Haines. Indeed, notwithstanding the huge inducements offered from Leeds to legendary centre Ron Gerrard in the 1930's (an offer he declined) no further player left the Rec to head North until centre Peter Fearis in the 1950's. However, in the early days of 1895 when the professional Northern Rugby Union was formed, it would be one hundred years before the Rugby Football Union in 1995 finally relented, bowing at last to the growing pressure to permit some form of professionalism into its own hallowed ranks. And when at the climax of season 1995-6 the hatchet was finally buried, two great teams were chosen from each code to meet at Twickenham in a game of friendship and conciliation. One team were Rugby League giants Wigan. The other was a once humble club from the West Country.... Bath, of whom a century previously it would have been fanciful to even have dreamed of such an extraordinary possibility.

Chapter 6. NEW HOME. NEW CHALLENGE. (1890's onwards)

The Great Schism of the mid-1890's, albeit dramatic, was merely one change during the final decade of the 19th century. Yes, the Schism certainly affected the Union game in the North, but there was no stopping its momentum taking place elsewhere and, perhaps contrary to common perception, rugby (not least in the West Country) was far from exclusive to the Public Schools and Oxbridge alone. Moreover, it was often a crowd-puller, particularly at the county level, with Devon's 3-0 win v Somerset pulling a 10,000 attendance (Chronicle, Football Talk, 12th Dec. 1895); while Cornwall's 17-3 County final triumph against Durham in 1908 drew a remarkable 17,000 attendance at Redruth (D. Mail, 31st Mar. 1989). Meanwhile, a hierarchy of elite club-sides was evolving, though not as yet including Bath. True, there were talented players at Bath, yet their main strength and tactics had for some years depended (although not entirely) upon their forwards, a pack usually good enough to hold its own in a rugby game that was becoming both better and faster. Indeed, they were known (and sometimes feared) for their much-favoured tactic of the combined forward 'foot-rush,' and the cry of *"Feet Bath, feet"* as a rush got going was a chant commonly heard from the Bath terraces during the 1890's and beyond.

Yet teams limited to a forward strategy would discover soon enough that such tactics were no longer sufficient to win the 'big' games against the leading clubs of England and Wales. Bath knew this only too well. Actually, they could hardly 'not' have known, located as they were near their increasingly powerful neighbours Bristol and those inspirational Welsh sides now joining the Bath fixture list. Ah yes…. Wales! Admiration for the back play among those sides from the valleys was increasingly recognised throughout the game. Moreover, by the turn of the century Bristol had already adopted the Welsh tactic whereby once the ball had reached one attacking wing, it would be re-cycled along the backs to the other wing, so sustaining that crucial momentum of a sweeping attack from one flank to the other. However, this additional dimension had yet to be developed at Bath. In addition, there were the leading London clubs such as Blackheath, the London Scottish and Richmond. For rugby union really was expanding into a national game, with many clubs (thanks now to an established rail network) able to travel the length of the Country to play fixtures. Meanwhile, another reason for Bath's somewhat pedestrian progress was the lack of satisfactory and permanent playing facilities. Good fortune intervened however when in 1892 there came that opportunity to move to Henrietta Park; and talking of the 'Park' it was a rarity in the annals of Bath rugby to see a team-sheet from this era of pre-1900's rugby. But thanks to an original post-card submitted to the Bath Chronicle by Mr Bob Tarrant, formerly Hon.Sec of St. Stephen's RFC (and later printed on 6th Apr. 1932) the names of **a team captained by Frank Soane when the club played at Henrietta Park (between 1892-4) was revealed:** *A.E. Pinch, W. Pattinson, B. Vincent, P. Dykes, B. Helps, T. N. Parham, and G.Vincent, F. Soane (capt.), Roberts, L.J. Fry, W. Coles, A. Timmins, R. Dykes, A.E. Clarke and Milsom.*

But while the Park was not without its advantages, a yet better venue became available, namely those 17 acres comprising the Pulteney Meadows (see Ch. 3) and situated in the very heart of the city. Just perfect! **But, could Bath obtain the 'rights' to play their rugby here?** The answer would be 'yes.' Because fortuitously Captain Foster, owner of Henrietta Park, now wished to convert the land for other uses; and Sydney College, who during this period had been playing on the Pulteney Meadows, now departed. As a result the '**Bath Recreation Ground Company Ltd**' was duly formed so as to purchase the land, and Bath successfully negotiated with the company **for long-term usage from September 1894 onwards.** Hopefully the nomadic days were over.

FRANK SOANE 1893

With the acquisition of Pulteney Meadows, soon to be termed 'the Recreation Ground' and then equally soon to be dubbed 'the Rec', the club now possessed a rugby venue of real potential. Alongside the Avon river (though initially playing on the far side of the field) and overlooked by the timeless beauty of Bath Abbey, some commentators have described the Rec as *'the most beautiful rugby ground in the world,'* (reportedly the 1912/13 Touring South Africans among them). Moreover, during this same era the club had the good fortune to acquire the assistance of John Townsend Piper. Devoted to the club, he was appointed Hon. Secretary in 1890, and among the first visiting club sides to face Bath on the Rec (possibly 'the' first) were Exeter. They were not new opponents but certainly strong ones. Yet on their visit on 6th October 1894, it was an on-form Bath who overcame their visitors 22 points to nil; and during this era Bath encounters against formidable Exeter did not always conclude as happily as that. So, with the Rec at their disposal, and hence able to attract bigger names to the Rec, no less a touring side than **the Barbarians** (founded 1890) played Bath on Christmas Eve, 1894 as follows: Gwynne, C.B.Fry, Baker (all Oxford), Tandy (Blackheath), Toller (Cardiff and possibly Blackheath), Biggs (Cardiff), Dyas (Sandhurst), Maud, Finlinson (both Blackheath), Dixon, Falcon, Tucker (all Cambridge), Todd, Carey (both Oxford) and Gould (Liverpool). Facing them was the following **Bath** team: **Barrett, J.Long, T. Fry, J.MacTier, F. Rowlett, Seers, G.Vincent, F.Soane, D'Aguila, B.Belsom, E.Taylor, L. Fry, W.Coles, J.Ruddock, W.England.**

Frank Soane was in fact Bath's first Barbarian in 1891, and while their 1894 team at Bath won 14-0, the benefits were twofold. First, the score was no humiliation for the hosts. Secondly, in an age of no radio and certainly no television, there was really only one way to learn about the best in rugby, and that was to play and watch the best in rugby. This 'did' matter, and the words of at least one admiring reporter for the Chronicle said it all: "...*how it opens our eyes and makes us realise what first class football is. The Barbarians are Par Excellence.*" A repeat of this 'Par Excellence' was seen again on 2nd Apr, 1896 (13 points apiece), and later on 15th Apr. 1897 with the visitors winning 3-8. In the following 1897-8 season the aforementioned Bath half-back G. Vincent was duly honoured as another Barbarian, followed by centre James Timmins in 1905-6.

But Bath could not afford to rest on their laurels. After all, their spacious new home required some 'extras.' **Hence, within a season of their arrival on the Rec the club completed a seated stand alongside the West side of the ground,** and though initially **bemoaning the annual rent of 20% of gate receipts to their Recreation Ground Company landlords (Chronicle, 8th Jan.1896),** this did not prevent the Bath committee from applying a touch of chivalry when permitting members to bring two ladies to watch the games on match-days…free of charge. Sadly, it was during this same era that Bath would bid farewell to an outstanding former player and England international, namely Herbert George Fuller (1856-896). A Bathonian, Fuller attended Christ's College, Finchley, then Cambridge University where he made a deep impression upon all those who knew him. An outstanding forward for Bath (also Clifton RFC), Somerset and England during the 1880's, his qualities both as sportsman and a born role model impressed all those who knew him. An academic, he would later become a proctor at Cambridge, and this in addition to his outstanding sporting prowess. In his last days, which were spent at the home of an elder brother in Streatham, Herbert finally lost his fight against a cerebral tumour on 2nd Jan. 1896. Buried in Bath (Lansdown) his loss was 'felt' by many. Later in July of 1896, the club would mourn another of their former internationals, namely Major Frank D'Aguila (and likewise the passing away of one of his two sons, namely J.B.S. D'Aguila in 1901, himself a popular Bath and Somerset player).

Now, there was no doubting that the likes of Frank D'Aguila, Fuller and Soane had helped to enhance Bath's reputation at forward. But finding good backs was another matter. And yet……at long last there were signs that this situation might be changing. In fact, come the mid-1890's there appeared signs of an exciting potential, not least by the arrival of co-centres Dan MacTier and former Welsh international 'Tich' Fry (a real 'jinking' maestro), while the long career of Bath and Somerset winger W. F. (Joe) Long had commenced on one wing, and that of his brother Jim Long on the other. And it was this additional talent that proved critical in victories such as Bath's rare uplifting 0-3 win at Bristol in the spring of 1897. Moreover, when a certain ex-Bath (Sydney) College schoolboy by the name of J.T. Timmins first slipped a club shirt over his back in season 1896-7, Bath had got their hands on another exciting young player. Because here was a newcomer whose abilities at centre three quarter (centre) would later inspire the one asset that Bath now craved and needed…..the complete all-round back division to lift them up a class.

Selwyn Biggs

That being said, one should not dismiss outright the abilities of certain backs of earlier years, among them the Hills brothers, two notable players of the Lambridge era (circa, mid-1880's). Long-time supporter Frank Melluish (letters, The Chronicle, 6th Sep. 1930) later recalled one brother sending over a 'drop-kick from just inside the touch-line from half-way.' He recalled too the famous Biggs brothers, also of Cardiff and Wales (Bath & W. Chronicle & Herald, 4th Sep.1930), and who graced the Bath backs in the Soane days (the 1890's era). While centre M. Baker, added an admiring Frank Melluish, *"would cut out some fine openings for Norman Biggs who, with his long stride making for the corner flag was a treat never to be forgotten."* Yet there remained the major task of strengthening the fixture-list, and furthermore to achieve results good enough to maintain it. Because make no mistake (as any fixture-secretary knows): 'there were and are other ambitious clubs always willing to take one's place.' So, when in the spring of 1898 the Hartlepool Rovers came south to play both Llanelli and Bristol, Bath negotiated a match with the north-east Percy Park club to visit the Rec on their Easter tour. The Newcastle team were class, sufficiently strong in fact to provide no less than seven players for the then current Northumberland team, who just happened to be that season's County Champions. Yet Bath, with that young man J.T. Timmins in the backs had cause for some celebration with their 8-3 victory, a result that hopefully promised much as they and the rugby game itself would soon bid farewell to the 19th century.

Yet victory or otherwise, rugby culture was/is invariably both fun and hectic, as was the case in late season 1898-9 when Bath found themselves (owing to the train timetable) in a tight race to reach their opponents Exeter (Chronicle, Football Talk, 14th Apr. 1899). Their timetable said it all: the train would not depart from Bath until 1.35pm and the team would be unlikely to reach the Exeter ground much before 4pm. Then there was the match to play, albeit on a reduced time-scale. Another hurdle was the return train leaving Exeter soon after 5.30pm, thus imperative that Bath must not depart from their opponent's ground for the homeward journey later than 5.15pm. This made for a stop-watch schedule, and that's putting it mildly. So, the team donned their kit while still aboard the train (reportedly changing in the saloon of all places), and miraculously they reached the ground for a 4.05 pm kick-off. Elsewhere there was more drama, far away 'up North' in fact, where Northumberland (winners in the previous season) were facing their challengers in the 1899 County Championship final, and the challengers just happened to be Devon. It would be symbolic indeed if they could capture the crown. Well, since it would be double cause for celebration if the hosts and their parent County could both win on such a day, then Exeter played their part to perfection. They won 11-0. But, come the final whistle Bath's own priority was now to catch that homewards train with barely fifteen minutes left on the clock to reach the station. Meanwhile, news (and what news!) had been signalled down from Newcastle, and it concerned that 'oh so special' County Championship final. Devon?... Devon had won! The news of the victory (by a goal) led to crowds thronging the streets, those same streets in which a Somerset club was now struggling valiantly to make headway towards St David's station. There was both joy and celebration, and Exeter, it was recorded, *"was mad with delight."* Moreover, could anyone have predicted the remarkable West Country 'enlightenment' that Devon's triumph would now help to inspire. For inspire it did! Indeed, the Western Counties were now poised to dominate the County Championship for near a quarter of a century, on occasions almost putting a stranglehold on it. And Devon were the first, on that glorious April day. Oh....and Bath did catch that train!

Chapter 7.   A NEW CENTURY BECKONS. (The early 1900's)

As dawn broke over Bath on 1st January 1900 the optimism of this era could hardly have been better demonstrated than by the celebrations three years previously for the Diamond Jubilee of Queen Victoria (later reported in the Chronicle, 8th Sep. 1905, p.13). Bunting and flags had adorned the streets of Bath on that glorious day of 22nd June 1897; a hot air balloon was launched from a packed Victoria Park; no less than 7,000 medals were gifted to the children of the city by direct order of the mayor, Mr George Woodiwiss; and Henrietta Park was gifted to the city. Iron-clad ships now crossed the seas; railroads criss-crossed the land, cars too had arrived, and soon the Wright Brothers would, quite literally, reach for the skies. Such transformation within barely seventy-five years since young William Webb Ellis reportedly picked up a football at Rugby School and ran with it. Since that dawn of the rugby age the game had 'come a long way, producing its own legends, among them Adrian Stoop (Oxford, Harlequins and England) whose creative brilliance would help transform half-back play in the English game. The Chronicle (and its sister papers) too was expanding their rugby coverage, usually under the pen-names of 'Football Talk,' 'Play Up,' superseded later by 'the Mascot' in the 1920's. As for the 'wannabe' sporting stars of the future there was the must-have bible of the Boys Own album. Describing the early days of rugby, the 1907-8 edition wrote thus: *"....the credit of its origins and development for many years was entirely due to Rugby School, until Marlborough College came on the scene and gallantly seconded the efforts of its notable rival....."* Understandably, admiration was expressed too for the Marlborough Nomads, the first fully established Old Boys team.

By the 1900's, as the pages further revealed, others had caught up. For instance, there was Bedford School who, as the Boys Own enthused, were by this time *"far and away the greatest of English schools to-day."* There were Fettes and Loretto in Edinburgh (who as the pages tell us) were so dominant in the rugby ranks of Oxford and Cambridge (and of course Scotland) as to be *"the subject of universal comment."* In Scotland in fact there had been occasions when schoolboys had actually gained full caps for their national team. In England too J.G. Milton (a Bedford School forward) would achieve this same remarkable distinction when selected for England against the iron men of Wales in January 1904 at a tender 18 years of age. Talk about a baptism of fire. University rugby too was covered, revealing that 'such was the 'domination' of Old Rugbeians and Marlburians at Oxford in the 1870's that they alone had been required to pay the university club subscriptions, all other students being regarded as honorary members of the rugby club and thus excused entirely the requirement to contribute towards membership funds.'

But what then did the immediate future hold for Bath? Well, the answer came on 16th April 1900, the occasion of the visit by Portsmouth rugby club for a late season game which, according to a post-match report from Portsmouth captain (Edmonds) was *"more free from rough or unfair play than any game he had ever played."* Playing too in that game was Portsmouth vice-captain George Llewellyn Trerise. A sail-maker, he was employed in the Government dockyards at the naval port. A Falmouth man from Cornwall by origin, Trerise played in the visitors' pack. Late in the game however he suffered a head injury (Chronicle, 19th Apr. 1900), yet was able to walk off the field at the final whistle without arousing serious concern. Indeed, he remained with his colleagues until reaching the Angel Hotel in Westgate Street, where the Portsmouth team had 'changed' for the match. Then suddenly concerns began. Trerise fell unconscious, his colleagues now realising that all was far from well. He was taken to the Royal United Hospital, for unknown to anyone he had suffered a fractured skull during the encounter on the Rec. Even so, nobody was fully prepared for the shock that would follow that same evening. For George Llewellyn Trerise, twenty-four years of age, single and vice-captain of Portsmouth, had died. For both clubs the news was numbing, now suddenly finding themselves having to come to terms with events so shattering and their unexpected introduction to the 20th century.

After this tragedy all else in purely human terms was mundane for the remainder of that season. Nonetheless, rugby continued and there were other matters to ponder, the respective strengths of Bristol and Gloucester among them. These two were getting better and better, while Bath by contrast were struggling to maintain equilibrium at the higher level to which they aspired. And should they fall too far behind, then sooner or later the stronger clubs could abandon them. Indeed, the contrast between the Bath results of the moderately successful season of 1900-1 (17 wins) and their worryingly low total of eight wins in season 1901-2 was early warning of uncertain days that lay ahead. Another reality was the growing dominance of Wales, fast proving themselves as natural born rugby players. True, Bath and other English clubs (if at home) did on occasions win against the Welsh guys. But in Wales it was usually a very different story. There was furthermore the question of tactics, a factor largely dependent on the respective abilities of those players available. Therefore, should (or even could) Bath attempt to emulate the adventurous style of Bristol? Or should they apply the rather different tactics of the likes of Lydney, for example? Because this small yet passionate rugby stronghold on the edge of the Forest of Dean (regular Bath opponents in the 1900's) might not have played the most attractive of rugby. But by heck (Chronicle, 12th Nov. 1903, p,5) *"with no brilliant men in their midst to inspire football ideas [could] by sheer determination and consistent preparation [bring] themselves into such proficiency that they made teams with considerable reputations lick the dust."* Two years previously, after a reverse at Lydney, Bath had decided that enough was enough, and commenced training twice weekly as a direct result.

Meanwhile then as now: 'tough' play can on occasions descend into 'rough' play (or worse). Even so a perhaps somewhat surprising feature of this era concerned not only excessive play on the field, but no little 'difficulties' among spectators off it (Chronicle, 14th Sep, 1899, p.2). True, Victorian and Edwardian England may indeed have been noted for its finesse and genteel behaviour in the Lords members' lounge and the Henley regatta, but such behaviour did not always extend to the rugby arena.....not by a 'long shot!' So alarmed in fact were Somerset County that in season 1899-1900 the committee had issued a circular to every member club, warning all concerned that adverse behaviour would be dealt with accordingly. Furthermore, posters were ordered to be displayed at every Somerset ground, duly warning clubs (and supporters) as to how seriously the Committee regarded the worsening situation. Nor would it have pleased these same good gentlemen when in the following season the Bath encounter at Taunton became so unmanageable that the game was actually abandoned, with one player from each side receiving marching orders for 'unacceptable' behaviour; in short: 'losing their cool!'

Nonetheless rugby grew in popularity. Indeed, by the turn of the century the membership alone of Gloucester totalled near twelve hundred, and the six thousand strong attendance at the drawn encounter at Exeter between Devon and Gloucestershire in season 1902/3 was nothing unusual in West Country county games. But these noteworthy figures did not only make good reading for the respective club treasurers, they gave a clear and simple message to the Game's governing bodies. And the message was this: that rugby attracted followers not in spite of, but partly because of the fact that it was a tough, physical sport. Paradoxically this same confrontational game on the field of play possessed (usually) an almost unique spirit off it, and the Somerset committee were doubtless aware of that fine line existing between hard play and actual dirty play. So, this was part of the rugby landscape surrounding Bath in the 1900's, a club already aware that its place in the hierarchy of the game would likely be judged by comparison with Gloucester and especially Bristol. True, Bath were generally strong at forward where a charismatic Frank Cashnella had now joined the ranks. Yet even here there was no certainty that sufficient quality-newcomers would be found to replace the old guard. Furthermore, this applied to the backs, as that reliable quartet of J. Long and W. Long and centres Dan Mactier and 'Tich' Fry were no longer available as a unit. Likewise, James Timmins would not always be on-call either, by now based in the capital and playing on occasions for London Welsh.

Yet behind the scenes the wider Bath rugby family were laying foundations that would help secure the long-term future of the parent club through thick and thin. First, the Bath and District Combination was formed in seasons 1901-2. Then in season 1905-6 a group of local schoolteachers founded the Bath and District Schools Rugby Union. Admittedly

James Timmins

the potential of these two fledgling organisations could only be guessed at. But as the seasons passed the club would have reason to realise that the launching of the Combination and the Schools Union would prove to be inspired decisions. Moreover, despite somewhat ordinary performances, the Bath seniors were still producing certain individual players of class. Somerset had noted this fact too and 'The Cidermen' (their oft used nick-name) were an outstanding county side in season 1902-3 that included Wellington (and England's) fearsome tackling full-back Herbert Gamlin and tenacious England forward Robert Dibble of Bridgwater Albion. Furthermore, this was a Somerset team (Bath's Cashnella and James Timmins playing) good enough to reach that season's County semi-final against Kent (though losing 0-12), Durham then winning the Championship final.

Then, in season 1905-6 there was to be a totally unexpected reason for not only Somerset, but for the entire rugby fraternity to sit up and take notice when British rugby awaited the first ever visit by our cousins from far away......**the New Zealanders!** Not much was known about the tourists on their arrival; after all, what did they know about rugby in New Zealand? Well, the answer to that query would soon be given when Devon, later County Champions that same season, would have the honour (for want of a better word) of hosting the tourists, and where any questions concerning the tourists' ability would soon be answered. The stunning 4-55 result to the New Zealanders was that answer! And, the reaction in the Bath Chronicle and in rugby circles everywhere to this first and totally unexpected result was naturally one of amazement. But the reality was that rugby football had already captured the imagination in Countries far removed from those playing-fields of Rugby School and Marlborough College. Moreover, our New Zealand cousins came with their own ideas and tactics that were exciting and challenging. Hardly surprisingly, following this first encounter the excitement aroused by the tourists was reportedly at 'fever pitch,' and the third game on their itinerary was Somerset at Taunton. Here, watched by a reported crowd of nine thousand the 'Cidermen,' fielding Bath backs R. Meister and J. Timmins (captain) limited the now fearsome tourists to a 0-23 defeat, an outcome that in the circumstances was deemed far from unworthy.

Predictably the tourists continued on their seemingly unstoppable way against clubs, counties and Countries: Scotland (7-12), Ireland (0-15), England watched by 45,000 at Crystal Palace (0-15) and France (8-38) would all fall. Indeed, only Wales would check the advance thanks to a try by Dr Teddie Morgan in a passionate 3-0 encounter at Cardiff Arms Park, 47,000 watching. This one upset, notable too for the disallowed Bob Deans try that New Zealand always insisted was genuine, did not disguise perhaps the most significant message of their eventful visit. Because though few perhaps at that time could have realised the long-term impact of this first New Zealand tour, hindsight provides a different perspective from which to make judgement. For the fact was this: that a mere five years into a new century, rugby football had taken its first real steps towards becoming global!

Chapter 8. IN THE MIDST OF WINTER. (The 1900's continued)

The sports pages of The Bath Daily Chronicle (Saturday 21st Apr. 1906) would have made for some depressing reading. For if the meagre return back in 1901-2 of a mere 8 wins from 30 matches had seemed bad, then the results of 1905-06 would prove that they could get even worse. Because from 33 games played, a mere seven were won, two drawn and no less than 24 lost. Small wonder then that morale was falling and 'dark clouds were descended over the Rec.' Meanwhile, with Bristol and Gloucester now establishing themselves firmly amongst the elite of the game, Bath could be facing the prospect of a second-class rugby existence at best. Furthermore, as if the results were not bad enough, those same sports pages concluded that the main problem in the side was a *"lack of a sufficiently strong forward rank and a lack of a permanently allied pair of halves."* A lack of a sufficiently strong forward rank! Surely not? After all, was not the strength in the pack the one saving grace that could always be relied upon? Well, with the exception of the likes of Cashnella the club now found itself unable to rely even on this once reliable resource. This, putting it mildly, was a setback with possible serious implications, because with rugby in the West Country and Wales no team could possibly succeed without a strong set of forwards.

Arnold Ridley ....a varied Career

Acknowledgements: Bath Chronicle

Furthermore, if this situation continued the stronger clubs might drop Bath from their fixture lists indefinitely. Confusing matters further was that in the previous season Bath had returned an encouraging total of twenty-one wins from 39 games. Yet was that just a 'one-off' during an otherwise seven-year struggle from 1901-1908 when crowds barely reached a hundred? Indeed, in the words of Arnold Ridley (actor, playwright and later club President): 'Bath came close to being disbanded' (Bath Centenary book, p.14). So, was season 1905-06 the mid-winter of Bath's misfortunes, the ultimate low point since their formation forty years previously? Yes! But the lone saving grace was the fact that though Bath were defeated far too often, only rarely were they defeated badly. Indeed, at times they got close against some of their strongest opponents; even defeating the likes of then highly rated Penarth (9-4) in the desperate 1905-6 season. But a genuine revival, rather than the occasional one-off success, depends partly on that vital ingredient of self-belief, and a large turn-over of players for 1st team duty was then an added drawback.

But, season 1906-07 would provide some relief, not only because the twelve-wins were an improvement, but because they included unexpectedly good victories over Neath and

30

Pontypridd (by 5-3 and 3-0 respectively). There were narrow upsets too, including the close 3-6 fall against Bristol at their former home on the County Ground at Ashley Hill. Nonetheless, one could not lightly shrug off the 15 defeats that season, including the 31-0 mauling at Pontypool, upsets that left Bath facing the reality that during the early 1900's they remained outside the boundary of first-class rugby. Indeed, among the few 'lighter' talking-points that season was probably the introduction of an all-white shirt replacing the dark blue and black hooped shirts worn previously. Yet it was not all gloom. For hidden behind the scenes there were a few (albeit only a 'few') signs for optimism. The pack was slowly responding to the inspiration of Cashnella. Utility player Fred Russell and ever-reliable Alby Hatherill were bonding at half-back, while R. Meister, H. Lewis, and Tom West (later a 1st teamer at Gloucester) were adding genuine pace into the back-division. The task therefore was to mould a successful team around such capable individuals. As for Meister, he gained selection for Somerset against the 1906-7 high-powered visiting South Africans at a packed Taunton, the 0-14 defeat hardly a disgrace. There was however one further event of season 1906-07 that would be long remembered, and this concerned *"the notorious county cup final against Bridgwater Albion"* (Bath Daily Chronicle, 20th Apr.1907). This competition, namely the then recently inaugurated Somerset Cup, had been launched for the best of motives, not least to channel the huge rugby enthusiasm in the County into a club knock-out contest; and initially there was considerable interest shown, not least at Bath. However, when at four minutes past seven on the evening of Saturday 23rd March, by which time Bridgwater Albion had secured victory by 5-0 against fellow finalists Bath, notice had been given that all might not run smoothly with this fledgling event. It had been barely ten minutes into this oft-interrupted match when Bath's T.B. Timmins (brother of James) was reportedly 'tackled with great violence' by Albion's England International forward Bob Dibble. The referee 'blew up,' but in the resulting uproar Bath's Loo Hatherill apparently 'did not hear it.' Albion's Parr then picked up the ball and was subsequently tackled by Hatherill, and to the great indignation of his team-mates, the Bathonian was given marching orders. Now, hard tackling is part of rugby culture, so whether or not Dibble's tackle on Timmins was actually illegal or otherwise (high perhaps?) was never fully clarified. But Bath were particularly upset, not so much by Dibble's tackle, as by their man (Hatherill's) dismissal. True, these were early days in this recently launched Somerset Cup and there was no immediate reason to doubt its long-term potential. But, as the seasons passed (and with Bath set to be embroiled in yet further fracas in the following year) the County Cup did not evolve into the success as initially intended. Instead, teams usually adopted the dour strategy of 'win it ugly beats not winning it,' and open, handling rugby was a rarity. It was of little surprise therefore that by 1914 the competition would be discontinued, and it seemed indefinitely.

Optimists on the Rec, perhaps not too many around at that time, would have hoped for better times come season 1907-8, in which three impending encounters in particular caught the eye. First there was the first ever game against the Harlequins. Secondly, the first ever visit of a French side, and a particularly good French side…..Racing Club de France. Furthermore, there would be a game against Bath's then arch rivals Weston super Mare in the First Round of that season's Somerset Cup, and it transpired that all three fixtures would be long remembered. The first of this trio was against Harlequins (founded 1866), with the match played in London on the 19th October. Originally known as Hampstead Football Club until 1870, by the late 1900's they had already earned a high reputation. Soon to depart from their Wandsworth ground to Twickenham, they possessed among their numbers one Adrian Stoop, an outside-half whose name would pass into England legend. Not surprisingly for Bath, this inaugural game was to be a salutary experience. They lost! In fact, they were white-washed 49-8! Could the West Countrymen possibly recover from so shattering a result, uncomfortably aware that this same 'Quins' club would later visit the Rec in March? Not many would have bet on it.

Come the New Year however, among the few brighter spots was a 0-0 draw at high-flying Bristol. Yet this hardly suggested that the visiting Harlequins could be overcome on the 21st March. Furthermore, Bath's preparations for the Quins game would now be affected by the ramifications of an earlier encounter, namely the 'small' matter of the Somerset Cup First Round game of 15th February. This had brought Bath 'head to head' with visitors Weston super Mare, and in all Somerset there were perhaps no fiercer rivals than these two clubs. Added to this rivalry were two sets of supporters known for their partisan feelings towards each other, and then as now, this heady mix can ignite the unwholesome events that took place in this particular encounter. One report estimated that some three thousand spectators attended the match, and what is near certain is that whoever did watch the game would probably never forget it, and for all the wrong reasons. The encounter was as tense as it was close (the visitors narrowly winning), and the trouble that erupted on the field then actually spread to the terraces. To make matters worse, the referee was mobbed at the game's conclusion, necessitating an actual escort to assist his safe passage to the dressing room. Indeed, so serious were these events that a full meeting of the Somerset Rugby Union (S.R.U.) was later summoned, and met on Tuesday, 3rd March at the Royal Station Hotel in Bath. The Union's highly respected president, namely Mr W.S. Donne was in the chair, and in the words of the Bath Weekly Argus (7th Mar. 1908. p.12) the *"report of the referee (Mr H. Smith, of Bridgwater) in the Bath and Weston super Mare Cup Tie on the Recreation Ground on February 15th was considered. He alleged that the spectators after the game mobbed and threatened him."* It was further reported that *"the referee, in his report, expressed his thanks to members of the Bath committee who came to his protection, and the Committee exonerated the officials from all blame in connection with the incident."* But the committee were not in the mood to let matters rest there. Players A. Fear (W.s.M) and W. Watts (Bath) were duly suspended for the rest of the season for fighting, while C. Perkins (W.s.M) was suspended until March 27th for the same offence. But perhaps most threatening for Bath was the real possibility that rugby on the Rec itself could be suspended, this when the club were preparing for the vital return against the Harlequins later that same month.

In fact the S.R.U. did place **a ban on the Rec!!** But perhaps mindful that Bath were due to host the Harlequins on 21st March, the ban was set only until the 20th March. So, to the club's huge relief, they were free to now play the visiting Harlequins in one of the most prestigious club matches yet played in the city. The Harlequins came, though this time they did not conquer. Bath ran home three tries; the Quins two with one converted; hence a home victory by 9-8! Yes, a close call, but no less sweet for that. Quins however would not be the only newcomers to the Rec that season, as four months previously (1st November 1907) Bath had hosted the Racing Club de France. It was just Bath's 'bad luck' however that on the morning of the match itself, due to illness, they found themselves short of a wing. There would have been a reserve in the 2nd string, but Bath 'A' had already departed for an away game. So, in desperation (literally desperation) Bath contacted Monkton Combe School asking if they could provide a player, be it schoolboy or master, who would be willing to accept the daunting task of facing a scintillating French side.

Well, the local school suggested one Alfred Kitching, an Oxford graduate (nor forgetting an ordained Minister) who had recently joined the school staff. Albeit there was no certainty that he could play at this level, he was nonetheless a wing when playing as a freshman at Oxford. So, this slightly built and kindly schoolmaster, whom no one at the club had ever heard of, would put on a Bath shirt for the first time. It would not be the last! While the 6-6 draw against Racing Club in front of a large and appreciative crowd could rightly be described as The Entente Cordial at its best, equally pleasing was the performance of Alfred Kitching. Quite simply he was the fastest wing Bath had ever seen and whose pace generated a similar impact to that of a young David Trick seven decades later. Yet 'The Season Review' of the Bath Weekly Argus (2nd May 1908) made no reference to Kitching, and the relief expressed at the home win against Harlequins was tempered by misgivings: *"There have been seasons,"* the report stated, *"when the Bath team has done worse than in 1907-8, but the record of the campaign just closed is one of the most unfavourable in the annals of the club. Altogether 33 matches were played; of these 10 were won, 3 drawn, and 20 lost."* Thus, a mere ten games were won (club records quote 9), and among them a 14-0 success against the Old Millhillians, a London side by now ranked highly among the leading Old Boys clubs in England. But yes, twenty games were lost....hardly a revival. But, could Alfred Kitching's arrival just prove to be the X factor so desperately needed, a wing whose speed might turn the excellent work of centres Meister and James Timmins into much needed tries, and transform some of those narrow defeats into victories? As this fraught era came to a close, time alone would tell.

Chapter. 9. WINTER TURNS TO SPRING. (1908-14)

Those uncertain years that had over-shadowed Bath since that dawn of a new century were not entirely fruitless. Nor did the club lose that precious thing called 'hope.' Moreover, adversity is an experience that can strengthen as well as weaken, and despite the many disappointments, there were those club 'servants' whose greatest gift was dedication. The aforementioned John Townsend Piper for instance, who served as secretary and later joint-secretary from 1890 until 1944; while the playing-ranks included highly rated centres J. Timmins and R. Meister, and not forgetting the ultimate utility player, namely Fred Russell, who over the years played in virtually every position on the field. And there was Frank Cashnella!

Ah, that man Cashnella! Now, when the going gets tough, it is said that the tough get going. Well 'Cash' was tough! From a youngish age he was to enter into folklore not only in Bath, but wherever Bath plied their rugby trade (Centenary book, 'from Arnold Ridley,' pp. 13-14). He was barely 5ft. 11in and weighed slightly under 13 stone, but he was as strong as he was tenacious. Arnold Ridley would speak in awe of the 'Cash' he once knew: *"ashen faced, black-haired and heavily moustached, Cash was always in the fore-front of battle and in that era of the Somerset Cup the word 'battle' can be taken pretty literally."* Then years later while Arnold Ridley and a former West Country England forward were deep in discussion concerning former playing days, the latter commented that *"Old Cash was the only man who had ever put the wind up him. Cash - he was ruthless – absolutely ruthless"* was the international's authoritative verdict. Such was his charisma that 'Cash' was hugely popular with friend and foe alike. Born in 1879, at fifteen years of age he switched from football (Association) and joined the former Widcombe Institute rugby club. This change was, to quote his own words, because Football *"was too rough,"* words that would soon enough arouse incredulity to anyone watching Cashnella perform on the rugby field. He first wore a Bath shirt in 1899 and from that moment he was set to make an immediate impact as a forward. Two seasons later in 1901 he commenced his County career with Somerset and his fearsome reputation would now advance to wherever he played. 'Is Cashnella here?' was the question always asked wherever Bath travelled. Twenty years after his Rec' debut the same question was again asked when Bath played at Leicester in their first major game since the 1914-18 conflict and Cashnella, now some forty years of age, played his irrepressible part in a 3-16 triumph. If this was not enough to achieve, Arnold Ridley adds that Cashnella *"made his last appearance for the 'A' team [later United] at the age of 51."*

Frank Cashnella

Of course, Cashnella was a mere 'youngster' of barely thirty years when Bath prepared for season 1908-09, and any thoughts of beating the likes of Leicester (and away from home) were remote. Time was running out and it was imperative for the club's long-term future that results improve and improve very soon. If not, then the day was approaching when major clubs might now decide to drop Bath from their fixture lists (once and for all). So, when the likeable Arthur Ford was appointed captain for season 1908-09, this powerful forward now shouldered arguably the heaviest responsibility of any captain in the club's previous history.

Alfred Kitching ....first demonstrated his searing speed against Racing Club de France

Acknowledgements: Bath Chronicle

The first hopeful sign of his captaincy was an immediate improvement in results from the previous season's nine wins to an encouraging eighteen. Further optimism resulted from the selection of not only James Timmins for Somerset against the 1908-09 touring Australians, but selection too of Bath wing Richard Ascott, a highly versatile back who was equally good at outside-half or centre. Nor did the match disappoint, with Somerset, led by England and Bridgwater Albion's Robert Dibble, losing narrowly 0-8 (barely different to England's losing score of 3-9). The following season showed improvement too, albeit the fifteen wins and the unusually high total of nine draws from thirty-six played might not at first glance reflect this. However, this was a much-improved win-lose ratio, a noticeable drop in the number of heavy defeats, and while the likes of powerful Pontypool were still able to show who was boss in Wales, Welsh clubs did not always have things their way on the Rec, as revealed by Bath wins that included Abertillery (5-3), Penarth (16-0), exiles London Welsh (11-6) and Pontypool (6-0). Furthermore, Alfred Kitching was indeed an outstanding asset on the Bath wing. *"This brilliant player"* was The Bath Herald's verdict of him in its introduction to the 1909-10 season, though the always modest Kitching insisted that much of his success was due to James Timmins at centre. *"I could wish no wing better good fortune than to have such a centre as I had in Timmins."* And adding to this improved back division, Bath would now reap the benefit of an outstanding Penarth recruit to their pack, namely W.H.Thomas (Billy), now based with the railways industry at Swindon. He too was poised to carve out a big reputation and was soon enough recommended to the Somerset selectors. His county debut on a January day in 1910 could hardly have been more demanding when playing against Gloucestershire at a forbidding Kingsholm. Moreover, added to the difficulties for Thomas and his colleagues was

Somerset's loss of their Bridgwater forward Walter 'rattler' Roman who had recently switched to the Northern Union (Rugby League). Both in psychological and physical terms this was a serious blow. The remedy however was to select W.H. Thomas as replacement. And the Welshman did not disappoint.

In fact, no fewer than six Bath players represented Somerset that day, namely E.C. Hartell, A. Kitching, James Timmins and Alby Hatherill (backs), with E. Cambridge and W. H. Thomas at forward. And their task was a tough one, namely to overcome a Gloucestershire side hell-bent on reaching that season's County semi-final, and watching the action was the rugby journalist of the Morning Leader, whose comments were then printed in the Bath Chronicle, 22nd Jan. 1910. There was much that impressed him about West Country rugby: *"well trained, the Somerset and Gloucestershire eights went all the way with an abandon that one does not always see in the London district…….the Somerset men, great big-boned fellows, were simply splendid for two-thirds of the match. One of them, Thomas, was irresistible….just the sort of man who would be useful for England to play against Ireland."*

Regrettably for Bath followers, Welshman Billy Thomas did not play for England against Ireland. But, he was selected for the 1910 British Isles touring-party to South Africa, alas an honour which owing to work commitments he was reluctantly compelled to decline. But, such tours at this period lasted for some four months duration, and for Billy Thomas this was four months too long. There was disappointment too for Somerset in that clash at Kingsholm. For Gloucestershire clinched a 16-8 victory in front of an estimated five thousand crowd, then next a semi-final win against Kent, prior to their capture of the coveted crown itself with an emphatic 23-0 triumph against Yorkshire. It was Gloucestershire's first County Championship title….it would not be their last! Bath too had reason to smile if only because their form, once so erratic and unpredictable, now appeared to stabilize. Furthermore, their representation at county level (usually a reliable indicator of form) now jumped to an impressive eleven Somerset players called-up for duty during the season; while a further indicator was the interest shown by professional Northern Union clubs as regards certain players on the Rec (see Chapter 5); albeit an interest that potentially threatened to deplete Bath ranks somewhat, which was the last thing Bath needed. It was this season too when Bath adopted the colours with which they have now long been associated. Originally wearing shirts of blue, by season 1892-93 this evolved into blue and black hoops. Then there was another change in season 1906-07 when Bath adopted an all-white shirt. But again, these colours failed to satisfy everybody. So, it seems probable that someone suggested that **the club should combine all three previous colours,** resulting with a shirt which was duly described at the time as ***"blue, white and black hoops."*** The strip (the hoops widened somewhat in the 1920's) met with much approval. Indeed the favourable reaction was best expressed in the pages of The Bath Herald, (4th Sep. 1909) which drooled at the transformation: *"the new jerseys…..look wonderfully handsome,"* and no one, but no one, has ever questioned the club colours again. By season 1911-12 the admirable James Timmins would soon be

Alby Hatherill .... They got him to
The church (and the match) on time.

Acknowledgements: Bath Chronicle

ready to hang up his boots from senior rugby. But, among those who would be donning those 'wonderfully handsome' jerseys were two newcomers whose prowess would soon enough be widely recognised too. Their names were Norman and Vincent Coates, brothers with previous experience at the Bridgwater club (merging with Bridgwater Albion in 1922) and who had arrived with their parents in the previous year to take up residence in Bath. Their impact on the Rec was immediate, and with Kitching and Vincent Coates on the wings, Norman Coates at centre, and half-backs Alby Hatherill and F. Hill, Bath had never possessed such quality of 'outsides.' Moreover, no one understood this better than Eddie Simpkins. A former student-teacher at St. Luke's College, Exeter, he would now, owing to injury, devote his tireless energies towards vital areas of administration. By now a master at Oldfield Boys School, Mr Simkins was imbued with a longing to see his beloved club both attain and then hold on to first-class rugby status; and his service to Bath that continued until 1957 would never falter from that time in 1911 when his secretarial partnership with John Townsend-Piper commenced. Not surprisingly the

Vincent (Left) and Norman Coates

need to develop the strongest possible fixture-list ranked high on their priority-list. For although barely five seasons previously the future had seemed so bleak, a transformation was taking place before their eyes, and with better results being achieved and more expansive rugby being played, Bath began to look like a first-class club. And....these factors were the magnet that drew stronger opponents to the fixture-list. In the four seasons from 1910 to the conclusion of season 1913-14 the number of wins increased from 16, 20, 21 and then 22 victories respectively. Contrast these results with the seven wins of 1905-06 and the difference is striking, not least as the fixtures were now growing progressively stronger. Indeed, the likes of Leicester, Llanelli,

Coventry and Northampton were among those added to the Bath programme during this same 1910-14 period.

There would be three players holding the captaincy during these years of increasing improvement. First there was excellent half-back Alby Hatherill (1910-11), followed by Norman Coates (1911-13) then Philip Hope and, this being rugby, affairs of the heart sometimes intervened, as they did in the midst of Hatherill's captaincy when the 'small' matter of his marriage to Miss Sutton clashed with Bath's home game with Abertillery. A tricky problem this one; but not too tricky for Alby. His wedding at St. Paul's church took place in the morning. Come the afternoon he then made a dash to the Rec for the game. And no doubt receiving a rousing cheer from his troops who would surely have wondered if the skipper would make it to the ground (hopefully sober), he proudly led his men out against Abertillery. Just one slight problem skipper! Abertillery took home a two try win into Wales (Ouch!). However, yet further recognition of the club's increasing status was emphasised when the Somerset RFU chose the Rec as the venue for the game against **the 1912-13 South African tourists,** a decision surpassing any honour yet bestowed upon the club. The match on Thursday, 3rd October 1912 was the first fixture of the South African tour, the visitors due at Southampton (28th September) the previous weekend and then reportedly travelling by train direct to Bath. There (Chronicle, Sep. 1912) they were received by a club determined to make the tourists feel 'at home.' A concert was arranged at the Roman Baths on the evening of their arrival; so too another evening at the Theatre Royal. The Rec was made available for the tourists' training programme, next a visit to Longleat (the incomparably beautiful estate of the Marquis of Bath). A motor-car tour of the city was planned (cars even then something of a novelty); so too a further informal concert-party in the Georgian splendour of the Assembly Rooms; "*entertainments which were much appreciated by [the County] guests*" (70 years of Somerset Rugby, 1875-1945, p.28).

Four Bath men played for Somerset that day, namely brothers Norman and Vincent Coates (backs), F. Hill (half-back) and W. F. Warde (forwards), and although the Cidermen never lacked for endeavour, the visitors (winning 3-24) were another team to demonstrate the impressive strides made by the Southern Hemisphere nations. Bath much enjoyed hosting their esteemed guests however, and the tourists reciprocated by expressing their much felt appreciation of the welcome shown throughout their stay. Interestingly prior to their departure, **the South Africans are reliably reported to have described the Rec as "*the most beautiful rugby ground in the world.*"** It was fascinating therefore that a rugby follower (Mr Vic Rosenburg) not only vividly remembered the occasion of the South Africans' visit in 1912, but six decades later (Bath chronicle, 26th Oct.1973) recounted his memories as follows: "*Sportsmen in Bath were delighted when Somerset's game with the Springboks was allotted to the Recreation Ground in October 1912. Before the 1914 War, only about a dozen counties competed for the county rugby championship and therefore each of them was given a fixture with rugby tourists from* *overseas. The Bath club had a powerful and versatile line of threequarters at this time consisting of the brothers Vincent and Norman Coates, J.T. Timmins and A.J. Kitching.*

Vincent Coates was a Cambridge Blue, a strong runner with a fearsome "hand-off." His brother Norman was a well-built centre with a safe pair of hands. Timmins, a local solicitor, was also a well-equipped and strong player. A.J. Kitching, a master at Monkton Combe School, was probably the most elusive runner to have played for Bath. He was a slim man of medium height, probably weighing ten stone plus. But what a runner! He was once likened to a hare as he weaved his way through an opposing XV. His defence was very good and he rarely failed to get his man.

It was generally expected that Somerset would choose the entire Bath threequarter-line for this Springbok game, but to the surprise and disappointment of every local supporter, Kitching was left out. The County selectors chose a wing named R.V. Knight (later killed in the 1914-18 War) who was then at the Wells Theological College, and who had played in the previous season for the East Midlands in the county championship. Knight was tall and well-built with a mop of fair hair. It was thought his physique would enable him to deal more effectively with the powerful Springboks than the lighter Kitching, who, 61 years later is quietly living in retirement.

*Fortunately the weather was dry and kind on the day. In those days the two teams changed in the cricket pavilion **and then walked across the Rec to the rugby area. There was a wooden stand on a brick foundation and about 50 yards long** running alongside the river bank, but otherwise there was no cover for spectators. The ticket enclosure for spectators began at the Johnston Street end and along the north bank and then parallel to the river. Temporary stands were erected along the north bank and down the popular side. And the crowds gathered six to eight deep around the ground. The Press were accommodated in the stand and everyone, Press and spectators, sat on long, hard wooden forms.*

***The Springboks,** a mixture of British South Africans and Dutch South Africans, looked a physically strong and powerful XV, wearing green jerseys bearing a badge showing a golden "Springbok." They included three players named Morkel. G. Morkel played at full-back and could kick goals from any angle. The two Springbok wingers were J. Stegmann and E. McHardy, and Millar was the captain. The game produced many shining moments and as expected, the Springboks won. But reputations were made that day. Stegmann was reputed to be a "flier" but that day he met his master in Vincent Coates. Whenever Stegmann got the ball, he was floored by Coates. Whenever Coates had the ball he tore down the wing and usually handing off Stegmann as though the Springbok was a bag of flour.*

The crowd roared and the English selectors then present selected Vincent Coates for all the international games played that season. The Somerset forwards, led by Dibble, a Bridgwater Albion player and current English international, harried the Springboks, but were finally worn down by the superior physique of the visitors. It was a great occasion. Bathonians were proud of their county that day."

As Vic Rosenburg related, Vincent Coates was a formidable winger, one who had risen fast in rugby ranks since his schooling at Monkton Combe, next onwards to Haileybury and ISC, and later winning his Blue at Cambridge prior to completing his medical studies at Bristol University. It was thus hardly surprising that he subsequently played for England against South Africa (the tourists winning 3-9) and again in all four Home internationals. In fact, his six tries in the Home Championship set a new record which was bettered the following season by fellow England winger C.N. Lowe of Blackheath. The following tale is told of Vincent Coates in England's win over Wales in Cardiff that season. The Bath wingman had got home with a typical Coates try of forceful power, causing the Welsh skipper to shout at his full-back: *"why didn't you stop him?" "Stop him!"* the full-back replied, *"why, it took me all the time to get out of his way."*

Barely three years later the qualities of Dr Vincent Coates would be displayed in a rather different theatre (see Ch. 10). But for now, his surging runs on the wing were among the reasons to bring a smile to Bath rugby. Indeed 1913-14, the season of twenty-two wins (from 35 played) was **arguably the most impressive in the club's history so far**, both in terms of the quality of opposition and the over-all success that was achieved. Neither was a Bath defeat any longer a cause for a loss of confidence (as had happened to often in former years), but rather reason to make amends the 'next-time.' So, Bath's first ever encounter with then awesome Coventry (season 1912-13) was indeed a salutary lesson, Bath losing away 23-0. Their first ever encounter against Leicester (13th Sep. 1913) was another set-back with the Tigers' 19-5 victory at Welford Road. But, come the last quarter of that season a home 9-0 win over Bristol was further confirmation of a Bath improvement. At home strong Welsh opponents from Pontypool (5-0) and Penarth (9-8) had already been overcome, and now as Easter approached, the Bath Chronicle headlines beckoned the faithful to witness *"the opportunity of seeing on The Rec three of the finest teams in England,"* namely Coventry, Leicester and Gloucester. Could it get better than that!?

Coventry were encountered first during that Easter rugby festival, the same Coventry who had convincingly defeated Bath in their first ever meeting in the previous season, and had furthermore defeated Bath again in February of the current season by 14-3; and where (Bath & Wilts Chronicle, 2nd Mar. 1914. p.4) matters had got somewhat 'heated' either side of half-time: *"language was lurid, tackling hard, and throws into touch forcible. Then after Harry Vowles, Bath's young and highly talented scrum-half, was downed with altogether unnecessary violence, matters deteriorated yet further. There was a succession of loose scrums just after, fists were flying, boots swinging, and had the referee ordered off every man who struck a blow there would have been not many left to continue the match."* Fortunately, in terms of sportsmanship the Midlanders' visit to

The Rec in April turned out to be different. There was much Easter cheer, an estimated 4,500 spectators (Bath & Wilts Chronicle, 14th Apr. 1914, p.4) and Bath defeated Coventry (wait for this one): 41-10! Next, Leicester arrived and….Bath ran home four tries (one converted) to win 14-3. Then next to arrive were Gloucester. Oh dear….it just 'had' to be Gloucester. And yes, not for the first time the Cherry and Whites arrived with their own script. Bath played well. Gloucester (3-10) winners, played better. But, there was hopefully now one significant difference from past years. Because as the 'Cherries' returned homewards they surely knew that easy games on the Rec were perhaps a thing of the past.

Meanwhile, as Bath's final game of their 1913-14 rugby campaign was an away encounter at Penarth (the Welshmen 'ungraciously' winning 16-0) it was reported that the club would celebrate their season by way of an after-match dinner in Cardiff. There, in the congenial atmosphere around the dining table the conversation no doubt flowed as delightfully as did the food, ale and wine. The upset that day against old friends Penarth, who had lost 9-8 to Bath in February, would hardly have dampened Bathonian spirits however. For this was a season of some big, big wins among those twenty-two victories, and that included a 5-0 success on the Rec in March against Llanelli, who, taking no chances fielded a full-strength side that included Welsh internationals Isaac Davies, the Rev. Alban Davies, and W. Watts in their line-up.

So, at long last there seemed reason to believe that Bath had climbed the proverbial steep and challenging slope since stepping into a new century. During this era they had experienced both the highs and the lows within that fabled rugby school of hard knocks. But setbacks notwithstanding, the experiences had taught them never, ever, to give up on their mission to build a first-class rugby team. And as Bath reportedly dined happily on that April evening in Cardiff to celebrate an often inspiring season, they were a club whose long and sometimes hazardous 'rugby winter' had indeed turned into a rugby spring.

Chapter 10. THE SUMMER THAT NEVER CAME. (1914)

It was the 1st August 1914 and there, featured among the pages of Keene's Bath Journal was the forthcoming Bath fixture-list for season 1914-15. It made for good reading, and local rugby followers would surely have been enthused by the prospects that lay ahead, thanks to a rugby programme that was arguably the most exciting and demanding that Bath had yet faced. The opening game was at Leicester, a team already rated among the finest in the Land, and yet such was the transformation at Bath over recent years that even this daunting encounter looked possibly winnable. Winnable at Leicester!! Merely a few seasons previously such a suggestion would have seemed fantasy. But how times had changed dramatically for Bath in a few short years; yet how times were about to change dramatically once again!

Because (as a result of the earlier assassination of Archduke Francis Ferdinand, heir to the Austria-Hungary throne, and his wife, on 28 June 1914), those same pages featured news of a rather different kind, both in tone and content: *"German and Russian mobilization….Extraordinary Precautions,"* proclaimed one headline. Other ominous reports followed: *"Great precautions are being taken to protect Home defences and no vulnerable point is to be left exposed."* It was further stated that at *"the request of the government the Great Western Railway are specially guarding their bridges and telegraphs;"* moreover that *"there are over a dozen men employed in patrolling Box Tunnel,"* adding that *"in the vicinity of Bath men were yesterday to be seen on duty protecting the bridges."* Meanwhile the First Fleet (at anchorage off the Dorset coast during the summer days of 1914) was believed to have already set sail from Portland under the command of Admiral Sir G. Callaghan, and with sealed orders.

On Saturday the 8th August further ominous news filled the pages of Keene's Bath Journal (Britain having already declared war with Germany on the 4th August). The British cruiser HMS Amphion, striking a mine, was reported sunk on 7th August with the loss of 131 lives. Bath seaman W.C. Comley (gunner) was one of the survivors. Sadly, C.D.Gedge, the nephew of the Mayor of Bath, was not. He was the lone officer-fatality in the crew. Meanwhile perhaps the one report most directly affecting Bath (and every sports club in the Country) was the statement reporting that on 6th August the sum of one hundred million pounds (an astronomical sum at that period) had already been granted by parliament, and with it the sanction of plans to increase the army by 500,000 men.

On 1st September the Bath committee, aware that duty would require the services of every sportsman in the Land to serve King and Country, met at the Red house. The mood was sombre. It was decided to cancel all fixtures until further notice. A telegram was duly dispatched to Leicester, stating that Bath (with deep reluctance) would not be fulfilling their away fixture on 5th September. It was furthermore decided that all club property would be stored at the Red House for the duration of the emergency. The committee, furthermore realising that the younger generation would now have a vital role to play in reviving the game at some future date, prepared accordingly. It was announced that the club would now unite with the Bath Schools Rugby Union so as to "*do everything in their power to train the lads at rugby.*" Meanwhile the North Somerset Yeomanry were granted the use of The Rec for military purposes.

Each and every rugby club in the Land, at the bequest of the Rugby Union (Museum of Rugby, Twickenham) was acting in similar mode with members requested to 'join up' with the Forces, likewise the Football Association and the Football League. Soon enough the harsh realities of the events now unfolding on the Continent would strike at the very heart of these same sporting families, though their French cousins would feel the consequences first. In early September it was learned that Sub-Lieutenant de Castelnau, among the most widely known rugby footballers in France and now serving under the command of his father, General de Castelnau, had been killed. And for Bath, one bleak day in November 1914, there was also news. *It concerned former 1ˢᵗ team player **Alfred Cleall**, who had volunteered for service with the North Somerset Yeomanry. At Vlamertinghe **on a Flanders Field**, he too was killed in action.*

He was the club's first recorded fatality of the Great War. He would not be the last. Thus, there would be no encounter at Leicester, indeed no rugby for four long dark years; and the summer for the hitherto most promising team in Bath's history would not arrive after all.

Chapter 11. A TIME FOR QUIET REFLECTION. (1914-18).

As the *'lights went out all over Europe'* in that autumn of 1914, Britain was preparing for a conflict without parallel in its history, and no one could possibly predict the outcome. Hence sport, not least Rugby Football, ceased completely at any official level, though not entirely at the unofficial level. For example, schools-rugby did continue; and with Dominion servicemen now stationed in the UK throughout much of the conflict, there were occasions when teams, including those schools XV's, who did compete with those hardened men from Australia and New Zealand. But there was no normal club or international rugby (see: Rugby Chronology, World Museum of Rugby, Twickenham). Hence, those who followed Bath at home or on 'The Front' could only ponder upon the rugby fortunes that might have been, including perhaps a development that reached back to the early 1900's (see too Ch. 3&7), one instigated by a group of rugby followers, the outcome of which would prove invaluable to the long-term future of a Bath club struggling to recover from its serious loss of form in the bleak mid-winter years of the 1900's. It had all begun with a meeting (reportedly on 24th November 1901) attended by representatives from junior clubs that included Walcot, Combe Down, Batheaston (now Avonvale), Oldfield Park and quite probably Fairfield Rovers respectively (see too Ch. 3) whose aim was to establish a rugby alliance of local clubs both in and around the city, and as a result of this meeting that the **Bath & District Rugby Combination** would be launched.

Bath were not in fact acting in isolation, the idea having already caught on, or was catching on elsewhere, and Bristol were forming just such a Combination during this same period. Indeed, the concept was entirely logical, with mutual advantages between both the junior and senior clubs. Thus, in the case of the Bath Combination for example it was accepted as a general rule that while the senior club (namely Bath) could in normal circumstances acquire the use of a Combination player (s) on condition that sufficient prior notification was given, there was a 'return' for the provider, namely a near certainty that a Combination player on his return to his junior club would now be a better player for the experience gained at the senior level. Bath were not strangers to this concept as indeed Walcot would have testified as far back as the 1890's when negotiating for partial use of the Kensington Meadows. Initially, Bath had held out for an annual rent of £5 (small change now, but not in fact then), and furthermore a claim for up to five Walcot players (yes five!) each week. Happily, commonsense plus not a little moderation intervened, and as a result the rent was subsequently reduced to £3 per annum, and Bath were limited to a more 'civilised' Friday night deadline for two (not five) Walcot players. Anyway, Bath's priority was not one of financial gain, but instead the need to cover for any sudden emergencies (i.e.; injuries) that might, and indeed do occur in rugby.

Early records are not always precise, nor clearly referenced, but what is certain is that in the early 1900's Oldfield Park (not to be confused with Oldfield Old Boys) won no fewer than three from four 'League' Championships, Walcot winning another. Moreover, an historically invaluable photo of the Oldfield Park club, ("*1901-2 Bath Rugby Champions,*") remains, indicating that the Combination and its League Championship competition commenced from the 1901-2 season, while an example of the sheer passion of this Combination competition was witnessed decades later in season 1983-4. Appropriately staged on The Rec on a balmy spring evening and watched by some 3,000 followers, Glyn Broom of Old Culverhaysians would get the clincher with a massive late penalty to beat Combe Down by 3 points to nil in a quite pulsating encounter. Talk about a vibrant hotbed of local rugby, one that on its long journey has included among its membership: 'Avonvale, Bath Civil Service, Bath Harlequins, Bradford on Avon,

OLDFIELD PARK RUGBY FOOTBALL CLUB
1901-2 Bath Rugby Champions

Acknowledgements to Ben Hartley (former Bath RFC player)

Corsham, Frome, Keynsham, Melksham, Midsomer Norton, Old Culverhaysians, Old Edwardians, Oldfield Park, Oldfield Old Boys, O Sulians and Stothert & Pitt's,' and drew reported crowds of three thousand plus to watch the likes of Walcot confronting their great rivals Combe Down in the 1920's and 1930's. Meanwhile, a century onwards from that inaugural November meeting of 1901 their successors would gather for the Centenary in the splendour of the Guildhall on 30th November 2001. That great servant of Bath rugby, namely Gerry Moore (Walcot), would be among those attending, and likewise Bath mayor Cllr Marian McNeir. Present too was no less a guest than the President of the RFU himself, Roy Manock, who spoke of the Combination (and indeed of junior rugby in general) as a part of *"the foundation on which the game stands."* True words indeed, for the Combination, despite many difficulties encountered, not least financial, would remain a bed-rock for local rugby and usually willing (sometimes at a moment's notice) to release players to Bath, a commitment moreover that continued until the latter's adoption of professional rugby in the mid-1990's.

Four years onwards from the launch of the Combination a further foundation-stone was laid, on this occasion due to the efforts of a group of local Bathonian schoolmasters. They gathered at Northgate Chambers on 16th February 1904, agreeing forthwith to found the Bath Schools Rugby Union (launched in season 1905-6) so as *"to foster the playing of the game among the schoolboys of the city."* Almost immediately this innovative project was endorsed by the senior Bath Club who, anxious to encourage a strategy of long-term rugby development in the city, underwrote the initial costs of this fledgling Union. Enthusiasm among local schools abounded too, and would include (inter alia) Oldfield Council, Widcombe, St Pauls, Weymouth House, Bath Forum, St Stephens, Batheaston and Walcot School. Barely stopping to take a breath moreover a Schools League Cup competition was launched, and with it a trophy duly donated by the supportive Egbert Lewis, a local JP and the Bath Schools Rugby Union's first president.

One school however would initially shine above them all, namely the East Twerton Council School. Playing in colours of black and red hoops and coached by the dedicated Mr R. R. Stephenson, they won every game of the League Cup competition launched in season 1905-6 without conceding so much as a single point, let alone a game. They played fourteen matches and won fourteen matches. They scored 441 points and did not conceded a single one. They topped the League with maximum points, and so became the first-ever winners of that much coveted Cup trophy. Furthermore, within the first three years of the Bath Schools RFU the East Twerton School (which almost a century later in 1999 would become the Oldfield Park Infants School) had produced two schools-internationals in forward C. Parsons and half-back Harry Vowles; while in the Schools Trial at Coventry of 1906-7 no less than four East Twerton Council School pupils played, namely Hingston, Brice, Love, and that youngster Harry Vowles, of whom much more later (see Ch. 12).

Not surprisingly Bath were not alone in their enthusiasm for schools-rugby. The Leicester & District Schools Union for example was formed during this same period, and it was their own Hon.Secretary (J.C.Cooper) who was prominent among other supportive clubs (which included Bath, Bristol, Gloucester and Exeter) who established **The Schools Rugby Union,** a national body with the aim of advancing schools rugby football throughout the whole Country. Yet Bath realised that yet further work remained, because (until the 1940's) the standard State School leaving-age was set at fourteen years and so a pupil's rugby progress could therefore stop abruptly when schooldays ended. Hence, the game was 'crying out' for Colts rugby. And, thanks partly to the dedication of club stalwart Harry Slade, the **Bath Ex-schools XV** was established in 1934, an innovation partly influenced by Cardiff's own system of post-schools rugby development. Next, to cover the equally crucial sixteen to eighteen years group, Bath would form their Colts team in the season following the establishment of the Ex Schools side. So, with a direct route from schools to senior rugby the bridge-building was now complete, another invaluable legacy of that small group of enlightened local school-teachers, whose foresight back in 1904/5 ensured that no barriers would prevent even the youngest of players from one day reaching the Rec.

Chapter 12. THE GREATEST DAY IN HISTORY. (11th Nov 1912).

On Saturday, 16th November, 1918, the headline of the Bath Weekly Chronicle spoke in effect a million words: *"The Greatest Day in History."* On the same page was a photograph of the Abbey churchyard now thronged with joyous people. Beneath were the following words:

"Monday, when the news arrived that the Armistice had been signed and that the "ceasefire" had sounded along the whole of our far-flung battle-line, has been described as the "greatest day in history." It was celebrated in Bath with an unprecedented outburst of rejoicing, and the inhabitants thronged to the Abbey to render thanksgiving to the Great Disposer of Events for the happy news the day had brought. So general was the desire to participate in such a memorable service that the Abbey was filled a few minutes after the doors were opened, and the Abbey Churchyard, as our photograph shows, was crowded with people unable to gain admission. The Mayor and Corporation attended in State."

Thus Bath, and countless other towns, villages and cities around the Country, stepped back into the 'daylight.' As for rugby football however (and the sporting world generally), their playing ranks were now alas depleted. Hence it remained to be seen exactly when any form of official rugby might be restored. Yet perhaps to the surprise of many, Bath had tentatively launched their own initial post-war rugby game (a trial match) as early as Saturday, 15th February 1919. The venue appropriately was The Rec, Bath's spiritual rugby home, a ground that during the conflict had been requisitioned for use by the Armed Forces, then vacated by the RAF (prior to April 1918 known as the Royal Flying Corps) as recently as the previous week. But notwithstanding that this would be an occasion for fresh hopes and a new beginning, there were recent memories that had yet to heal. Such sentiments moreover found expression in the sporting columns of the Bath Chronicle reporting on that trial game, and few stones were left unturned: *"included in the teams turning out for the Bath Football 'trial' were many who have suffered torturing wounds, and others who have tasted the cruelties of Hun internment camps, while the committeemen looking on to select the wherewithal for "reconstruction" mourn two gallant colleagues blown to atoms or buried by German shells, for their fate had never been actually known."*

In fact, there were to be rather more than 'two' gallant colleagues who would alas not be returning from the Front, among them Bath's **Alf Cleall, Loo Hatherill, Tom West (Rifle Corps), Douglas West (Manchester Regiment), lieutenant-Colonel Gustavus Perreau (Indian Army) and not forgetting sub-Lieutenant Frederick Hill who as a half-back won schoolboy international honours in 1905-6.** Furthermore, there were **the twelve fatalities suffered by the former Widcombe Juniors,** who partly as a result of their terrible loss would never recover, and from whose ranks many a Bath player had previously come (Bath & Wilts Chronicle, 5th Sep. 1919). Mercifully there were those former players (thankfully reasonably unscathed) yet to return from war-time action, but whose availability nonetheless remained uncertain. Captain Vincent Coates for example (decorated with the Military Cross for gallantry in France, later posted to the Balkan Forces for research as a bacteriologist and then transferred to the Croydon Military Hospital) and who would not arrive home until the Autumn of 1919, but who if fit could add inspiration both on (and off) the field. Fortunately, others (and not forgetting new arrivals) were available to step onto a rugby field once again, there to feel after four long years the sheer elation of freedom.

At this same period the Bath Chronicle (15th Feb. 1919) reported that among the guests residing at Bath's Empire Hotel (later the Admiralty building) that overlooked the Rec and perhaps casting a watchful eye, was no less an icon than Rudyard Kipling; and as befits an author of the exploits (inter alia) of British soldiery, he doubtless would have understood the poignancy of this particular encounter….Bath v Bristol, two rivals, but two rivals sharing a unique bond, not least in the aftermath of the shattering events of the previous four years.

For the Bristolians too had suffered grievously in the recent conflict. Indeed, it is recorded that they had lost no less than fourteen players killed in action. In fact, so severe was this depletion that the club did not play as Bristol for fully another season, and instead played as Bristol United (their reserve team's title). Thus, in Bath's first inter-club game since World War 1, played on the Rec on 22nd February 1919, there could be no more worthy opponents. The result (Bath won 8-3) was really of secondary importance. What did matter was the fact that one's thoughts were no longer of deep and muddied trenches in places far away, but instead of a regained liberty to play rugby on the playing fields of England. Other fixtures duly followed, including Bath versus a New Zealand Services side (lost 3-13), a further upset in front of a large Rec crowd against Abertillery (lost 0-14), and an end-of-season home victory against old adversaries Pontypool (8-4), again attracting a large and enthusiastic attendance. There was one further victory for followers of rugby to cherish, namely the fact that within barely three months since the Armistice the rugby game was active, in some form at least, across much of the British Isles. While in Bath's concluding match against the hard men of Pontypool, the club were to witness the first appearance of a young outside-half by the name of S.G.U. Considine. In his late teens and still at Blundell's School, reports of his rugby prowess had nonetheless reached the Rec. He looked a smart little player of exciting promise did this young S.G.U., and around his later partnership with former schools' international scrum-half Harry Vowles (now returned from four years military service in France) a 'special' team was to be forged; and notwithstanding that few if any would have dared to raise their expectations too soon, halcyon days now beckoned.

Chapter 13. THE RESTORATION. (1919-1920)

On the evening of Tuesday, 26th August, 1919, members of Bath Football Club gathered at the Red House, there to attend the 'after-the-war-dinner.' Originally planned to celebrate **Bath's Golden Jubilee in season 1914-15,** the War had delayed the occasion. Now however there was reason to smile again and the mayor, who submitted the toast at this emotional gathering, commented to the assembled party that *"they little thought that this time twelve months ago they would see such a revival of sport this year."* But a revival there was, and at this gathering there was opportunity for speeches, for music and of course song. Mr W.E. Angell was at the piano, so too the delightful presence of Miss Appennea Roberts and Miss Lily Morgan adding singing and charm to the happy occasion, while among those present was a certain Mr T.J. Gandy, no less than one of the original founder members of the club (Bath Centenary Book, pp. 25-26). Maybe the conversation amongst the gathering included reference to the brothers James and Christian Pitman of Bath (grandsons of the late Sir Isaac Pitman). Still at Eton, their prowess was now attracting serious interest among sporting journalists. Both outstanding middle-distance runners, hurdlers and sprinters, James Pitman had won the 880 yards event at the 1918 Public Schools Championships. But rather less was known about his rugby potential. Small wonder, because Eton was a soccer school, although soon enough any doubts as to whether young James might have a future in rugby were cast aside….and in some style too (Bath Chronicle, 5th Apr. 1919, p.1).

Almost certainly news of another Bathonian, one **Arnold Ridley,** was discussed. The one-time school teacher and graduate of the Bristol University Dramatic Society was earning commendable reviews that year with the Birmingham Repertory Theatre, and like so many of his generation he too had a tale to tell. Serving with the 6th Somersets, he was reportedly engaged in a deadly hand-to-hand encounter with a German soldier near Delville Wood during the Somme offensive of 1916. It was here that a resulting bayonet wound would cause a long-term handicap to his left arm, a wound moreover that would require much skilful make-up whenever Arnold 'trod the stage.' But the kindly actor was already laying the foundations for a notable theatrical career that would span five decades and include the stage success of his own creation '**The Ghost Train'** (he wrote over 30 other plays) and not forgetting his appointment as club president of Bath (1950-52), nor later the national acclaim for his role in 'Dad's Army,' the much loved World War Two television comedy series, and furthermore his award of an OBE in 1982 two years before he passed away at 88 years of age (see too: review of *Godfrey's Ghost; From Father to Son, by Nicholas Ridley*), the Bath Chronicle, 24th Sep. 2009. No doubt discussion would have included the hopes for the future of the club, and the key question as to whether or not the momentum of that fine pre-war team ('when winter turned to Spring') could continue despite the four years curtailment of rugby football. So now only those hastily arranged matches in the spring of 1919 provided any clues as to Bath's future prospects, while lying in wait for them in their opening game of season 1919-20 was one of the greatest names in rugby….Leicester!

Happily, there were no worries regarding the use of **the Rec. A further ten-year lease had been agreed with the Recreation Ground Company, partly because Bath had been 'good paying tenants ever since the Company was formed.'** Finances too had been helped if only marginally by those matches played in the previous spring, though to the club's regret it was financially imperative to increase season tickets from six shillings annually to twelve shillings (men), and five shillings for ladies. Today such prices seem the proverbial 'give-away,' but not in those post-war straightened times. Fixtures too required a revamp, as not every club had yet recovered from the effects of the War. Hence to fulfil Bath's season of 1919-20 no fewer than four games with Bristol were arranged and a number of less-known opponents were added, including Paignton and Burnham.

The captaincy was offered to, and accepted by, winger Philip Hope, while new faces in the backs appeared, among them centre Harry Richardson, the athletic utility back Clarence Whittaker, and young wingman Tom Fry, nephew of 'Tich' Fry who had so delighted Bath crowds in the 1890's. In addition, there was the potential brilliance of half-backs Harry Vowles and Blundells schoolboy S.G.U. Considine. But, for a club elated by its acquisition of top-class outsides in the run-up to World War One, the vital question was: could the post-war arrivals aspire to such standards? Meanwhile, at forward it was decided that W.H.Royal (an Old Monktonian) would lead the pack, and finally there was the one man whom Philip Hope (and others) still felt was indispensable. That man was Frank Cashnella, now forty years of age, yet often worth points on the score-board simply by 'being there.' After all Bath, notwithstanding possessing some players of proven experience (including forward Fred Russell) were pinning their hopes on a number of new faces. So off to Leicester on the 6th September 1919, where striding out at Welford Road to the accompaniment from a local band playing 'Should auld acquaintance be forgot' and the applause of a reported ten thousand crowd, the following Bath team (no less then eleven Bath born) braced itself for one of the truly historic encounters in the club's entire history: *C. Whittaker, P.P. Hope (Capt.), A. Hope, H. Richardson, T. Fry, S.G.U.Considine, H. Vowles, W.H. Royal, W. Worger, E. Hodges, F. Russell, W. Harding, J. Pope, L. Richardson, F.J. Cashnella.*

It need hardly be said that only an exceptional performance would ever win against the Tigers on their home territory. But Bath did not just win, they triumphed 3-16 thanks to four tries (two converted) against Leicester's one. Skipper Philip Hope clinched two touchdowns, his second an absolute gem launched from his interception inside Bath's 25 yard line to scream off for a scorcher that no defender could stop. New boy Tom Fry then caught a cross kick to jink over for another, before Cashnella (who else?) crashed through some three opponents to bludgeon over the line, dropping the ball but enabling Harding to touch down for Bath. Subsequently described by the Bath & Wilts Chronicle (6th Sep.1919) as *"a finer result than ever before recorded in the Club's long history,"* this was no ordinary success. Moreover, the fact that two weeks later Leicester would defeat Coventry 39-3 simply confirmed the sheer scale of Bath's achievement, one that would inspire that critical factor of self-belief among the team, a victory whose long-term effect would help inspire the finest Bath team yet seen. As for the homewards train journey from Leicester, jubilant Bath spirits were not to be dampened by a three-hour delay at Didcot, since by happy coincidence a travelling fair just happened to be visiting nearby. And surprise, surprise, to that same fair did the Bath team now made tracks, whereupon with commendable understatement the Chronicle (13th Sep. 1919) commented thus upon this same opportune visit: *"there was more fun at that fair than its proprietors could ever have contemplated."* One needs no convincing! Nor is it any exaggeration to add that something almost spiritual was happening that day. An horrendous war was thankfully over. Leicester had been beaten at Welford Road. The Bath club was bonding again, and each and everyone was soaking up the atmosphere ('living the dream' if you like) that only a sense of a renewed post-war euphoria could bring. Thus, amid the carnival atmosphere of a travelling fair at Didcot a somewhat tired yet truly joyous rugby team were experiencing one of the most enchanting days in Bath rugby history.

Yet in this of all seasons **tragedy** would later strike! Once again, memories of a grievous injury would haunt the Rec, where twenty seasons previously Bath and the Portsmouth club were confronted with the numbing experience of the fatal injury to the visitor's vice-captain George Trerise. Now, with the visit of Welsh side Cross-Keys on 27th December 1919, those same memories would return with a vengeance, when midway through the second half of this Christmas holiday game George Greenslade of Cross Keys tackled Bath utility back Clifford Walwin. A violent collision resulted and both men fell unconscious. Walwin, after initial attention from the St. John's Ambulance Brigade, returned by taxi to his Lambridge home accompanied by his wife who had been watching the game. But soon enough (Chronicle, 3rd Jan. 1920) it was learned that Clifford Walwin had suffered a serious injury. On the following Monday fuller details would be described at the inquest requested by the Bath City Coroner. It was stated (inter alia) that the injured Clifford Walwin, shortly after arriving at his home

Clifford Walwin
'Tragedy on the Rec.'
Acknowledgment :Bath Past Players

was then attended professionally by Dr James Lindsay. He instructed that the injured player be taken immediately to a nearby nursing home, whereupon Mr Forbes Fraser (in consultation with Dr Lindsay) decided that an operation was now necessary. By 9pm, with surgery now completed, witnesses were able to speak to Clifford, and it was stated that they were hopeful of a recovery. But as the inquest would later learn: *"About five minutes to mid-night he simply collapsed."* Then, five minutes after mid-night, Clifford Walwin, 29 years of age, died suddenly. To many, it must have seemed that 'only yesterday' a similar incident had cast its shadow over the Rec with the fatal injury to Portmouth's George Trerise. The feeling of sadness throughout the club was palpable.

Born in Gloucester and educated at the Crypt School, George Trerise had played with distinction for Bath as early as season 1911-12 under the captaincy of Norman Coates, who ironically (as a guest player) was co-centre with Walwin on that fateful day against Cross Keys. Walwin (a trained pharmacist with a Bath practice) was a player good enough in fact to have represented Somerset against Devon and Middlesex respectively in 1914. The War then followed (in which Clifford lost a younger brother) and he joined the Somerset 35 Red Cross Voluntary Aid detachment. He had married Hilda Blake, a well-known Bath soprano, on 4th October 1914 at the Walcot Wesleyan church, and they would later have a daughter, two and half years old at the time of the tragedy. An indication of the deepest affection he attracted was shown by the packed church on the day of his funeral, held on the Wednesday after the accident; it was shown too by the words of the Rev. A. G. Tuck (the officiating minister at that service) who spoke of his grief when he heard of the tragedy; it was revealed again by "*a great crowd*" who assembled outside that same church to show its respects; and not least by the words of The Bath Chronicle in describing Clifford Walwin thus: "*there was no man who has ever donned the Bath jersey who was more generally beloved.*"

It is imperative to add that the Coroner-jury were unanimous in finding that this had been a case of accidental death and that the Cross Keys player was exonerated from all blame. Indeed, Bath regarded Cross Keys as the cleanest side in Wales, and the referee (schoolmaster George Hancock from Bristol) stated to the inquest that "*the game was peculiarly free from anything like rough play.*" Just such sentiments were readily supported by Bath official Mr W.F. Long; while Mr William Edwards (secretary, Cross Keys F.C.) spoke of the deep sympathies of the Welsh club for both Bath and the bereaved relatives. Nor should it be forgotten that George Greenslade too had been seriously injured in the collision and it was later reported that he himself did not recover for at least another two seasons. Hence there was no animosity whatsoever between the two clubs, and it was former Gloucester and England half-back D.R. Gent, who as a correspondent for the Sunday Times (and reported in the Chronicle, 5th Jan.1920) expressed just how widespread was the resulting sense of loss with the following eulogy: "*I knew Walwin (an old Gloucester boy by the way) well, both as a player and a man. A more genuine sportsman never played for Bath or any other club. He was not quite a first-class player but he was a first-class sportsman, a man the club could always rely upon to turn out, even at the last minute, and every minute of the game he was heart and soul for his side. What admirable fellows these are: always at their club's disposal, consistently good in their play, and ever clean in their tactics. They are to be found in every club – its backbone, really. They do not get the plaudits of the crowd or Press, like the "stars," but their worth is appreciated by players, officials, and all who understand the stuff of which the torch-bearers of the traditions of Rugby are made. Of such was Walwin.*" Come the following Saturday and the Rec was silent, the club withdrawing from all rugby activity. Bath hockey players did likewise and a sorrow hung over the sporting heart of the city.

However, the next encounter following the tragedy was at Gloucester, ironically Walwin's city of birth. That Bath lost heavily by 24-0 was in the circumstances understandable, a situation not entirely helped by the fact that the team were weakened through call-ups for Somerset on the same day. And anyway Bath 'would' recover, as Clifford Walwin would only have wanted, while strong rumour that scouts from Leeds (Northern Union) were watching certain Bath players with more than a passing interest was evidence, although not entirely welcome, of the talent down on the Rec. Certain results however of the 1919-20 season revealed one of the puzzling traits that characterised the club for literally years to come. For example, Bath encountered Bristol on four occasions, winning only once, but with an outstanding 9-19 success 'away,' a top result similar to 'that' great day at Leicester. And, as the years passed Bath would not infrequently reveal this similar trait, reaching the heights then resting on their laurels and let 'smaller fish slip through their fingers.'

Yet this conundrum notwithstanding, the over-all performance of the 1919-20 side suggested that the club could continue to live at the first-class level of the game. Admittedly 15 games were lost, 4 games drawn, but a healthy 21 victories recorded from 40 played (the Centenary Book quotes 20 wins from 39 played); while included among notable successes were wins over London Irish (37-8), Leicester again (8-16) and London Welsh (18-0). Thus, this crucial season, upon which so much would depend, achieved its mission, namely to re-build the broken pieces resulting from the Great War and establish a solid foundation for the future, a task that would yield an immediate post-war win-tally of 20, 21, 25 wins from 1919-1920, 1920-1921 and 1921-22 respectively, and to be followed by arguably the most exciting team yet to be seen in Bath colours. Yes, the Restoration had begun!

Chapter 14. 1922-3….WHEN BATH CAME OF AGE.

Looking back through the previous decades of rugby it was the season of 1922-3 under captain Harry Vowles (and thanks not least to the legacy of his predecessor Philip Hope) that could be described as that season when 'Bath came of age,' albeit a culmination of growing improvements either side of the Great War, with a list of prestige victories that included the 11-3 win (admittedly at home) against Stade Bordelais in the previous 1921-22 season. Yet something extra 'stood out' in the 1922-3 campaign, and that something was glamour, brought about not least by Bath's critical role in bringing the Holy Grail of the County Championship to Somerset. The side (later called 'squads' in future rugby decades) was built around the outstanding (and sometimes brilliant) half-back partnership of scrum-half Harry Vowles and S.G.U. Considine. Secondly, talented players were in abundance, not least the brothers Joe Richardson (forwards) and Harry Richardson (backs). Third, Bath no longer felt out of place amid the demanding Anglo-Welsh first-class ranks of the game, while 'that' 11-3 victory (see above) over French team Stade Bordelais in April of the previous 1921-22 season would have provided yet another confidence-boost. And what a season that one proved to be, with 25 wins under its belt….the best yet. Now the challenge was to better it.

In fact Bath's start to the 1922-3 campaign that included away upsets at Leicester (16-8) and Gloucester (17-5) respectively was somewhat inauspicious. But later in the month (Bath Herald, 23rd Sep. 1922) *"W.J.A, Davies, England's premier rugby exponent, brought his then famous side of United Services [Portsmouth] to Bath…."* Like the Devonport Services club, another forces side, United Services ranked high for decades amongst the first-class game. They produced legions of county players and not a few internationals that during this era included the acclaimed England half-back partnership of scrum-half C. A. Kershaw and W.J. A. Davies, although Kershaw's late withdrawal that day was doubtless a deep disappointment to a reported four thousand plus crowd. Meanwhile, a small group of gentlemen was present among that same crowd, a group with more than a passing interest in Bath and with a mission to find a Somerset team capable at long last of capturing that long-sought trophy….the County Championship.

Their presence was hardly surprising, as Bath were by now ranked among the strongest teams in the West Country, with a number of potential candidates for Somerset, not least in their backs! These included wingers James Pitman (also a Harlequin, Oxford Blue and by now England), W.J. Gibbs (already a Warwickshire county back), L.V. Burt, G.Woodward, Bert Morgan and Harry Richardson; likewise the ever-improving Bert Comm at full-back (later signing professional) and the brilliant half-backs of Vowles and Considine. A further significant factor during this era was Bath's adoption of the 'five-eighth game,' originally a New Zealand formation that had found favour with certain clubs in the British Isles in the 1920's and involved playing a seven-man pack (rather than eight) and a back-division of eight rather than seven. The five-eight operated as an additional outside-half, and even now is a tactic not entirely consigned to history (for brief periods of a game admittedly) when an attacking team close to their opponent's try-line calculates that seven forwards are sufficiently strong to reinforce their backs with an additional player. For the Somerset selectors therefore Bath's 5-8th experience provided an extra string to their bow, not least should the county find itself facing opposition applying this same tactic. And crucial it would later prove to be! Meanwhile the 9-4 win against US Portsmouth was to be Bath's first major win of a memorable season, one that included victories against 'big guns' such as Aberavon (18-3) in October, a match that

The Vowles Team was always a team of excitement, win or lose

L to R Back Row (standing): W.T. Davis (Touch Judge), F.J. Cashnella (Committee), L.J. Richardson, L.W. Bisgrove, W.H. Sheppard, J. Dobson, C.C. Wills (Vice-Chairman), R.S. Chaddock, J.T. Piper (Hon. Sec.), C.E. Carruthers, C.Mannings, E.F. Simpkins (Hon. Sec), A. Hatherill (Trainer). Middle Row (Sitting): H.J. Comm, H. Richardson, G. Woodward, H. Vowles (Captain), Dr. F.A. Meine, W.J. Gibbs, G.A. Roberts (Hon. Treas.). In front: L.V. Burt and S.G.U. Considine.

witnessed an 80 yard dash by England wing James Pitman for a try so spectacular that it raised a roar from the Rec that was reportedly heard on the Odd Down golf links two miles away (Herald, 14th Oct. 1922). Pitman would likely have run home many more but for the curse of a leg fracture that would shortly halt his rugby for the remainder of the season. But, injuries are a well-known occupational hazard in rugby, and Bath knew that they must simply 'get on with it.' They did, and marched onwards and for the most part upwards. Further high-profile victories followed, including home wins over London Welsh (20-0), Cross-Keys (4-3), while in December the notable 9-6 victory over Gloucester was the latter's first defeat by English opponents that season.

Acknowledgements to Bath Chronicle
April 1925 (Football Herald) Bath 18 vs U.S Portsmouth 10.
C. Mannings scores. Note original seated West Stand.

Meanwhile arousing excitement throughout Somerset was the red-hot form of their county in the County Championship, a competition won by Gloucestershire for the past three years, now hell-bent to increase that total to four, a team moreover generally selected around the formidable Bristol and Gloucester duo, though not forgetting talent to be found in the ranks at Cheltenham, Clifton and to a lesser extent Lydney. Somerset by contrast were generally chosen from a wider rugby parish stretching from Bath in the East to Wellington and Wiveliscombe in the West, whilst mid-way lay Weston-super-Mare, Bridgwater and Taunton, though occasionally Bristol and Clifton players qualified too. Thus, as a result of this more scattered rugby community Somerset-selection tended to be less straightforward than that of their Gloucestershire neighbours. Meanwhile, Bath's increasing improvement was confirmed by their unprecedented ten players (a mix of both forwards and backs) chosen for the county during that season, as Somerset blazed a trail through the South West division with wins over Cornwall (21-7), all-powerful Gloucestershire (10-8) and an 0-14 away victory over Devon at Torquay watched by a reported seven thousand crowd. All then was set for a semi-final at Taunton (17th February) against Kent, an encounter reportedly attracting a nine thousand crowd. Kent, formidable and former County Champions themselves, would run home a Jacob try converted by McLennan, while Somerset went two better with three tries (Reg Quick, J. Reed and F. Spriggs), and adding a Gaisford penalty for a 12-5 victory, so opening the way to the County Championship final, the ultimate test of their pedigree.

Bath now continued to enhance their own reputation with a string of high profile victories that included home wins over Plymouth Albion, Pontypool and Blackheath, all then top opposition; and likewise a narrow 5-4 win over Devonport Services who provided no

57

less than four players in that season's final England Trial, of whom both fullback F.G.Gilbert and forward William Luddington would be selected for England. Furthermore, there was to be an eye-catching Bath away success against Oxford University (28th Feb. 1923), where it was realised from the outset that if the Dark Blues were to be beaten then it was absolutely imperative that their international outside-half Harold Kittermaster must be watched like a hawk. So, a tactic was devised whereby this danger-man would be tempted to turn inwards through a seemingly unopposed corridor whenever receiving ball from his forwards. In fact it was a trap, and Oxford fell for it! For ready and waiting at the far end of that corridor was the highly effective Bath back-row of Carruthers, Dobson and Humphries. The ploy worked like a dream. The Oxford attack was blunted and the visitors duly ran home three tries (none converted) by Considine, Joe Richardson and F.A.Meine, so gaining a prestigious win (0-9) where Bath in the words of the Chronicle were *"full value for their victory in a game very brilliant in patches."*

Sometimes it is not only prestigious victories that are long remembered, but valiant defeats, and especially so if facing among the best sides in British rugby, as indeed was the case with Bath's agonisingly close 10-9 upset at Llanelli in November; while on 10th February 1923 Newport arrived on the Rec. Hailed by the Chronicle as *"perhaps the most famous side in the world"* the visitors drew an estimated 7,000 crowd, an attendance that included some hundreds arriving on chartered trains from Wales. And, without a weakness anywhere, the question depended on whether Newport could be held at forward. The watching 'South Wales Argus' reporter provided the answer: *"Bath have a fine pack of forwards. They made good at the line out, quick to get away with footwork, clever in supporting each other in combined rushes. They were often dangerous."* Of the outsides The Argus further noted that *"….the backs of both sides did their utmost to attack by running and passing, and both put in movements which were excellent…."* Newport however came unbeaten, and with a lone drop goal ensuring an 0-4 victory they departed unbeaten. But as at Llanelli Bath had got close, albeit "not quite close enough." Yes, they were moving in the right direction, though yet to actually reach their long sought destination….namely defeating those 'top' Welsh sides.

On Saturday, 14th April 1923 at Bridgwater all eyes were on Somerset, now carrying the hopes of an entire county on their shoulders. Facing them would be Leicestershire, a team ominously selected entirely from the Leicester club with the exception of Nottingham's C.J. Burton in the backs. It had therefore been unwise (to put it mildly) for county skipper R.G.B. Quick to have played for Bristol in their 3-0 mid-week home win against (ironically) Bath, and this just three days prior to the final. A shoulder injury resulted, just about the last thing the selectors needed, and this to a player then rated (see; Seventy Years of Somerset rugby, p.34) as *"among the finest wings we have ever had."* Clifton's E.H.Esbester was then hurriedly chosen to fill the gap, and the captaincy switched to Bridgwater half-back J. Jarvis. Yet another late quandary for the Somerset selectors concerned the use, or otherwise, of the unorthodox 5-8th formation then currently played at the Leicester club, and equally successfully utilised by the Leicestershire county side. Yet while one view among Somerset selectors considered it too late to switch to these unorthodox tactics, the opposing view held that it was a risk that simply 'must' be taken, and not forgetting Bath's own 5-8th experience. Furthermore, with half-backs Considine and Vowless and the entire Bath back-row of Sheppard, Bisgrove and Mannings all experienced in these tactics, Somerset were a team equipped to deal with a Leicestershire side certain to apply them. So, the selectors gambled on risk and opted for the 5-8th.

Without doubt Somerset's back division looked impressive. Centres E. Hammett and A.E. Thomson had previously played for England and Scotland respectively, and Vowles and Considine ranked among the best halves in English rugby. Meine too was a proven wingman, and not forgetting the probable psychological 'lift' provided by Bath's recent 17-3 home win over the Leicester club, **Somerset** took the field as follows: *W. Gaisford (Clifton), F.Meine (Bath), E.Hammett (Blackheath), A.E. Thomson (Wellington), E. Esbester (Clifton), J.Jarvis (Bridgwater, capt.), S.G.U. Considine (Bath), H. Vowles (Bath), backs. A. Spriggs, F. Spriggs, P. Lewis and J. Reed (all Bridgwater), W. Sheppard, L.Bisgrove and C. Mannings (all Bath), forwards.*

Facing them for **Leicestershire** (with former Bath favourite Norman Coates *now* of the Leicester club in their ranks) were: *L.C.Sambrook, E. Haselmere, P.Laurie, N. Coates, A.M.Smallwood, C.J. Burton, G.J. German, T.F.Taylor, G.Ward, J.C. Davis, C.Cross, H. Grierson, D.J. Norman, M.T.Thornloe, H. Sharratt (all Leicester except back C.J. Burton of Nottingham). Referee: Mr T. Vile, Newport.*

An estimated ten thousand crowd filled the Bridgwater ground to witness the most important encounter so far in Somerset's rugby history, one that according to county records (Seventy Years of Somerset rugby, p.34) was *"an intensely thrilling match,"* with home captain J. Jarvis scoring the opening try within seven minutes (W. Gaisford converting superbly from wide out) to set pulses racing. Winger F. A. Meine (Bath) then sent them racing yet further ahead when running home for a second score, although an 8-0 lead in rugby was easily catchable as Leicestershire soon showed. Having absorbed the earlier Somerset pressure, the visitors then settled into their stride, replying with a Smallwood try and then another by Burton far out, and sheer relief rose from the Somerset crowd as Thornloe's attempt at conversion missed its target....just! With the Cidermens' lead now hanging on a thread, the closing phase featured ever more determined Leicestershire attacks that drove Somerset into desperate defence, while two further Thornloe penalty attempts again fell just short. That would prove however to be the Midlanders' last throw of the dice. Somerset held on to that 8-6 lead in the remaining nail-biting minutes and with it captured the coveted Championship trophy that every county treasured. It was to be their finest day....ever!

Bath, with six players in that county side played a key role, while that same season achieving their highest total yet of 26 club victories, albeit many would argue that the October win at Blundells (0-17) with a purely 'schools visiting side' should not have been included as a 1st XV fixture. But it was not merely the number of wins, but the quality of rugby played that made things so special. True, three games were drawn, sixteen lost, and if discounting London Welsh then fortress Wales remained just that….a fortress. True also that Bristol (beaten 6-3 on the Rec in the last game of the previous season) could not be beaten either. Yet some of the best sides in England and Wales (including Leicester at home) were overcome on the Rec, and the home and away double was achieved against both London Welsh and Moseley. *"Better rugby has never been seen in Bath,"* wrote The Mascot, adding that *"the splendid crowds which have witnessed the home games are evidence of the popularity of the game in Bath."* The further news that the forthcoming 1923-4 season would commence *"with the fixture list [yet]strengthened"* would have resonated too with those who remembered those bleak days when many had feared whether there would be a rugby future at all for Bath. Now the Rec was home to a genuine first-class side, and following in the footsteps of Philip Hope, this Harry Vowles team of 1922-3 was confirmation that Bath had 'come of age!'

Chapter 15. A CHALLENGING MID-TWENTIES.

Following the leadership of Harry Vowles (1922-24), the captaincy passed to S.G.U. Considine with Bath's momentum continuing for another season with a healthy total of victories, some of which got the pulses really racing, not least Bath's first ever away triumph over Bristol at the Memorial ground (7-11) in early December, and the later defeat of Newport 6-3 on the Rec watched by a reported 7,000 spectators (Bath Football Herald, 14th Mar. 1925). The return from injury of James Pitman was an added bonus, not as a wing (his England position), but this time as centre. Moreover, he adjusted to this position so well that Bath would rate him in the same company as the likes of James Timmins and Norman Coates, no mean comparison! Meanwhile a rather unexpected (yet highly valuable) late season recruit to make an appearance in the backs was outside-half J.R.Wheeler. Now, Mr Wheeler was not only a practicing doctor, but an Irish international, and since his parent club (the London Hospital) had already concluded their own rugby season, this allowed players in the then amateur game to guest for another club. He chose Bath and the four cap Irishman was excellent. As for genuine utility players they did not come much better than Combe Down product Harry Slade, who could play literally anywhere in the backs, And, it was with this versatility that he would develop into one of the great Bath stalwarts of his era.

S.G.U Considine ....outhalf artistry.

Acknowledgements: Bath Chronicle

1924-5 was the season too of the second New Zealand tour to these islands, where the 'Invincibles' would remain unbeaten, albeit (20th September) at Weston super Mare Somerset, with Bath's Considine and forward L.W. Bisgrove included, 'gave it their all,' only falling 0-6 to prove it. Meanwhile the long-awaited international call-up of Considine for England against France (13th Apr. 1925), though as a wing rather than at outside-half, was an honour felt throughout the club. He learned of his selection (Chronicle, 11th Apr. 1925) by telegram from the English Rugby Union, and his reaction was typical of this calmest of sportsman. He placed the telegram in his pocket and departed for a game of golf. Born in Darjeeling, India, on 11th August 1901, Stanley George Ulick Considine had completed his schooling at Blundell's (Tiverton) after his junior schooldays at St. Christopher's, Bath. An outstanding sporting talent, he played for Bath when still at Blundell's, while his Irish background had allowed him to play in the Irish Trial of 1920. Arnold Ridley later spoke of the *"audacity of Considine's play, the instantaneous nature of his reactions,"* adding that some colleagues claimed that *"with Consi' it was as difficult to play with him as against him."* Excelling furthermore at cricket, Considine had played for Somerset since 1919 as a 'splendid bat,' and proved to be a fielder of such quality that at cover-point he was acknowledged by some commentators as *"the finest in the Country since the days of Gloucestershire and England legend, Gilbert Jessop."*

It was at the Colombes stadium however where Considine would reach both the zenith and yet the demise of his otherwise supreme sporting career. England would triumph 11-13. But the victory came at a cost, namely a wretched first-half injury to Considine. He refused to leave the field (no subs allowed in rugby union until the later 1960's), though the second-half would be an ordeal. And while the advances in surgery in later decades may have ensured a full recovery, this wasn't yet those later decades. Thus, one of the finest backs ever seen in Bath colours would never again play a serious game of rugby. "How good was he,?" A question hardly better expressed than in the words of a colleague on that fateful day in Paris, namely Bristol centre L.J. Corbett. Writing four decades later (Bath Football Club Centenary book, pp. 8-9) and by now rugby correspondent for the Sunday Times, he wrote thus: *"on his day "Consi" was surely the most brilliant player behind the scrum ever to wear the Bath jersey……...whose genius in attack was quite outstanding."* No words therefore need be added to such unstinting praise. This loss of his silky skills was therefore the one serious set-back in an otherwise successful 1924-5 season, and there could be no complaints about the 22 victories gained at this level of rugby; wins moreover that included notable away success at London Welsh, Bristol and Richmond. While the eye-catching late season 5-3 home win over a Llanelli side fielding no less than nine internationals was further proof that by this stage, Bath when at their best (and admittedly at home) could compete against any side in the Country.

But, after ten seasons riding the crest of a wave, Bath experienced an unexpected jolt to their confidence in the following 1925-6 season. This just happened to be the 20th anniversary of season 1905-6 when it seemed that Bath (with a total of a mere seven wins) had faced the nightmare of possible oblivion. Yet with an identical seven wins in 1925-6, this was hardly an ideal start for W.J. (Bill) Gibbs's two years of captaincy. Yet though depressing, the situation was not identical to those alarming days of the early 1900's. The cause moreover was identifiable, one that included the departure of the excellent full-back Bert Comm into professional ranks at Oldham and in addition the departure of other former stalwarts, and of course the loss of Considine! Meanwhile over the years the club's experience had grown in tandem with its on-field progress, and so setbacks could now be better cushioned from shocks, and a recovery more speedily launched. And, exactly this did happen just one season onwards. But there was no denying that the 1925-6 campaign was an uncomfortable ride with a truly demoralising 27 defeats; and not only upsets away at tougher opposition such as London Welsh, but defeats at the hands of the likes of the Old Blues (normally a victory), adding to the disquiet.

Yet there were rays of sunshine. First, Bath celebrated their Diamond Jubilee (15th Oct. 1925) with a game against the combined Western Counties, albeit losing 3-19. While later, again on the Rec, Bath hosted the **England Trial** of 19th December with their **new North stand** now open for business. Not surprisingly perhaps, in a season in which the club was performing below its potential, no Bath player was selected. Yet this disappointment apart, the Centenary Book (p.28) records that 8000 spectators attended, there to witness the Probable's led by England legend W.W. Wakefield unexpectedly lose 14-22 to the Possibles. However, if there was a hint of a recovery, then it showed with the first ever visit of Cardiff on 16th January, the inaugural game between the clubs held in the previous season (24th December 1924) with a 22-6 result for the Welshmen. This time Cardiff, among 'the' best in the British Isles, were held to a 13-13 draw, three tries each, two conversions apiece. So, satisfaction for Bath from arguably their best performance on the field that season; and not forgetting Cardiff's diplomacy off it, their committee expressing thus in their post-visit letter to the club: *"The genial hospitality only proves what a wonderful club of sportsmen you have. Gatherings of the sort that took place on Saturday last only tend to bring us closer together;"* (Football Herald & Chronicle, 23rd Jan.1926). This improvement against Cardiff, one of Wales's finest, followed by a January 14-6 home win over Cross-Keys (that season a powerful team fielding three Welsh internationals), nor forgetting a later 3-0 home victory over Gloucester, raised pertinent questions: because if Bath could win victories such as these, then how come so bleak a season as 1925-6? Well, one reason is that a largely new roll-call of players needed time to blend into a team, and excuses aside, a similar loss of form occurs to most (perhaps all) clubs at some stage in their history. And sure enough in the following 1926-7 season a noticeable recovery 'did' follow under Bill Gibbs (again skipper) as another generation stepped up to the starting-blocks. They included H. Burgess, W. Hancock, Norman Matthews, A.F.Lace, R.S. Chaddock, E. Chard, W. Banyard, D. James, R. Collett, A.Milsom, E. Dunscombe, G. Nudds, and not forgetting powerful running three-quarter J.B. Hannah. Albeit mostly new names on the team-sheet, they bonded quickly and within a year the decline was reversed, Bath notching some impressive results that included victories over Plymouth Albion (home and away), Moseley, the Royal Air Force, Leicester, Blackheath, U.S. Portsmouth, London Welsh, London Irish and Newport. Confidence had returned.

Yet while no club would ever underestimate a challenge from the likes of Cardiff, it could also be unwise to underestimate the challenge posed by certain London Old Boys clubs. Corinthian in outlook, teams such as Old Merchant Taylors, Old Millhillians and Old Blues (Christ Hospital School) played much of their rugby in the Home Counties, but would willingly travel westwards, especially so during the Christmas and Easter holidays. Cavalier almost to a fault, such teams were justifiably ranked as senior clubs, and remained so regarded until the late 1960's. A glance at the Taylors' team-sheet on their Easter tour match at Bath in mid-April 1927 confirmed just this fact, with a line-up that included full-back R.Melluish (Cambridge Blue and England Trials), centre W. Cheeseman (Oxford Blue & England), F. Collier and D. Hodgson (Middlesex half-backs), and county forwards G. Bryant (Kent), H. Fagrari (Middlesex) and G.H. Earle (Surrey). If this was not impressive enough, they were led by forward R. Cove-Smith, one of the England greats of the 1920's. Meanwhile Bath, who prior to the Old Merchant

Taylors' arrival had put all their efforts into notching four straight wins over U.S. Portsmouth, Bridgwater, London Irish and London Welsh, unwisely rested certain players from their own line-up. This was asking for trouble, as O.M.T.'s proved when winning 8-18. Yet the over-all results of season 1926-7 were confirmation of a swift turn-around in fortunes, with 21 wins, one draw and 13 defeats, not by any means a poor record at the first-class level of the game. G. Nudds was proving to be something of a discovery at scrum-half, while forwards R. Collett and W.B. Wake joined Bath centre H. Partridge in the Somerset line-up during the season, all four then called-up for county duty against the formidable touring Maoris at Weston-super-Mare, though losing 8-21. L.H. Scott, when available, proved to be a genuine speed-merchant in the backs, while skipper 'Bill' Gibbs again demonstrated his leadership during a time of transition and topping Bath's try list with 16 scores that season, notwithstanding missing 12 matches.

It was during this same era that the game witnessed the **emerging role of club coaches**, in Bath's case Alby Hatherill and Jack Cutting, as the Bath Chronicle duly confirmed in their fulsome end-of- season review. Admittedly coaching was not fully recognised as an integral part of club rugby until the 1960's. But coaches were nothing new, as records clearly show, including fortuitously the following letter previously sent to the Bath Herald on 5th February 1910. The writer, having returned from India to whence he had journeyed in the 1880's, now exclaimed, with no little disapproval, that the changes he found were not to his liking. He wrote disparagingly of *"huge stands, huge attendances, players found in everything, not wearing anything they have paid for, with trainers to look after them as though they were prize fighters or gladiators."* Well, if those were our complainant's feelings in February 1910, it is just as well he didn't arrive from India come February 2010.

Finally, season 1926-7 had introduced a largely new generation of players to the Rec who would themselves step back into the past with a concluding match against Wellington. Not seen in the city since October 1906, Wellington's presence stirred memories of their 19th century pre-eminence, their string of county players, and their iron-tackling England full-back Herbert Gamlin. For years past the West Somerset club had expressed a wish to play Bath again, and now that wish was granted. So it was that two rugby families who by now occupied two different spheres of the game celebrated a common friendship; and that mattered, not the fact that Bath (in a carnival atmosphere) won 16-8.

Chapter 16. THE 1920'S – A LANDMARK DECADE?

At the culmination of the 1920's the overall results achieved (notwithstanding the disappointments of season 1925-6) exceeded those of any previous decade in the club's history, this in both quantity of victories and quality of opposition. Furthermore, the turn-around that followed the mid-20's 'dip' with returns of 21, 22, 17 and 19 wins respectively from seasons 1926-7 to 1929-30 displayed a capability to recover from setbacks. Another feature of this decade was that Bath (apart from a few exceptions) were rarely a team of nationally known stars, though not infrequently they were a star team, as some of their best results proved. While the 1927-8 team captained by England winger James Pitman was arguably as good as any during the 1920's.

Yes, Bath lost fourteen, drew another three, but importantly won twenty-two victories, and this included a highly prestigious 9-5 triumph over Cardiff, where of the four tries ran home that day Bath scored three. Indeed, this performance equalled any they achieved during the 1920's, and it was noticeable too that Pitman's side got the double against the likes of Moseley and London Welsh; and Bath were fully aware that beating the best demanded that they must prepare accordingly. Hence rotation of players (by no means a later practice in rugby) was not uncommon at the club during the Twenties, and Bath did rest key players in supposedly less demanding fixtures (sometimes losing as a result) so as to enable selectors to field full-strength sides to face opponents such as Leicester and Gloucester (Pitman's team winning both). However, for Pitman (likewise previous Bath captains) it too often remained a different story on 'foreign fields,' and his side experienced some painful lessons from upsets that included defeats at Leicester (0-33) and an inexplicable home defeat to Bristol (0-32) against whom Bath had only narrowly lost (6-3) away in that same season. It hurt! Yet, such sobering defeats notwithstanding, the overall results of the 1920's indicated that Bath were a genuine first-class club, who on occasions looked a very good first-class club but: it was 'just their luck' that by stint of geography they could not escape the shackles of comparison with nearby rivals Bristol and Gloucester! And what rivals...nothing less in fact than two of the best and most consistent teams in the Country!

But to their credit Bath did not forget their humble origins, part reason for their willingness to arrange fixtures from a 'broad church.' Hence alongside the Big Guns of Leicester, Cardiff (et al) less glamorous teams featured in the typical Bath season too. During 1927-8 for example Bath met Old Alleynians (Dulwich), Old Paulines (St. Pauls),

James Pitman ....a soccer background at Eton, a Blue at Oxford, a cap for England.

Acknowledgements: Bath Chronicle

Old Blues (Christ's Hospital), Old Dunstonians and Old Merchant Taylors; while Edgware (little known nowadays) were then an ambitious club who were mustard keen to strengthen their own fixture list. Furthermore, in this same season and despite earning a pittance 'from their own home gates,' (Football Herald, 28th Feb. 1925) this North London rugby family could certainly cause a fright or two, pushing Bath uncomfortably close with their narrow 6-5 defeat down on the Rec in October 1927. St. Thomas's Hospital were visitors too. Arguably an equal match for Guys (a major first-class team in the 1920's), this pair had played a notable part in forging a hugely respected London Hospitals rugby tradition, producing numbers of internationals that any club in England would have been proud of. So, it was as a result of playing amongst this wider rugby family, that Bath would grow into a class-less rugby club. They were easy to live with, with a distinctive West Country character that was nonetheless comfortable amongst the wider echelons of rugby. As regards the Dressing Room, James Pitman (Centenary Book, 1965, pp. 9-10)) gave it to us in poetry: "*Happy times! Those luncheon baskets at Bath station. Solo! Cashnella; Eddie Simpkins. The smell of embrocation in the changing room; the band. The hot bath afterwards. Our home ground was the most beautiful by far. Only did the Oxford ground and Torquay among all the others stand out at all. Our surrounding hills; the greenery everywhere; Sham castle high above and the Abbey's tower close at hand. What a glorious setting.*"

Yet and yet again, the Bristol/Gloucester remained the yardstick by which others judged Bath, and Bath in fact judged themselves. After all, the Bristolians (growl) usually did win! However, at the Memorial Ground (28th Nov.1929) they didn't! It was an absolute nail-biter, the score balanced at 3-3, when the ball reached the eager hands of Bath's young nineteen years old winger Bill Hancock. Suddenly, this former England schools Trialist switched on the gas and sped clear. Clear that is save for Bristol full-back Jim Watts. It was now man against boy and it looked odds-on that the boy would probably come off worse (a whole lot worse). Sure enough the menacing Watts closed in for the 'kill' and……Hancock had other ideas. He literally leaped over the off-balanced Bristolian to notch a gem, a try so unusual that it reportedly startled a full-house Memorial Ground and was still recalled decades later in Bath (if not Bristol) rugby folklore. More importantly still, it clinched that rarity, a Bath away win at Bristol by 3-6 and the first part of a cherished two-timer for that season. Moreover, as if one high-profile double was not enough for season 1929-30, another was achieved with the club's home and away pair against powerful Northampton.

However, in this significant 1920's era for Bath there was one unnoticed event in Autumn 1927 that initially would unlikely have aroused even a ripple of interest. Indeed, it was merely the arrival of a fifteen years old schoolboy, Ron Gerrard, at Taunton School. The youngest of five children (two girls and three boys) he had journeyed with his recently widowed mother from distant Hong Kong where his late Scottish father had risen to the position of Assistant Superintendent of Police. The boy was both new to England and new to rugby football. But soon enough, this being Taunton School, a rugby ball was put into his hands. Almost immediately he displayed a natural-born talent for sports and within two months of his first autumn term he was fast-tracked as a three-quarter into the senior colts XV. Come the Spring term he went one better, namely selection for the 1st XV. It is safe to assume that few if anyone beyond the confines of Taunton School knew much about young Gerrard, that is until season 1929-30 when Somerset, owing to a late withdrawal, found themselves short of a centre to play against Gloucestershire. Then someone, possibly a schools-referee (see 'Men of a Stout Countenance,' p.29) notified the County selectors about a promising schoolboy centre: R.A. Gerrard! What is positively recorded nonetheless is that Gerrard *"was spotted by the [Somerset] County selectors as a player of the greatest promise"* (Seventy Years of Somerset Rugby, p.36). Thus, at short notice this 'mere' schoolboy stepped out into the 'take-no-prisoners' cauldron that is Kingsholm. And although Gloucestershire won a narrow, grimly fought victory, the fearless schoolboy never shirked a tackle, nor wilted under the intense pressure suddenly placed upon his young shoulders. A wider audience now 'did' know about this young protégé, and would soon learn much more. Fortunately, it was Bath that would be both his chosen home and chosen club, and as the rugby world moved into the next decade the young man from Hong Kong was destined for rugby legend.

Bath would now move onwards into the 1930's, having answered important questions. For that rugby Spring from season 1909-10 onwards (halted temporarily when 'the lights went out all over Europe') was not a false dawn, and Bath would indeed continue that momentum (bar one brief season) throughout the 1920's. Fine victories against the best in England and Wales were recorded. Crowds of 6000-7000 sometimes filled the Rec (Centenary Book 1865-1965, p.28). And the club had played a crucial role in Somerset's victorious County Championship team of 1922-3. So yes, the 'Twenties' were a landmark decade. Even so, one other issue remained. For while Bath often won 'big' at home, they too rarely won 'big' away. And this left another question to answer: "were Bath now regarded the equals of West Country powerhouses Bristol and Gloucester?"

Not yet!

Chapter 17.   A COUNTRY WITHIN A COUNTRY.   (1930-35).

On Monday 7th April 1930 the Bath & Wilts Chronicle & Herald (Chronicle & Herald) reported the events of the club's annual dinner held on the previous Saturday at the Fortts Restaurant, Milsom street, where numbered among the eminent guests were former Bristol outside-half Mr W. Pearce (by now president of the RFU) and Mr Frank Cowlin (President of the Bristol club). Various toasts were made, and it was the RFU President who would refer to certain characteristics of the rugby game, among them the sacrosanct principle of that era, namely that rugby football was *"for the amateur and the amateur only."* But it is doubtful that any of the two hundred plus listeners that evening would have envisaged how half a century later this principle would so torment that same rugby union game. Mr Frank Cowlin spoke too, arousing laughter when stating that *"Bath had done the dirty on Bristol that season by winning the double over their great rivals,"* adding that rugby *"is one of the cleanest, if not 'the' cleanest of sports."* Well….yes and no! For the truth is that rugby history (including Bath's) is not without its own rogues-gallery, and ironically the 1930's would witness at least two occasions when Bath (not for the first time either) would find themselves embroiled in fracas both on, and off the field! That being said, as the glasses clinked amid the rugby-banter, Bath, with a mix of youth and experience in their side, had reason for optimism as they stepped into a new decade. Indeed, having achieved a moderately good 1929-30 season with nineteen wins under their belts, the club would now enjoy five seasons of rugby that on occasions would compare with anything the club had achieved before. The wider game too was moving onwards in addition to a recognised hierarchy of first-class clubs (to which Bath now belonged) and of course a thriving County Championship. Indeed, as early as January 1927 the England v Wales game at Twickenham had been the first international to be broadcast **live on radio;** while the England v Scotland encounter of 19th March 1938 (again at Twickenham) would be the first to be screened **live on television**. Another feature of the first-class game throughout the 1930's was the continued influence of the leading Services clubs, namely U.S. Portsmouth, Devonport Services and the Aldershot Services. All three competed at the senior level of rugby, and the inclusion of Services players (likewise the Hospital and the London Old Boys sides) in the Home International teams was the norm, not the exception.

Bath too continued to attract the attention of international selectors, and they did their reputation no harm with their 3-3 draw at Leicester to kick off the 1930-31 season. Not quite a perfect result, yet a performance that hinted at the success that would shortly follow. Scrum-half and Cambridge Blue E.Benson had now arrived, his half-back combination with Charles Gough proving highly effective. In the backs Herbert Buse (a full Somerset County cricketer like Considine previously and Gerrard later), Louis St. V. Powell, Albert Merrett and Billy Hancock could cause real problems for defences; and come the 11th October 1930 the young R. A. Gerrard would make his debut for Bath at Plymouth Albion. Albeit that his new club lost 6-5, he looked 'one' for the future; indeed

England selectors would soon be taking a closer look. Equally satisfying for prop forward Ian Spence (captain,1929-1931) was the performance of his pack, one that would be strengthened furthermore by D. Crichton Miller (previously Gloucester and Scotland) and G.G. Gregory (previously Bristol and England). They would now team-up with England Trialist Mervyn Shaw and local hero Norman Matthews. Furthermore in E.G. Haydon (strong and very fast) one saw the personification of the modern-day wing-forward. A player of perpetual motion, he created club history in season 1930-1 when running home for a remarkable 29 tries, a record that would stand for some half a century until wing Barry Trevaskis (1982-3) ran over for 32. Crichton-Miller and Gregory would then make their own

Ian Spence

contribution to Bath rugby history. For the club had yet to field two players in the same international and certainly not two players representing opposing sides. But at Murrayfield (21st Mar.1931) in a Scottish 28-19 victory, Crichton-Miller packed down for Scotland and G.G.Gregory for England. Now it seems puzzling that Bath have never

Norman Matthews ….minutes from England's cap at Cardiff.

Acknowledgements: Bath Chronicle

fully claimed either player as Bathonian internationals, and one can only hazard a guess at the reason; but since both players had already arrived on the Rec as fully-fledged internationals, it seems possible that Bath considered that their former respective clubs (Gloucester and Bristol) should alone be accorded recognition for their international status.

One player who 'did,' but then did 'not' receive international honours was Bath's lion-hearted all-round forward Norman Matthews, who, impressive in recent England Trials, had accompanied the England team as travelling reserve for the 18th January 1930 encounter against Wales. Suddenly, it was realised that forward Harry Rew (Army) would not be match-fit and as a result Matthews was immediately called-up to deputize. Simultaneously however efforts were made to contact experienced Bristol and England

forward Sam Tucker, and literally at that moment when England (including Matthews) had changed and were now preparing to step on to the Arms Park, Sam Tucker arrived in the dressing room, having been flown from Bristol to Cardiff. And Matthews? He never did play for England that day in their 3-11 victory, Sam Tucker did, and one wouldn't want one's worst enemy to go through an experience like that. Yet Matthews….he just took it on the chin like the man he was.

69

However, Bath's following 1930-31 campaign was regarded as *"one of the best-if not 'the' best [season] in the previous history of the club"* (Bath & Herald, 14th Apr. 1931), and home wins against Moseley (27-0), and later against Leicester (19-9) emphasised just how formidable Bath could be at home. Even away, always a bigger challenge, Bath overcame the likes of then formidable Devonport Services (6-10), though on the minus side slipping up 8-0 at Llanelli, 14-3 at Neath and later 18-0 at Pontypool. So, with 22 wins and three draws from thirty-seven games, the question remained: 'where exactly did Bath stand in the rankings of the English first-class game, and how did they compare with rivals Bristol and Gloucester?' This question was tricky since the Bath - Bristol - Gloucester triangle created a Country within a Country, an island separated from the rest. So whatever Bath achieved outside this island mattered less than what Bath was seen to achieve within it, and this long-held perception could only change by domination over both their two great rivals, a task lest it be forgotten that was as difficult as any faced in English rugby.

Yet Bath were as ever a happy bunch of souls, and in the words of international Crichton Miller (Centenary Book, (1865-65, p.12) the club played *"neither with the humourless intensity that is met further west, nor in the irritating happy-go-lucky style that characterised some of the London clubs……it was serious rugger, but jolly."* And considering that the Bath & Herald had rated the 1930-1931 season in glowing terms, then arguably what followed under new captain Mervyn Shaw in the next two seasons (1931-1933) was even better. Now, Shaw was a previous England Trialist with Bristol, a club whom he had captained with distinction. Yet, he arrived on the Rec as an exile, and this was unusual, because only rarely did Bristolians ever leave the Memorial Ground. Indeed, he was believed to have been the popular choice of both players and committee to remain as captain. But a faction within the wider membership begged to differ; and they got their way. Thus Shaw, chastened by this rebuff but nonetheless the nicest of men, felt it only diplomatic to depart. His destination would be Bath, where he would prove himself both a magnificent player and an admired general during his two years captaincy. However, notwithstanding that at home his adopted club could beat some of the best in the Land, London rugby rated Bath in a somewhat different 'light' compared to their high regard for Bristol (and not forgetting Gloucester). Reviewing the begrudging reports on Bath wins in the capital the Chronicle & Herald (21st Oct, 1931) asked: *"Why are Bath's wins always lucky?"* Why indeed, for surely a win is a win?! But London rugby remained unsure as where exactly to place Bath in 'the order of things,' and rightly or wrongly it would take literally years for Bath to overcome this obstacle. Nonetheless, Bath did not need much time to assess the potential of a recent arrival playing in their ranks for the 1931 Boxing Day visit of the Old Blues. A Christmas holiday game (Bath not at full strength winning narrowly 15-11), the visitors would reiterate their view that they *"always looked upon [their] game at Bath as the most enjoyable of the season."* A Rec crowd of 6,000 plus (yes, six thousand!) witnessed a match described as a 'thrill a minute' and notable too for the performance of that recent arrival. His name was H. Minte who had joined without ceremony on a temporary basis (while serving with the Army nearby), and initially played with the 'A' XV. But with a 'man of the match' performance against Old Blues, some further enquiries were made, and it was learned that Minte was a fully-fledged Scottish Trialist. His days as an 'A' XV player ended promptly!

Likewise, England selectors needed precious little time in assessing the potential of young Gerrard, already an England Trialist, and who in late 1931 received a telegram: *"Heartiest congratulations…….from your club-mates, friends and admirers in Bath"* it read. There then followed the **England team to play South Africa** in the forthcoming international at Twickenham on 2nd January 1932: backs: ***R.Barr (Leicester), C. Aarvold (Blackheath, capt), R.A. Gerrard (Bath), J. Tallent (Cambridge Univ), C.Tanner (Gloucester),* half-backs: *R.Spong (Old Millhillians), W. Sobey (Old Millhillians),* forwards: *D. Norman (Leicester), G.Gregory (Bristol), A. Carpenter (Gloucester), R.G. Hobbs (Richmond & Army), C. Webb (Devonport Services & R. Navy), L. Saxby (Gloucester), A.Rowley (Coventry), J. McD. Hodgson (Northern)."***
So began the international career of 19 years old Ronald "Gerry" Gerrard, who a mere four years since first touching English soil would pull the white shirt of England over his shoulders to face the might of South Africa. Could England triumph? Well, not quite, as the tourists (whose defeat by the Midland Counties would be the sole setback of their tour) commenced their clean sweep of the Home Nations with a 0-7 triumph over England. But defeat notwithstanding, the National press as reported in the Chronicle & Herald (4th Jan. 1932) spoke thus: *"Gerrard proved the big success of the line ....."* (Daily Mail); *"Gerrard in attack was the best of our threequarters"* (Sunday Express); *"R.A. Gerrard made a splendid first appearance, a couple of dashes of his in the second half being wonderfully good"* (Sunday Times). Thus, spoke the press, unanimous in their collective praise for a young protégé set to gain fourteen caps for England.

For Gerrard's parent club too the 1931-2 season was 'up there' with Bath's best: 38 games would yield 25 victories (plus one draw), and significantly five of those wins would be 'away' at Bristol (8,000 attendance) and the double over US Portsmouth, Northampton, Devonport Services, and an emphatic 7-21 win at the London Welsh that included a try hat-trick by Bath wing-forward Leslie Moore. In addition, Pontypool, Llanelli and Leicester were among those defeated on the Rec, as was an eye-catching 28-0 victory over London Irish. In fact, such was the rugby-fever gripping the city that even the recently founded United side was attracting crowds of 2,000 plus (Chronicle & Herald, 4th Nov. 1931). And then, in 'the' perfect finale to any Bath season, the club clinched an 8-3 victory over Gloucester; while in addition were the individual honours of Gerrard's call-up for England, the selection of forwards Norman Matthews and Derek Wilson for the England Trials and the call-up of seven Bath players for Somerset. Indeed, only the sad news on 2nd April 1932 that former Bath international Frank 'Buster' Soane had lost his brief battle against a sudden illness would dampen the spirits; while a post-card printed in the Chronicle & Herald (6th Apr. 1932) listed a team that played under his captaincy 40 years previously: *A.E. Pinch, W. Pattinson, B. Vincent, P. Dykes, B. Helps, T.N. Parham, G. Vincent, F. Soane (capt.), Roberts, L.J. Fry, W. Coles, A. Timmins, R.Dykes, A.E. Clarke and Milsom.*

The following 1932-3 campaign mirrored very closely the outstanding previous season, led again by the inspirational Mervyn Shaw, whose still-close bond with his former club and their captain and England centre Don Burland helped arrange a Bath v Bristol Friendly (yes 'friendly!') to celebrate the opening of the **Rec's new West stand** (6th Sep. 1932) with a 6-3 home win. Further happy days then included Bath's October tour of 1932; and when one reads of journeys to the likes of Marazion, Gweek, Manman's Smith, Elford Passage, Swan Pool and Port Leven, one soon realises that much (though not quite all) took place down Cornwall way. The opener was a close-run 6-7 win over the Devonport Services. Next on the agenda came the farmers and miners of Redruth, a team fielding England Trialist centre Roy Jennings and eight Cornish caps, and despite the fearsome roar of a reported 3,000 Cornish crowd, Bath 'just' clinched it 8-10 with Rec favourite Albert Merrett swooping over for an absolute gem on the wing. Then followed Penzance (merging as Penzance & Newlyn in 1945) where Bath *"throwing the ball about in brilliant style"* ran home 5-24 for a more comfortable victory. So, three wins on the trot, and for many perhaps the one opportunity to cross the Tamar into King Arthur's kingdom, that forbidding Bodmin Moor, that awesome Saint Michael's Mount, and not forgetting Jamaica Inn! Oh, and Poldark! Yes…those tours were magical times.

Not conspicuous on the field naturally, but highly active off it was the Bath Supporters Club, with an admirable remit that included efforts to enrol every club in the Combination to 'insure' their players for injury-cover (Chronicle & Herald, 3rd Jan. 1933) with *"each club getting the [Bath] supporters 12 new members, thereby having the whole of their insurance premiums paid for them."* Injury payments of £3 per week (maximum) for married players and £2 weekly for single players would appear trivial in later decades, but not so in the 1930's, and anyway it was a world away from previous days when rugby injuries could sometimes subject a player to life-changing consequences. Former player J. Humphreys for example had been rendered near helpless when playing for the Widcombe Institute club in the early 1900's. The Club's efforts included (inter alia) the January 1933 trip to Twickenham for England's clash with Wales, with some one hundred members departing from Bath Spa station, travelling in 'reserved' saloons and arriving at Paddington at 11.45, where awaiting buses transported the merry band to the Regent Palace Hotel for luncheon. From thence to Twickenham; the buses wedged amongst the infamous 'crawl' for the last three miles but fortunately reaching their destination by 2pm, and duly packed amid a 60,000 crowd for kick-off! 'England's day?' Not a good question, with Wales (fielding schoolboy centre Wilfred Wooller) winning 3-7 and Bath's Gerrard receiving a potentially serious, but mercifully not long-term eye injury. But upsets apart, it was into those buses again, dinner at the Regent Palace Hotel and then an evening spent among the bright lights of the big city. At midnight the party returned to Paddington for the homewards journey, and as luck would have it the train was packed with (you've guessed it) joyous Welsh supporters in full voice. But win or lose, rugby folk live for such times as these, and on arrival at the Spa station the ad hoc choristers of the Supporters Club reportedly interrupted a by now peaceful, slumbering city with their own somewhat inferior rendition of a traditional Welsh choir.

And, there were other reasons for celebration in season 1932-3, among them Gerrard's performances for England, forward Peter Clothier's selection for England Trials and the perfect climax to any season with a 15-8 home win over Leicester. Twenty-four Bath victories and one draw were gained from thirty eight played, and among the headline wins was the 9-17 success over Moseley (away!) where *"Hancock's try after a brilliant break by Charlie Gough was the best outside move of the whole game...."* Moreover, the victory was all the more laudable since backs R.A. Gerrard, Louis St V. Powell and Albert Merrett, plus forwards Peter Clothier, Derek Wilson and Norman Matthews were representing Somerset that same day.

GREAT GOUGH! ....Bath's outstanding utility back takes two Llanelli players over the line for a try against 'the Scarlets'. Bath 21-Llanelli 3 (8th Sept 1934).

Acknowledgements: Bath Chronicle

But of the Bath 1932-3 highlights there were at least three candidates for 'the win of the Season Awards,' the victories over Newport and Leicester among them. Indeed, in the case of the Welsh, Bath had triumphed only twice in the ten previous years, but now would gain a 12-5 win by four tries as against a try-goal by Newport. Meanwhile the 11-9 success in January over powerful Coventry had clearly demonstrated the strength of the Bath pack. And, if ('if') such results of this quality could continue, then it seemed a possibility that it might be only a matter of time before Bath could be spoken of in the same breath as rivals Bristol and Gloucester. Two further satisfactory seasons of twenty wins apiece in 1933-4 and 1934-5 followed under the respective captaincy of B.C.Barber and Gerrard; and it was the name of Gerrard in particular with whom Bath were by now most commonly associated. By now a national rugby figure, his abilities had been noted by the Rugby League, with offers that included one 'approach' of a four-figure signing-on-fee that in the 1930's amounted to seriously 'big' money, though one which Gerrard declined. But Rugby League interests in the South were not confined to the recruitment of players. In fact, **the League code now sought to establish a club-base in the South,** and there was nothing 'amateurish' about their ambitions or preparations. Indeed, on 13th September 1933 at the White City stadium (and under floodlights) an exhibition League match was played between the first and reserve sides of the recently launched London Highfield RL club; and taking more than just a passing interest in the matter, the Chronicle & Herald referred to a 'number of prominent Union players taking part, among them former Plymouth Albion and England scrum-half Eddie Richards who had already signed for London Highfield.' The Paper further enquired if *"those Union players in the White City game would henceforth be classed as professional?"* adding that *"in the North anyone over 17 years playing Rugby League would be professionalised, whether or not receiving payment."* The answer to this query later come loud and clear when one Thomas Brown's request for reinstatement to the Union code was firmly rejected. Of course, one could understand the concerns that such a situation might arouse among the amateur RFU hierarchy, with the possibility of players criss-crossing unconditionally from Union to League, but their sheer intransigence over the matter would leave the RFU little room for manoeuvre when facing challenges to its authority from within the Union game itself some fifty years later, challenges moreover that the governing body would find increasingly difficult to defy.

Meanwhile another opportunity to spot possible future internationals was provided in February 1934 when Bath hosted an international Schools Trial between England and the Rest. Here, local boy Tommy Hicks played on the wing for the Rest XV (who won 7-12), an already 'rated' young back who by the late Thirties would be a Bath 1st teamer and who would form an unshakeable friendship with a yet unknown half-back by the name of Norman Halse, both remaining Bath rugby stalwarts into the following century. Season 1933-34 under new skipper B.C. Barber could not have started better with an opening morale-booster of a 5-3 win over Swansea, a win partly inspired by out-half discovery Lance Wardle. But, a month later Bath fell 8-10 to Guys Hospital on their first visit to the Rec, and although Bath were five players short on county duty it was a result suggesting that a season of the unpredictable lay ahead. And, you can say that again! Gloucester, 23-8 winners at Kingsholm, fell 13-8 on the Rec. Bristol, 0-3 losers at home, avenged Bath 0-12 on the Rec. Bath won 0-7 at Coventry. Coventry won 3-13 on the Rec. Bath won 8-7 against Llanelli at home, then fell 20-3 at Neath. That was not the end of it. The inconsistencies continued, and would continue into the following 1934-5 campaign under the captaincy of Ron Gerrard, clearly demonstrated in the opening fortnight of the season. Bath fell 14-3 at Llanelli. But a week later and with recently joined wingers J.S. Bartlett and G. Wynne-Jones revealing scorching pace, Bath triumphed 21-3 with a four try blitz against Llanelli on the Rec! Indeed, the Scarlets and Wales scrumhalf Dai John later commented that he had *"never seen Llanelli more completely outclassed."* Outclassed! Few clubs ever outclassed Llanelli. And if Bath could just carry this form with them when they travelled away then arguably they would be right 'up there' with the 'big guns,' including Bristol and Gloucester. If!! Another Bath characteristic was mentioned almost as an afterthought in the Chronicle's post-match report of the Bath v Aldershot Services match in Autumn 1934 where the visitors earned some high praise: *"Apart from the Harlequins, Aldershot Services were the best side Bath have met this season....behind a pack of huge fellows......their backs threw the ball about in a way that often changed the point of attack with breathless rapidity from one flank to another. If the exceedingly mobile back division were not brought down on some part of Bath's line, giant forwards came smashing through."* Nonetheless, Bath dug their heels in for a 11-3 victory, with the Chronicle concluding thus: *"That Bath were so well fortified against these battering attempts to score was due to the yeoman way all took part in the robust business of defence......"* Ah yes: the 'yeoman way!' Of this more later.

Later that month, it was most fortunate for a party of young friends frolicking by the Avon that a strong (and courageous) swimmer was nearby. Because, one eleven-year old (a non-swimmer) suddenly lost his balance and fell into those icy, deep waters at Batheaston. Nearby, there just happened to be a small group from the city's engineering staff to whom a companion of the stricken youngster called out: *"Quick, he can't swim."* Aware now of the danger, a member of that group plunged into the river fully clothed (save for his coat) and brought the young schoolboy safely back to the bank. And that rescuer just happened to be R.A.Gerrard (Chronicle & Herald, 17th Jan. 1935), who politely dismissing all attempts to publicise his potential life-saving action, joined his colleagues two days later when Leicester were in town. The result.... a four try Bath victory without reply! One week onwards this dazzling form was repeated with a 3-14 win at Moseley whose match programme-notes generously acclaimed their visitor's win over Leicester as *"the outstanding result of last Saturday's games."*

But somewhat less generous it must be said was the reaction of certain Bath supporters on the popular side when Norman Matthews seemingly crossed the line to score for Bath against Blackheath on 16th March 1935. The referee however saw things differently, disallowing the try and ruling that Matthews had first knocked over the corner flag. The popular side did not agree, believing (almost certainly correctly, with archive photos suggesting that the corner flag had indeed been knocked down, but by a Blackheath player), and duly voiced their disapproval in no uncertain terms at the decision. Nor was the volatile situation helped by the fact that Blackheath won the game 8-13. In fact, so angered was a section of the home crowd that come the final whistle they held a demonstration outside the entrance to the North stand changing-rooms. This was hardly the reaction expected of a city where the likes of, among others, Jane Austen (domiciled at Sydney Place) once trod. But the fact is that happen it did and…lest it be forgotten, had previously happened (on 15th February 1908 to be precise) against then arch-rivals Weston super Mare in a Somerset Cup match. Furthermore, the club would have been only too aware that since the Somerset RFU could ban rugby on the Rec in 1908, then they could ban it again in 1935. Yes, Bath did 'have' to tread rather carefully to avoid such incidents occurring again. Ironically only one week prior to the Blackheath encounter Bath had hosted the **County Championship final** between Somerset and Lancashire. A record crowd estimated at 12,000 packed the ground and four Bath men wore Somerset colours that day, namely **Gerrard (centre), H. Davies and J.H. Bailey (scrumhalf & out-half respectively) and J.S. Wood (forward),** and though the 'Cidermen' had previously beaten Eastern Counties 11-6 in their semi-final at Bridgwater, they harboured no illusions about this particular challenge. The Lancastrians were strong, not least with international centres **Leyland and Heaton** in their line-up, although it would not be until the closing stages that Lancashire's domination would be really felt. Then suddenly it happened! Lancashire struck with a devastating final burst, adding eleven points in ten minutes to win 14 points to nil. It would be their day, their triumph, and their time to raise aloft the County Championship trophy.

This deep disappointment apart, Bath achieved some impressive results during the 1934-5 season in addition to the aforementioned wins over Leicester and that away success at Moseley. But despite twenty victories (with one drawn), nineteen were lost, and of these one in particular was a shocker, and in more ways than one. This was a late season game at Llanelli, where Bath's reputation would have soared sky-high after their superb 21-3 early season extravaganza against the Scarlets on the Rec. Indeed, it was a certainty that with Bath's return to this proud Welsh stronghold, their home supporters would have wanted to see the Bath team that had so impressed Llanelli's genius of a scrumhalf, Dai John. Yet the reason for Bath's agreement to play three games against the Scarlets (two away) was frankly, anyone's guess. Needless to say: agree they did! A less than full-strength side then departed for Wales and putting it bluntly, got trounced, and the club's hard-earned reputation suffered an equally hard 42-0 defeat, one that according to Hon. Secretary Eddie Simpkins was the biggest defeat so far in the club's history. And the result was that setbacks such as this and a lack of consistency (despite some outstanding performances during some twenty years from 1910 onwards) explain why Bath could not shake off that tag as the junior partner of the West Country Triangle. But then few clubs could. For this was a Country within a Country, and the only way to escape the shadow cast by these two giants was (one repeats): 'to better them, a challenge so demanding as to seem virtually impossible.'

The 1934-5 season of highs and lows had experienced **one further occurrence that would affect both club and the** city on the night of 13/14th November 1934 (Chronicle

& Herald, 14th, 15th, 16th November 1934). It was now half-past midnight as the night train steamed out from Paddington to the West, and among the passengers was a Bath doctor now described as *"among the foremost young physicians of his day."* He was already an assistant physician at Bath's Royal United Hospital, a Fellow of the Royal Society of Medicine and furthermore the Medical Society of London; and since 1921 he was a physician at Bath's Royal Mineral Hospital where he had founded a post-graduate course for the study of rheumatic complaints. His name was Vincent Coates (son of a Bathonian but born in Edinburgh) who had three brothers, among them former Bath captain Norman Coates, and a sister. Previously an acclaimed Bath and England winger, he had married the former Miss Ethel Bertha Longuet Layton of Essequebo, British Guiana (now Guyana) on July 1915 at Charlcombe Church. They were now resident at No.10 the Circus (Bath). When qualifying as a doctor in October 1915 he had joined the Army the next day. In October 1916 he then won the **Military Cross for bravery** during action on the Western Front. However, on the evening of November 1934 Dr Coates (now forty-five years of age) had been invited by an 'influential and grateful patient' to a banquet at the Mercers' Hall, London, an event reportedly attended among others by the Lord Mayor himself. As on previous late-night return journeys from London, Dr Coates had asked the train guard if he would kindly call him at Bath, for it was not uncommon (then as now) for late night passengers to sleep en route. But as the midnight express *"was passing Maidenhead East signal box the signalman noticed that a carriage door was open. He stopped the train at Twyford, a search of the line was made,"* and Dr Coates was subsequently found lying injured *"at the side of the line."* First aid was rendered by ambulance men, Dr Coates was taken to hospital. But Dr Coates had not long to live. The news when reaching Bath was received with shock.

The inquest was held at Maidenhead on 15th November by the Coroner (Mr W. Owen Stuchbery) and a jury of eight. They were mindful of evidence that barely a month previous to the tragedy a guard who had been requested to call Dr Coates at Bath had forgotten, and the doctor *"had to get out as the train was leaving Bath."* And the jury verdict was indeed *"accidental death,"* the Coroner concluding that the doctor *"might suddenly have seen the light from the signal box (and) ..... drowsy from sleep, he could have suddenly decided that he was at Bath station and that it was time to get out."* Dr Vincent Coates, a rugby great whose skills in medicine would later attract to his clinics numerous patients from home and abroad, including South Africa, Canada, USA, Holland and France; whose kindness ensured that others unable to afford treatment nonetheless *"had the best for nothing;"* these were among a legion of people now mourning his loss. A throng packed Bath Abbey on the morning of 19th November 1934 at the service performed by the Archdeacon of Bath (the Ven. S.A. Boyd) and the Vicar of St. Stephen's, Lansdown, (Rev. G.L.Fitzmaurice). Outside in the Abbey churchyard another crowd watched silently as Dr Vincent Coates was then driven to his resting place high upon the hill above the city at the Lansdown cemetery. Thus, not only a rugby club, but a city he had served so well, were now united in their grief.

Chapter 18. A SEEMINGLY IMPOSSIBLE CHALLENGE. (1935-39)

Ron Gerrard : Classic Bath and England centre.

Acknowledgements: Bath Past Players

Following the Great War there would be (see too Ch.16) fifteen seasons of near uninterrupted success. Though Bath did not break into the highest level of first-class rugby, they nonetheless anchored themselves into the then unofficial mid-table rankings. However, with the departure during the mid-Thirties of a number of established players, the momentum slowed down. Surprisingly the pack, so often a strong point in any Bath team, initially suffered most from this exit, though the invaluable Norman Matthews and Peter Moon remained to mentor the newcomers. In the backs things did look more promising with the superb Gerrard playing outside the exciting potential of out-half Roy Harris; while the scintillating J.S. (Jack) Bartlett of the RAF and B.V. Robinson would make a noticeable mark. But backs can only thrive on good ball and they simply weren't getting enough of it. This drawback was evident in the opening exchanges of season 1935-6 when not a single win was recorded until 28th October with Bath's 28-5 home victory over Clifton, so ending a litany of defeats that had included a home 0-34 September horror-show at the hands of Llanelli. Thus, confidence gave way to uncertainty; while rumblings of discontent among followers (perhaps not surprising in the circumstances) were once again reported in the Chronicle pages; and forcefully expressed in the letter of 'F.S.' (Chronicle & Herald, 30th Sep.1935) when asking *"What's wrong with Bath rugby,"* and what he described as a possible reluctance of some players to travel to Wales which could then lead to a loss of those leading Welsh fixtures. Too true it could!

Yet not for the first time Bath pulled one of their surprises out of the hat, and Boxing Day was as good a time to start as any. Following their Christmas holiday 8-5 win against the Old Blues, a suddenly inspired Bath team sprang into action and proceeded to defeat Bridgend (3-0), Richmond (9-8), Northampton (11-0), Leicester (14-0) and Bedford (8-3), six straight victories, admittedly at home, but against quality opposition and followed furthermore by home draws against Gloucester and Bristol. While during this run of unexpected yet welcome success a delighted Chronicle & Herald (20th Jan. 1936) pin-pointed the *"growing striking power of the young players,"* among them scrum-half arrival Dai Davies and utility back 'Bud' West. Others too were now showing promise, among them the Rev. John Downward (lock) who rather interestingly *"was always in the thick of the fight,"* and front-row men Les Phillips and A. Ash, soon joined by prop Harry Oak, flanker Bill Gay and lock Kenneth Foss. But the post-Christmas uplift was short-lived, this one swallow alas did not herald a summer, and the club could only reflect on a deeply disappointing season's total of 13 wins (none away)), 3 draws and a worrying 18 defeats.

That said, 'Gerry' Gerrard remained a shining example, and seen at his finest in England's 13-0 triumph over the New Zealand All Blacks (4th January 1936) in the following English line-up: *(backs): H.G.Owen-Smith (St Mary's Hospital), A.Oberlensky (Oxford University), P. Cranmer (Richmond), R.A. Gerrard (Bath), H. Sever (Sale), P. Candler (St Bart's. Hospital), B.C. Gadney (Leicester, capt). (Forwards): D.Kendrew and E. Nicholson (both Leicester), R.Longland (Northampton), C.Webb (Devonport Services), A. Clark (Coventry), E. Hamilton-Hill and P. Dunkley (both Harlequins), W. Weston (Northampton).* As reported in the Chronicle & Herald (6th Jan,1936), Gerrard received unreserved plaudits in a game famous (inter alia) for the startling two try performance of England winger Alex Oberlensky. *"Nicely fed in the first instance by a suddenly swift burst of passing by Candler, Cranmer and Gerrard, Oberlensky went galloping ahead....he flashed past Gilbert for his touchdown"*(News Chronicle). Then there was the impregnable defence of the England backs: *"New Zealand would concentrate on mid-field attack. Very well, Hamilton-Hill, Candler, Cranmer and Gerrard would be there to stop them, and stop them they did, with a vengeance"* (D. Telegraph). *"For this [victory] no praise can be too high for Candler, Gerrard and Cranmer"* (D. Mail). *"But New Zealand failed badly outside. Praise here for the English defence, Cranmer, Candler and Gerrard, deadly tacklers, every man"* (Daily Express). Ah, the elation in overcoming 'the' **All Blacks!** But....how many knew then (or now) of **the origin of that fearsome New Zealand trademark?** Well, one month prior to England's encounter against the Tourists the Chronicle & Herald, 'Sports Gossip' (6th Dec.1935) reported the following communication from Reuters: *"The man mainly responsible for the nickname "All Blacks" has just died at Christchurch, New Zealand.......he was Mr E.E. Booth, a member of the New Zealand side which toured England in 1905, and was out training one day by himself and wearing black elastic knee bands and anklets in addition to a black vest and shorts. Asked the reason, he made the jocular reply, "Oh, just to be all black."* But is this, one asks, 'the' authentic story? Do not others perhaps exist? Well, who really knows. However, Reuters had specified an individual's name from Rugby's past. For that alone the archivist can be grateful.

The same season was memorable too for the 100th official match between Bath and Bristol (29th Feb.1936), a rivalry where, to put it mildly, Bristol had enjoyed something of a monopoly. Suffice to say that in 99 previous outings Bristol had won 71 matches to Bath's humble 17 (with 11 games drawn), while the 100th encounter (on the Rec) was another draw. In fact, the 3-3 result, thanks to tries from Bristol's P.J. Haskins and Bath winger Les Matthews, would mirror the same 3-3 result of that first derby game in 1888, when according to Bath records, a draw resulted from three minors each. The statistics of that 1888 encounter were quoted in the programme notes **for the 100th game**. But so too was another matter, concerning the brother of Bath try scorer Les Matthews, and referred back to a painful memory that seemingly was not yet fully exorcised. Yes, there was praiseworthy reference to (inter alia) Bristol internationals L.J. Corbett and Sam Tucker. But, a further reference to Sam Tucker was included: *"Much as we admire "Sam" here in Bath, we can never forgive him for flying to Cardiff and robbing us of another international player, Norman Matthews."* Now, six years had passed under the proverbial bridge since that day when Matthews was stood down literally minutes before running out with England; six years in which to air this grievance. Yet now, on this historic 100th occasion between two uncommonly fierce yet friendly rivals the 'Cardiff incident' was briefly, yet noticeably, highlighted. If this reference was intended in jest (as it may have been) then it did not quite read that way. Indeed, it suggested that Bath (who had never born a grudge against Bristol) could not as yet entirely forget or forgive. Yet in truth Sam Tucker was absolutely 'not' the villain that day, but to be quite frank, the decision-makers, namely the England hierarchy (see too: Ch.17.). But one performance in a season of sparse success was that Neath, already victors over Swansea, Bristol and Llanelli, were defeated 11-6 on the Rec. Now, that 'was' something to remember as the Chronicle & Herald duly noted (7th Apr.1936) when reporting thus of Bath's *"wonderful forwards...and a rock-like resistance under the severest pressure;"* adding too that this victory *"proved what a tremendously difficult side [Bath] are to subdue on their own ground."* So, with this re-built pack seemingly beginning to gel, could this be one of those results that can 'lift' a team, which in Bath's case would mean rising to the level of near twenty seasons of success on the field? Well, such hopes would doubtless have been in the forefront of Eddie Simpkins' mind (he of the 'unruffled temperament'), he who had now completed twenty-five years as club secretary, he whom the Bath Chronicle wondered *"if anyone [else]has done so much for the club as he has."*

The eighteen wins (six away) of the following 1936-7 campaign that included home victories over Harlequins (6-5) and Northampton (15-0), did suggest that fortunes might be on the upturn. The pack responded positively to the captaincy of the great all-round forward that was Norman Matthews, and consistency was improved from the previous season. While among the backs those stalwarts Billy Hancock and Les Matthews remained good value (and fast enough) to get past defences when good ball came into their hands. Les Matthews (*"once he is off, there is not much stopping of the winger"*) got a brace in Bath's January 15-0 home win over Northampton; where the Chronicle further noted the highly promising influence of Roy Harris, a new out-half discovery who *"took the ball at speed, and his masterly cuts through, with pace, dummy and swerve, were a treat to watch."* Yet doubts persisted. For though certain away performances showed an improvement, indeed Bath came close at Cardiff in a 3-0 nail-biter, drubbings at Llanelli (27-0) and 29-3 at Bridgend hardly made the best headlines in Wales. After all, the Welsh judged what they saw! No guesses needed therefore as to where the Principality placed Bath in the 'order of things,' notwithstanding that for many years Bath at home could beat some of the best that Welsh rugby could throw at them. That being said, it was in south Devon, not south Wales, that Bath would find themselves embroiled in an incident at Torquay Athletic that would lead to totally unexpected ramifications. Now, regular fixtures between these two clubs had commenced only one season previously, and Bath's 21-6 defeat at Torquay's beautiful ground in April 1936 showed the hosts were not a side to underestimate, albeit Bath won 8-3 on the Rec come the following September, leaving matters balanced at one apiece. But any supposed *entente* would change on Bath's visit to Devon on 20th March 1937. On this occasion Torquay, with some 1500-2000 spectators present, did not have things their own way, and in the closing minutes Bath's Peter Moon scored a try to effectively settle matters beyond Torquay's reach at 4-14. Moon however was clearly off-side, as Bath openly acknowledged later. Nonetheless, a small section of the home crowd now took matters a 'little further,' and the Chronicle & Herald (22nd Mar. 1937) reported thus: *"As the teams left the field a crowd congregated in front of the main stand, booing and hurling derisive comments at the referee. One or two adopted a threatening attitude and to avoid any possibility of a serious incident, the players closed round Mr Newcombe, forming an escort to the dressing room."* *"It is to be hoped,"* added the Chronicle, *"that the matter will be speedily forgotten."* Wishful thinking. Because 'forgotten' it was not!

In fact, the Bath committee met the following Monday and within a week it was announced that future fixtures with Torquay Athletic would be cancelled! That's right….cancelled! The decision seemed draconian, not least since the Devonians were a much respected club with an impressive record in West Country rugby. But, it is highly probable that uppermost in the minds of the Bath committee would have been the need to avoid any risk of further trouble, either home or away. Moreover, the incident raised awkward questions. First, the next visit of Torquay to the Rec would undoubtedly arouse wide interest and almost certainly a large crowd. Secondly, there was the sensitive issue occurring two seasons previously against Blackheath, when a small Bath post-match demonstration had occurred on the Rec for reasons similar to that at Torquay. Nor was an 'event' from season 1907-8 likely to have been entirely forgotten, when following a violent home Somerset Cup match against Weston super Mare trouble had spread to the terraces, resulting with a temporary ban imposed upon Bath. And some or all of these factors may have influenced the Bath-Torquay decision, one made quickly and decisively.

Now it is near certain that Weston super Mare would have followed this situation with more than a passing interest. Indeed, in recent seasons hints had been raised concerning their wish that the historic Bath v Weston super Mare crowd-problem of the Somerset Cup era be forgotten, and that their once regular fixtures be restored. Rotarian T.B.Butter from the seaside town had expressed just this desire when visiting Bath Rotarians in January 1936. Emphasising to the Chronicle that *"the seaside town were somewhat peeved that Bath would not give them a match,"* he added humbly that *"Weston did not expect any of the best dates, but were nonetheless anxious to have the opportunity of renewing a sporting occasion."* Naturally with the cessation of Torquay fixtures, Bath suddenly found themselves with blank days to fill and so decided to adopt some 'realpolitik.' The hatchet was buried almost immediately and 'normal service' with the

GOTCHA! ....just as well for Leicester. Even Prince Alex Obolensky (far left) looks back in alarm as jinking Bath outhalf Harris leaves three Tigers sprawling (result: Bath 17, Leicester 13, season 1936-37)

Acknowledgements to Bath Chronicle

'Seasiders' was resumed accordingly, their team now rated by the Chronicle as "*a very fine side, worthy to rank with the best.*" And the goodwill with opponents that season did not stop there, with the letter that season from Sale following their tour match at Bath to prove it. Albeit losing 11-3 they expressed their warmest gratitude for the hospitality shown to them. "*We [Sale] were splendidly entertained by the Bath club, and Mr Simpkins, their secretary, made every effort to see we had a wonderful time. Their hospitality did not cease on the Saturday. We had an invitation for every member of the side to accompany some of the team and officials on a visit to the magnificent Cheddar Gorge and the noted Cheddar Caves;*" and adding that on the final morning "*we left the city that had shown us such exceptional hospitality.*" (And thankyou Sale for those kind words).

When Bath launched their 1937-8 campaign with a 19-17 home win over Llanelli, the signs looked promising. So too did the qualities of some of the Bath backs, Roy Harris in particular. The Bath Chronicle, reporting the Llanelli match, were again among those singing his praises: "*His darts, fast and unexpected, nonplussed the opposition. They got [Llanelli] on the wrong foot, hopelessly beaten.*" And wing B.V. Robinson showed that Harris was not the only star on show. "*Astonishingly quick at the uptake and amazingly determined in his running. His four tries will be long remembered.*" Four tries against

Llanelli? A winger's prayers answered. But early hopes were soon followed by disappointments, and despite the renewed captaincy of Gerrard, it became clear that wishful thinking alone is no guarantor of success. While, disconcerting questions once more arose around Bath's forward strength: *"Wanting in weight and height, [they] do not get the ascendancy in the tight and in the line-out one would wish to see...."* (Chronicle & Herald, 4th Oct, 1937). Even so, Bath continued to display their curious unpredictable character. The January 11-0 win over Northampton was, in the words of "The Captain" (Chronicle & Herald) 'astonishing,' as Bath *"swept [the visitors] off their feet."* Foss got the first, and Lance Wardle and Jack Bartlett the others: *"the outcome of dashing passing and glorious running. Bartlett's was a splendid affair. He ran like a deer and with beautiful judgement. A hand-off, a swerve, and a change of direction and he completely hoodwinked the defence.* That was not all. The 8-0 win over Bristol in early March again brought out the superlatives from the "The Captain" (7th Mar. 1938). *"[Bath] wiped out the memory of indifferent performances this season, touched heights almost unsuspected, and made the opposition look very unimpressive."*

There would be victories too over Gloucester and Moseley. But....how then could one explain the season's woeful total of 13 wins only and the final three home defeats against Headingly, Old Merchant Taylors and the 0-27 loss to Leicester respectively, three matches where Bath failed to score so much as a single point. And no one, but no one, could put their finger on the reasons for such unpredictably. However, there was certainly off-field cheer provided by the marriage between the striking Molly Taylor and Bath's revered Ron Gerrard. Molly, like her father, was already a qualified architect and the wedding (19th November) was described in the Chronicle as a *"brilliant affair."* Best man was H.G. Owen-Smith, Gerrard's England colleague, and some four hundred guests attended the service at St. Mary's church, Bathwick. Then following the reception at the Pump Room, an ancient Bath Chair 'miraculously' appeared in the Abbey churchyard awaiting one R. A. Gerrard, who was thus *"conveyed through cheering crowds along Stall Street to the waiting honeymoon car."* It was a wedding fit for a sporting hero whose example had won the hearts of countless rugby followers, nor forgetting the heart of a beautiful young woman.

Ken Foss was then handed the captaincy for season 1938-9 with a squad still somewhat short on experience and a lack of old hands with experience, albeit the inspirational Gerrard was still good enough for an England Trial, though at full-back, not centre. But it would be events elsewhere that would shortly dictate matters, and not just at Bath. Meanwhile, the late September defeat at Devonport Services reported by "The Captain" (Chronicle & Herald, 26th Sep, 1938) outlined both the frailties and the potential within the side. In the backs the only regulars were scrum-half Norman Halse and centres Bud West and G. Forster. But youngster Tom Hicks looked one for the future, so too winger Fred Hayman (all 15 years of him) who come the conclusion of World War Two would again appear for Bath still a youth of 22 years. Scrum-half Halse, schoolboy international Tom Hicks and wing Jack Arnold would likewise resume their promising rugby careers some six years later, and like Hayman all still young men. At forward the front-row of Unwin, Brown and Ash, with Foss and Grundy at lock, and Weiss, Bill Gay and Phillips *"[looked] a pack good enough for any opposition, but there is not the fire, the team-work – anyway not till too late."* One of the exceptions was Bill Gay (father of Bath and England No.8 David Gay). *"A great forward"* wrote "The Captain."

The final total however of a mere nine wins could not be shrugged-off as simply bad luck (though to be fair there were six draws) and the victories did include Bristol and Northampton, while Bath's 3-5 success at Kingsholm on 19th November 1938 was the club's **first ever away win at Gloucester**, one elevated into an elusive Double when Bath triumphed 6-5 at home on 18th February 1939. Yet the season ended on a losing run of seven straight defeats that culminated with a 20-3 defeat at Neath. Some comfort could be drawn however by the selections of three-quarter A.V. Rogers and forward Bill Gay for **Somerset in the 1938-9 County Championship final** at Weston-s-Mare against Warwickshire; albeit that with the score poised on a knife-edge at 3-3 the Midlanders clinched victory literally with seconds to spare thanks to a Bruce-Lockhart try under the posts (Seventy years of Somerset rugby, 1875-1945, p. 44).

And yet…. during the season eyes were now looking elsewhere, to the Continent to be precise, and the world was about to change again; thus time once more for reflection on two decades of rugby that had promised so much, not least at Bath when from that day in September 1919 and that joyful 3-16 victory at Leicester they would thrive with more than fifteen years of success and record crowds, albeit followed by four less certain seasons of re-building. Usually, they held out the hand of a welcome friendship. Occasionally (Blackheath, March 1935) they had shown a more questionable side of their nature. Curiously a club who always held their great rivals Bristol in the highest regard were nonetheless the same Bath who since Somerset Cup days until the mid-1930's had long shared a somewhat uneasy relationship with Weston super Mare. So it was that Bath continued with their contradictions. Their strengths included their warmth, a sense of family and at home especially their capability to beat some of the best sides in England and Wales; while their weakness included a lack of confidence away from the Rec, a drawback especially evident when in Wales. Yet their geography was a help, not a hindrance, the city conveniently situated between the top clubs in London, the Midlands and Wales. But, they could not shake free from that continued comparison with Bristol and Gloucester, and from this there was 'no' escape. For they must (but must) turn the status quo on its head, reach heights never yet achieved and dominate Bristol and Gloucester….simultaneously! Even the top sides of England and Wales might shudder at the thought.

Yet that remained the challenge, and though on rare occasions it seemed that Bath had got close to this goal, close was not good enough. Again, it seemed an impossible challenge.

Chapter 19. IN THE LAP OF THE GODS. (1939-45)

In mid-summer 1939 the everyday life of the city seemed normal….on the surface. On the Rec the training had commenced by early August; it was learned that Lt. H. Withers (Army, Blackheath and Ireland) and Bryan Wallis (R.A.F. and Irish Trialist) were set to join Bath; numbers of former players were intending to team up with the coaching staff; and talented scrum-half J. Parsons (Leicester & Cambridge Blue) was a definite recruit whose presence promised a brilliant half-back partnership with Roy Harris. While high up on Lansdown (16th August) jockey-legend Gordon Richards ran home four winners at the Bath races. So, all seemed like any other normal August day, except it wasn't. And come the 24th August, the Chronicle & Herald headlined conclusive news that things were anything but normal: *"Bath ready if the worst comes,"* it proclaimed. Then in words that would have prophetic significance for the city, the report added: *"Bath, in common with the rest of the country, has received its special instructions to be prepared to affect a black-out in the event of need."* The particular need in this case referred to the possibility of air-raids, and Bath with an Admiralty Headquarters right in its midst was potentially a strategic target, one situated barely a stones-throw from the Rec.

Thus, following Britain's declaration of war with Germany on 3rd September the preparations for the Bath v Llanelli curtain-raiser of the 1939-40 season on 9th September were brought to an abrupt halt; while on the eve of this prestigious encounter those typical pre-season forecasts and team reports were absent from the Chronicle & Herald. Instead the front page showed a striking photograph, not of the Bath rugby line-up, but of the Somerset Yeomanry parading in immaculate order prior to their departure for a destination as yet 'unknown.' So, there would be no Bath v Llanelli clash in September 1939. Indeed, there would be no Bath v Llanelli clash for another six years, and as with the outbreak of conflict in the 1914-18 war, this new emergency threatened the continuation of any official form of sporting activity. But remarkably, rugby did continue in those early Autumn days, though admittedly not on a nation-wide format. Instead, matches were initially arranged on an 'ad hoc' basis with fixtures planned regionally, and for Bath this ranged as far as Exeter in the South West and to Newport and later Cardiff in Wales. However, although Bath played their first war-time game on 7th October, winning 30-6 on the Rec against an Admiralty XV, it was soon obvious that owing to military call-ups there would be a shortage of available players. Acting promptly therefore, the club and that same Admiralty XV agreed to join forces, and as a result (and for the duration of the war) the **Bath & Admiralty RFC** played as a combined club-team. Their baptism (14th October 1939) was a home 17-15 win over a Mr McNamara's XV. One week later they hosted Exeter with a reported two thousand crowd watching. They lost 9-20, a defeat that signalled a losing run that continued until the 18th December when Bath won at Cheltenham with a 0-23 away win. But although winning is always pleasing, actually 'playing' was now the top priority in times so threatening as these; it was an act of defiance; a message for friend and (especially) foe: 'we'll play our rugby come hell or high water…so get used to it!'

But, in view of the emergency there were doubts as to whether or not this hastily planned war-time rugby programme could continue into a second season. In fact, such were the omens by the New Year that it seems that there were doubts that rugby could get beyond half a season, let alone a full one. Indeed, there was no rugby for Bath come January 1940, nor rugby for Bath (or for many other West Country clubs) for the first seven weeks into 1940, such were the uncertainties caused by the on-going military preparations and not helped either by the sometimes severe blizzard-type weather conditions sweeping across parts of the Country. On the 24th February however Bath & Admiralty travelled to Stroud. Again they lost. But what the 'heck'….they played; and it was smiles all round in late March (1940) when not only did they actually win (6-4), but their change of fortune was at the expense of an Army XV led by, of all people, home favourite R. A. Gerrard.

Yet the task involved in continuing rugby in war-time cannot be underestimated, and the decision of the RFU to grant a two week extension to season 1939-40 extended a life-line to many clubs struggling to keep the show on the road, not least the gate-taking clubs so dependent on attendances. Another difficulty during a major war lay in actually obtaining sufficient players to field a team, let alone a competent one; likewise the 'back-room' task of administering a club in times of constant change. For example, the difficulties of obtaining transport, the uncertainty of player-availability and the often unreliable means of communication were all problems confronting any club operating in such a predicament. In addition, there was the critical financial shortfall caused by loss of gate-money. But it was the final game at Weston super Mare on 20th April that was perhaps the most poignant for the Bath & Admiralty in season 1939-40, not least because Jack Arnold, G.C. Foster and Roy Harris were all preparing to join the RAF, the Armoured Corps and the Royal Artillery respectively. That the Seasiders won that day mattered little, because for the Bath lads this was an occasion to bid farewell to their fellow team-mates, none knowing when (or if) they might ever meet again. So ended the fraught and far from normal season of 1939-40, whose significance is perhaps easy to overlook, while in fact it was nigh on a miracle that it even started, let alone finished. After all, those now struggling to organise rugby during a full-scale war were frequently compelled to make things up as they went along. Yet, in defiance of all temptation to simply throw in the towel, the organisers stuck to their guns, if one will pardon the pun.

Yet, so uncertain had been the situation in the final week of this opening season that the "The Captain" (Chronicle & Herald, 15th Apr, 1940) had ruefully commented that the *"future of war-time rugby was in the lap of the gods."* And yet, unlike 1914-18 when official rugby was abandoned completely, the Bath and Admiralty among a number of clubs would continue to function throughout the war, and once again the reason was partly one of geography. For the city was situated within a reasonable distance to several nearby RAF bases and furthermore to the large military garrisons now stationed on the Salisbury Plain. It was these centres in particular that provided eager and willing sources of opposition, and not forgetting players. Furthermore, at the national level not only did the prestigious Barbarians play on occasions, but a number of unofficial international games were held. Sevens too proved popular, not least at Bath, where both inter-club and Services 7's tournaments provided a highly successful feature of late season rugby. And remarkably in such critical circumstances, the Middlesex Sevens (then England's premier inter-club tournament) would continue throughout the entire War. But other (not always obvious) difficulties arose in maintaining an effective rugby side, not least the captaincy factor; and for the first two war-time seasons the leadership of Bath & Admiralty was often dependent on who might be available at any given time. Fortunately come 1941-2 the amiable John Wass was able to skipper the team on a more regular basis, thanks partly to his role as a civil engineer based at the Admiralty. From 1943 onwards it was the equally affable Austin Higgins who then took up the reins, while John Wass dedicated his efforts to the considerable task of club secretary. Meanwhile another difficulty that sometimes required a 'quick fix' was obtaining a referee. They too were subject to the 'call of duty,' leading to a predicament typified on 12th December 1942 when Bath hosted an RAF XV. The opposition arrived, but the referee didn't. So, Dick Chaddock, Bath's otherwise indispensable treasurer suddenly discovered that he was now an equally indispensable referee. By all accounts he didn't do too bad a job either!

Then there was the normally sensitive matter of the Rugby League factor, or to be precise, the 'removal' of the Rugby League factor. This after all was war-time, and in view of the exceptional circumstances now prevailing, **the RFU withdrew all Union barriers to those League players involved in Services rugby.** True, there probably wasn't much else they could do in the circumstances, and such a barrier was virtually unenforceable in war-time anyway. Moreover, clubs such as Bath sometimes faced Services teams literally packed with League players. But! Bath not only played against League players, on occasions they even played 'with' them. S.Morgan (R.A.F.) for example, otherwise of Hull Kingston Rovers, earned considerable praise at scrum-half for Bath in their win at Bridgwater on 9th December 1944. And his appearance raised several pertinent questions. First, while the Union-League truce permitted League players to represent Services teams, it was not certain whether the RFU intended this liberty to extend to the selection of League players to represent non-Service teams? Whatever the answer may have been, it appears that Bath were 'openly honest' about the matter and, apart from the 1939-45 period, the club followed the standard RFU ban regarding professionals. The matter did not stop there however, because the Bath & Herald's report of Morgan's debut for Bath (11th Dec, 1944) suggests that in addition to Morgan, other rugby League players might have represented the club: *"It is a rare occurrence for a Rugby League player to figure in the Bath side...."* the Chronicle wrote. A 'rare' occurrence yes, but perhaps not an entirely unknown one (interesting)? But it seems reasonable to draw the following conclusions: namely that the war-time Union and League truce was in practice more far-reaching than perhaps has been realised; that on occasions some clubs (including Bath) had on occasions fielded League players, and that the RFU (assuming that they were aware of this fact) took no action to stop it. If this was the case, one can only wonder at the contrast with the RFU's refusal to compromise on this issue in later decades, a refusal that would cause such divisions within the Union game itself towards the end of the century.

The aftermath of the North Stand following night-time bombing raids on Bath
Acknowledgements to Bath Chronicle

Meanwhile that other conflict of 1939-45 continued, and much of the time the threat lurked high above in the skies, hence the air-raid warning (printed on Bath match programmes) as follows: *"In the event of an alert, spotters will go on duty. If danger becomes imminent they will blow 3 blasts on their whistles. Play will then immediately cease. Shelter guides wearing white armlets will be available to direct spectators to shelter."* Furthermore, the threat was always there, and on the nights of 25th/26th April 1942 it struck directly at the heart of the city. *"Three air raids over two nights took the lives of more than 400 people,"* headlined the Chronicle, while *"900 buildings were destroyed and some 12,000 more were damaged."* Among this destruction was the home of Eddie Simpkins (and alas the loss of a treasured photo-history of the Bath club), while the Rec took several direct hits from bombs most probably intended for the Admiralty building across the river, leaving the West and North stands nothing more than heaps of mangled wreckage.

Then….there was the fate of those serving beyond these shores, not least the loss as reported in the Chronicle & Herald (10th Feb. 1943). It duly announced the *"grievous news"* that had arrived in a War Office telegram on the previous night, one that was subsequently diverted to the club chairman Capt. Stanley Amor who undertook to break the news to a suddenly bereaved family. For 'Gerry' Gerrard (now Major, Royal Engineers) had been killed four days after his 31st birthday at Alamein in January 1943. The Chronicle expressed its deepest and sincere sympathies, and those of all Bathonians, to Molly Gerrard and her baby son Duncan, whose godfathers were Wing Commander B.V. (Robbie) Robinson, D.S.O. and D.F.C., and Capt. Pottinger who saw action against the Graf Spee in the battle of the River Plate. For Ronald Anderson Gerrard was the classic schoolboys' hero. There was the outstanding all-round sportsman whose sporting prowess included county cricket for Somerset and rugby for England. In addition there was the fearless soldier who in his final days would lead his sappers out into hazardous night-time operations on vital mine-field clearance tasks and who 'for his bravery in the push from El Alamein received the immediate award of the D.S.O.' But now….it was farewell to a rugby legend, one whose qualities had proved an inspiration to a generation of Bathonians, and it was the Chronicle again who would provide the near perfect yet heart-rending lament: *"Now he sleeps on the battlefield in a spot that will be forever England."* Naturally in a conflict of six years duration there were other Bath players who selflessly gave their lives for their Country, among them Royal Air Force wingers J.S. Bartlett D.F.C. and the aforementioned B.V. Robinson. In addition, the Roll of Honour included half-back John 'Freddie' Rhymes, forwards Peter Moon and Leslie Phillips, George Nudds (Royal Navy), and 1920's three-quarters H.C. Partridge and Lt. Colonel 'Dick' James (Somerset Light Infantry). Their loss too was great.

Rather more comforting however were the events unfolding abroad during 1944 indicating that the end of the conflict in Europe was within sight. Indeed, the 1944-5 rugby season would close just five weeks short of VE Day; while another highly promising outside-half had now arrived in the city, namely Edinburgh University medical graduate Ian Lumsden, a young Scot who had impressed from that moment of his Bath debut in December 1943. Of steady hands and composure and an excellent long-range kicker, the young doctor possessed a natural ability to tactically dominate a game. He was destined to be **Bath's first club-produced Scottish international.** Austin Higgins continued as skipper, although if one anecdote is to be believed, it was only Lady Luck who ensured that he was. Because according to Jack Simpkins (son of Eddie) 'the redoubtable Austin managed to sleep peacefully through an entire night of the Bath Blitz only to awake the following morning to discover that half his house no longer existed.' Thus Austin, neither 'shaken or stirred' from the visit of the Luftwaffe, was obviously 'the' man to lead the club through their final war-time season; one that in early September would include a 5-24 upset against the **R.A.A.F.** (Royal Australian Air Force) whom Bath 'rated the best team of the War seen on the Rec,' and then culminate with a 0-3 upset at Nuneaton who (Chronicle & Herald 27th Mar. 1945) claimed to be the only Midland club to continue throughout the war without a break, and Leicester (Bath winning 5-3) known during the conflict as Leicester Barbarians.

Five weeks later (8th May) it would be VE Day, and the official rugby game would resume in the Autumn. At Bath however the game had never stopped for the six years of conflict, an era when players from here, there and just about everywhere had carried the colours of the Bath & Admiralty. **As for the Rec**, *bombs had been dropped right on top of it. As for the club treasury, the coffers were all but empty. But it was home! Bath had played on this green meadow* **since 1894** *and not even the Luftwaffe was going to stop them playing on it! It was, apart from anything else, a show of defiance. The Ritz had never closed throughout the War.* **Nor did Bath!**

Chapter 20.   BATH (1945-50)......RUGBY YEOMEN.

It was during the late 1770's (Georgian Summer, by David Gadd, p.124) that the architectural genius that was Thomas Baldwin 'redesigned the Cross Bath one hundred yards west of the pump room.' Fast-track to the rugby season of 1945-6 and that same Cross Bath conveniently provided emergency changing facilities for Bath RFC as they embarked upon their first season of post-war rugby, one beginning with their encounter against Welsh giants Llanelli. So far, so good; but the Rec was another matter altogether, because the ground that in those pre-war days had sometimes hosted crowds of thousands now possessed not a single enclosure and the club were seriously short of money. Nonetheless, a temporary West stand would soon be open for business, and a rugby family that had played the game throughout the war, sometimes with bombs 'dropping on their heads,' would allow nothing to spoil the party for the Scarlets' visit. Yet while a temporary enclosure was one thing, something to actually wear was quite another, with government issued 'clothing coupons' required (almost gold-dust at the time) before the club could purchase so much as a single shirt, and it was doubtless much to the relief of Bath when 36 extra coupons landed on the secretary's desk prior to the start of the new season. Unfortunately (Chronicle & H, 3rd Sep. 1945) the club colours of blue, white and black were not immediately available, and for the following three seasons it was to be white shirts only, blue shorts and red socks....actually, quite smart. Yet even at this most austere of times Bath chose to donate the proceeds of this first game to the Alkmaar Fund, so providing financial aid to post war-stricken Holland. It was a gesture (Chronicle & H, 4th Sep.1945) that said much about Bath.

But, it was difficult to predict how any team would perform after a lapse of six years of official rugby. This much was known however: Austin Higgins (yes, he who reportedly had slept peacefully throughout a night-bombing raid) was a morale boosting skipper. The admired 'Bud' West of pre-war days was yet again to prove a steadying hand at fullback. Furthermore, centre Joe Bailey (who had played for Somerset in their County championship final in 1935) could still live in top-class rugby despite his thirty-six years of age, and out-half Lumsden, when available, was truly a master of his craft! Alas, the flying Scotsman was not available for this emotional post-war opener on 8th September 1945 among the following **Bath line-up: *B. Capon, F.W. Thomas, J. Bailey, Les Moores, Pat Leahy, Tom Cuff, J. Parkin, C.P. Hosking, L. James, W. Barrow, J. Owen, C. J. Stewart, Tom Smith, Kenneth Weiss, Austin Higgins (Capt.).*** An estimated two thousand crowd attended that day, including perhaps the unofficial winner of the club's 'most dedicated war-time follower award,' namely Bristol (yes Bristol!) domiciled Mr A.E. Ley. His round journey to the Rec covered no less than 26 miles of travel. But 'have wheels-will travel,' and as the Chronicle (10th Sep.1945) admiringly reported, he had for many years regularly biked some 300 to 500 miles each season to support his beloved Bath. What a star!

Others, among them Llanelli loyalist Gareth Hughes (see: 'One hundred years of Scarlet') would learn of the outcome by other means: *"....I know exactly what I was doing [he wrote]. I was glued to the wireless, waiting impatiently for the result of Llanelli's first rugby match after the war. And I still recall the pride and exhilaration when the news was broadcast to an expectant nation-or at least the part of it which I, as a third former at Llanelly County School, represented. "Bath nil, Llanelly 16 points." My joy was boundless: and my pride was confirmed a few days later when a headline in a local newspaper proclaimed, "Impressive Start to Rugby Season." No addicted supporter at Stradey will be surprised to know that the Scarlets' margin of victory would have been greater "but for the inconsistent decisions of the referee, who twice disallowed spectacular, and what appeared to be legitimate, scores by Gerwyn Rees." The newspaper files of more than a century provide staunch evidence that every referee who ever set foot at Stradey should properly have been consigned to the nearest lunatic asylum. "Bath nil, Llanelly 16 points." A simple statistic, in my case never to be forgotten. Yet, in general terms, I have never been much interested in the general statistics which attach to the game. It has always seemed to me that the sociological aspects of rugby are very much more interesting than the arithmetical ones. That man of steel went straight from a hard shift in the heat and glare of the furnaces to play against a major touring team at Stradey seems to me to be the real stuff of rugby history...."*

But after their opening season defeat notwithstanding, it was still a case of wait-and-see as to whether a new post-war Bath could repeat the exhilaration so often witnessed following the Great War of 1914-18. Moreover, a new West Stand was an absolute 'must' if the club was to continue attracting gate-paying attendances sufficient to support the running-costs of a first class, gate-taking club. And it hardly helped that money was tight in those post-war days of limited means, albeit the price then of Bath season tickets of £2 and 2 shillings (men) and £1 and 1 shilling (ladies) seems trifling now, but not in the 1940's it wasn't! Though with luck a few good crowd-pulling seasons could hopefully bring a smile back on the treasurer's face. And, there were potentially encouraging signs with wins over London Scottish, Northampton, Moseley (a double), Wasps, and an 11-13 win at fortress Kingsholm (16th February 1946), a prized scalp and furthermore Gloucester's first defeat at the hands of a fellow English club that season. Yet, this huge victory came at a fearful cost. For Roy Harris, he of sublime skills, was injured so seriously it would put him out of the game for the rest of his life. It was no surprise therefore that despite a follow-up win over Moseley, a visibly despondent Bath would slide into an alarming run of nine defeats on the trot, save for victory over the O.M.T's, before a further home 5-17 upset against Leicester closed a modest sixteen win season.

Furthermore, of the respective season-totals from 1945-50 of 16, 18, 15, 19 and 15 victories respectively only two suggested that Bath might rekindle some of the dominance often seen in pre-war days, and of these the 1946-7 campaign under new captain Ian Lumsden would be the first. Things took time to warm up however, with a 3-3 home draw against Llanelli and Joe Bailey (days from his 37th birthday) deputising as captain for Lumsden. Then narrow defeats at Leicester and Swansea followed before Bath (admittedly seven 1st teamers short) were literally swamped 45-3 by a rampant Devonport Services in late September. So, now it seemed again that dark clouds might be approaching, and not for the first time either. But then this was Bath, and in that not untypical way there would be signs of daylight when least expected. Bristol were appropriately the turning point thanks to a close mid-October 8-6 win and the Chronicle enthused over the abilities of new skipper Ian Lumsden: *"He often saved his defence by his positional play, tackling and kicking, and often his pack by use of the touchline. He was not spectacular, but he was amazingly sound and a 'tower of strength' at many critical points of the afternoon."* This victory was followed later with an exceptional team performance that clinched a January 8-5 win over Cardiff, while in late season Bath hit dazzling form. Harlequins were defeated (3-0), then London Scottish (6-3) and Leicester (12-8); while Newport were held 13-13 away, Northampton fell (16-13) and Moseley (11-0). Finally, Bath concluded their season with an 8-3 success against Gloucester, and only Bristol's 9-3 revenge win interrupted the seemingly unstoppable late run of success.

IAN LUMSDEN ..... from Watsonian to Bathonian.

Yet while Lumsden (gaining 7 Scotland caps) was undoubtedly a key individual of this team, the noticeable factor in a season's total of 18 wins and 4 draws was the pack. This was a new generation of forwards, and what forwards! *"No pack in England could have excelled Bath's in their match with Harlequins...."* enthused 'The Captain,' in his Chronicle report (3rd Apr.1947) of the one try to nil win over Quins (see above). *"Austin Higgins – could you find his master anywhere; – D.S Beard who is worth a place in any first-class side; W.G. Jenkins, a top-top aggressive wing forward; Dr [Allan] Todd, medico, like Lumsden at the Royal United Hospital, who appearing in his first game of the season was magnificent in the middle of the back row....and Farmer Bland from his broad acres on the Wiltshire Downs."* Nor were they the only ones, because chasing 1st team places were powerful Arthur Burcombe (later to captain Somerset), Len Harter and Bill Barrow. While with the home 8-3 victory over Gloucester that brought closure to Lumsden's one-year captaincy the Chronicle (5th May 1947) was moved to comment thus: *"If [Bath] can keep the present players together and introduce some new blood in the United to fill the future vacancies in the Firsts [then] the record of this season, magnificent as it has been, will be beaten."*

Now, if that 'new blood' was to include a back-division equal to those sometimes seen during the 1920's and 1930's then that really could set pulses racing. Moreover, with three-quarters Kevin O'Shaughnessy and Stan Ascott the club was already equipped with several highly capable outsides, including Jack Arnold at fullback. Yet the emphasis continued to focus mainly, though not entirely, on the pack, and rightly or wrongly Bath's post-war reputation as a no-nonsense, forward-dominated side would remain for the next two decades at least.

Newport and Wales wing legend (Ken Jones) heads for Bath line. Bath in white shirts (l to R), A. Higgins, F. Hayman, S. Spence-Meighan, I. Lumsden.

Acknowledgments Bath Chronicle

Meanwhile the Chronicle & Herald's report (11th Oct. 1946) of the Somerset v Middlesex county match had explained a query that had long gone unanswered, namely: 'why did Bath number their team-shirts from 1 to 16 (not 1to15), omitting shirt 13?' 'Suspicion,' as is often the case with this unjustly maligned number, was the cause, but one that resulted from this same county rugby match played on 10th October 1946. On the face of it the drawn 13-13 result seemed harmless enough but, the equalising third Middlesex try that levelled the score was run home by centre A.Venniker (St. Mary's Hospital) wearing shirt number 13 and, for the suspiciously minded Bath committee watching this game on the Rec (Somerset to the core), this coincidence could not be brushed off lightly. And their problem was that 'damned' No.13 shirt. It just 'had' to go. Loyal Cidermen, their feelings were expressed the following day no less in the Chronicle with the following statement: the "Bath *club are excluding No.13 from the numbering of their players."* Nor were they joking! And although the change was not immediate, not least for administrative reasons, the fact is that during season 1951-2 the switch was completed, with Bath teams now numbered from 1-16 and omitting number 13 altogether. So, laid to rest was one long-held assumption, namely that the number had long been rejected in the belief that shirt 13 was worn by Clifford Walwin on the day of his fatal injury (27th. Dec. 1919), an era anyway when a different shirt-numbering system applied.

For 1947-8 skipper Tom Hicks (awarded **the Military Cross** in the War) there would be the major task of filling the gap left by Lumsden's frequent unavailability owing to his National Service call-up at RAF Cranwell. Yet it was not for nothing that the Chronicle had commented thus in the final days of the previous season: *"The fact remains that the better the opposition the better the Bath performance and the more uphill the struggle the more they seem to be able to pull out.* There was 'some' truth in this. Yet, this was another post-war season with a confusing lack of consistency, yielding a lowly 15 wins and 2 draws from 37 matches played. But it did not lack for poignancy, as revealed when prior to the Boxing Day 9-8 win against Old Blues the club flag was flown at half-mast and the players quietly lined up for a short silence in memory of James Timmins, Bath's England Trialist centre (late 1890's to 1910) who had recently passed away. He had not been forgotten. However, the following 1948-9 season, though commencing ominously with a draw and three defeats, would then herald a landmark win that perhaps surpassed any in the club's previous history, and whose impact would be heard from the joyous reception awaiting the team's return at the Western Station on the night of 2nd October. Ringmaster was club president Capt. Stanley Amor, supported by chairman B.C. Barber, the committee and a large and a joyous crowd of supporters. Cyril Bailey (heart and soul of any gathering) became impromptu Town Crier. Former secretary Victor Smith played a portable harmonium, and all around was music and vociferous song. Oh, and crates of beer were available, and in 'healthy 'quantity. Small wonder....Bath at long last had achieved their **first ever win in Wales**, and won it at Llanelli!! Nor did things stop there, because Bath once again wore their traditional club shirts of blue, white and black. It could hardly get better than that. Meanwhile amid the gathering there stood skipper Dr Allan Todd clutching a doll. It was not the prettiest of objects, hence long known as '**the Rag Doll.**' But the obscure history surrounding its origins was later explained in the Llanelli v Bath match programme of 29th November, 1978: a '*Mrs Rosina Rothery of Bath had made the original soon after the First World War to be presented to the winners between Bath and Llanelli,*' and since then (until the professional era) it would hang from a cross-bar in the current victor's

The Rag Doll ....has never backed a loser.

Acknowledgements: Reg. Monk

94

colours whenever the two rivals met. There was one further piece of information, explained on the eve of the post-war Bath v Llanelli match of September 1945 by the Chronicle & Herald (7th Sep. 45) that referred to the *"celebrated trophy, the 20 year old doll, given by Bath for annual competition by the two clubs."* Assuming this to be correct, this indicates that the Rag Doll was first contested circa 1925, another fact not widely known.

But it 'was' long known that to win in Wales demanded total discipline and concentration, for there was no harder arena in rugby. But this success would be remembered not least for a superb solo try more typical of Welsh three-quarter wizardry when Cornishman Michael Terry shot away, *"beating three opponents before searing down the middle to score beneath the bar."* New Cornish arrival Terry, a Physio' trainee at the RUH, was indeed a centre of exciting potential, and not surprisingly soon to be an England Trialist. Equally interesting was that another discovery was made that day, a centre-cum-wing-forward by the name of Alec Lewis. He too was about to attract much interest. Another high-profile win against Harlequins (18-13) in October on the Rec thanks to a drop-goal and no less than five tries, as against two goals and one unconverted try by Quins was proof to all those present that a post-war Bath 'had it in them' to play 15-man rugby. The pack as shown at Llanelli was probably the equal of most, and now the outsides were strengthened by the further acquisition of 'utility' backs such as Michael Hanna; and so reliable was Graham Hawkes at out-half that against Harlequins it was Ian Lumsden who was paired at centre with Terry. Oh! And what a clever selection this proved to be. The Quins (Chronicle & H, 1st Nov.1948) *"muffed their passes under the devastating tackling of the Bath centres. Though Lumsden did not score himself, he played the role of opening-maker to perfection....his beautiful cross-kicks to the open side - these contributed handsomely to Bath's victory."* And, the *"match was a personal triumph for Terry, his fleet-footed resourceful running - once covering three-quarters the length of the field brought him three glorious tries."* Meanwhile Hawkes flighted home a drop-goal and skipper Todd notched a try-brace to complete a near perfect Bath exhibition. Even so, there remained the query (yes, 'that' query) from which Bath as yet could not escape: could Bristol and Gloucester be upstaged? Well, Bath would hold Bristol 3-3 at home, then defeat them 0-3 away; while Gloucester's Autumn win at Kingsholm was conclusively avenged 13-3 in February on the Rec. But was that enough to draw Bath level in the bragging stakes? Frankly, not until such results became the norm; not merely 'one-offs.'

Meanwhile Christmas came, Llanelli soon arrived and Bath (with tries from Wilfred Williams and K. O'Shaughnessy) joyously sealed the Double over the Scarlets with a 6-0 home win on 28th December. Boy....was that some Christmas! Not without significance either was Bath's 13-8 victory over Wasps in February, not least as the Londoners (a recent addition to Bath fixtures) were now described by the Chronicle 'as the fastest improving side in the capital, who in the previous season had won the Middlesex 7's for the first time in their history.' Noticeable too was the 3-5 February victory at unfashionable but dangerous Newbridge, a side virtually unbeatable on their home territory. Yes, another win in Wales! And, despite lacking a truly reliable goal-kicker during the 1948-9 campaign, Bath's 19 victories (some outstanding) and 5 draws from 40 games ranked as the best of their first five post-war seasons. Furthermore, Allan Todd's team (he gained a Scottish Trial that season) was only badly defeated on one occasion with Newport's emphatic 34-8 win in April, a harsh warning from the Valleys that Wales was only too capable of exacting heavy retribution upon any English side that had the temerity to trample on Welsh pride, as had Bath at Llanelli.

So, the final season of the decade beckoned, notable for the guest-visit of Hylton Cleaver's International XV (15TH September 1949), a team packed to the rafters with internationals, Trialists, Blues and Barbarians, an occasion moreover for followers to actually see the 'stars' for 'real.' Few surprises then that the visitors won (6-21), but that neither dampened the enjoyment nor overwhelmed two young props alongside Bath hooker Jack Francis, namely Tom Smith and John Roberts, a duo who would soon forge a front-row partnership that would become a part of Bath rugby folklore. Meanwhile, the fluctuating fortunes since the war continued, and a mere fifteen wins and three draws from 39 matches was a disappointment following the previous season that had suggested that Bath were on 'the up' once again. True, under Len Harter's captaincy there were wins to savour, not least the forward inspired 6-3 December success against highly rated London Scottish and the late season home 8-3 victory over Newbridge. But there were 21 defeats, and it seemed an uphill struggle lay ahead as Bristol and Gloucester (usually deservedly) continued to attract the accolades. Yet in the Chronicle's own words (Ch. 17) Bath *"played the yeoman way,"* a thought-provoking comment, since it was/is the yeoman who learns his trade from the bottom upwards. Often 'long' on experience, he remains in the background, little noticed. And though on occasions the yeoman climbs up through the ranks to the top, they are never expected to do so. Neither for that matter were Bath.

Footnote: Photo on page 93 is from the Bath v Newport match of 9th March, 1946 (result: Bath: 5 Newport; 20).

Chapter 21. GREAT DAYS! (1950-55)

Since the end of World War Two, both Bristol and Gloucester (the occasional threat not withstanding) could still sleep easily in the belief that Bath would be unlikely to disturb their peace any time soon. And yet, could Bath really produce 'that' something to emphasise loud and clear that this was a three-horse race, similar to those glamour days seen on occasions during the 1920's and early 1930's? Well, the answer would now come with the appointment of the lion-hearted Alec Lewis as captain, plus a pack that few would equal and even fewer would surpass.

The 1950-51 season for Bath, a club saddened by the untimely loss of S.G.U. Considine (a war-time squadron-leader) who had unexpectedly passed away in late August, opened

Alex Lewis steams away from Bristolians Woodward and Bain (white shirts) Robin Hambly (far right)
Acknowledgements: Jack Simkins

with narrow defeat at Leicester, followed by a 0-16 upset against Hylton Cleaver's International XV on their second visit to the Rec; and though by no means clear of their own financial difficulties, Bath again shared the gate-profits, this time with the National Playing Fields Association and the club's own Memorial Fund dedicated in part to the families of Bath and District players who had lost their lives in the War. There then followed an 8-8 home draw against Llanelli (18th September), a result against those men of steel where the Bath pack did not merely look good, it looked potentially awesome, a fact demonstrated when their second try resulted from a full-blooded push-over try! An

Autumn 13-6 home win against Bristol was then as good as it gets against the best, with the exception that is from victories away from home against the best; and the January success at London Welsh, who already that season had defeated both Coventry and Llanelli, really did send out a signal that Bath must be taken seriously. Then, as the season progressed the leadership of Alec Lewis (not to be confused with Trevor Lewis, another excellent back-row forward) became ever more evident. The Bath Chronicle, at first cautiously optimistic, now sensed something was 'really happening.' Thus, the victory at London Welsh had resulted by way of a pack that "*shone in the line-out and was devastating in the loose;*" while ex-Bristol full-back Pat Sullivan won the unofficial 'Man of the Match' nomination for the Chronicle & Herald (15th Feb. 1951) in the 8-3 victory against Gloucester. "*No one shone better than Sullivan. His catching and kicking and his positional play were immaculate;*" and not forgetting winger Donnelly's try "*that really won the game. It was typical of this flaxen haired speed merchant....taking advantage of a mistake by the other side and that race for the line.*"

A cherished Double (thus 'full-on' bragging rights) was then achieved with Bath's 6-9 win at Bristol in early March, where the Bath pack "*under Alec Lewis worked like a machine.*" While a potential problem owing to injury to scrum-half Mike Hanna was solved by the simplest of solutions within the club's own resources by recalling 'A' team skipper Halse (by now both a war and a rugby veteran), who it was duly discovered could still rough it with the toughest, as he proved again when facing England's Pat Sykes in Bath's 8-3 victory over Wasps when "*Halse's experience at the base of the scrum was invaluable.*" Now, a seven-win surge took off that included the away success at Bristol, another at Saracens, while the 8-6 victory over Swansea (not beaten by Bath since 1930) drew an ovation at the final whistle, where the performance of Bath's other Lewis (namely fellow wing-forward Trevor) "*was exceptional.*" The all-time club record meanwhile stood at 25 victories previously achieved by the Philip Hope side of 1921-2, and surpassed by the 26 wins if (but only 'if') one accepts as valid an exhibition game at Blundell's School by the Vowle's side in the following season. Whatever one's judgement in this matter, Bath's form in season 1950-1 was now so hot that not merely 26, but an even higher win-total looked attainable; and on their final offensive there would be one defeat, two draws, and crucially three victories. First, the home 23-5 success over Moseley brought the win tally to twenty-five, while a Thursday evening 6-11 win at Taunton raised that total to twenty-six. Then two days later the matter was put beyond doubt when in the return at Moseley **(21st April 1951) an undisputed new club record of 27 wins** was achieved, and gained in the perfect way, with the Midlanders' lone drop-goal bettered by Bath's three tries, the last from highly promising back Alec Poulson. It was significant too that Bath were playing at the highest level of the first-class game, and there being no rugby union 'league' tables at this stage, standardised or otherwise, it was not possible for the rugby fraternity to accurately judge and compare respective strengths. Nonetheless, the Chronicle calculated that the club's 1950-1 performance would have placed Bath not only in the top half, but in the top quarter of an unofficial first-class Table.

So ended an epic season where the pack had been a key strength, a pack where in the record winning game at Moseley bludgeoned over for yet another of their now almost predictable push-over tries, scored on this occasion by 6ft 4inch lock John Dingle. Five years earlier in December 1945 his first-class baptism had been delivered in blood (literally) when Bath, a forward short, plucked the talented line-out jumper from the King Edwards School XV and pitched him straight into the arena at Llanelli... of all places! He then stepped on to Stradey Park as a young 17 years old boy. Eighty minutes later of a pulsating 3-3 draw young Dingle strode off the park.... a Man! As for the individual appearances made in season 1950-1 the Chronicle named the **most regular Bath team as: *P. Sullivan, R. Hambly, G. Addenbrooke, R. Todd, W. Donnelly, K. Wilcox, M. Hanna, T. Smith, F. Hill, J. Roberts, J.Dingle, G.Brown, Trevor Lewis, Allan Todd, Alec Lewis (capt.).*** Others too played a prominent role, among them the brilliant young **Welsh back Glyn John** prior to the welcoming arms of London Welsh, but who, when with Bath had: *"set the Thames on fire when he ran from halfway right through the heart of the London Scottish side at Richmond to score."* Talent (especially at forward) seemed to be everywhere, so too experience, and it proved to be a highly potent combination. A return of 27 wins (an impressive 13 away from home) and 4 draws from 41 matches was proof enough of an excellent season.

Even so questions (sometimes justified) remained concerning Bath's style of play. Yes, the back-line were frequently lethal in the tackle, but as early as the October 8-8 draw with Llanelli the Chronicle had expressed one reservation: *"....back play is not yet Bath's strong point. If only the three-quarters were equal to the pack, well, Bath could beat any opposition they are likely to meet."* It was this one deficiency that on occasions would leave the team short of options, as was the case in defeats at Gloucester (27-3), likewise 11-25 at home to Cardiff, followed later by a fearful 39-9 drubbing at Newport! And yet just to complicate matters there was 'individual' ability outside the scrum. Pat Sullivan, wings Guy Addenbrooke, Robin Hambly and Brian French, centres Bob Todd and Alec Polson, halfbacks Hanna and Kenneth Wilcox, and especially the brilliant Glyn John, would challenge for places in most first-class sides. Though, if there was one type of player missing then it would have been play-makers in the mould of Roy Harris and Lumsden, international standard outside-halves who would have thrived outside a pack so powerful and galvanised the back-division accordingly. Meanwhile, it was during the close season that the 'Bath Old Players' was founded (later renamed 'Bath Past Players' in June 2005), while Alec Lewis accepted the team captaincy again, leading Bath (a

John Kendall-Carpenter
Bath and England

reported 7,000 watching) to face H.B. Toft's International XV among early season challenges. And Bath put up 'some' fight, albeit losing 9-17, and playing with 14 men after a wretched broken-shoulder injury to centre Robert Todd after 28 minutes. Yet utility back Guy Addenbrooke was then seen at his best with the game's opening try: *"clever interceptor, vigorous and determined in his bursts for the line, a danger point at all times. He survived two tackles before he forced his way doggedly over the line;"* (Chronicle & H, 21st Sep. 1951).

John Roberts, part of an immovable front row

In January Alec Lewis was honoured with his first cap, paired alongside Kendall-Carpenter (a try scorer for H.B. Toft's international XV and destined to join Bath) in England's back-row against South Africa at Twickenham. First however there would be the 'small' matter of a home encounter against Gloucester ('the' perfect warm-up) and Lewis, after *'glancing through another batch of congratulatory messages in the dressing room,'* duly led Bath to a 3-0 victory over one of the toughest opponents in England. Against South Africa, one of the toughest opponents in the world, things ended a little differently, England losing 3-8. But Lewis had impressed. He would gain another nine caps for his Country. Meanwhile with Bath and Bristol sharing bragging rights with each winning at home and Wasps, now very much a leading club held 8-8 by the Lewis side in London, it was a narrow home 0-5 defeat against Cardiff in January that demonstrated both the strengths and the one drawback during this era when Bath faced opponents capable of 'spreading it wide.' Not for the first time the Chronicle & Herald (21st Jan. 1952) emphasised the point that the *"Bath pack was as good as any in the Country."* [But] *"while the backs tackled extremely well....little constructive play emerged from the backs as a whole and Bath badly need an opening-maker, which they now lack."* That opening-maker was of course another Roy Harris or Lumsden.

Nonetheless, one could hardly begrudge a total of 21 victories and 3 draws achieved that season, though one could understand the deep regrets throughout the club at the decision of Alec Lewis to resign the captaincy, brought about by his ever-increasing business commitments. Who could replace such a man, described by one of the leading judges as *"the greatest skipper in the history of the club"* (Football Herald & Chronicle 5th May 1951)? Who indeed? The answer was prop forward John Roberts; and encouraged by wins that included a 3-11 away victory at the sometimes top-notch Devonport Services, the Roberts side prepared for the visit of Llanelli in early October 1952, along with an advance warning from the Valleys: *"Expect fireworks from Lewis Jones."* Ah Lewis Jones (centre), destined for greatness in a Welsh shirt and later Rugby League stardom at Leeds. So, Guy Addenbrooke, ex Swansea and Welsh Trialist, was rushed into the centre to stiffen Bath in mid-field, though switched to out-half on the day, while John Kendall-Carpenter, now at Bath, was immediately called-up for his club debut. Yet nothing, but nothing, could stop Lewis Jones from casting that same awesome Celtic magic over the Rec that he was in the habit of doing wherever he played; kicking (from all angles) two conversions, two penalties and crossing over for a try with a tally of 19 points from Llanelli's 25 overall total. In reply Bath salvaged a lone Sullivan penalty, and the Chronicle again pin-pointed a not unknown weakness: *"Bath had as much of the play as [Llanelli], but the backs were uninspiring."* This shortfall furthermore was a factor when losing 3-16 at home against a Cardiff team complete with out-half genius Cliff Morgan in its ranks; evident too when Harlequins visited the Rec in April with England centres W.P.C. Davies and A.E.Agar in their line-up for their 3-14 victory. And why did these opponents win?....*"because 'on the day' they were just too good outside the scrum!"*

But to further to confuse critics, on occasions the Bath backs 'did' perform, and not just against the minnows. Bristol, exponents of open rugby, would have testified to this fact in their 9-3 Autumn defeat on the Rec. Admittedly all scores came from the boot (one a 40 yarder from Sullivan). But the Bath outsides in the words of the Chronicle *"were brilliant."* Mick Hanna and Clifford Weston shone at half-back, while Addenbrooke, O'Shaughnessy, Hambly and impressive new arrival Peter Fearis looked top grade. Again, Bath were at their 15-man best with a sparkling four-try total in their early April 16-3 win over the highly rated London Scottish, having previously struck perhaps their finest form of the season with ironically a defeat, not a win, at Neath in mid-March. Admittedly they fell 15-14, but Eddie Simpkins, who had followed Bath for some forty years rated their performance as simply *"the best display ever given by Bath in Wales."* A reported 4,000 crowd doubtless agreed and on the final whistle there was a loudspeaker request for *"three cheers for Bath for a wonderful exhibition of rugby football;"* proof that Bath could play the open, running game and…. play it in Wales! Furthermore, a new scrumhalf discovery had arrived on the scene, namely ex-Bristol player Gio Sidoli!

True, the 19 wins (and 6 draws) of 1952-3 could not equal those 27 victories of the 1950-51 record season, yet the final home game (an 11-0 win over Gloucester) was headlined a *"Real Thriller."* Yet it was abundantly clear that John Roberts was already stamping his own character upon Bath, as the Chronicle had noted at Neath, where the *"result was a tribute to John Roberts's spirited and inspiring leadership."* Indeed, even the supremacy of the Alec Lewis record was in due course to be threatened. Nonetheless, on paper at least, the 20 wins (and 4 draws) from forty games of the following 1953-4 campaign and summarized by the Chronicle as *"one of outstanding wins mingled with defeats,"* typified many a season of this most unpredictable of clubs. Again, the principal strength was at forward with a pack among the best in their history so far. The drawback too often remained in the back-line. But, as demonstrated at Rosslyn Park in November, (whom Bath last played and defeated in 1924), Bath would win again, and P.J.M. (Chronicle & H, 30th November 1953) reported thus: *"though they failed to score, it was the Bath backs who impressed;"* adding that it was the re-appearance of England Trialist centre Mike Terry that proved crucial to his fellow outsides, among them centre Len

Hughes who *"put in some powerful dashes,"* and winger Hudson Adams, who *"played his best game since joining the club"* and *"stuck grimly to his [exceedingly difficult] task of marking English international Chris Winn."*

So just one player, in this case Terry, proved capable of transforming the backs, while the 3-3 home draw against Leicester in early January was headlined as follows: *"Bath backs superb in defence."* Defence was another Bath strength. In the January away encounter against London Welsh, already victors over Coventry, Neath and London Scottish, P.J.M. again spoke glowingly of the Bath 'outsides.' Of special note in their 6-8 win was 18 years old Welsh outside-half Royston Collins, taking ball *"brilliantly"* from scrum-half Mick Hanna. The pack too were outstanding; they 'had' to be at London Welsh, and Dennis Mattingley and Eric Hopton were *"so prominent....that Alec Lewis and Kendall-Carpenter were hardly missed."* And as P.J.M. so fittingly added: *"When two strong packs get the ball back as often as possible, it is at outside-half that the match is won or lost. Collins hardly wasted a ball."* Too true!

Yet such victories were, as the Chronicle openly admitted: *'mingled with defeats,'* and one of those defeats was a mid-January 0-29 and seven try upset against Cardiff on the Rec. Bath accepted defeat without excuses, notwithstanding their England Trialist flanker David Naylor missed most of the second half with an eye injury; and though Bath supporters would have wished to forget such a debacle as quickly as possible, their next home match (6th March) was a performance that they would wish to remember for as long as possible. The opposition just happened to be Bristol, a club poised on the verge of another great era of open rugby; but who doubtless to the surprise of many had not won on the Rec since 1937! Neither did they win in March 1954. Oh no! They lost 16-6, and their *"all-star back division,"* wrote P.J.M. (Chronicle & H, 8th Mar. 1954) *"was completely over-shadowed. It was a tonic to see two home-bred centres in [Cliff] Weston and [Tony] Guest playing like world-beaters."* World beaters....and against Bristol! How fitting therefore that a large contingent of supporters remained to witness the opening of **the club's first permanent club-house at the North end of the Rec.** Former player and then current committee member Mr Bert Anderson cut the ribbons, **expressing thanks, among others, to the Recreation Ground Company for their co-operation. Thus, it appeared that the Rec (Bath's portion at least) was truly their permanent home;** and surely no one would wish things otherwise. The season now entered its final phase with home wins over Newbridge and Harlequins; while the warm gratitude expressed in Bedford chairman Peter Perkins's letter to Eddie Simpkins spoke much for the ethos and warmth that underpinned the rugby game during this era. He wrote thus: Bedford *"very much enjoyed the renewal of our fixture with Bath, and thank you all for your generous hospitality....;"* humbling words indeed in view of Bedford's 21-5 defeat in Bath's final (and successful) home game of the 1953-4 season.

Yet one more objective remained, their **first ever overseas tour.** The destination was South West France, the challenging opposition a trio of first-class French sides, the tight schedule consisting of three games in three days with departure from Bath at 4.25am on

Friday, 30th April, and the first match scheduled to commence the following afternoon (Saturday) against St. Claude. But, there was a surprise awaiting the tourists, and after the Channel-crossing arrival from Southampton and two hours spent lying 'flat out' on their beds at the '*hotel de ville*', Bath awoke to learn that the opposition had mysteriously transformed from St. Claude into a full Jura-Lyonnais combined side (and surprise-surprise) were to be boosted by five 'guest' French 'B' internationals for good measure. Sacré bleu! It was fortunate therefore that Bath had travelled with a near full-strength squad, including big-guns in the pack such as lock George Brown, Frank Thomas, the increasingly impressive Eric Hopton and the now irrepressible Bryan Peasley, a recent Bath wing-forward acquisition from Maestag. The pack, as so often during this era, was outstanding, likewise the backs, who unrecognisable from the outsides who had struggled against Cardiff, threw caution to the wind, and enjoying the time of their lives threw passes here, there and just about everywhere. Their haul that day was six tries with Weston, Naylor, Guest, and Jim Vaissiere each scoring one apiece and wing Richard Bassett (exceptionally fast, barely 18 years) running home a brace. Meanwhile full-back Phil Hardy duly banged home three conversions to complete Bath's 3-24 rout, a victory duly described by the Chronicle as the *"near-perfect text-book style of the Bath XV."*

Against Givors on Sunday, and with French hooker Dupinay in their ranks, the task could be no less demanding. They too were tough, and in French rugby terminology that means 'really' tough. Meanwhile the news of the sheer scale of the tourists' win the previous day had put the home side on full alert. In fact Bath were the first English club to visit the town and the fixture duly attracted a record 4000 crowd to their impressive Olympic stadium. Mr Landsdown, British Consul at Lyons (and related to a Bath family) honoured the encounter with his presence and he was doubtless as relieved as Bath that the John Roberts side just, but only 'just,' managed to squeeze home for a 6-9 victory in what proved to be their hardest game on the tour. On Monday the tourists moved on to play Tour du Pin led by French international L. Junquas. But any hopes among the hosts that Bath might now be nursing one too many bruises were to be rudely dismissed. Emotion too was 'written' on Bath faces that day, as Alec Lewis, having recently announced his retirement from senior rugby, now led out his beloved club on to the field for one last time. It was to be an apt occasion for a Bath and England great, for his team played like men inspired, winning 0-17 with non-stop attacking rugby literally set ablaze by the flamboyance of Gio Sidoli at scrum-half. Alec Lewis appropriately was among the scorers, so too Peasley, Vaissiere (2) and Roy Collins, with Phil Hardy slotting home a conversion. At the tour's conclusion Bath were both happily exhilarated and happily exhausted. They had been greeted by warmth, champagne receptions and post-match celebrations in the unmatched tradition of French hospitality. In return Bath, under skipper John Roberts, had produced displays of vintage attacking rugby that raised again an important question: 'why, since Bath could play open running rugby (and in France!), did they not do so more often?' One answer was that sometimes they did. But....due West lay Bristol, still casting its shadow, from which it seemed there might never be an escape. Unfortunately, the home Bath v Cardiff fixture in the following 1954-5 campaign was cancelled owing to serious weather conditions, an occasion that otherwise would have filled to capacity **the new (previously bomb-shattered) 1,100 seated West stand officially opened on 2nd October 1954.** But since Bath would complete this season only two victories short of the 27 club record, there would be much for the Bath Chronicle's new rugby correspondent, namely **John Stevens (W.J.S.), to talk about**.

As expected, Bath continued with a largely forward-based strategy, and by early February following wins over London Welsh (13-11) and then 0-3 at Newbridge (only the third Bath win in Wales since the War), John Stevens gave his 'guarded' praise for the overall 'teamwork' of a side, now *"settling down into a solid – if not – brilliant team;"* and if anyone doubted the difficulties of winning in Wales then they need only ponder Bristol's own 38-3 crash at Cardiff earlier that season. Meanwhile on the 12th February following Bath's win at Newbridge the Rec and much of the West Country was covered in a blanket of snow; visitors Gloucester arrived; but two players had travelled separately by car, and perhaps not surprisingly their car broke-down. So, Bath kindly offered to loan them two players (namely lock Angus Meek, and winger Brian French from Old Sulians). Gloucester then expressed their deep gratitude, as well they might, since they proceeded to thump Bath 21-0! ("Thanks for that Glos.").

It was a different story however with Bath's inches-close 9-8 defeat at Llanelli in early April, very different in fact, and summed up by an admiring John Stevens thus: *"if the pack played such a large part in Bath's fine showing, so did the outsides. Shuttleworth [brother of England scrumhalf Dennis Shuttleworth] and Weston formed a fine combination at half- back, both using the touchline to great advantage. The threes, Guest, Curtis, Trenchard and Leonard all threw everything into the game and Hardy must be congratulated on his five points."* Such a performance at daunting Stradey Park, invincible to all that season save Cardiff, proved not least to Bath themselves that they could play expansive rugby.

Other impressive performances of which any club would have been proud included home wins over Swansea, Harlequins, Northampton and *"in one of their finest performances of the season"* (W.J.S.) was their 11-0 victory against Neath in late April. While further proof of another season to remember, not least for the twenty-five victories (and two draws), was a second unbeaten tour of France that saw wins over Dijon (0-14), St Claude (8-13) and Macon (3-8). So ended a five-year era that had seen Bath produce results, despite pitfalls, that emphasised their rightful place in the rankings of first-class rugby. Some critics questioned a reliance (not entirely fairly) on a tight forward game and sometimes their lack of enterprise outside the scrum. But a team must play to its strengths, and as many of the strongest sides in England and Wales would testify during this period, Bath could be one hell of a problem on the field. And John Roberts, when years later recalling this same era, spontaneously repeated but two words: *"Great days!"* he said, *"Great days!"*

BATH AWAY! ....scrumhalf Gio Sidoli spins out the 'leather' as Bath attack St Claude.
Colleagues (left to right) B, Peasley and D. Beard.

Chapter 22.   ERA OF UNCERTAINTY. (1955-60)

As Bath stepped into the second half of the 1950's, and despite their sometimes impressive form of the previous five years, the Chronicle & H (9th Sep. 1955) advised caution: the *"team must to some extent be experimental, for the backs in particular."* Too true, as shown with a win-total return from 1955-6 onwards of 17, 15, 11, 12 and 16 respectively. So, what caused this lapse? Well, first and foremost was the loss of much of their pack, that all-powerful mean-machine. Secondly, the player-pool was smaller than previously, not least because a headline grabbing Bristol at this period were pulling in players from far and wide, of whom some may otherwise have joined Bath. And yet, during this same five-year period there would be those occasions when the club revved-up into top gear to gain victories that turned the form-book completely upside-down. For instance, the side of the inspirational John Kendall-Carpenter (captain, 1955-56) rose to the occasion come Bath's inaugural game against Ebbw Vale (unofficial Welsh Champions two years previously) with an Autumn 6-3 home win. A further victory was a 20-nil home win over Devonport Services who in those National Service days could frequently field a team packed to the gunnels with class, and it was the performance of the outsides, not least scrumhalf Ron Shuttleworth and Cornwall out-half John L.Thomas who, wrote W.J.S: *"showed some of the best half-back play by Bath for years"* And speaking of National Service days, young Second Lieutenant Robin Hambly, a former Bath winger whose call-up with the Somerset Light Infantry was deferred to allow for completion of his law studies, saw action during emergency operations in Malaya (Chronicle, 21st Oct. 1955). Noticing a dissident preparing to open fire on his unit the young officer *"got in the first shot,"* and that as they say 'was the end of the matter.' Amazing what rugby does to a man!

Back to the rugby field meanwhile and Bath again upset the odds with a January 11-0 win over Leicester, with notable performances from backs Wyn Holmes, Malcolm Smith (very fast) and Mike McCarthy, and likewise lock John Ramsay (former Watsonians) and prop Bill Law, all more recent 'faces.' But if one performance topped the lot then that would be the 3-15 away victory at London Welsh. Bath (wrote W.J.S.) *"served up champagne rugby;"* running home three tries plus two penalties, as against a single try. So, they 'could' play top-class rugby against top-class opposition. Yet, as would become all too apparent, they lacked that essential depth in player-resources to sustain this capability throughout a full season of rugby. And this pattern would continue under the captaincy of John Roberts for the following two seasons, though Bath's 3-13 win at US Portsmouth in November 1956 came with the welcome bonus of a new discovery in their backs. The name was Ken Miners, and (wrote I.J.T.) it was: *"after 15 minutes that the Services [and Bath] first saw his great potentiality. An orthodox movement developed swiftly. Miners raced past his opposite number with a deceptive swerve, and as he drew Bell, the full-back sent out a scoring pass to [6ft, 4in] John Dolman on the right wing."* Boom-boom, Try! Moreover, another back with plenty of tricks up his sleeve was John Rees. Fast and elusive, he was class, and further evidence that Bath did not so much lack individual ability, as a failure to develop an all-round team, shown by the 1956-7 season's total of a mere 15 wins, five draws and 19 defeats, including a 27-6 fall at Kingsholm. Though if it was any comfort, Gloucester later walloped Bristol 21-3. However, Bath and Gloucester were (and remain) the bookmakers' headache, and if the Kingsholm result was Bath's worst defeat of 1956-7, then the best result was their 11-0 revenge in the return match. It was some day, noted I.J.T. (Chronicle & H, 11th February) writing thus: *"Bath's finest hour of the season,"* a day when formidable Gloucester appeared *"strangely subdued against the furious but calculating and efficient home eight;"* and where the performances of prop Fred Book, lock Frank Thomas and flanker David Naylor among others stood out. While if scrum-half Paul Dart had yet to earn a reputation in Bath colours, he did now; and David Curtis, the recalled Addenbrooke and recent arrival Dennis Silk (Cambridge Blue) *"on the day were far more convincing than their*

Dennis Silk

opposite numbers." And there was another player *"whose positioning....handling, economical touch kicking and occasional enterprise warmed the heart,"* a Marlborough College schoolboy who seemed completely unfazed by the opposition. However, he was already a Dorset & Wiltshire County player, later a Cambridge Blue full-back and a National Hunt jockey. His name was Ian Balding, a future horse-race trainer to the Queen.

But as regards the haphazard results during this period the Chronicle (25th February) prompted by Bath's one try (3-0 win)) against Wasps wrote thus: *"Take a Cambridge Blue named Silk, [wrote I.J.T.],*

Eddie Simpkins. Devoted his life as secretary to Bath RFC.

place him alongside three-quarters of average ability, and you have a back division capable of holding the best sides in the Country. Add another Cambridge Blue and England player named [Ian]Beer, place him in the back row, and you have a set of forwards which will rank among the best in the Home Counties." But was it really that simple? Well, in Bath's case the theory was not as yet fully tested.

However, despite the all too short presence of Barnstaple's young Devon (and later England Trialist) wing Mike Blackmore and the leadership of John Roberts, the results of the following 1957-8 season of 11 wins, 4 draws and a numbing 27 defeats that included a 34-5 crash at Stradey Park in October by Llanelli was hardly likely to raise the morale-barometer. Even so, there were those performances to raise hopes, and when (February 1958) and despite the absence of Dennis Silk (injured) and Ian Balding required by his brother's racing stable to ride National Hunt at Lingfield Park, Bath hosted the Welsh emerging side that was Bridgend. Not a chance in hell, surely? Well, not least thanks to the composure of outside-half Treleven Thomas, and winger David Ogden who (I.J.T.): *"scored two of the finest tries seen on the Recreation Ground in this or any other season,"* Bath did go to hell (and back) with a 6-3 victory in their hands.

Ian Balding

Yet another result to make critics really sit up and take notice was the 10-6 victory over Llanelli in mid-March, those same Welsh wizards who had humbled Bath in early Autumn. Now, despite a try from Scarlets wing Roberts and *"an amazing cork-screwing drop-goal from centre David Evans...."* the home tries from Peasley and then lock Tony Jacob who completed a *"brilliant run by Trelevan Thomas,"* (both converted by skipper John Roberts), would bring the Rag Doll back to the Rec, though simultaneously pose that same puzzling question. For if Bath could not as yet build a new team to compare with those of 1950-5, what made them click on occasions to beat the best in the game? It was a simple question to ask. It was far from simple to answer. Meanwhile, yet another schoolboy would catch the eye when playing at outside-half for Bath in their customary Boxing Day match against visitors Old Blues, watched by a reported 2,000 crowd perhaps not yet aware why this Prior Park pupil was already a Dorset & Wilts county player. Well, the reason was revealed soon enough with young Ian Reid's *"foxy breaks, his canny turns and his great burst of speed when it was most required, [which] were all painful thorns in the Old Blues side."* Bath duly won 15-6 and, this young Scotsman was one to watch.

Another name 'was' widely known, namely Eddie Simpkins, who sadly passed away on 1st February (Chronicle. 3rd Feb. 1958). 'E.F.S.' as he was affectionately known, was true 'blue, white and black.' Born in the city, he trained at St. Luke's College Exeter before returning to devote his entire teaching career in Bath, initially at Bathforum School, and then some 40 years at Oldfield Boys School. A promising centre at both St. Luke's and Bath, injury curtailed his active playing at 24 years. E.F.S. then, as previously mentioned, turned his attention to administration and became joint secretary in 1911 with Mr J.T. Piper until 1939, then later from 1948-1957. He had witnessed Bath play on no less than 66 grounds in England and Wales, and it is said that he never missed a single committee meeting. Much admired, much loved, what more can one say.

The following 1958-9 season under Gordon Drewett with 12 wins from 39 played was barely an improvement from the eleven wins in the previous season, albeit no less than eight matches were drawn and defeats were reduced from a numbing 27 to 19. Yet it was an ominous warning of 'more of the same' when Llanelli kicked off the new season with their 25-11 win over Bath at Stradey Park. Nonetheless, a narrow 6-6 draw at Clifton in October revealed another unexpected talented arrival now at Bath's disposal. *"Remember the name, Ray Gazard, because I can assure you that more will be heard of this blond, crew-cut winger with the velvet smooth running style"* wrote R.N.M. (Chronicle 2nd Oct. 1958) of this former Welsh Empire (now Commonwealth) Games long-jumper and considered *"one of the Army's crack sprinters."* Few at Bath knew much about him however, though that changed when seeing him against Llanelli following the draw at Clifton. He scorched over for a brace on his home debut within the opening 20 minutes *"that knocked much of the wind and confidence out of the visitors and gave Bath an initial advantage which they fought like Titans to maintain."* This inspired that crucial self-belief, whereupon *"Gordon Drewett was brilliantly efficient and Joe Colford at stand-off made the utmost of the first-class service which the skipper threw out;"* while *"Barry Richards at full-back had another great game."* Moreover, thanks to locks Frank Thomas and Tony Jacob, and back-row men John Jacobsen and Brian Peasley the Scarlets did not dominate the game at forward either. For this was a '15 man-Team-Bath' 8-6 victory, and as R.N.M. concluded: *"This was their finest hour."*

But a week later this same Bath slumped 21-nil at Bridgend and it got worse in December when falling 30-nil at London Scottish. Yet, come February it was 3-3 against Gloucester and where "Pat Hill's hooking was perfect and in Beer, Phil Winchcombe and Malcolm Martin selectors have definitely found the best available backrow. But wrote R.N.M.: *"if there is any man who has played a harder game on the Rec this season than did Peter Parfitt, I should be pleased to meet him."* Ah Pete Parfitt…a legend in the making. And his younger brother Alan would prove himself a pretty useful talent too. More praise then followed with the 19-nil win over powerful Wasps in February, and so impressive were the Bath outsides that (wrote R.N.M) this *"was the finest exhibition of constructive and class back play that a home side has produced on the Recreation Ground for possibly two or three seasons."* Then how could one explain such unpredictability? In truth with difficulty! But the question is likely best answered thus: "because of a lack of self-belief!" Nonetheless, in April the club was not disinclined to take risks and gamble on youth, selecting Paul Masters (18), Brendan O'Mara (17), Terry Hopson (19) and Peter Robinson and Gyn Robins (both 21) for the encounter at Torquay Athletic, the Devonians having already that season won an impressive 23 games from 28 played. The game *"ebbed and flowed like the spring tides and the largest crowd of the season must have wondered why the two teams hadn't played each other for 30 years."* In fact, it was not 30 years, but rather 22 years (see Ch. 18) when on 20th March 1937 a late controversial Bath try had led to a post-match demo' by a small group of home supporters, resulting in a long cessation of fixtures. Well, no one at either club seemed aware of the fracas of long ago, moreover when literally in the final seconds Paul Masters hurled over for his debut try for his club that would clinch an 11-12 Bath win, there was no demonstration, but applause instead.

Finally, the 1959-60 captaincy of John Jacobson (16 wins, 5 draws, 20 lost) was an improvement, bringing the curtain down on five seasons of lows and the occasional highs that included his own team's hugely prestigious September 3-11 victory at Llanelli and later their 6-10 success at London Welsh. Yet no one could (or would) deny that this was a period of disappointment, since from 1950-1955 Bath's beacon had often shone so brightly, that an assured future among the higher ranks of the post-war first-class game had seemed tantalizing close. Then the landscape changed, and in retrospect one would see the chief causes of this downturn: the player-pool that diminished in size, the subsequent loss of confidence, and despite occasional sparkling wins, the sheer numbers of defeats that adversely effected morale. So, an era that had promised so much became an era of uncertainty. And there remained one further conundrum to ponder: 'Should Bath attempt to adopt the expansive tactics of Bristol, yielding them a mouth-watering 36 victories in this same 1959-60 season, or those of Gloucester whose style (W.J.S.) was based on *"steamroller forward tactics backed up by clever half-back play and an adequate three-quarter line."* No guesses which options during the 1950's most suited Bath. Nonetheless, there 'was' to be a third option, one that five seasons later would unexpectedly be part-influenced from London club rugby, an influence moreover that would change the course of Bath rugby forever.

Chapter 23. THE ULTIMATE CHALLENGE. (1960-66)

At the dawn of the 1960's the comparison between Bath and their main West Country rivals Bristol and Gloucester could hardly have been greater. While in the previous 1959-60 season Bristol had attained (as mentioned) a stunning 36 wins, Bath had struggled to win 16, and unless things dramatically improved it seemed that fate as the permanent underdogs of West Country rugby stared Bath in the face. Indeed, the first five years of the new decade mirrored uncomfortably close to the last five years of the previous decade. True, season 1960-1 under skipper Angus Meek raised hopes with a more respectable total of 21 victories and some high-profile ones at that, not least their mid-season 11-3 success over an increasingly strong London Welsh, a performance notable too for a stunning 50 yard try by wing John Cousins, a towering 6ft. 4in newcomer and then current Gloucestershire County sprint champion. A 15-3 win over Llanelli was then followed by Bath's 13-3 defeat of Swansea (wing Alan Howard-Baker hitting form) But, could Bath raise their profile in relation to Bristol? Not a chance!

Laurie Rimmer: exceptionally fast wing-forward

That aside, the January 1961 selection of flanker Laurie Rimmer for England against South Africa at Twickenham (England 0, South Africa 5) and prop Pete Parfitt's nomination as an England reserve (non-travelling) for the 1961 February international against Ireland in Dublin confirmed again that Bath did not lack for individual talent. But on the downside the club suffered twenty-one defeats; some literally embarrassing, that included the 29-11 defeat at Bristol (Oh dear) and the Easter collapse by 12-62 at Harlequins, Bath's biggest defeat in their history (yes, another

Brendan Perry: an often brilliant outside– half.

embarrassment). Did Bristol suffer such defeats? No! Even so there would be the occasional interest shown by Rugby League scouts, as happened with the arrival of RAF and Orrell full-back Bob Randall in Autumn 1960. Physically strong, tactically assured and an excellent goal-kicker, he impressed from day one. But after a mere eight games for Bath the talented Randall switched codes to join Widnes, the first Bath player to 'go North' since three-quarter Peter Fearis joined Blackpool Borough in 1950 and then onwards to St. Helens. However, other talent arrived, few better than young St. Brendans (Keynsham) schoolboy Brendan Perry. A gifted athlete, he was already the 100 and 220 yards England Schools sprint champion and an England (over 15's) international outside-half against France and, had already guested for Bath in the previous 1959-60 season.

But predictably, interest came from another source….Bristol! And as their own inspirational captain John Blake (also an outside-half) just happened to teach at St. Brendan's it seemed that young Perry was bound for the Memorial Ground. Bath could but pray therefore and, 'lo and behold,' their prayers were answered. Perry chose a Bath shirt, and proceeded to gain just about every representative honour in the book save a full England cap. Elsewhere **Floodlight rugby**, first experienced by Bath in their 16-3 defeat at Llanelli (Friday, 19th Jan. 1962), became increasingly commonplace, and likewise televised rugby, especially at the international level. Meanwhile when new skipper Roy Farnham's team opened the 1961-2 campaign with a run of seven straight wins that included the 'big' names of Leicester, Llanelli and Bridgend, one could have been forgiven for hoping that a breakthrough was nigh. The 11-12 win at Welford Road for example, where the Bath pack *"gained such a stranglehold that Leicester's undoubted talent at the back of the scrum could do nothing to open up the game"* would be Bath's first away win against the Tigers since that historic victory of 1919.

Meanwhile a top-rate 13-6 win over Llanelli revealed encouraging signs among the younger backs with Geoff Frankcom (King Edward's School, Bath), O'Mara (now a Somerset centre) and Brendan Perry showing that they already had the quality to perform at the top level. In addition, John Hawgood was everything one would expect of an experienced former Northampton full-back, and expectations were further raised with the arrival of former Rosslyn Park wing Nick Bruford and Irish Trialist back John Keepe. The 'Heavies' looked promising too, with Pete Parfitt and hooker Pat Hill now reinforced with back-row cover from Cornishman Paddy Mulligan and Lance Clark, nor forgetting the youthful North Midland's lock Kevin Andrews. Indeed, the overall quality among the 20 wins and three draws (albeit 20 losses) of the Roy Farnham side suggested that the dire situation since the second-half of the 1950's might have been halted. Significant too was the fact that Bath ran home one hundred tries for the first time since the War. Meanwhile, young flanker Phil Hall, a former England Schools International from Chipping Sodbury Secondary Modern, commenced an illustrious career on the Rec; while 19 years old Geoff Frankcom (the lone freshman on the day) won his Cambridge Blue at Twickenham and scored the crucial winning try from a lightening dash and pounce upon an Oxford defensive handling error. Furthermore, among the Light Blues that day was another Bath player, namely Ian Balding. Hardly surprising then that when Bath (6th Jan. 1962) completed their first Double over Leicester since season 1919-20 with an 8-5 home victory, the Chronicle went into over-drive with its plaudits, and not least for the laser-fast service of Bath's young Dorset & Wilts scrum-half Jamie Spencer! An enigma both on and off the field, for Spencer was an accomplished avant-garde artist, he would later return to

Geoff Frankom : electric speed

Harlequins post his National Service days in Wiltshire and in 1966 gained an England cap against Wales.

To the casual observer the following 1962-3 season under the captaincy of Laurie Rimmer would appear to be one best forgotten. After all, a mere 14 games were won, one drawn and 24 games lost, but unavoidable factors intervened. First, of 39 matches played no less than fifty-nine players were called-up for first team duty. So small wonder the Chronicle concluded that the team *"never really had a chance to settle down."* And how does any team cope when to Bath's acute embarrassment against Harlequins at Twickenham their scrum-half failed to arrive, skipper Laurie Rimmer nobly taking over this key role, while Bath's young linesman Bill Sykes was pressed-ganged into the back-row, never having played anything approaching first-class rugby in his life. Then within minutes Bath prop John Lacey retired hurt. Small wonder then that 'Quins,' fielding England internationals John Young (wing) and scrum-half Johnny Williams, coasted home to a 29-3 win.

Yet poor team performances obscured the fact that individual-ability was not lacking, not least wing-prospect John Edwards (student teacher, St. Luke's College, Exeter), hooker Colwyn Owens, prop John West, nor forgetting the recent arrival of Warwickshire lock Phil Hall. Nor was there anything sub-standard about full-back Hawgood, backs John Edwards and O'Mara, plus an effective half-back combination of young Julian Darling (son incidentally of Lord Darling) and the charismatic Brendan Perry. Furthermore, despite an Arctic freeze-up that wiped no less than eight games off the fixture-list, Bath proved themselves good enough to beat the likes of Neath (13-6) and Richmond (17-12). So, did this signal a sustained revival? If only! Instead, Bath lost four on the trot that included lowly (though likeable) Stroud, before Rimmer's side produced another turn-around with a late season run that was pure Bath in its contradictions. First Llanelli fell 6-3, then bogey side Exeter (19-3), and finally a 3-3 draw at Coventry, a team nigh on unbeatable on home soil, so concluding a season that like so many before showed the yawning gap between Bath at their best and Bath at their worst, a gap seemingly as wide as the Grand Canyon at its widest.

Come season 1963-4 new captain Kevin Andrews's first game in command saw a sparkling Bath team race to a 30-0 win over the touring West German Representative XV. But this bright curtain-raiser notwithstanding, seasoned Bath-watchers could easily have predicted the following scenario: embarrassing defeats followed by sometimes exceptional victories. Indeed, with away set-backs including Leicester (22-3), Llanelli (32-3), and Swansea (36-3), no guesses how 'their' respective club-supporters rated Bath. But then just to confound their critics, Bath then beat powerful Pontypool (3-0), and next won away at Wasps (9-14). There was even competition for some 1st team places (usually a healthy sign), and it was an immaculate display against 'Pool' by newcomer Chris Harvey that would see him supersede even the outstanding Hawgood as first choice fullback. Meanwhile, in early season wing Richard Andrew celebrated a two year lay-off with form so impressive that Somerset immediately snapped him up for county duties.

Another bonus was the arrival via Orrell, Sheffield University and Loughborough College of wing-forward Tom Martland, whose qualities caught the eye of the Chronicle in Bath's late December 9-3 success over Northampton thus: *"Leighton Jenkins [former Welsh international] as ever utilising his experience, [and] Tom Martland a bundle of non-stop energy and Phil Hall hunting tigerishly after the ball."* No less emphatic was the 11-0 win over Leicester, with the Tigers *"continually held in a vice-like grip and had the life slowly squeezed out of them."* Here Club legend Peter Heindorff played No.8, then a lean and fast back-row forward, a surprise to many who later remembered him as a mighty 2nd row giant of a man. Equally impressive was that owing to a Brendan Perry injury, flanker Laurie Rimmer proved his top-notch all-rounder status when playing at outside-half against both Northampton and Leicester. Some player was Rimmer!

By the New Year John Millman established himself as first-choice scrum-half, and in April prop Bill Carling, (a subaltern in the Welch Regiment whose son Will later captained England to a World Cup final at Twickenham) made his Bath debut at home against Llanelli. But it was the final game of this 20 win season against a then top rated Bedford club that would inspire John Stevens (Chronicle) to reach for the superlatives thus: *" if ever Bath, in all their long history, have scored three more brilliant tries in one match than those which helped them to a sensational [14-9] victory over Bedford, no-one on the Recreation Ground can remember them,"* In particular, Stevens spoke of Brendan Perry, whose *"amazing acceleration left England wing-forward Budge Rogers standing and staring and provided the launching pad from which Bath rocketed into unbelievable heights."* Stevens spoke too of another Perry burst that *"enabled Frankcom to dart through, as only he can, for the try which made him the leading try-scorer in the country this season."* Perry it was who then scored a further gem from a Leighton Jenkins pass on half-way, and Perry once more in the final minutes when breaking from his own line to the half-way, there to feed Frankcom to race another 50 yards to score the winning try. Breath-taking stuff, it earned a spontaneous standing ovation from the crowd on the final whistle.

Yes, this was a day when Bath had indeed reached the heights but, however ungracious it may sound, realism determined that such standards must (and here one repeats 'must') be repeated throughout each and every season if the club had even a chance to be compared with their two closest rivals, and there was no need to repeat who those two rivals might be. And notwithstanding the optimism resulting from the dazzling Grand finale to season 1963-4, the following 1964-5 campaign had barely begun before the club landed with a hard thump. It was not only that Bath fell 35-5 in early season at Llanelli, then 8-31 to Leicester, but rubbing salt into wounds were further Autumn defeats at Devonport Services (25-6) and a 22-14 fall at usually less difficulty opponents Bridgwater, setbacks that frankly would leave the club with precious few, if any, answers for a season's tally of 15 wins, 3 draws and no fewer than 28 defeats. "Where," one asked, "was that display of exuberant self-belief shown in that glorious 14-9 victory over the then highly rated Bedford that climaxed the previous season?"

The business re-location of Kevin Andrews to the Midlands in January hardly helped, his regrettable departure necessitating a change of captaincy to a comparative (albeit excellent) newcomer, namely Gordon Margretts. He in turn faced a problem created by continual team changes (53 players called up for the season's 1st team duties), nor forgetting many poorly attended training nights. Furthermore, until a reliable replacement for Millman at scrum-half was found, even Brendan Perry had problems getting his outsides moving. 'Could things get worse?' one asks. Indeed, they could, because until the arrival of lock Clive Armstrong, Bath were bereft of that vital role in rugby, namely a consistently competent goal kicker. Small wonder therefore that John Stevens (Bath Chronicle) concluded that the Bath side of 1964-5 were *"a collection of individuals rather than a team,"* an opinion so evident when in their final game of the season they literally collapsed 33-0 at Coventry.

It was at this point however that Roger Whyte, a former Harlequin, would now contribute invaluable coaching assistance, while hooker Clive Buckle in the absence of Pat Hill, would prove to be invaluable cover for both Bath and Somerset, while props Roger Smerdon and Peter Jenkins showed that they too could handle the rough stuff up front. Even the high turnover of players yielded occasional dividends. John Monahan for example, a young schoolboy wing at Kingswood School was one discovery, so too Fettes School captain and three-quarter Alexander Russell whose stay at Bath was alas too short-lived. Recently arrived scrum-half Jim Galley showed promise, and again there was the not unknown Bath recovery. It commenced with a 6-6 draw at powerhouse Newbridge, a typical Welsh side unbeaten at home for 18 months and where full-back Allan Gay on his Bath debut proved himself steady as a rock at a venue known for 'not' taking prisoners. Next, Bristol's ten-year reign of near total supremacy was halted in April by Bath's 17-12 victory on the Rec, and for those detractors dismissing the win as a fluke there would be Bath's 19-6 victory against a Llanelli side fielding out-half genius Barry John (later Wales and British Lions), a victory that included three tries and two drop-goals, one a superb 45 yarder from Brendan Perry. Meanwhile, there was the selection of Geoff Frankcom for that season's Home internationals, and England's 9-6 victory at Twickenham over France saw the Bath centre at his superb best, his smooth and effortlessly gliding speed one highlight of a triumphant day.

Ironically, come the final stage of the season Frankcom featured in a situation resulting quite innocently from his new teaching appointment that necessitated a move to the Bedford club while simultaneously remaining a Bath player. Hence, he played in Bedford's late season 17-12 home win over Bath, while one week later (and quite legitimately under the then amateur rules) Frankcom ran out at Twickenham for Bath in their first ever attendance at the by now hugely successful Middlesex 'Sevens.' In fact, and perhaps half expected, Bath fell 13-0 to Rosslyn Park in the opening round. But in truth 'Sevens' was not yet a perfected art in the West Country, where even the likes of Bristol had returned empty handed from a previous foray into this now classic event. Nonetheless for the following **Bath** team of: *'Frankcom, Brendon O'Mara, Brendon*

Perry, Tom Martland, and forwards Phil Hall, Clive Buckle and John Parsons,' and not forgetting several coach-loads of Bath followers, it was a new experience to savour.

And as Bath reached **their Centenary of 1965-6** there was hope that this would be a season to remember. Those early pioneer-nomadic years would later **lead them (1894) to their home on their beloved Rec.** Slowly they developed an increasingly demanding fixture list and by 1900 they had produced three international forwards, namely F. D'Aguila, H. Fuller and F. Soane. Joyful revival then followed a desperate slump during the early years of the 20th century, and either side of the Great War Bath had produced two generations of outstanding backs. A downturn then occurred from the mid-1930's prior to **World War 2, during which time the Bath club (like the Ritz) never closed, notwithstanding that their stands and facilities were literally bombed to pieces.** Revival again followed, and one of the mightiest packs in Bath history stormed relentlessly onwards during the first half of the 1950's. Then followed a decade of trial and error, plus a lack of any consistency or a standard pattern of play, with too many heavy defeats and too few notable victories. And when at the outset of their Centenary Season the news broke that Brendan Perry had now switched to Bristol (temporally as it turned out), a disconsolate Bath Chronicle commented thus: *"his decision will come as a great shock and bitter disappointment to Bath members who have often been delighted by his brilliant attacking play."* As for the Centenary season itself (Margretts continuing as skipper) there seemed little to write home about with 19 wins, 1 draw, but an ominous 28 defeats, and even the win-total included a post-season 3-15 victory against Chateau Renard in France (Bath next losing 17-9 at Nice). Nonetheless, among the modest total of domestic wins there were a handful that justifiably 'caught the eye,' not least those against Oxford University, Wasps, Gloucester and Harlequins. Furthermore, there was pride with the selection of Bath three-quarter Alexander Russell for a Scotland Trial, and further England Trials for Geoff Frankcom and former Bath captain Kevin Andrews. Yet, as their Centenary neared its conclusion, the club could only reflect on another campaign so typical of those of the last decade. That is, until the very last game of this same Centenary Season and the visit again of Bedford, when by the end of a rugby extravaganza an irresistible and almost unrecognisable Bath had swept to a stunning 51-3 victory by way of eleven tries to a single score against an admittedly below-par Bedford.

The inspiration for this triumph had sprung not least from the mesmeric performance of a young Millfield schoolboy blessed with a precocious talent, namely out-half Vaughan Williams. Already a Somerset cap and a half-back partner to his fellow Millfield School colleague Gareth Edwards (later a Wales and British Lions legend), Williams ran home two outstanding tries and landed no fewer than nine conversions. Then partly thanks to a highly effective combination at centre of Gordon Margretts and Combined Services player Bob Stevenson (RAF) a seriously fast John Monahan shot over for four more tries. Thus, by the second half (wrote John Stevens) Bath *"were tormenting Bedford.....and their forwards began to frolic around like extra three-quarters."* Meanwhile other recent newcomers suddenly emerged on the scene to stamp their own signatures on the game, James Monahan (brother of John) for instance, No.8 David Gay (brother of Allen) and Bob Orledge, all members of *"Bath's ruthlessly efficient eight."*

It was an intoxicating brew producing a tonic of a win, and even though years of dashed hopes had taken their toll on the loyalties of even the most hardened of supporters, this time the doubters need not have worried. For as the curtain came down on one hundred years of Bath rugby, all those present on that sun-drenched day were perhaps unknowingly witness to the future. And the timing was positively exquisite. Uncertainties would be swept aside, confidence would be renewed, and 15-man rugby would now be the order (and practice) of the day! Indeed, a second 'coming of age' beckoned. And come one distant day Bath would meet head-on that awesome and ultimate challenge……and overcome it!

Chapter 24.   THE ENLIGHTENMENT. (1966-69)

Come the season of 1966-7 the rugby-game was continuing to widen its profile, with increased TV exposure that included not only international, but both county-championship and club rugby. In addition, there was a far greater emphasis on coaching and tactics, nor forgetting the advent of league tables (though as yet unofficial). There was another aspect, namely an emphasis on 15-man running rugby, because by this stage the successful sides, bar a few exceptions, were 'all' playing it! So too, on occasions, had Bath, that 51-3 win against Bedford for example that brought the curtain down on last season. Yet such performances were a rarity. But, what if they became the norm, because it is at this point from 1966-69 that one Peter Sibley as club captain stepped into the pantheon of Bath history and who in the words of the Chronicle's John Stevens built the foundations for a *"revolutionary era of Bath rugby."* Profound words, but they did not exaggerate one iota the sheer scale of the transformation that would sweep through the club from those early September days of 1966-7.

Certain factors lay behind the achievements that would now unfold, not least the fortunate coincidence of a number of talented young players arriving on the Rec, of whom at least six (Brian Collins, David Gay, Ian Duckworth, Bob Orledge, Mike Hannell and Mike Beese) would soon prove to be of international potential. Secondly, and crucially, Bath now possessed an actual surplus of class half-backs, a luxury for a club who had often struggled in this key department of the game. Third….there was Peter Sibley! This thoughtful and quietly spoken winger from Blackheath, a recently arrived Monkton Combe schoolmaster who had only joined the club in the previous Centenary season, was fast-tracked into the captaincy one season post his arrival. So, what were the qualities that led to such swift promotion? After all it was rumoured that he never relished marking an opponent who was both big and fast; and it was said jokingly that without his contact lenses there was a possibility that he might run off in the wrong direction and score a gem….for the opposition. Yet, there was just something about Sibbo' that impressed all who came to know him, and whose qualities of calm, yet firm leadership would now galvanise a 'rough and ready' bunch of footballers into a fully functioning 15-man rugby-machine.

Sibley the scholar, whose rugby CV included some forty games for Oxford University (though agonisingly never gaining a Blue) quietly promised all those who were prepared to listen (and initially many didn't) that his Bath team would forthwith adopt a strategy of open rugby (no 'ifs,' no 'buts') and a mere four matches into Sibley's reign an emphatic 14-8 home win against Leicester would cause the doubters to think again, among them the Chronicle's John Stevens, who described the half-back pairing of Jim Galley and Vaughan Williams as a *"highly explosive mixture who proved lethal."* He wrote of the back-row of Fred Hicks, England Trialist Geoff Hines and Phil Hall who *"were in the midst of every facet of play, constructive or destructive;"* and he approvingly 'spoke' of a Bath side that by the interval had stamped their dominance with *"three spectacular tries."* Ah but, was this merely yet another of those 'one-offs' Bath followers wondered? No!

Soon the player-pool was increased further with the additions of scrum-half Malcolm Lloyd, No. 10 Jack Thomas, Bryn Jenkins (Birmingham University) and later the return of Terry Hopson from Gloucester. Equally fortunate was the healthy competition for back-row places, with a strong list of 1st team candidates that included Keith Richardson, Ian Holmes and the ever-improving teenager David Gay. In December the promise of 20 years old Bath winger John Monahan, now an undergraduate at Cambridge, was acknowledged with his selection for the Southern Counties against the touring Australians. Of utmost significance too was the fact that the 15-man strategy that had achieved the emphatic win over Leicester would set a long-term blueprint with Sibley's signature writ large all over it. Within barely two months Bath were confidently applying the rugby philosophy of their 'rookie' Home Counties skipper. Within one season commentators were re-appraising a Bath team they had tended to regard as solely forward-oriented. Within three seasons the 15-man running game was expected of Bath wherever they played. Not everything of course was plain sailing in Sibley's first season of captaincy, after all Bath conceded 20 defeats. But among the many positives was the achievement of their 27 domestic victories (29 if including two wins on their German tour) that equalled the club's all-time record. Not bad for a captain with only one season's experience on the Rec prior to his call-up to now lead his adopted club. The general quality moreover of the 27 victories (not least away successes) was hard evidence of a club with a renewed self-belief, victories that included Bath's 0-3 away win at powerful Pontypool, thanks not least to faultless performances at full-back by David Dolman and also Brian Collins who was selected that season as a reserve hooker for England Trials. The transformation was further emphasised by a post-Christmas run of four consecutive away victories at St. Mary's Hospital (0-20), Rosslyn Park (6-8), Gloucester (14-19) and Cheltenham 6-9 respectively, followed later by an impressive 3-16 triumph at Sale that sent news to the north of a Bath revival. Meanwhile even the Welsh genius of Barry John could not prevent Llanelli falling 11-3 to a clinical Bath home performance in April, one highlight of a season that would prove to be literally a life-changer in the club's history.

However, the best of the best was perhaps the aforementioned 14-19 away win against Gloucester in February, Bath's first victory at Kingsholm since 1948, and where *"Bath held [Gloucester] magnificently in the set pieces where Heindorff injected great fighting spirit and outplayed them in the loose where Gay, Hall and Martland latched on to the ball in a flash."* Away scores don't come easy at Gloucester, yet Bath ran home *"three cracking tries"* from Ian Duckworth (2) and Hillyard, while full-back Gordon Mobley was a revelation, the modest Kingswood School teacher having previously played only a handful of first-team games since his arrival in 1963, in effect third choice full-back, yet who calmly struck home two conversions and two precision penalties from the touchline. Thus, The Chronicle harboured no doubts at what they and others were now witnessing: *"Bath took their biggest step yet towards re-establishing themselves in the top flight of English clubs....and the mere fact that they did win was less important than the way in which they won....by persevering with that positive and imaginative football which Sibley has been emphasising all season."* Yes, the new skipper had seen what others had not, that Bath 'did' possess the pedigree to play open 15-man rugby. It was opportune too that Sibley's inspirational captaincy coincided with far-sighted changes at the national level, among them the first of the R.F.U.'s ten pamphlets on coaching, a development suggested John Stevens: *"believed to have been a dirty word at Twickenham"* (Chronicle, 21st Dec. 1966), while adding that while some clubs had already appointed coaches, others had not, and that when one former international of a senior club was asked if they had a coach replied (apparently in all seriousness): *"of course not, we all have cars."* Come the following 1967-8 season representative call-ups further reflected the Bath resurgence with six Bath players called-up for Somerset's 9-3 win over Cornwall, namely backs G. Francom, Ian Duckworth, Vaughan Williams and forwards Peter Parfitt, Bob Orledge and David Gay. Dorset & Wilts (whose County division played mid-week) meanwhile called upon seven Bath players, including former Somerset backs Sibley and Galley, and forwards John Parsons, Dave Robson, Pete Heindorff, Bill Lye and Phil Hall. England selectors too were now taking a closer look at the club, and brilliantly fast winger Ian Duckworth, lock Bob Orledge (an outstanding line-out jumper) and No. 8 David Gay were each selected for full England Trials.

Adding further publicity was the **televising of the Bath v Devonport Services match** on Saturday, 18th November 1967 for BBC 2's Rugby Special, the first Bath game to be so televised. Five tries crossed the line that day, one by Services wing Bardwell, four from Bath (Duckworth and Martland) and two from newcomer Leigh Robinson (RAF), who ran home for a brace on his debut. Further individual honours materialised with Bath prop Jamie Monahan (brother of John) winning the first of his two Blues for Cambridge in the 1967 Varsity match; while the selection of No. 8 David Gay (a mere 19 years old) for England against Wales (20th January 1968) stamped the club's imprint yet more clearly upon the National stage. There was drama too involving winger Ian Duckworth, arguably the club's fastest winger since the War, when with fitness doubts concerning Rod Webb (Coventry), selectors had placed Duckworth on stand-by for the England v Wales encounter. On the eve of the international, Bath were booked over-night at a Teddington hotel, so enabling a Saturday morning fixture with Metropolitan Police prior to Bath watching the international at nearby Twickenham. Webb failed his late fitness test and Duckworth was duly requested to step into the England side. But the winger, literally on the verge of an England cap and in the view of many commentators good enough to hold his place in the National side, had cried-off from the trip to London with flu.

Nonetheless with his Twickenham debut in the 11-11 draw with Wales, David Gay did play in all four Home internationals that season, including England's always tricky encounter in Paris, and though the hosts won 14-9, certain French observers spoke admiringly of two English back-row teenagers: *"This David Gay; this Bryan West [Northampton].....how will we cope with them during the next three or four years?"* commented French rugby supremoes Jean Prat and Guy Basquet, adding: *"They are veritable young lions;"* Yet, to Bath's bewilderment, and no doubt to Jean Prat and Guy Basquet, Bath's young lion gained no further caps for his Country. Meanwhile in December, Bath embarked on a nineteen-match phase that involved as daunting a set of fixtures as it gets. Their first opponents to fall were Northampton (8-3), as others then followed with a string of top-grade victories that seemed to run off a conveyor-belt, including: Rosslyn Park (22-15), all conquering Moseley (12-11), Harlequins (21-8) and Llanelli (17-9). While those most notable (and noticed!) of achievements, namely actual 'away' victories, included wins at Liverpool (0-9), London Irish (8-12), Bristol (6-8) and Gloucester (6-18); and it was success at on-form Richmond (3-8) in late March, that inspired the Chronicle to comment thus: *"if further evidence was needed of what an improved side Bath are these days, it came on Saturday at the Athletic Ground where they effectively destroyed Richmond, one of London's most successful clubs."*

David Gay ...."England's veritable young Lion" (Jean Prat, French rugby supremo).

Acknowledgments: Bath RFC

That same season the touring New Zealand All Blacks arrived in the British Isles. Formidable opponents as ever (and 11-23 victors over England), their team-work in ruck and maul and all-round off-loading was awesome, though with increased televised rugby coverage these same Kiwi advancements could now be studied more closely, not least by the emerging generation of UK coaches. Thus, the positive approach was replacing the negative, and the successful sides would prove to be those (as Sibley predicted) who *"sustained continuity through on-going phases."* And what Sibley preached he practiced. No surprises therefore that by virtue of their free-flowing style Bath would not lack for new talent drawn to a club that now seemed 'the' place to be, with at least two players for every one position. Thus, John Parsons stepped effortlessly into the prop vacancy caused by Weston-super-Mare bound Peter Jenkins. At hooker both Harvey Hill and young Alan Parfitt (brother of Pete) proved top-class back-up to Brian Collins, and with David Lewis (in addition to Orledge and Heindorff) Bath possessed a trio of first-rate locks. Meanwhile Bath selectors could hardly believe their luck when post-Christmas former England scrum-half Simon Clarke arrived on their doorstep for the remainder of the season, a period when Bath possessed the luxury of three (yes three) pairings of top-class half-backs.

The season concluded with 24 Bath wins, 5 draws, and 14 games lost. But in view of the sheer quality of many of the victories, and they included the Double over Bristol, there was little doubt that Bath had established their right to play again at the top flight. Even so Peter Sibley was under no illusions. Elected unopposed to skipper the club for a third successive season, he spelt out 'in plain English' the scale of the task now facing a senior club. Yes, he was confident that Bath *"have the right basis to play the sort of game that will be needed, but we shall need to improve our continuity of moves;"* and fortuitously **a rule-change was introduced for season 1968-9** that enabled a Sibley led side to do just that! The law drastically limited the scope to kick directly into touch beyond one's own 25 yard (22 metre) line, because to do so would now lead to an opposition throw-in at right angles from that position from where the player kicked the ball into touch. Basically, this consigned negative kicking tactics to history and proved to be a gift from Heaven for attacking teams, a group that now included Bath.

The vital need for a specialist goal kicker for season 1968-9 appeared to be solved with the arrival of Redruth marksman Mike James. But on the centre's sudden departure in mid-season this role (often the difference between victory and defeat) was handed once more to the ever-versatile Tom Martland, and not without some success either. But goal-kicking aside, Brendon Perry (he of the electrifying bursts of speed and the lightning breaks) was coming home! The prospect therefore of Vaughan Williams, Jack Thomas and now Perry at outside-half, and not forgetting further cover at scrum-half post-Christmas with the arrival of the RAF's Tim Keane, emphasised yet further the club's wealth of talent at half-back. Bath duly opened their 1968-9 season with a promising 13-9 victory against Italian side Roma, the visitors travelling with twelve internationals in their squad. But after a month of mixed fortunes that included a two win and one defeat tour of Ireland, Bath's season did not really hit full throttle until the visit of then powerful Aberavon on 5th October. It was here that Bath expressed every quality that Sibley had instilled into the team, and among those reporting on the encounter was the Sunday Telegraph's Eric Hill who commented thus: *"a match to stir, almost fatally, even the most sluggish pulse, was magnificently won by a goal, two tries and a penalty, to a try and two penalties...,"* Observing too was an enthralled John Stevens. He described a team who won with *"a glittering, bubbling display of best champagne vintage, outplayed Aberavon in the finer arts of handling, passing and backing up;"* and adding that *"one lost count of the number of times that the ball was moved first one way and then brought back the other, passing through seven, eight and even nine pairs of hands with ease and assurance."* He continued: *"At times one might almost have mistaken them for the Bristol of three or four years ago and their endeavours were rewarded with three cracking tries."* An exaggeration? No! Sibley had simply unlocked a latent talent at Bath that he, perhaps alone, had recognised on his arrival at the club. Two weeks later Bristol were beaten 9-14 at the Memorial Ground, with a commanding Bath running in three tries as against one in reply. Neath then fell 10-8 on the Rec, before Pontypool (early season 25-15 winners in Wales) suffered a similar fate, losing 21-6 by a Bath team *"who dominated proceedings to a degree which would never have seemed possible a few years back."*

However, one club now looking virtually invincible were the brilliant London Welsh, who arrived on the Rec in January with their 'turbo-charged' team of Welsh internationals and British Lions. They had already humiliated some of the biggest names in British rugby that season, including taking 30 points off Newport and another 23 off Northampton, and now all eyes were on Bath. In a titanic struggle London Welsh would triumph 14-23 in a contest that produced three Bath tries (one by newcomer centre Mike Beese) and four by the Welsh, a team so skilled in *"repeatedly switching the direction of attack,"* a team *"so adept at turning defence into devastating counter-attack...*and not forgetting *"their quick second phase possession."* In short, it was London Welsh who at this stage were the supreme masters of the new modern game. A similar spectacle was later witnessed at Easter (Good Friday) when Harlequins, beaten that season only four times prior to their visit to the Rec, arrived with six internationals in their line-up. But on a glorious Spring evening, as the Chronicle noted, it was now to be *"Bath's superb second phase football, backing up and switches of direction"* that inspired a three to one try count and a 15-5 home victory. Noticeable too was the performance of centre David Wilce, yet another gifted student-teacher from St. Luke's College, Exeter, whose strong, straight running added real mid-field punch as he and his colleagues put a stranglehold on the game *"by outplaying their star-studded visitors at their own open game."* And if any among an estimated 4000 crowd had initially questioned Bath's ability to beat some of the very best teams in the Land by the use of positive, creative rugby, then any doubts now would surely have vanished. Indeed, it was fortunate that the Sibley era coincided with an age of rugby innovation, where new forward-tactics arrived (and duly adopted) by courtesy of the 1967 New Zealand tourists, where long-needed limitations on direct kicking into touch were introduced, and where the RFU's positive encouragement of coaching would all yield a faster and more scientific form of rugby. For Bath therefore it was a case of the right captain at the right time.

There was however one administrative item of news that seemingly raised little attention during the season concerning the question of **Sponsorship**, though duly reported (Chronicle, 18th February 1969) thus: *"The committee of the home unions wish to make it clear that in accordance with the international rugby football board resolution on this subject, no club or other body under their jurisdiction may accept any commercial sponsorship and that the strict principles of amateurism which are fundamental to the game of rugby union must be upheld."* The Chronicle duly added that 'the International Board had already ruled against any form of sponsorship in 1966.' But, those wide-ranging developments in the late 1960's that would inevitably increase the popularity of the club-game (yet also its running-costs) would in time lead to an inevitable challenge to those R.F.U. administrators who would not countenance any flexibility to their rigid interpretation of 'amateurism.' A clash it seemed was inevitable.

Sibley's Men (1967-68) L. to R standing: J. Messer (official), A. Gay, J. Monohan, P. Parfitt, R. Orledge, J. Parsons, D. Gay, J. Thomas, J. Galley, R. Ludlow (physio) sitting: W. Lye, G. Frankcom, P. Hall, P. Sibley (Capt.), P. Peindorff, J. Donavon, B. Hartley.

Acknowledgements: Bath Chronicle

Meanwhile Bath were adapting rapidly to the new developments, albeit that their otherwise creditable 24 wins of season 1968-9 were perhaps rather modest by Sibley standards. Yet their 645 points-total was a new club record, resulting furthermore from six fewer games than the previous record of 628 achieved by the Sibley side of 1966-7; and though 17 games were lost, the quality of the victories confirmed again that this was a Bath team capable of playing top rugby at the top level. John Stevens (like Gloucester, a strong advocate of the then novel idea of a 'squad system,') openly suggested that *"whatever the diehards may think, [rugby union] is becoming more professional in outlook."* Moreover, regarding Sibley's captaincy, John Stevens (Chronicle, 3rd May 1969) continued thus: *"His three years in command have been among the happiest and most successful Bath have known in recent years. More than that....Sibley, bred on the firmer fields of Oxford and Blackheath and coming West late in his career, revitalised Bath rugby, lifting it out of depression, sweeping away old negative attitudes and restoring players' faith in their own ability."* Now, the reference to Sibley's previous experience at Blackheath (nor forgetting his Oxford rugby) is a reminder regarding an often overlooked aspect of his days at Bath. For Sibley's rugby philosophy and influence was partly of a London origin, whereas in the West Country there was a tendency to regard London rugby (rightly or wrongly) as physically less demanding and so vulnerable to a more aggressive brand of the game. Indeed, with the exception of Bristol players, West Country internationals had tended to be forwards (not backs) and West Country clubs (again with the exception of Bristol) as forward orientated. The effect of Sibley's London influence on Bath however was sudden, dramatic….and certainly unexpected, and under his influence the club had travelled on a journey of self-discovery. Yes, the hardness at forward remained, but virtually overnight Bath discovered an ability and confidence to play open, expansive rugby too. Thus, a remarkable future lay ahead.

There was no going back now!

Chapter 25.   MIXED SIGNALS. (1969-75)

Tom Martland: injury curtailed his captaincy.
Acknowledgements: Bath Past Players

In his summary of Bath's 1968-9 season, John Stevens emphasised that the **'squad system'** (previously a loose general term referring to a collective group of players) now effectively removed *"the concept of first team and reserves."* His prediction would be confirmed soon enough, not least at Bath where Tom Martland was elected captain for season 1969-70. An inspirational wing-forward (he could play full-back at senior level if needed), he was an ideal choice with a talented pool (i.e.: a squad) in support. It needed to be, because a succession of injuries, some serious, would hit the club almost immediately, and later described as the *"worst injury list experienced in 105 years of rugby at Bath"* (John Stevens, Chronicle 2nd May. 1970). As luck would have it, one such casualty was Martland, a knee injury causing his absence from October to March and requiring a captaincy-change to former West German international Peter Heindorff. Matters then got worse. Orledge required a cartilage operation, followed in due course by Chris Perry (broken ankle), wings Peter Glover and Harry Barstow (broken legs), vice-captain Brian Collins, Brian Fear and David Wilce (all cartilage injuries), and Ian Duckworth (fractured cheekbone). And yet, despite this toll a new club record would be achieved, so hardly surprising that John Stevens would further conclude in his end of season summary (2nd May 1970) that: *"much of the credit must go to Heindorff who, with a mixture of determination, encouragement and almost bullying, made a fine side out of what remained."* Ah yes, and 'what remained' included the recently incorporated squad system, and not forgetting an indispensable source of local players from the Bath Combination.

However, the season had commenced with the unexpected announcement by Ian Duckworth at the club's first trial (Thursday, 28th August) that he and the former Miss Sandra Wood had married at noon that same day. But this did not deter the happy couple from delaying their honeymoon for two days until the second trial on Saturday, nor to Duckworth's willingness to play in Bath's 12-5 victory against visiting La Rochelle come the following Wednesday (3rd September). Now *that's* dedication! Meanwhile results, not surprisingly in view of injuries, were mixed, the later December 39-13 crash at Gloucester for instance, yet the earlier September 14-13 near miss at Newport, the first meeting between the clubs in seventeen years. By contrast one witnessed Bath's stunning 10-17 October victory at then powerful Aberavon, where notwithstanding injuries to Barstow (leg fracture) and Martland (knee injury), Bath produced *"wonders of determination and team spirit."* And amid the turmoil, flanker Roger Walkey kicked two penalties (one from 45 yards), a touchline conversion, and as an emergency wing ran home two 70 yard tries. Then in November, with Bath less five players on Somerset duty, young colts player Alistair Watson (son of actor Jack Watson) was thrust into 1st team action at Saracens who had not lost at home since February 1968. No matter, with Watson playing *"his part in a pack it was difficult to fault,"* Bath triumphed 6-11. Then there were the performances of supposedly reserve players in Bath's numbing 14-35 win at Pontypool in November, the biggest win in Wales in the club's 'previous' 104 years history, where among notable performances was former Cheltenham full-back Walt Casey, whose *"strength and attacking ability.....brought him two most splendid tries....,"* and Ian Holmes showed that he (like David Lewis) could handle impressively the No.8 role vacated by David Gay's departure to Harlequins. Indeed, as John Stevens commented, with Bath it was now *"difficult to assess exactly what is the strongest line-up,"* another vindication of the New Model Squad system. Oh, and how Newbridge must have cursed centre Roger Elliot in Bath's 24-16 victory in December, where despite the Welshmen topping the try count three to one, Bath (or rather Roger Elliot) won the penalty count with seven 'beauties' through the sticks.

Representative honours too resulted during a season that included the visit to the British Isles of the sixth South African Springboks. Both Jim Waterman and Geoff Frankcom played in the Western Counties 3-3 draw with the Tourists at Bristol (31st December). While in January the Southern Counties faced the Springboks at Kingsholm with Bath's John Donovan, Mike Hannell and Phil Hall playing. Against such demanding opponents few gave the Counties much hope, drawn as they were from this less fashionable division of Dorset & Wilts, Berkshire, Hertfordshire, Buckinghamshire, and Oxfordshire. Yet the narrowness of their 0-13 defeat belied predictions that they would be trounced, nor did Bath's contingent (as John Stevens reported) disappoint: *"Phil Hall, a blend of patient watchfulness and natural improvisation,"* and *"Mike Hannell augmented his sound scrummaging with some enterprising contributions to the loose exchanges,"* and *"none of the backs were out of their depth....but rising above them all was centre John Donovan. His attacking flair as he occasionally swirled away with phlegmatic poise was a source of comfort to the Counties."* Furthermore, perhaps two more Bath players might have played at Kingsholm that day but for the terrible misfortune that struck on 1st December when Bath's Irish Trialist prop James Monahan, following a strenuous training session, died at his parents' North Wiltshire home. Both James and his brother John had played for Bath, London Irish and Cambridge (James gaining his Blue), and it is understood that each was on the shortlist for selection. Save for the tragedy, both might have played that day.

Meanwhile Bath continued to rely heavily on the player-resources of the Combination, and not forgetting the staff-room of Marlborough College. Indeed, in the 19-21 victory at Metropolitan Police in January three Marlborough schoolmasters represented Bath, namely prop Mike Hannell and colleagues Alan Conn (also prop), and No.8 Ian Murphy. One week later and Walcot's Brian Fear (lock) and Oldfield Old Boys Brian Eames (wing) answered the S.O.S. when making their debuts in Bath's January 9-20 win at St. Mary's Hospital. A further newcomer was scrum-half Robbie Lye (brother of club flanker Billy) from Walcot Old Boys, yet immediately converted by Heindorff into the back-row. Two weeks later he was sent into 1st team action against Rosslyn Park. So, despite all the odds, the season would prove inspiring, and those difficult away wins would surely have delighted any first-class club: Aberavon (10-17), London Irish (9-11), Pontypool (14-35), Saracens (6-11), and not forgetting Bath's first ever win at Swansea (9-11), all stamping the Bath trademark throughout England and Wales. The home wins too were often outstanding. A fine London Scottish team who fell 32-11 was to be at this juncture Bath's biggest-ever win over the Exiles; while Leicester (13-9), a totally dominated Harlequins with 5000 watching ((27-6) and Llanelli (16-8), were all grade one victories. Early April moreover welcomed the return of Tom Martland to face Sale where he duly banged home a 35 yard drop-goal in Bath's 16-6 success against opponents consistently rated among the best teams in the North, and when Bedford (already crowned as unofficial club Champions of England & Wales) were overcome 20-6 in late April, Bath had achieved a new club record of 28 victories. In fact, they promptly created another **new record of 29 wins** when beating Exeter in the following week, prior to travelling to friendly Holland for a two match and two victory tour.

Peter Heindorff not surprisingly was elected to continue the captaincy in the following 1970-1 season, a campaign that led to 26 victories (some outstanding), two draws and 13 defeats; and much credit for this continued success resulted from that 'new' Bath (Sibley) style of rugby, bringing with it an added bonus of attracting quality recruits, including an impressive quartet from Clifton, namely lock Ken Plummer, hooker Mark Robinson, and centres Graham Steer and Mario Polledri, all proof 'writ large' that those clubs on the outer edge of the first-class sphere could produce players capable of 'living' at the highest level of the game if supported by experienced colleagues around them. In fact, Polledri (likewise Steer on his debut in Bath's victory over Llanelli in the previous season) was thrust straight into first team action in Bath's home 11-9 victory over Leicester. Impressive too was the mature performance of young Combination scrum-half Bob Ascott (Stotherts), perfectly at home throughout Bath's April 12-8 victory against Newport, their first win against the Welsh giants since 1933.

Ironically, the scrum-half slot could have caused nightmares for selectors following the hamstring injury to Malcolm Lloyd, but seemingly from nowhere John Deverell and Tim Lerwill (both Army), Chris Perry, Bob Ascott, Millfield schoolboy Richard Harding (later Bristol & England), all filled the breach with a competence so assured that Bath barely noticed the difference. In fact, so well did these and other squad members fill the gaps, that Bath overcame Saracens 9-6 on the Rec in November despite supplying nine regulars to Somerset. Even when outstanding centre John Donovan departed for Torquay Athletic mid-season, Simon Burcher (the previous season's Welsh Secondary Schools captain) and medical student Peter Burrowes (formerly Rosslyn Park) suddenly appeared 'out of the proverbial blue' to stabilise the situation. Furthermore John Tredwell

(Cambridge Blue) and John Ashcroft (Army) proved outstanding back-row cover, so too 'outsides' Neil Mathias-Williams (down from Oxford) and former Newport and Rosslyn Park's Geoff Phillips.

Peter Glover: Effortless speed

Acknowledgements: Bath RFC.

Thanks not least to that 'squad' concept there was all-round cover, with a pack (wrote John Stevens) that, was *"unbeatable in a season in which the club's power was recognised and opposition tended to spoil and cover accordingly." While* Bath's 14-11 Autumn win against Neath led John Stevens to further comment thus: *"what a devastating side they can be, with right-wing Glover [soon recalled by England] once more the outstanding try-grabber."* Previously however another encounter had occurred at Kingsholm, namely Western Counties (Somerset & Gloucestershire) versus the touring Fijians, who had already demonstrated their dazzling rugby ability, but who would now demonstrate something a little different. Bath's Jim Waterman and Mike Beese both played that day (actually 10th October, Fiji's Independence Day) and as the Chronicle reported it was a certainty that neither they nor their colleagues *"will ever wish to take part in anything remotely resembling such a holocaust again."* Strong words indeed (nonetheless justified); and despite frequent injuries the Western Counties did win (25-13), while Mike Beese (now at Liverpool RFC), played an eye-catching stormer of a game; a performance that did not go unnoticed by watching England selectors.

In fact from the mid 1960's onwards there had been growing demands on players in senior rugby regarding fitness levels, tactics plus the speed of the game, and the wisdom of the 'end of season tour' now came under scrutiny at Bath following their late campaign trip to the French strongholds of Angouleme (losing 33-12) and La Rochelle (losing 17-6). 'Lightweight-games' these were not. Furthermore, the club still faced a Somerset Cup final to play on their return. Little wonder therefore that some commentators argued that pre-season tours (offering valuable warm-up team-practice) were the better option; and as it happened, would become the preferred choice anyway for many first-class clubs in the future. As for the present, on the evening of 8th May 1971 the club concluded its season when facing the 'Somerset & Bath Police' in the final of **the now restored Somerset Knock-Out Cup, not played since pre-World War One days.** The task may have looked easy, except it wasn't, although as expected Bath did win a dour struggle 13-8 on the Rec. The close result however was a timely warning that in K.O. Cup competition there is no second chance. The fitness levels too could frequently be the deciding factor, and it was in this context that the arrival of Tom Hudson as director of physical education at Bath University in January 1971 could not have been better timed.

A British pentathlon champion who had represented Gt. Britain in the 1956 Olympics, Hudson arrived with an impressive CV. A former physical education lecturer at Sheffield and Swansea universities, a rugby coach at Llanelli and who had served with the Guards Independent Airborne Company, his experience was invaluable. Initially, his first priority would be devoted to his new role at the university. But come the mid-1970's Hudson would be forming one part of a remarkable coaching triumvirate.

When Bath reached season 1971-2 the Sibley philosophy of open rugby was embedded in the club's soul and everyone knew that there must be no return to negative tactics. So, leading the club at the culmination of five seasons of unrivalled success would be no easy task, and there were two outstanding candidates, namely Phil Hall and Roger Walkey, for the captaincy. Walkey got the 'nod,' the demanding role hardly helped by the early departure of Bob Orledge to Bristol and a temporary move by Jim Waterman to Clifton. However, early season home wins against Pontypool (12-6) and an emphatic 23-13 success over Moseley suggested it could be 'business as usual.' But defeats soon followed, some heavy. Cheltenham (they clinched the 'Double' over Bath) and a string of upsets that included defeats by St. Mary's Hospital, Exeter and U.S. Portsmouth would dent Bath's reputation in the first half of the season; so too did the away 30-7 drubbing at Saracens and an ominous home 0-34 loss to Llanelli.

Roger Walkey: showed huge promise since arriving from London Welsh.
Acknowledgements: Bath Chronicle

Yet Bath (not uncharacteristically) launched yet another sudden recovery (post New Year) commencing with a 17-15 win over Leicester, and a haul of wins that included Ebbw Vale (19-6), Harlequins (27-13), Sale (20-8) and a notable 15-6 triumph against Northampton in April. Furthermore, the departure of Waterman to Clifton was cushioned by the arrival on the Rec of former Bristol full-back Bruce Thompson, whose performances were sufficiently impressive to gain him selection for Somerset and nomination as a reserve England Trialist that season. Impressive too was former Walcot wing Terry Norris, a classic example of the quality in the Combination, and whose 20 tries topped Bath's points scoring-list in this, his debut season in first-class rugby; **the season (1971-2) moreover** that saw the **introduction of the four-point try.** Invaluable during this period was the presence of those now elder statesmen, including hooker Alan Parfitt, Brendan Perry, and not forgetting winger David Taylor (ever steady and ever reliable). Encouragingly, locks Radley Wheeler and Brian Jenkins matured noticeably as support for Heindorff, and further recognition of the class in Walkey's team was the selection of wing Peter Glover and prop Mike Hannell for England's three-match early season tour to Japan (though sadly two years later Mike lost his fight against serious illness). Happily though new talent to Bath continued to arrive; with Oxford Blue Peter Binham at centre, and for a short period former Moseley and England wing Martin Hale.

So, season 1971-2 was a journey of highs and lows, of bumps and bruises, of a salutary 27 defeats and yet 23 sometimes inspiring victories. In short, it was a season of mixed signals and in fact the first of a trio of uncertain years. But never for one moment did Bath abandon Sibley's legacy of the 15 man running game.

The same philosophy continued under the Phil Hall, skipper from 1972-74, alongside ex club full-back David Dolman (cousin of former wing John Dolman), who during Walkey's captaincy had been nominated as **Bath's first officially appointed coach**; and among Hall's first duties was to lead his side against the visiting President's XV that bore the name of Molly Gerrard (widow of pre-war great Ron Gerrard). President of Bath from 1971-3, and **believed to be the first Madame president of a rugby union club** in England, her guest team captained by Bristol and England hooker John Pullin included 13 internationals, and (watched by a reported 4000 attendance on the Rec), won 15-30. But this result was immaterial. However, since the Sibley days expectations had risen sharply and other results were not treated quite so kindly. Indeed, the creditable 24 victories of Hall's 1972-3 campaign was summarised by the Chronicle thus: a *"season with little more than an average record."* Average record?! Never in the club's previous history had 24 wins been treated as merely 'average.' Meanwhile, for reasons of necessity Bath took a gamble when in February young King Edward's schoolboy Andy Sparkes was thrust into action at Gloucester for his senior debut. Now Kingsholm is no place for a boy, especially one wearing a Bath shirt, yet alongside the hard tackling Nick Hudson at centre, Sparkes showed himself a man as Bath closed in on Gloucester to within two points in a narrow 18-16 defeat. Meanwhile the departure of brilliant runners Peter Glover and Ian Duckworth had left Bath seemingly vulnerable on the flanks. Yet, David Flower soon proved his worth, while Tony Hicks (son of Tommy) was recruited from Walcot Old Boys in mid-season, yet another astute piece of Bath scouting among the Combination ranks, and his 12 tries at wing placed him second only to David Gay in Bath's try-list that season.

Meanwhile in 1971-2 the Rugby Union had introduced the **National Club Knock-Out Cup (K.O. Cup)** with the final staged at Twickenham, a competition that soon enough would have an electrifying effect upon the English game. However, any club intending to reach the dizzy heights of Twickenham would have to be 'dead' serious about getting there. So, for Bath, though now transformed since the mid-1960's, the question was this: could they adopt a touch of the Machiavelli? Because if not, they were unlikely to ever get near to those same dizzy heights. Moreover, could they shed their historic faultline that separated their (sometimes) outstanding home performances from their (sometimes) woeful away form? And the early indications were hardly encouraging, since in their initial forays into this new competition the club appeared not unlike a group of innocents abroad, whose visit to supposedly lowly Matson (Gloucestershire) in the preliminary round for the 1972-3 K.O. Cup revealed some of the pitfalls. Yes, Bath made it home by 6-18. But an overwhelming victory this was not! Instead, this was another warning that reaching the gates of Twickenham, let alone actually getting through them, was not going to be easy. Fortunately, Phil Hall knew only too well that for donkeys-years Bath had been a club mocked one week, yet praised the next, and few encounters in season 1972-3 would more vividly show these two sides of their character than their mid-October visit to the Memorial Ground. Prior to the start of this flood-lit encounter the Bristolians (losing only at Cardiff so far that season) were proud recipients of the twin pennants for winning both the English and the Anglo-Welsh unofficial championships of the previous season. Yet by the end of the evening Bath had inflicted (in John Stevens' words) a *"superb demolition job against a side which began almost arrogantly, but by the end were reduced to fumbling ineptitude."* and there were two newcomers running over for converted tries in Bath's 7-12 win. First winger Geoff Hughes (ex Pontypool) scored, then tough-tackling centre Edward Holly (ex Esher) climaxed a 70 yard Bath surge *"to score another try of classic simplicity."* This victory of such quality suggested that Bath might be capable of overcoming 1971-2 National Cup holders Gloucester nine days later in the 1st round proper of the competition. But street-wise Gloucester, doubtless alerted by Bath's result at Bristol, had prepared accordingly. Primed and ready, they repelled all that Bath could throw at the castle walls of Kingsholm to gain a 16-0 home victory.

Yet this was not a season confined solely to learning painful lessons about National cup

Phil Hall ....led a dramatic 42-0 revival against Leicester.

Acknowledgements: Bath Chronicle

rugby, because there were times (as at Bristol) when it was Bath who, far from being the pupils, were instead the masters, and rarely was this more devastatingly shown than in their remarkable home victory over Leicester in early January. The encounter followed a dismal December month that included defeats at Llanelli, Northampton and a Boxing Day 18-22 humiliation against Clifton. Hardly surprising therefore that barely a handful of spectators braved the atrocious elements that descended over the Rec for the visit of the Tigers. But what a treat awaited those brave souls who did. Because a seemingly over-confident Leicester (34-4 victors at Welford Road in September) and possibly confused by the presence of identical twins David and Peter Jenkins in the Bath backs (their brother Brian was playing at lock) were now to be put to the proverbial sword. For at the culmination of eighty minutes of pulsating rugby that witnessed eight Bath tries (yes eight!) that included a hat-trick from an inspirational Phil Hall, it was Leicester who were subjected to one of the biggest defeats in their proud history by 42-0! Ah Bath....masters of the 'Big' surprise!

This surge of form continued with a 25-3 win over Wasps in February emphasising that under Phil Hall and Walkey the club had not, would not, abandon the Sibley philosophy of 'open' rugby. It was not merely that Bath would win impressively (assisted by the immaculate goal-kicking of Bruce Thompson) against the likes of Richmond (31-12) and Harlequins (37-10). Rather it was a trio of March victories over major Welsh opponents Swansea (15-9), Ebbw Vale away (21-22) and Bridgend (21-0) that provided the vital clue, results that would doubtless have brought out the flags in the capital if achieved by a London club. For it was this continued experience against Welsh opposition, then consistently the toughest in the British Isles, that was producing long-term dividends. The victory over Bridgend, recent victors against Cardiff, was but one example; and albeit that this hard-fought encounter was marred by a fractured jaw injury to Bath Prop Bill Mottram (*"a sad episode for which neither side was blameless,"*) John Stevens concluded that this powerful Welsh club were overcome *"in a superb display of modern rucking....by a Bath pack which is now an awesome force."* Stevens in fact had now seen Bath's future, if not before. It was informative too that in their penultimate match of the season Bath not only defeated National K.O. Cup holders Gloucester by 16-7 on the Rec, but did so fielding an entire reserve front-row of R. J. Elliott, Martyn Gould and Frank Carter, and this against opponents whom Bath had not beaten since 1968. So, the 1972-3 campaign concluded with 2 draws and 24 victories, with some wins so impressive as to suggest a place for Bath should rank among rugby's Ivy League, but for the fact that it was also a season of 23 defeats, none more severe than a 59-4 humiliation at Moseley in September. And again this pointed the spotlight on that difference between Bath at their best and Bath at their inexplicable worst? It raised too another important question in this new age of increasingly competitive rugby union: could Bath ever have the confidence to match away performances with those at home, and could they adopt a more 'professional' and frankly downright 'bloody-minded' approach to their rugby? Because frankly, unless Bath could improve their consistency and furthermore export their Rec form into the most hostile arears in the game (and there were plenty of those) then even getting close to winning the National K.O. Cup would remain the proverbial pipe-dream.

And, rarely have Bath experienced so chequered a rugby season as the following campaign of1973-4. It had literally everything the script-writer could wish for: despair, elation, low farce and high drama. Defeats?....there were 28! Wins?....there were 26. A popular captain was suspended by his own club. A sickening injury ended a promising rugby career. A National Cup match was literally thrown (and blown) away. A charismatic full-back re-established himself from days spent mainly in the rugby-wilderness. A brilliant half-back arrived, and a helter-skelter season duly commenced. Two early defeats against Pontypool (0-7) and at Leicester (16-3) were compensated with a startling 43-7 home win over Moseley who one season previously had thrashed Bath 59-4 at the Reddings. Here new faces shone, including centre Vince Gaiger (formerly Devizes), back-row man Andy Mills; and on the Rec again was the mercurial talent that was Jim Waterman. Against Moseley he kicked superbly for nineteen points and ran home a scintillating try, and as the Chronicle enthused: *"it all added to another of those remarkable displays which Bath manage to produce periodically over the past few seasons."* 'Periodically' yes! But only consistency at the highest level would get Bath anywhere near a Cup final.

Anyway, celebrations post the Moseley victory were to be short-lived with Bath falling 22-4 at old foes Exeter. Worse still, after a 'robust retaliation' on an opponent who had *"perpetrated on him a particularly painful foul,"* skipper Hall got his marching orders! *"Hall is no angel,"* rued the Chronicle (24th Sep.1973) *"but this time he was more sinned against than sinning."* Unfortunately for the ever-popular skipper, the committee did not see things quite so sympathetically, and with a decision unprecedented in Bath's then 108 years of rugby history they suspended their own captain for two matches. Hall, whose *"first reaction was to resign,"* then decided otherwise (to the huge relief of both players and supporters) and accepted the judgement gracefully, as he did the 'one-week ban' later imposed by the Somerset R.U. for the same incident. Next, in late September a sickening injury to young three-quarter hopeful David Jenkins occurred during the United XV's encounter with Harlequin Wanderers. As sometimes happens in sport, the cause resulted from a seemingly innocuous collision with an opponent. But almost immediately onlookers feared that something was amiss from the manner that Jenkins collapsed in agony. Nor were they mistaken, for the youngster had suffered a seriously damaged knee injury, and fatefully he would never play serious rugby again, a shattering blow for one so young and of such glowing promise.

Four weeks later (27th Oct.1973) the club for whom David Jenkins had promised so much hosted the South & South Western Counties against the touring Australians, the first international tourists to visit the Rec since the South Africans in 1912. This mercifully was a happier occasion, with no less than a 15-14 prized victory over the tourists. While in early January there followed another uplift when Bath, inspired by sparkling performances from their new Lancashire and England Under-23 outside-half John Horton and centre Mike Beese (now an England international) overcame Leicester 20-3 at home, just the kind of form that augured well for the National K.O. Cup, in which Bath overcame R.M.C.S. Shrivenham 27-6 in the preliminary round. Next, Bath were drawn at home against Cheshire side Wilmslow. But, incessant mid-week rainfall was turning the Rec into a quagmire, indeed by Saturday it was effectively unplayable and Bath would have been perfectly justified to demand a postponement. Instead, on the morning of the match club officials made frantic overtures to secure another venue, and in so doing committed the team to play a crucial first-round National Cup game at Kingswood School. Situated high up on the Lansdown Hill, the pitch was admittedly firmer than the Rec, but totally exposed to gale force winds and rainfall now sweeping across Lansdown heights. Hence the committee, in the words of the Chronicle (11th Feb. 1974) had *"merely exchanged one set of farcical conditions for another."* Moreover, there were no enclosures for spectators, assuming that any would have braved the elements anyway, while any hopes of benefiting from an otherwise lucrative home Cup tie was to be one more item on a long list of self-inflicted damage. Making matters even worse was the fact that the captain was not even consulted about the matter, while some players (none of whom were even remotely familiar with the Kingswood pitch) only learned of the transfer to Kingswood when arriving at the Rec. Small wonder that to everyone, apart from the committee, this decision to literally throw away home advantage was simply inexplicable.

The effect furthermore on the morale of the Bath team, now effectively condemned to an away fixture on Lansdown Hill was frankly unprintable. Confidence gave way to sudden doubts, and before a mere handful of spectators the storm-lashed game subsided into a chaotic version of a rugby match. Bath meanwhile, notwithstanding their potentially match-winning backs, subsequently lost 6-17 in a game summed up by the Chronicle as nothing less than a *"morale shattering defeat."* But the fact was that it was 'off' the field where this vital game was lost, and the whole experience was a profound jolt for a club who, sometimes quite outstanding, appeared to be mere novices when faced with the harsh realities of the National Cup. For in this recently launched competition there was but one over-riding priority, namely 'winning!' Indeed, Wilmslow could hardly have believed their luck when the Bath committee literally exhausted themselves on the morning of the cup game frantically searching for another venue (literally any venue), so throwing away their vital home advantage. Adding yet more discomfort was the painful fact that if Bath wanted to learn how to win in Cup football, then two nearby rivals were exceptionally well qualified to teach them......Gloucester (winning finalists in 1972) and Bristol (finalists, albeit losing, in 1973)! Fortunately, Phil Hall was a strong leader, qualities rarely more needed than in the aftermath of the Wilmslow debacle. Nonetheless, following the cup defeat there was a shake-up of the Bath front-row. Geoff Pudney (formerly Saracens) and ex Welsh schoolboy international Bob Hawkesley were introduced at prop and young Devizes recruit Steve Horton was given an extended run at lock; and in their first ever Sunday home club game a still shell-shocked Bath somewhat cautiously overcame Cheltenham 6-4, scant reward for a committee-blunder that bordered on the inexcusable. Stern tests meanwhile still lay ahead, not least at Wasps. But fielding young Downside schoolboy centre John Bramall and John Horton oozing class at outside-half, an inspiring Phil Hall crashed over for a winning try and Bath had secured a confidence restoring 15-16 away win. And....the ability and confidence to win away was an essential quality on the long, hard road to cup glory at Twickenham.

With much credit now owed to Walkey and John Hall for maintaining the 15-man Sibley approach and achieving many a top-class victory, Chris Perry, formerly of Oldfield Old Boys, whose sporting skills had been fine-tuned during a two-year sports-scholarship at Millfield School, was handed the captaincy for 1974-5. He had already played first team rugby for Bath at full-back, centre, scrum-half and even wing-forward, not bad for a sportsman who was also a Somerset (2nd X1) County cricketer. Such all-round prowess furthermore seemed barely possible with one so mild of manner and of such youthful appearance. Yet he was not elected captain for nothing. *"Spoil and hit 'em hard,"* demanded Perry of his Bath 'infantry' prior to their October clash at Bristol, and that is exactly what they did, winning a 9-10 nail-biter. They did it again in March, their 13-4 victory securing their first Double over Bristol since 1967-8. But things would not always run quite so smoothly for the new skipper, albeit that Bath had stormed off the starting blocks with victory in the Cheltenham Sevens (beating favourites Bridgend 18-16 in the final), and concluding the season with a 41-3 success over Old Redcliffians to win the Somerset Cup….again. But these two trophies notwithstanding, Bath would continue to send out those same mixed signals, not least in terms of the National K.O. Cup. Here, Bath were drawn to play their first-round encounter at Falmouth in mid-November, well aware that they had only narrowly won 13-11 at home against the Cornishmen in September. But now this would be cup rugby, far from home, and Bath knew that Kernow is a lonely place to be for outsiders who threaten their fierce rugby pride. Not surprisingly this match was NOT a 'vicar's tea party.' Indeed, by the closing stages the clash (for 'clash' it was) ended *on a thoroughly bad-tempered note with some ugly brawling in the packs.* Fortunately from a Bath perspective it was Radley Wheeler and Robbie Lye who steadied matters with their domination of line-out play, while a re-called Heindorff set about *"generating a massive shove….that helped push the Cornishmen yards back in the scrums."* But it was uncomfortably close, finishing at 9-9 by way of three penalties apiece; and by sole virtue of the K.O. Cup tournament's away side rule Bath now advanced into the next round.

Next stop was Liverpool RFC for round two in February, and as Mike Beese could have told anyone: 'Pool were not to be taken lightly, especially at home,' and this time Bath were taking no chances. Any thoughts of open rugby were discarded. Instead, Bath set out to *"smother Liverpool into mistakes, coupled with some good cover and hard tackling."* No, it was not attractive, nor this being a cup-match was it intended to be, and the end justified the means with a 6-12 win. It brought Bath further reward: a home-advantage for their quarter-final tie against supposedly lowly Morpeth from distant Northumberland, that is until approximately one hour prior to the match itself on 8th March. Then suddenly recent haunting memories stirred when literally *"the heavens opened….producing mud, the great leveller."* And naturally such conditions are a godsend to any would-be giant-killers. So it was that on a rain-soaked Rec the weather once again fatefully intervened, so too that haunting spectre of Wilmslow, and this time Morpeth returned homewards with the only thing that matters in Cup rugby….a 9-3 win! For Chris Perry this defeat would remain the one great regret of his captaincy. A leader from the front, he could only reminisce from the side-lines as his Morpeth opponents strode onwards into the semi-finals, though they too would lose at home to Rosslyn Park, who themselves would fall at the final hurdle against Bedford (28-12) at Twickenham. And Bath? they could but ponder again what might have been.

The club scene is a different 'world' however, though the gulf between Bath at home and Bath away remained glaring at times. In December for example they fell 49-4 at London Scottish (losing 1974 Cup finalists). Two weeks later such woes went very public when, by way of the BBC's televised Rugby Special, Bath were seen to slide and slither upon a rain-soaked Llanelli pitch and endure a 30-0 drubbing. While in early February London rugby would doubtless have taken another critical note of Bath's 21-0 defeat at Rosslyn Park. Yet such upsets obscured a quite different 'picture' at home. Leicester, London Irish and Gloucester were among Bath's home victims in the first part of the season. While post-Christmas Bath's victory toll included victories over a still superb London Welsh (13-8), Saracens, Wasps and Harlequins. And perhaps Bath's finest performance of the season was their February 12-6 victory over a Newport club who had lost just once previously that season. Yet *"Bath not only outplayed them up front but produced far more enterprise outside."* And doing the outplaying up front were Bath props Pudney, Meddick, and hooker Alan Parfitt, a trio ably supported by locks Brian Jenkins and Mike Plummer, plus a back-row of Robbie Lye, Clive Harry and Phil Hall. As for enterprise outside, there was John Horton and: *"the artistry of Bath's Lancashire-born fly-half was there for all to see."* Such sparkling performances ranked among the commendable 28 victories that season, an unthinkable total for most of the post War years until Sibley's arrival, and moreover one in which the club's capital-base was strengthened considerably with the **introduction of floodlights,** a facility initially launched (1974) for the Boxing Day win against Clifton, and followed in January when successfully hosting the Royal Navy. Secondly, Bath welcomed a number of 'interesting' new faces to the Rec, including Peter Fryatt from Hampshire club Tottonians, teenager Mike Richardson, and John Davies from St. Brendan's Old Boys.

All three were top-class goal kickers. All three topped over 100 points that season. All three occupied one third each of the season as Bath's designated goal kicker. Fryatt (full-back or wing) arrived on the recommendation of Hampshire County and dominated the opening third of the season. Richardson followed until ruled out by injury. Then Davies fulfilled the kicking role. Their impact was profound. Indeed, Bath's final tally of 647 points included a huge contribution of 347 from goal kicks alone; while the 74 penalty goals attained was a hit-rate unprecedented in the club's entire previous history. And the fact was that in first-class rugby the 'boot' was now vying to be king. Others would now come knocking on the club door, including Bristol centre Dave Alred (a future specialist international goal-kick coach), and two young backs who in April were given their baptism in Bath's losing 15-3 encounter at Northampton. One was St. Luke's student Steve Donovan (brother of John); the other was Prior Park College all-round back John Palmer, and come the following season of 1975-6 Bath would be fielding a back division of lethal potential. Horton, Beese and Palmer were players any side would give their proverbial right arm for. In addition, the compulsive genius that was Jim Waterman (now an Oxford Blue) would be lining up alongside them....as captain! And from Falmouth a strong-running young wing by the name of Barry Trevaskis had not forgotten that Cup game with Bath.... nor Bath him. He too would soon make the long journey from Kernow to the Rec. And though few perhaps at the club would have dared to dream, the foundations for the most remarkable era of Bath rugby were quietly being laid.

Chapter 26.   AGE of PROMISE. (1975-80)

It was fitting that season 1975-6 would prove as colourful as new skipper Jim Waterman's colourful nature, now inheriting a club packed with talent, not least thanks to the graft of previous captains Heindorff, Walkey, Phil Hall and Chris Perry who had (some mishaps notwithstanding) maintained the momentum set by Peter Sibley. Indeed, the new campaign started like a rocket with a 3-35 win at Taunton (their Centenary year), followed by a 30-15 victory over Pontypool that typified one side of Bath. The other side

Jim Waterman ….brilliant attacking player

Acknowledgements: Reg Monk

was shown by a 30-12 defeat at Newport, next a 37-7 salutary lesson at Leicester and a 40-18 drubbing at a *"superbly drilled Moseley."* Ah yes, Bath's erratic form away from home. Would this change one wondered? Nonetheless, thoughts soon switched to the National K.O. Cup in October, now sponsored and known as **the John Player Cup (J. P. Cup);** with Bath drawn for a home-tie for their first-round encounter. So far so good, but for the fact that they were drawn against Bristol. Worse, Bath lost 15-24 in a contest remembered especially for *"some ruthless tackling…..and sadly some fearsome displays of temper."* Yet, with their cup ambitions finished for another season, Bath worked-off their disappointments by concentrating on non-cup games, 'landing' some very big fish

indeed to achieve **a new club record of 31 victories.** Moreover, the Rec remained virtually impregnable against Welsh opponents, with that earlier success over Pontypool and wins over Bridgend (10-9), Neath (15-9), South Wales Police (22-15), Cardiff (9-4), Ebbw Vale (15-6) and sweet revenge over Newport (9-4). And, those victories against Cardiff and Newport deserve a special mention.

First it was Cardiff, an estimated 4000 watching, in part to witness Wales scrum-half great Gareth Edwards. But on this day, in the words of John Stevens: *"even the legendary Edwards was over-shadowed as Horton….first toyed with Cardiff, then destroyed them with his superb kicking and running…."* Against Newport in April an early second half injury to Phil Hall depleted Bath to thirteen fit players. But *"in a bruising, sometimes brutal affair"* the defiant Waterman inspired a never-say-die defence that subsequently thwarted (just!) everything that Newport could throw at them. It certainly was tough-going playing against the Welsh, and there was only one way to do it...their way! Yet the season's impressive seven home victories against Celtic opponents was evidence that Bath 'could' do it their way, save for one important factor; namely Bath's six forays *'into'* Wales that season had led to six defeats and Llanelli (victors at Stradey Park) did win at Bath. But, if that psychological barrier that thwarted numerous English teams when venturing into the Valleys could be overcome, then there might be no mountain that Bath could not conquer one distant day. It was a tantalizing thought.

Fortunately, there was a rich seam of talent for this gruelling fifty match season, with Bath able to select both Oxford Blue wing Ian Dunbar and Army prop Rod Campbell for the opening victories against Taunton and Pontypool. Soon youngsters Chris Thomas from Wales (wing) and out-half Mark Sutton would be thrust into the deep end; and later invaluable contributions were provided by, among others, centre Robin Hone, winger Rob Wyatt (RAF & Combined Services), scrum-half Tim Lane (ex Bristol), and locks Hugh Leman and former Sale forward Peter Boyle. Another unforgettable discovery was 24 years old, 18 ½ stone and 6ft 5in lock giant Adam Litowczyk who made his debut under floodlights in Bath's November revenge 12-6 victory over Bristol, a senior baptism to remember and this from a supposed 'rookie' who in the previous season was playing for Cirencester RFC. Another surprise was Bath's selection in November of Avonvale hooker Tony Edwards. There was nothing unusual of course in Bath fielding Combination players. But to draft them immediately into first-team duty against top opposition usually was. However, with Alan Parfitt injured, Bath thrust Edwards straight into the senior side that narrowly overcame powerful Bridgend. That the 30 years old Edwards would then demonstrate that he could 'live' amongst opponents that included Bristol, Gloucester and Cardiff was proof of his ability. That Bath possessed the intuitive judgement to make so bold a selection was proof of their long-standing knowledge of those strengths within the Combination.

By now Horton was on the verge of an England cap and likewise John Palmer, while Nick Hudson, Mike Beese and Horton in the backs, and forwards Bert Meddick and Ken Plummer all appeared for Somerset. David Gay too remained a class player. Furthermore Phil Hall, Robbie Lye and Geoff Pillinger could handle any opposing back-row in first-class rugby. They needed to be, because since losing narrowly at Richmond ten matches from the end of the season, Bath knew they simply must win at least seven of their remaining nine encounters to beat the club record of 28 wins (29 if Somerset Cup finals included). And standing in their path were the likes of Newport, Llanelli, Harlequins and bogey sides Bedford and Exeter. Notwithstanding this daunting challenge they won not seven, but eight more matches, and literally blazed a trail through Harlequins (35-9), Bedford (35-7) and Exeter (37-6). The Rec was literally buzzing! And…on the final day of the season Bath had to honour not one, but two important engagements. There was the visit of a fast-improving Nottingham, while simultaneously Bath would be a guest side in their first-ever participation in the prestigious **Snelling Sevens at Cardiff.** By coincidence this final day was in fact May Day, and Oh.... what a day! In beating Weston-s-Mare 22-7 four weeks previously Bath had already won the Somerset Cup for the 5th time, while their victory over Exeter had 'guaranteed' their entry into the following season's John Player Cup. Master-kicker John Davies would complete the season with **a remarkable club record of 425 points** that consisted of 7 tries, 53 conversions and 97 penalties; and the now legendary Phil Hall would be retiring with a new official record of **580 first-team Bath appearances** under his belt. Moreover, despite key players on Sevens duty at Cardiff, Bath defeated Nottingham 10-6 and established that **new record of 31 victories** (excluding the Somerset cup final). While in Cardiff a 7000 crowd attended the Snelling Sevens; and **Bath, travelling with a team of J. Palmer, M. Beese, J. Horton, T.Lane, D. Gay, A. Parfitt and R. Love (with reserves J.Roberts and M. Richardson)** won applause when initially overcoming Welsh Merit Table champions Pontypridd 16-6, next defeating fellow guest side Moseley 30-16, before losing 24-12 to a Newport team who fell 18-8 to hosts Cardiff in the final.

Two weeks since Bath attained their new club record, readers of the Bath Chronicle (15th May) were treated to an eye-catching headline. It stated thus: "*Can Bath become the best rugby club in England.....?*" For thus spoke Tom Hudson, now a part of the Rec coaching set-up and who challenged the club to "*win the John Player Cup.*" However, with Bath's sometimes embarrassing track-record so far in National Cup rugby, this sure was some 'tall' order. Yet, as the Chronicle wrote: he had helped lift Llanelli "*to probably the best club side in the world.*" Moreover, he would introduce the most demanding training schedule that Bath had ever known. Even so, harsh reality soon intervened come season 1976-7. Pontypool struck first, winning 46-6. Then upsets followed at Newport (22-3), Neath (35-19), Llanelli (36-0) and Bedford (44-15). Worse was the March 51-7 nightmare at Gloucester, though Bath's immediate response was to trounce Richmond 25-4 on the Rec. Indeed, at home things were often very different, with new captain John Horton's side chalking-up a not

Tom Hudson ....knows how to train a rugby team
Acknowledgements: Reg. Monk

insignificant 26 Bath wins that included big guns Leicester, Harlequins, Wasps and Welsh opponents Aberavon, Newbridge and a 7-9 away success at Bridgend. New faces arrived too, among them prop Dougal Spaven, former Gloucester scrum-half Richard Nichols, Old Whitgiftians hooker Tony Mason, ex Newbridge wing-forward Roger Hill and powerful centre Chris Bird. Further talent meanwhile travelled along the well-trodden Combination 'corridor' to the Rec, notably young winger Gary Townsend (Trowbridge), centre Andrew Smith (Chippenham) and outstanding scrum-half Paul Smith (Combe Down).

Yet perhaps predictably there was to be yet another chapter to the on-going saga of Bath and the Cup, now fast becoming either a farce or a nightmare, depending upon one's sense of humour. Horton's men had been drawn away in a demanding (but highly attractive) first-round tie at London Welsh in December, and on the morning of the 'big day' Bath and some two hundred supporters headed for the Old Deer Park. Nonetheless, although no warnings had been announced, there were certain reservations about the supposedly hard surface of the pitch. But the first that Bath knew about it did not occur until both teams were actually on the field of play waiting for kick-off. It was then that host captain Jim Shanklin *"indicated he considered the pitch was too hard to play."* Though Horton begged to differ, Shanklin promptly led the 'Welsh' off the Park. The home captain *"was roundly booed by his own supporters,"* while Bath were absolutely seething. As club secretary Jack Simpkins said: *"if we had known we might have at least have been able to stop supporters travelling up for nothing."* Not until the 8th January was the matter resolved (for want of a better word) when, with the original sense of cup expectancy now evaporated, London Welsh won 18-3. But they too did not reach the final, Gosforth winning 27-11 against Waterloo. Meanwhile the 1976-7 season's decision by the **RFU to accept sponsorship** (with 'John Player') for the National K. O. Cup, effectively opened the door for clubs to follow suit, as did Bath in March 1977 by courtesy of local stockbrokers Godfrey, Derby and Co. of George Street. However, the future of Bath 'end-of-season tours' was a different matter. For starters, following an intense season there was a shortage of players, though despite a second-half injury to prop John Cunningham, Bath won 19-10 against Libourne. Next it was powerful Begles, a very different proposition, not helped either by the fact that Bath struggled to even raise a team of 15 fit men. No surprises then that Begles walked it 52-6, and one really did wonder if such tours for Bath might now belong to history.

However, Jim Waterman's appointment for his second term of captaincy in season 1977-8 again ignited expectation, because like Horton, he never disappointed his many admirers, and though but an injured spectator for Bath's 27-9 season-opening victory against Pontypool, his team (in cavalier form) had the name of Waterman written all over it. But again, there would be a mix of top victories yet some truly embarrassing defeats. Coventry in November was one example, with Bath overwhelmed 42-4, a trouncing partly resulting from *"Bath's powder-puff pack which was shoved back yards in the set scrums."* But come the return in March the tables were turned as Bath with *"thrilling attacks which often started deep in their own 25"* gained revenge with a 21-13 victory. And having defeated Exeter 16-25 away in September, an expectant Bath had journeyed to Exeter again in January for their 1st round John Player K.O, match where the hosts applied *"a commonsense display suitable to the trying conditions,"* winning 20-6 on a quagmire pitch that left Bath pondering if their fortunes in the National Cup would ever change. And in truth, they still had cup-rugby lessons to learn, not least adapting to bad conditions!

With some among the seniors now departing from the game, a younger generation of forwards would now be arriving on the Rec in the coming months and seasons. Among these was young prop Gareth Chilcott from Gordano (Bristol), hooker Chris Legg and lock Neil Spencer, all impressive in Bath's inspired October 25-9 victory against Neath.

It was encouraging too that a front-row of comparative newcomers, namely Peter Ford (ex. Salisbury), hooker Chris Legg and Phil Davies (ex. Penarth and Llanelli) proved equal to top opposition not only in Bath's home 28-16 victory over Leicester in January, but in the outstanding 11-17 away win at Bristol in March. Later former Bristol prop Rod Speed, lock Colin Chappell and flanker Gerry Parsons (all newcomers) stamped their own mark in Bath's overwhelming seven try and 9-39 win at Richmond in April; an impressive demonstration for a London audience and partly inspired by John Horton, now a full England international since his February 1978 debut at Twickenham, albeit a narrow 6-9 defeat by Wales. Another achievement was the earlier debut of Alan Jenkins at centre in Bath's 0-26 win at U.S. Portsmouth in November. Albeit a rare first-team appearance, Alan was the fourth and youngest of the Jenkins rugby-dynasty to play at senior level for Bath, a record believed to be unique in the club's entire history.

But sentiment apart, by the late 1970's rugby was taking itself ever more seriously. Coaching was developing more 'professionally,' so too administration, and not just among senior clubs either. In addition, the commercial sector was now taking a closer interest, and while in the mid-1970's the RFU had agreed that sponsorship deal with John Player, certain leading Welsh clubs later commenced their own **separate sponsorship deals** with Adidas, although *"officially deplored by the Welsh Rugby Union."* Several English clubs then made similar agreements, among them Bath, who at the start of the 1977-8 season also negotiated a sponsorship deal with Adidas worth approximately £3,000 over the following three seasons. To be precise (Chronicle, 6th Sep. 1977) this involved the annual supply to Bath of no less than *"40 complete sets of shorts, jerseys and socks – 12 [rugby footballs] and, to start with, 40 hold-alls."* Such a deal seen retrospectively may seem a pittance, though not then, and its long-term significance was considerable. Indeed, later much larger sums would flow into the game. And interestingly, despite the initial disapproval of the Welsh RFU to shirt sponsorship, Bath faced no opposition whatsoever from the Rugby Union for their own similar arrangement.

Another professionalism-issue arose (Chronicle, 20th Apr. 1978) when Bath full-back Dave Alred revealed that he had signed a three-year contract with Minnesota Vikings to play in American [grid-iron] football. Crucially, it was Alred's ability to kick goals (and quickly) that had attracted the attention of his intended employers. Indeed, such was the value attached to a reliable kicker in US football that Alred revealed he would *"earn more in four months there than I would get in eight years as a teacher here."* But speed would be of the essence, since to quote the Bath full-back: his sole role was *"just to kick-off and kick the goals,"* adding that in grid-iron you *"have about 1.3 seconds to kick at goal before the opposition gets to you. That means two steps and bang."* There were however two hurdles now facing Alred. First was the need to obtain a US work permit. That was the easy bit. Then, he would require RFU clearance that playing pro' grid-iron would not prevent his return to rugby union football. That would be the tricky bit. Bath meanwhile concluded their 1977-8 inter-club programme with a winning-trio. First Newport fell 15-9 on the Rec, next Taunton 0-56, with Bath's Jonathon Roberts (son of ex skipper John), Robbie Lye and **Geoff Pillinger** causing havoc among the opposition. Finally, against Bedford on the Rec, Bath completed their campaign of 28 victories with a 45-28 win and "*another marvellous feast of open rugby and a glut of spectacular tries,*"

with Bedford's England wing Derek Wyatt, joining Bath the following season, scoring two. Their final event of the season however would be the Middlesex Sevens, and having already won the earlier Oxford tournament with an emphatic 32-6 win over Oxford University in the final, Waterman's men headed for rugby HQ in high spirits. Before a packed 'house' Bath reached the last eight with their 18-12 win over London Scottish; though progress stopped in a 14-6 defeat to Rosslyn Park, with Harlequins the stars of the show with their victory in the final.

Derek Wyatt: Oxford Blue and England, later MP for Sittingbourne.

Acknowledgements: Bath RFC

But the serious business is the 15-man game and former England centre Mike Beese was skipper for 1978-9. A leader of quiet determination, his one-year captaincy would be among the most exciting in the club's history. Despite four matches cancelled, there would be a total of **31 victories,** three draws and a mere 10 games lost; and again specialist kicker John Davies, albeit playing in barely a third of the fixtures, would be the leading points-scorer for the fourth year in succession with his tally of 133 goals. It was the season too when a new coach from the North East (**Jack Rowell,** all 6ft 6in of him) would arrive. Moreover, it was a season when Bath would prove beyond doubt that they could 'handle' the very best that even Wales could throw at them (well, usually!).

Even so, fortunes in the Cup would again disappoint, this time on a grim February day at the London Welsh, whose 28-18 win brought Bath's cup hopes to a shuddering halt. Adding to the disappointment was the intended departure of Bath's England Trialist scrum-half Steve Lewis, soon to return homewards with his considerable talents to Ebbw Vale. Yet the season had kicked off with a cracking 10-26 win at Pontypool, and in late September Bath triumphed 8-12 to gain their first-ever away victory at Neath. Meanwhile when Bath later hosted Cross-Keys in March, the clubs not having played regularly since pre-First World War days, this match (or rather dual) between presumed Old Friends was to be an encounter that "*flared fitfully into open warfare,*" albeit that Bath won 22-0. But in truth matters could get equally non-friendly in England, as happened during Bath's visit to Plymouth Albion (10th Oct. 1978) to play a South West Merit Table encounter and where clubs in the top four grouping at the end of season would be guaranteed an automatic place in the first-round proper of the John Player Cup the following year. But this, as the Chronicle explained, hardly justified the events that followed. For while there was precious little rugby, there were numerous *"late tackles, flying boots, flurries of fists and blatant trampling. Neither side was blameless."* Indeed, the Chronicle described the match as nothing less than *"reminiscent of the bloodbath West Country derbies of old."* Bath, fortunately capable of looking after themselves, squeezed home by 12-13. But this was no 'vicars tea party;' nor was it a surprise when two players after an 'exchange of pleasantries' received marching orders. And yet. there was a twist to the tale. For the players involved were flankers Simon Jones (Bath); and the flaxen-haired Roger Spurrell (Albion), who soon would not only join Bath, but later captain them.

Mike Beese ....one of the most successful post-war captains.

Acknowledgements: Reg Monk

Meanwhile, Bath by now were growing noticeably more confident when away from home, as shown with a number of highly significant results during the season, not least their first ever win (4-15) over Harlequins at Twickenham. And there was another reason to remember this particular encounter, because with only five minutes remaining Bath touch-judge David Jenkins **managed to get himself sent off!** In fact, he had made a *"light-hearted remark to someone in the crowd,"* but one that referee Mr Williams *"thought was aimed at him."* Thus former Bath player David Jenkins, who had never been dismissed as a player, now received his marching orders as a touch-judge instead, a 'feat' that has remained an all-time club record, and likely to remain so....forever! Humour aside, other results caught the eye pre-Christmas: Coventry were overcome 23-3 at home, likewise both Gloucester (20-10) and the return against Harlequins (21-10). But a key feature was that Bath now ranked among a small group of English clubs capable of matching top Welsh teams, albeit there had been glimpses of this potential in the past. Yet of the 13 matches against Celtic opposition only two, namely Newbridge on a County day and at Bridgend, were lost. In addition, Bath drew at Newport and at Llanelli, defeated both Pontypool and Neath away, and likewise overcame Aberavon, Cross-Keys, Swansea, Newport, Pontypridd, South Wales Police, and Llanelli at home. Few if any English clubs could match such a record as this.

Ignoring his own contribution to the season's achievements, Mike Beese instead heaped praise not least on the younger players in the ranks, among them out-half prospect Neil Hopkins (soon to be capped for England colts), and who as a Millfield schoolboy in the previous season had helped Bath defeat the RAF on his debut that included a superb 45 yard penalty goal. Wing Simon Jarvis, himself ex-Millfield, impressed on his Bath debut in the 25-10 Autumn win against U.S. Portsmouth. In addition, prop Gareth Chilcott and backs Mark Sutton and John Palmer all received the call-up to the England U.23 squad, and the line-out ability of Derrick Barry was proving invaluable. Beese furthermore described winger Paul Simmons *"as the most improved young wing in the country,"* praise indeed when considering two other wingers now carving out big reputations. Of these the first was 18 years old Bryanston schoolboy David Trick, already an England U.19's international of stunning speed, who 'screamed' over for a hat-trick on his debut in Bath's 36-16 defeat of South Wales Police. Another winger was former St. Luke's College Exeter, Bedford, Oxford Blue and England international Derek Wyatt. Now a master at Dauntseys he was quality, so forthrightly demonstrated in Bath's superb late season 23-6 win against Llanelli. Watched by the club's biggest crowd of the season, Bath *"produced some quite glorious running and handling,"* and Wyatt ran over for a hat-trick, taking his season's total to 29 tries, a tally that **equalled the club record set by Bath utility forward George Haydon 48 years previously.**

Another factor was **the coaching-trio of former Bath forward Dave Robson, Tom Hudson and Jack Rowell,** now evolving into a triumvirate so successful that during the following decade it would attract not only domestic, but international recognition. And, it was partly this coaching input that led to this outstanding 1978-9 campaign, where from the start to the finishing-line Bath strode onwards like the US Cavalry in full charge-mode. Indeed, the pace never ceased, and only after a nine-win blitz commencing in March and concluding with a 13-21 away win at Bedford did Bath even pause for breath. Yet success did not change one iota the essential sense of family at the club; and two players expressed such sentiments with John Stevens (Chronicle, 23rd Apr. 1979). First, Welsh-born England Trialist flank-forward Gerry Parsons commented that he had seriously considered retiring at the end of the season since by now *"the demands of first-class rugby were a bit too much,"* and yet *"I think I would miss it terribly, especially at Bath, which is just about the most friendly club one could imagine."* Likewise, Mark Sutton, who had played superbly in Bath's early season 18-6 victory over Romanian side Bucharest, duly concurred. Notwithstanding that in the following season this highly promising England U.23 squad member was not guaranteed a regular place, Sutton announced that his future was on the Rec: *"It's simply that it's such fun being involved in the sort of rugby Bath are playing at the moment that I wouldn't dream of going anywhere else."*

The 'professionalism' saga meanwhile would not disappear off the radar, and in April 1979 Alred, having actually completed a season in USA football, received the RFU reply: he 'would be suspended indefinitely from the game.' Whatever their reasoning (professional cricketers were not so affected for example) the RFU's verdict turned out to be, in American jargon, 'a great career move,' though the time for Dave Alred to dispatch his thankyou-letter to Twickenham for their ultra-strict ruling would come later.

Come the final season of the decade (1979-80) John Horton was elected to the captaincy for a second time, his side achieving **a new record of 37 victories**, one draw and a mere 10 defeats, with the aforementioned flanker Roger Spurrell and wing Barry Trevaskis in the ranks and both making their 1st team debuts in Bath's 58-0 win over Seahawks, the early season tourists from California. Alongside these two Cornishmen was former London Scottish prop David Butcher, soon to catch the eye of England selectors, and England Schools star Brian Kenny at hooker. Meanwhile young prop Richard Lee from Wellington RFC proved his potential against the might of Bristol, and strengthening the pack yet further were lock giants Michel van der Loos from Holland and former Loughborough Colleges Welshman Howard Thomas. Never, but never, had the club been so blessed with such an abundance of ability.

Naturally, possessing a surplus of quality is the one headache that selectors rarely complain about. But it calls for leadership at the top, and a willingness among players to accept that literally no one is guaranteed a first team place as of right. The squad understood this and morale remained extraordinarily high. Waterman at 35 years of age was still regarded by John Stevens as a player of an *"undying genius, "*and Derek Wyatt as a *"try-scorer extraordinaire;"* while skipper John Horton after a year in the wilderness *"finally came of age internationally"* when marshalling his England backs to a 24-9 win over Ireland at Twickenham in January. No fewer than five Bath players had been called-up for the South and South West team to play the New Zealand tourists in November (though losing 0-16), namely **Mike Beese (captain), John Palmer, John Horton, Damien Murphy and Simon Jones.** Four Bath players were called-up for the England U.23 squad, **namely: John Palmer, David Butcher (prop), Mark Sutton and Bryanston schoolboy David Trick.** While wing-forwards **Simon Jones and Gerry Parsons featured in the final full England Trial at Twickenham.** As for results, some victories were simply dazzling. Indeed, one wondered if any side would be safe from a potential Bath onslaught. Certainly not Pontypool, beaten 16-9 in the season's opener, nor current JP Cup holders Leicester beaten 9-10 away, nor Moseley beaten 22-11 on the Rec, and not forgetting Bath's first ever Double over Newport (3-6 away, 17-7 at home). For Bath devotees it was like walking on air. Budge Rogers, chairman of the England selectors, watching the 22-11 victory over Moseley, pin-pointed the sheer energy that Bath now brought onto the field of play. Bath he said *"just don't know when to stop attacking....even when things aren't going right for them....and they're a very exciting side to watch."* Soon it would be Bristol's fate to experience not only this same non-stop wave of attacking football, but also the electrifying speed of 18 years old David Trick. Surging to a try hat-trick in Bath's 38-17 win, John Stevens (Chronicle, 22nd Oct. 1979) wrote in awe of his *"remarkable pace and attacking skill."*

Yet perhaps no performance could better the November 17-41 win against Harlequins at Twickenham. For this, as John Stevens reported (Chronicle, 5th Nov. 1979) was undoubtedly among the most brilliant and significant Bath victories of the decade: *"[Bath] produced the sort of rugby which the London public has often read about but so seldom seen in a devastating period at the end when they scored five of their seven tries."* Wyatt and Trick bagged a brace of tries apiece, and the schoolboy's second was *"a superb 60-yard run outside his opposing wing and back inside the full-back"* and was simply *"the score of the match."* Though as Stevens cheekily added, prop Bert Meddick would disagree. He after all completed the rout with his score in the closing minute *"with a try he will cherish above any other."* Indeed, by clinching the double over Harlequins with a home 27-10 win in December, Bath looked unstoppable; and when in early December the London Scottish had been humbled 36-7, former Bath international Alec Lewis was moved to acclaim Horton's side as the *'the best ever in the club's history.'* Not surprisingly, interest now came from another direction, namely Rugby League, and their attention was focused on two players in particular. The first was England B international John Palmer, and the second was David Trick. As the Bath Chronicle reported in mid-December, the offers made to both these outstanding backs were not in fact accepted, but it is not difficult to understand the reasons that led some Union players to switch codes. Young Trick after all was but an 18 years old schoolboy when first invited to go North with a seven thousand pounds offer from Widnes in cash literally placed before his eyes. Then one year out of school, Oldham offered the young wing a then mouth-watering offer of twenty thousand pounds; and such a sum in the late1970's was very serious money indeed!

Nonetheless, this same period was not without some heartfelt regrets, and among them was the occasion of Bath's Autumn 6-28 win at St. Mary's Hospital. The victory apart, this was to be the last time that these two clubs would ever meet again on a rugby field, and among those who came to bid farewell to this remarkable Hospital side was Arnold Ridley. He would feel the poignancy as keenly as any, since it was Arnold himself who as a former Bath fixtures secretary had initiated this annual meeting half a century previously in the late 1920's. But there was an inescapable reason for this parting of the ways, namely the growing gulf between the upper echelon of first-class clubs and those now finding the pace a little too hot. These included the London Hospital sides and the leading London Old Boys clubs that until the 1970's had played with such distinction at the highest levels of the first-class game. Meanwhile this would be another season when it was advisable to whisper softly any mention of Bath when in Wales. True, they did not win everything when confronting the fearsome Dragon, and fell at Llanelli and Aberavon. But they overcame both Newport and the South Wales Police away, and apart from a 22-22 draw at home against Neath, Bath proved that the Rec was an uncomfortable place for Welsh teams. Here they overcame many of the finest in the Principality, and it was sure some hit-list! For Pontypool, Newbridge (Bath less ten players on County duty), Bridgend and Ebbw Vale would all return homewards empty-handed.

And yet the curse that bedevilled Bath vis' the John Player Cup continued. For in March, albeit hot-favourites and at home, they lost 3-6 in the quarter-finals to London Irish who then strode onwards to a Twickenham final, albeit losing 21-9 to Leicester. Thus. a Cup run that had commenced with a sweeping 30-6 away win at Marlow, followed by an impressive 12-19 away victory at Liverpool, now ended once more in bewildered dejection. If there was any consolation it was provided by Bath's guaranteed entry into the 1st round proper for the following season thanks to an unassailable position in the top four of the South West Merit Table; to record the aforementioned **record of 37 victories,** clinched in late April with their home 22-16 success over Bedford.

How the late Eddie Simpkins, those National Cup defeats apart, would have loved such times as these, not least when on 14th February his son Jack Simpkins (Bath's general secretary) was honoured, alongside Coventry secretary Alf Wyman and former Bristol and England forward David Rollitt, at the annual dinner of the Rugby Writers Club at the Press Centre in London; all duly praised by the Writers Club chairman Tony Bodley (Chronicle, 15th Feb. 1980) for *"the stalwart service of the trio to the game over many years."* But after a season of such dazzling rugby, could Bath's momentum continue? Or, would they fade under the sheer pressure of maintaining the exacting standards that they had now set themselves. 'Could something go wrong?' Could they really win that treasured National K.O. Cup? Well, this much one could say: since the mid-1960's Bath had undergone an initially little-recognised transformation. But now the whole rugby community was judging this enigmatic rugby family far more seriously. Just one vital question remained however: 'could the still happy-go-lucky Bath actually take *themselves* more seriously?' It was precisely this same question that Tom Hudson five years previously had 'dared' the club to confront. The following decade, a tumultuous one as it happened, would provide an empathic answer to this most crucial of questions.

Chapter 27. COUNTDOWN TO THE SEASON THAT CHANGED EVERYTHING. (1980-3)

Season 1980-81, and a new decade under new skipper Robbie Lye now leading a club with one of the most challenging fixture-lists in British rugby. England Trialist full-back Charles Ralston (ex Rosslyn Park) had arrived, likewise lock Andy Marriott (ex Swansea), prop Kevin Neale (ex London Irish), while hooker Simon Luxmore and lock Nick Williams (both Somerset players) joined from Clifton, and Penryn full-back Chris Martin (on a sports-scholarship at Bath University) joined too. What odds then of reaching Twickenham and clutching that prized John Player (JP) Cup? Would inter-club results provide any clues? Would fate intervene yet again? Anyone's guess! But Lye's squad made a good start. Wins at Moseley, Neath and home success against the calibre of Leicester, Aberavon, Maesteg (their first ever visit to Bath), Coventry, Harlequins and London Welsh was 'some' hit-list. Then late season came a brilliant treble over Wales's finest. First Newport fell 9-3, where Phil Turner (ex Bristol) showed the sheer strength in depth at Bath's disposal with a rampant back-row performance alongside Gerry Parsons. Then there followed wins over Llanelli (16-3) and Cardiff (18-11) for a season's total of 30 victories. But, there was no reason for complacency either as upsets at Pontypool, then home against Wasps, and home and away defeats to Gloucester were a warning-signal that nothing could be taken for granted.

In March 1981 however the committee (to the bemusement of many, and that's putting it mildly) withdrew Bath from the Somerset K.O. Cup (not to be confused with the South West Merit Table) for the following 1981-2 season, notwithstanding that victory in the Somerset competition guaranteed entry into the 1st round proper of the 1982-3 National K.O. Cup. True, the withdrawal allowed for a degree of respite from the growing intensity of senior rugby. But Bath had best keep their fingers crossed that they would gain a top-four Merit Table place come season 1981-2, as this too ensured entry to the 1982-3 National Cup; because if they didn't there would be no Somerset Cup to rescue them since they had already withdrawn from that competition, although they could probably have won it with reserves. As for the current 1980-1 John Player Cup campaign, Bath travelled to Nottingham, having overcome Richmond in a Horton-inspired 6-12 away victory in January. But the Nottingham game was played on a quagmire of a pitch covered completely under water until only hours prior to kick-off. Even so *"Bath dominated most of the match."* With half-backs Steve Lewis (now returned from Welsh club rugby) and Horton controlling tactics with *"sound kicking for position"* they led from a Charlie Ralston penalty. But, with ten minutes remaining the referee, according to Bath, *"indicated he was awarding them a penalty when Nottingham strayed offside at a ruck and hounded Horton into error."* However, the referee then *"deferred his decision for advantage."* But since *"Horton's clearance went straight to an opponent"* Bath claimed that there 'was' no advantage. Worse followed when Nottingham's Baron Bedford collected Horton's clearance and countered with a speculative kick ahead from which home winger Clive Pitts ran on to score an unconverted try for a 4-3 cup victory.

Would that 'damn' Cup curse ever go away? Would dreams of John Player Cup glory ever be fulfilled?

The following 1981-2 season would again be both eventful and painful. A prestigious England Trial (Chronicle, 10th Dec. 1981) was re-located to the Rec, only to be re-directed back to Twickenham come the following week, and it was already confirmed by early Autumn that club captain Damien Murphy (cartilage problem) would likely miss most if not all the remainder of the season. This proved especially regrettable for Damien Murphy personally, but disruptive too for a club whose pre-season preparations had included a carefully planned rugby tour of Florida, but who now were saddled with a major captaincy headache, temporally solved by a somewhat ad hoc arrangement with vice-captain Spurrell taking over at the helm. Complicating matters further he too suffered a fractured jaw, and Horton stepped into the breach on a temporary care-taker basis until Spurrell's return. Not surprisingly, captaincy-changes combined with injury problems disrupted on-field performances, though by no means always. Indeed, despite heavy defeats that included a 41-0 drubbing at Swansea and a 57-15 shocker at Llanelli, wins against Moseley, Neath, Harlequins, Coventry and Newport for example showed that Bath had not lost their winning touch. Moreover, during this same period the committee showed its faith in its coaching triumvirate by granting Rowell, Robson and Hudson the unqualified freedom to decide team tactics, strategy and training for the foreseeable future.

Their task of moulding an English club (in this case Bath) with long experience against Wales's finest would shortly come to magnificent fruition, and helped not least by the arrival of Scotland B hooker Rob Cunningham from Gosforth, highly promising England Colts back-row forward Jon Hall, nor forgetting lock Nigel Gaymond from Bristol; although it would be some three months (Chronicle, 1st Mar. 1982) before Gaymond sensed that he was now fully fledged 'blue, white and black,' and so in a position to make comparisons: Bath *are a different club with different attitudes.....perhaps even friendlier though not always quite as competitive. They have their own ways of doing things here and it takes time to acclimatise. Now I'm beginning to enjoy it."* Gaymond's words would have resonated with many newcomers and his switch to Bath was soon rewarded with an established place in the Bath 'engine room' alongside another recent arrival, namely Irish international and line-out specialist Ronnie Hakin. A vital new second-row partnership had thus been discovered at a critical time. The arrival too of Oxford Blue centre Simon Halliday, a fast and superbly balanced runner and Halliday's Dark Blue colleague and back-row forward Tony Brooks was an added bonus. Bath's open-house recruitment policy further attracted others from less fashionable rugby backgrounds too. Indeed ex St. Luke's student Mitch Patching arrived as an established soccer player good enough to have run-out for Eastbourne (Borough), a club that at times had competed in the ranks of the National Conference League. Yet Patching, in leading the pack in Bath's January 27-0 rout of Northampton, proved he sure could play a 'mean' game of rugby too. Furthermore, Berkshire county utility forward Roy Matthews (formerly Maidenhead RFC) who, though not a regular 1st teamer, would then perform like a seasoned veteran in Bath's November 18-22 victory at Coventry, an encounter that Matthews stated was *"a memory he will always treasure."* *(Remarkable how some players from so-called Junior clubs perform so well when thrust into the Senior rugby game!).*

Yet while new players arrived, others were departing, among them the seemingly ageless Jim Waterman who in September at Newport had played his 415th game for Bath at 36 years of age. By now deputy-headmaster at 950-pupil Stockwell Hill school, Bristol, he spoke warmly of his days on the Rec, remarking that *"Bath's rugby has certainly changed over the last 14 years, and mainly for the better,"* though adding that the game is now *".....more competitive, winning is more important than it used to be, and no club can afford to stand still or they could be left behind."* Leaving too was the forthright Derek Wyatt (a future MP for Sittingbourne, (Kent)) who suggested that the game should adopt 'professional administrators, club officials with relatively recent playing experience, fewer games and smaller committees.' And he concluded (Chronicle, 8th Apr. 1982) with these challenging words: *"Professionalism is coming, like it or not. Rugby is lagging behind and changes may not arrive until the 1990's....but there is no doubt that they are on the way."* His predictions would prove to be uncannily accurate. Furthermore, the perceptive winger had already raised an issue that would now 'hit the club for six' during the same current 1981-2 season when stating: *"We still, amazingly, do not have all our merit table matches on a Saturday, [and] thereby put at risk our considerable reputation, not to mention endangering our bank balance."*

And, as sure as night follows day, Bath not only dropped out of the JP Cup by way of their opening round 9-11 defeat at home to Rosslyn Park, they would then learn that the South West Merit Table was anything but a 'level playing field.' Yes, they had comfortably defeated Plymouth Albion and Camborne, who ironically both qualified for the 1982-3 JP Cup along with Bristol and Gloucester. But unlike Bath, Camborne did not play Gloucester. Moreover, Albion's request (owing to four players on County duty) for their game with Gloucester to be excluded from the table was granted; notwithstanding that Gloucester (with ten regulars absent) chose from the outset to accept the result and duly won. It was literally beyond parody, yet so avoidable. For if Bath had won the Somerset Cup in season 1981-2 (highly likely), another direct route into the National Cup in season 1982-3 would have been their's on a plate. Just one problem: the committee had *not* entered the club for the 1981-2 Somerset Cup. Yes, the farce continued; and it wasn't particularly funny either.

Therefore, despite the season's highly commendable 29 wins, Bath could only feel a sense of under-achievement; and it hardly helped matters that rivals Gloucester reached Twickenham for their third final, sharing the spoils from a 12-12 drawn game with Moseley. But if nothing else, the Bath committee had at long last learned salutary lessons. They promptly took out the 'insurance-policy' offered by the club's entry to the Somerset Cup for the following 1982-3 season, and credit where credit is due, they would rarely, if ever, put a foot wrong again. Indeed, by the conclusion of the following 1982-3 season the media in general rated Bath among the best club-sides in England, though at the outset it seemed best to hedge one's bets when skipper Spurrell's team were *"crushed 37-16 by [the] Pontypool pack"* in September. Within a week however calm was restored with a 24-15 home win over Leicester, then a 3-12 success at Newport; and aside from the fact that this was only Bath's second win at Rodney Parade in their history, it was the sheer quality of this performance that gave hint of the events that would follow in the second half of the season. Trick too had returned from a gap-year in the U.S.A., and John Stevens (Chronicle, 23rd Sep. 1982) duly described the impact of the winger's return at Newport. Within seven minutes Trick's *"smouldering pace burst into flame when he was launched into flight almost from his own line by the combined skills of John Horton and Alun Watkins. Horton played a miss-ball move to Alun Watkins who drew the opposing wing brilliantly before setting Trick away on a blistering 60 yards run deep into the home half. He wriggled out of one cover tackle and then outwitted the defence before his inside pass sent centre Alun Rees away for a crucial try score."* Trick was back! And when in October he bolted over for a try-treble with an England XV against the touring Fijians at Twickenham he duly confirmed the faith of then England skipper Steve Smith, who previously had proclaimed Trick as *"the fastest man I have seen on a rugby pitch for ten years."* One now dared to hope that perhaps everything was 'coming right' for a serious JP Cup challenge, and talent continued to make a pilgrimage to the Rec, including back-row forward Paul Simpson (Gosforth's 'player of the Year' the previous season), Young England Colts lock John Morrison, and later hooker Kevin Adams (Avon & Somerset Police), plus brilliant scrum-half prospect Richard Hill from St. Luke's College, Exeter. However, the RFU's announcement that 'all' County Championship games must in future be played on pre-set Saturday dates divided opinion. So Bath for example, from whom Somerset now relied for most of their County side, found themselves depleted of no fewer than 21 players on certain County weekends, supplying thirteen for Somerset, five for Dorset & Wilts, two for Cornwall and one to Northumberland. It was a heavy drain on player-resources. But then that's success for you!

Come November and with County duties now receding, two notable away wins against Harlequins (7-21) and at still formidable London Scottish (9-21), suggested that Bath might be set for a highly successful second half of the 1982-3 campaign, save that in early December one mighty test for supremacy remained in their path.....Gloucester! That Bath possessed the better backs was not in dispute. But that was no guarantee of victory against such formidable masters of the forward game, not least since in recent years some doubts remained concerning Bath's own strength at forward. Another question remained as yet unanswered regarding the leadership-style of ex-paratrooper and Bath skipper Roger Spurrell. Indeed but for injury, Damien Murphy would likely have remained club captain, and the flaxen-haired Spurrell himself admitted in early season that *"the responsibility of captaincy got to me and perhaps I was thinking about it too much....I was more worried about what people were doing around me than what I was doing myself. I forgot to play my own game.*" In which case against Gloucester he was about to remember how to play his own game, because instead of relying on the backs, Spurrell's Bath went straight for the jugular and chose instead to battle it out at forward, and battle it was! In previous years such a strategy would likely have been suicidal. But not this time, not with this headstrong Cornishman in charge, and on a cold winter's day two packs proceeded to 'slug it out' with no prisoners taken. As John Stevens reported, the "*game wasn't so much full-blooded, but rather full of blood, with punches being thrown with abandon, boots used for anything but the purpose intended and ugly brawls reviving memories of the bad old days.*" In addition, Bath prop Richard Lee and Gloucester flanker Mike Teague got marching orders for fighting "*in a bruising encounter in which no quarter was asked or given.*" This was as hard as it gets in West Country rugby, and that 'is' hard! For not since the 1950's and the teams of Alec Lewis and John Roberts had a Bath captain so much as dreamt of challenging Gloucester in a trial of strength at forward. Yet this was the strategy that Spurrell chose to adopt and without a second thought. Moreover, the resultant psychological effect from this 21-12 victory was to be profound. Thus, a front row of Gareth Chilcott, Rob Cunningham, Richard Lee, supported by locks Nigel Gaymond and Ron Hakin, and the back-row of Roger Spurrell, Phil Turner and Paul Simpson had given notice of Bath's ability to match head-on arguably the most feared pack in England. And on that same dank December day a unique Cornish captain had been born.

On New Year's Day 1983 Leicester avenged their earlier setback on the Rec with their own 21-9 win at Welford Road. Yet Spurrell's team would never look back from that moment; instead, they were now set to add a new chapter to the story of not merely Bath, but English rugby too, and arguably it was to be among the most remarkable (and certainly the most unexpected) chapters ever written. It commenced with a 16-11 home win over still impressive London Welsh, and would then lead to a 26 match unbeaten run that apart from two draws would scatter all opposition to the four corners of England and Wales. Northampton (16-19), Ebbw Vale (3-7) Plymouth Albion (3-30) and the final 15-30 success at Bedford ranked among the away wins; while Rosslyn Park (35-12), Swansea (30-14), Llanelli (31-28) and Maesteg (45-10) were included among a galaxy of home victories. Indeed, even at fortress Kingsholm the hard men of Gloucester could get no closer than a 7-7 draw; while Bristol, destined for a 28-22 JP Cup Final triumph against Leicester, were defeated 21-16 in their April run-in to Twickenham. However, it was John Mason's report for the Daily Telegraph following Bath's emphatic 28-9 win over Cardiff in late April that typified the reaction of the National Press to a West Country revival that could no longer be ignored. "***Mighty Bath bring back the smiles***" was the banner headline, John Mason writing thus:

"*Bath are proud of impressive statistics that reflect a successful season. But the figures alone convey only part of the commitment and little of the enjoyment a well-drilled side have created for all concerned since early January. On Saturday Bath demolished Cardiff, which few English clubs ever do.....*" "*So even before Jack Simpkins, Bath's secretary whose family have been associated with the club for generations, says simply: 'this is the best side we've ever had in my time,' there is a temptation to sit up and take notice. The manner of the dissection of Cardiff bore out practically every expectation. Bath's players have confidence in themselves and in each other. There is a warming team spirit readily obvious and, dare I say it, they have re-learned to play with a smile. That the match also had explosive moments of temper told a story too. To assert a waning authority Peter Hughes - at his best one of England's better referees – had to lecture the captains, neither, presumably, entirely used to the role of gamekeeper.*

Martin, Bath's fullback, Halliday, maturing splendidly, and the canny Horton, cleverly pulling the strings, headed the better attacks, while opposite them, Ring showed plainly why the Welsh selectors promoted him for the match against England. Then there was Trick, full of running and the searing speed to go on the outside. Nor did Lakin and Golding cease in their efforts in Cardiff's back row. Yet of all the medals I would cast, the most handsome would go to Hakin and Simpson, sterling Bath forwards." Trevaskis, Halliday, Trick and Martin scored Bath's tries, Palmer converting three and landing two penalty goals. Cordle got across for Cardiff on the right, a forward pass having been permitted on the left, and Ring kicked the conversion and a penalty goal."

Barry Trevaskis: The Cornish flyer became a record try scorer.

Acknowledgements: Bath Past Players

Thus Bath would then complete the most successful season in their history, a season too when David Trick in March against Ireland would win the first of his two full England caps at Lansdown Road. And fortuitously, Bath's non-appearance in the JP Cup had allowed them to concentrate solely on blending a squad into near perfection. In fact, they cruised home with both the South West Merit Table and the Somerset Cup, a **new club record of 38 victories**, 3 draws and a mere 9 defeats. No fewer than 205 tries were scored, a new record of 1,278 points was amassed and **the 32 try total of wing Barry Trevaskis broke the previous 29-try record** held jointly by George Haydon (1930-1) and Derek Wyatt (1978-9). Indeed, as John Steven's concluded, this was a *"rugby season to savour for years to come."* Yet it would prove to be even more than that: because it was the season that literally changed everything!

Chapter 28. THE YEAR of DESTINY. (1983-4)

As Bath launched their campaign for 1983-4 it seemed that this was a club with everything, including their flamboyant rugby that could often brighten even the darkest of winter days. Yet one task remained....triumph in the National JP K.O. Cup! And until they captured this trophy they would remain indefinitely under the shadow of their closest and greatest rivals....Bristol and Gloucester! Moreover, doubts still persisted, since so many pitfalls had befallen them, some self-inflicted, some not. Furthermore, would call-ups for the re-vamped (Thorn EMI) County Championship exhaust Bath resources to breaking-point, or, might this updated competition provide invaluable knock-out cup experience that could enhance the quest for JP Cup glory?

As regards the County front, Dorset & Wilts would play in the 4th Division grouping; Somerset (virtually a Bath team by another name) playing in the First Division. And fascinatingly, Somerset's County Cup progress would run almost parallel to that of Bath in the JP K.O. Cup. Indeed, the first signs of this came with Somerset's 15-12 win over Lancashire in October on the Rec. It was close, though achieved against one of 'the' best county sides in England, and the post-match assessment of Red Rose skipper James Syddall was pertinent: *"they [Somerset] were superbly disciplined and deserved to win."* Furthermore, Somerset coach Jack Rowell was moved to add that *"We've finally learned how to play cup rugby...."* And since 13 players in Somerset ranks that day hailed from Bath, Rowell was surely referring to both county and club.

The County's next stop was partisan Exeter (Devon) in late October, returning home with a commendable 18-27 win under their belts. There followed a narrow 10-9 defeat of Middlesex at Bridgwater in November, though a win at a sickening price, one evident from the moment that the brilliant Simon Halliday dropped like a stone with *"a horrendous dislocation and double fracture of the left ankle after 32 minutes."* It was freakish, but side-lined Halliday for the remainder of the season, delayed his already predicted international career and left his Somerset colleagues visibly shaken by the event. Neil Hopkins, now with Weston-super-Mare, deputised commendably, but the serious injury had cast a shadow over the Somerset post-match dressing room. The subsequent semi-final 15-12 win against Yorkshire in November on the Rec did not come at a price, but rather a controversy, when a drop-goal attempt from John Horton failed to carry over the bar, albeit allowed by the referee. So, 'what's to do' in such situations? True, one could inform the referee that 'he's got it wrong!' Yet, how many tries for example are claimed and awarded that are not tries? Or how many tries are fairly grounded but are disallowed? Who really knows? All one can do, and in this case the media and many in a four thousand crowd indeed 'did do,' was to point out the error. But for hapless Yorkshire, who played bravely and sportingly, there was honour in defeat. For Somerset, openly admitting that luck was on their side, there would be their first county final since 1939.

Bath, not least thanks to experience where they least expected to find it, namely the re-vamped County Championship, now turned their efforts to the JP Cup; and two impressive victories in October and November respectively demonstrated that they had not lost their dazzling touches of the previous season. First Neath were overcome 67-0 (then Bath's biggest-ever win over Welsh opponents), and a total so remarkable that BBC Wales phoned back to the Rec to have the score verified before announcing the result. Eleven tries were grounded, John Palmer converting ten, and the Bath Chronicle's John Stevens was left near speechless, although sufficiently composed to report that it was simply a *"day when the superlatives ran out."* One week later and Bath headed for Newbridge, unfashionable maybe but a highly dangerous outfit. Indeed, having dispatched the proposed South and South West team (now preparing for action against the touring All Blacks) with a 21-6 win only days previously, Newbridge looked good enough to avenge Bath for daring to inflict such humiliation upon Welsh reputations. But Bath duly proved to a large and sporting home crowd 'exactly' why they had overcome Neath, and with supposedly reserve back-row forward Phil Turner playing as if he was an international regular, Bath put a stranglehold on the game to secure a highly impressive 12-22 away victory.

There was nonetheless one team during this period, perhaps the only team, who were capable of 80 minutes of rugby-power such that no team could hold them. They went by the name of Pontypool, pride of Monmouthshire and a side formed around men who crafted steel in the mills and hacked coal deep down in the mines; and only days before Christmas they departed from those same mills and mines to avenge those 'English upstarts' who had ran amok against Neath and then on sacred Welsh soil had overran Newbridge! Furthermore 'Pool' had come prepared with a strategy, one brilliant in its simplicity. So it was that these visitors from the Valleys duly controlled the entire match around the might of their forwards, an eight so dominant it had to be seen to be believed. Welsh international forwards Graham Price, Eddie Butler and Jeff Squire looked world class, while the tactical kicking of halfbacks Dave Bishop and Mike Galsworthy was simply copybook precision. Their grip was vice-like. They dominated the line-out for their half-backs to boot kicks 40-45 yards upfield. Then when near the Bath 25 they struck, sending the ball out wide and four 'Pool' tries resulted that included a hat-trick for young debut winger Pat Hayes. It was stunning. It was thought-provoking, and Bath were left to ponder a 6-23 defeat on home soil. And....when the final whistle echoed into the dark night sky the Rec fell strangely quiet. With Bath less than four weeks away from their opening (3rd round) JP Cup clash with Headingley, this scale of upset could hardly have come at a worse time. Or so it seemed. But, the indelible Pontypool footprint of that chastening defeat was to swiftly reveal that Bath were a highly adaptable team, one able to employ these self-same ruthless 'Pool' tactics when deemed necessary. In fact, barely one week later powerful Northampton were overcome 16-6 on the Rec, with forwards Chris Folland, Gregg Bess, Nick Maslen and Oxford Blue Tony Brooks prominent in a pack that, with Horton's astute kicking, adopted a game-plan strikingly similar to that so forcefully employed by Pontypool. While come January Bath gained another tonic of a win with a highly impressive 9-40 victory at London Welsh, their first success at The Welsh for twenty-four years.

Two weeks later Headingley arrived, and this time Bath were taking absolutely no chances whatsoever. The Yorkshiremen were highly rated, though not seen in Bath for over thirty years. Moreover, if Northern sides Wilmslow and Morpeth had proved capable of overcoming Bath in the K.O. Cup, then a major club such as Headingley posed a real danger. So, Brendan Perry, now a selector, was dispatched to Devon, there to attend an Exeter v Headingley game and prepare a pre-match dossier. Firstly, wrote Brendan Perry, Headingley were coached by former Scotland three-quarter Ian McGeechen (later a British Lions coach) and the experienced Peter Nash. Secondly, they possessed a rich seam of county experience that included England back-row forward Peter Winterbottom. Third, three players (members of the Yorkshire semi-final team against Somerset) were now acquainted with the Rec. Not surprisingly therefore, Perry advised caution: *"Don't underestimate them. They are nobody's fools."* There was a further warning: *"if we decide to mix it with them, I think we could be in for a tough time....I feel we will do better if we run the ball wide."* Running it wide!? Then Bath, haunted still by memories of rain-soaked Cup encounters in seasons gone by, could only pray that the conditions would be kind to them. Headingley, *"whose pack, under the tireless Winterbottom, did a great disruptive job in the scoreless first half,"* were eventually overcome 17-0 in an encounter played on a damp surface that nonetheless allowed for a degree of open rugby. In the second half Bath tightened their grip as Barry Trevaskis stormed over for the opening try. Richard Hill then struck for home with a 40 yard burst to launch Horton for a second try, Ralston converting. Finally, Bath stamped their overall superiority with a perfectly executed try by Chris Martin. *"It was perhaps [Bath's] best-ever cup performance,"* commented Jack Rowell.

Another performance in November, with a TV audience of millions, saw England conclude a 15-9 victory at Twickenham against New Zealand and a performance that would earn national media acclaim for Bath's unstoppable flanker Paul Simpson. Come February and Simpson was picked for England again, this time against Scotland in Edinburgh, with Jon Hall, 21 years old, duly winning his first cap as a replacement, and Richard Hill then capped by England during their summer tour of South Africa. That made it a trio of new Bath internationals in one season, an honour they had never achieved before. Honours notwithstanding, nothing would diminish the club's hunger for JP Cup success, and not even the psychological 'lift' from their commanding 13-6 home victory against Gloucester in early February would allow Bath to fall into the fatal trap of over-confidence when heading to Blackheath for further cup action with ten straight wins behind them. The 'Club' would now be the eleventh, albeit a biting east wind swept across the Rectory Field with only a modest crowd of 1500 brave souls present to witness the hosts closing the first half with a 12-7 lead. Come the restart however Spurrell's team cut loose. Six tries were run home, John Palmer kicking conversions and penalties galore, and Bath swept to a 12-41 victory. Another mission accomplished, leading Blackheath chairman of selectors John Williams, formerly of Bath Combination club Old Sulians, to comment thus: *"I just can't see anyone touching Bath on this sort of showing. What a back row they've got and what pace in the back division."* True, one London club had been overcome away. But the next would be London club Wasps, thankfully on the Rec,

There now followed a brief period when Bath could relax (well sort of) from the pressures of Cup campaigns, so allowing a happy crew to journey westwards in late February for an evening floodlit game at Exeter. Charlie Gabittas, a recent recruit from Plymouth Albion, was awarded his debut for Bath and the Devonian county out-half promptly returned the compliment with his own converted try, a second conversion and a 40 yard penalty gem from wide out. Meanwhile at both forward and outside a victorious Bath dictated events throughout, and until late into the game it seemed that an equally happy Bath would travel back home again that same evening. That is until minutes from the final whistle when something (or possible nothing) caused a flurry of fists involving just about everyone in the two packs. However, to the utter dismay of Bath someone got their 'marching orders,' and that someone was prop Gareth Chilcott. At the very least an automatic 30-day suspension was an absolute certainty!

Now, despite that twice during his six previous seasons at Bath this courageous player had been lifted from the base of a collapsed scrum with knee injuries so severe that his entire rugby career had seemed threatened, Chilcott had what is commonly termed in rugby circles as 'previous.' Moreover, this opinion was partly based upon a near one-year suspension in season 1981-2 for 'dangerous use of the boot' during a Bath v Bristol derby on the Rec. That was not all, because the Somerset disciplinary committee had emphasised that if Chilcott was sent off again then he 'could expect a very long sentence indeed, and much longer than the previous one imposed.' This caveat in particular filled Bath supporters with trepidation, because if applied then Chilcott, assuming that Bath reached Twickenham, would be side-lined. On the homeward journey there were simply no words in the English language that could comfort a totally disconsolate Chilcott. There was just one glimmer of hope however, namely that the Bath prop was by no means the only sinner in 'that' rumpus nor was he necessarily the culprit who even started it, so providing at least one mitigating factor that might just influence the decision of the disciplinary committee. Indeed, all the circumstances were taken into consideration, though Chilcott did not escape entirely since his otherwise certain Somerset selection for the Thorn EMI County final was blocked by the additional two weeks added to the 30-day suspension. But crucially, if Bath should reach Twickenham then Chilcott would be available.

Two weeks later in March a tense crowd of 6,000 witnessed two of the top performing clubs in England contest the JP Cup quarter-final. The atmosphere was electric; the Wasps pack commented Jack Rowell was *"one of the biggest collection of opponents I have ever seen;"* and the teams 'on paper' were so evenly matched that it was virtually impossible to make any meaningful pre-match forecast. But there was one strategic decision that was to prove decisive, namely Rowell's insistence that in the event of Bath requiring replacements, specialist cover must be available at both scrum-half and at hooker. Sure enough, within 30 minutes Bath replacements Chris Stanley and Greg Bess (scrum-half and hooker respectively) were required to fill the key gaps left by injuries to scrum-half Richard Hill and hooker Rob Cunningham. This proved critical as Wasps, on losing scrum-half John Cullen in the first half were now dependent on out-half replacement Mike Boyd, and the change to the balance of the two sides was immediate as Boyd for all his efforts was not comfortable at scrum-half. No such problem hindered Bath however. Instead, they now looked the more confident team, since both the experienced Stanley and Bess knew their respective trades well. Even so Wasps proved mighty opponents. Out-half Mark Williams sent home a smart drop-goal, likewise Nick Stringer a conversion and penalty, while their immense pack steamrolled over for a push-over try by Andy Dun (and not many sides did that to Bath). Yet Spurrell's men maintained their composure despite huge Wasps pressure. Horton, (diagonal kicks here and sudden breaks there) was a master tactician as always. Nigel Gaymond crashed over from a tap penalty (and not many players did that to Wasps). Then with tensions mounting in the final period and the result still wide open, Horton suddenly created space into the right flank 'box' for David Trick to race home for his first try. Next, with a crucial victory within their sights, but not as yet certain, the excellent Stanley chipped over a perfectly placed drop-kick into the same box for Trick to pounce for Bath's third try. Meanwhile John Palmer, a picture of calmness throughout, accounted for four penalties and a conversion. The final whistle then blew, bringing the curtain down on a day that brought credit to the game, utter dejection to Wasps, yet sheer elation (and relief) among a winning Bath team.

A semi-final away at Nottingham now beckoned, but for the fact that a storm sweeping across their Beeston ground was so intense that the tie was postponed. So, priorities immediately reverted back to the Thorn EMI County Championship, and a spate of late injuries within the Somerset camp led to a county debut for Bath prop Chris Lilley and further late call-ups for Chris Stanley (scrum-half) and hooker Greg Bess on the eve of the final. Furthermore, Bristol wing Gareth Williams was side-lined by injury and so Bath winger Paul Simmons was rushed into the Somerset line-up. Hence on the day, with Twickenham blessed with Spring sunshine, fourteen Bath players strode on to the field for **Somerset: *C. Ralston, D. Trick, (R. Hopkins, W.s.Mare, 75 mins), J.Palmer, A. Rees, P. Simmons, J. Horton (capt.), C. Stanley, C. Lilley, G. Bess, R. Lee, P. Stiff (Bristol), R. Hakin, J. Hall, R. Spurrell (P. Turner, 55 mins), P. Simpson.*** The encounter, watched by an estimated 20,000 West Country crowd, was to be a day that undoubtedly belonged to Gloucestershire. For Somerset, their revised front-row facing a Gloucestershire eight that included the awesome front-three of Phil Blakeway, Steve Mills and Malcolm Preedy, it was to prove too much. It was no surprise therefore that Gloucestershire took try-count honours with six from backs Ralph Knibbs, Stuart Barnes, Alan Morley (2), Richard Harding and forward Simon Hogg. While despite a lone late try (and a good one) from Alun Rees, Gloucestershire coasted home for an impressive 36-18 victory. Somerset nonetheless were humble in defeat, acknowledging the strength of their opponents, and as John Horton commented post-match: *"We were beaten by a far better all-round side on the day."*

Now however attention turned to the J.P. Cup semi-final at Nottingham, a strong all-round team without any weaknesses. Forwards Neil Mantle (England), Gary Rees (later England cap) and not least future England full-back Simon Hodgkinson were class. In addition, not only did Nottingham enjoy vital home advantage, their Beeston ground was a place of painful past memories. But on 7th April Beeston conditions were suitable for open rugby and albeit scrum-half Richard Hill and hooker Rob Cunningham were side-lined by injury, their respective deputies Chris Stanley and Gregg Bess had already proved against Wasps that they could 'handle' the demands of the big occasion. Likewise, young lock Nigel Redman, already an England U.23 international, was drafted into the Bath pack owing to Ronnie Hakin's withdrawal with flu. Bath's strategy, despite dry conditions, was only partly based upon the 15-man running game. Instead, it was more orthodox, with a front-five containment of Nottingham's formidable forwards, supported by the back-row mobility of Spurrell, Jon Hall and Simpson, and not forgetting the astute tactical kicking of the peerless Horton. Bath took few risks and the encounter developed into a grim struggle of attrition. Specialist kicker Hodgkinson then put the home side ahead with a penalty after 30 minutes, with the score remaining on a knife-edge until the final 15 minutes. Meanwhile, though second-half injuries had led to the retirement of John Palmer at centre and lock Nigel Gaymond, Charlie Ralston and Jon Morrison proved excellent cover, and crucially Bath maintained their composure. Indeed, during the last quarter their game-plan paid off! The Nottingham pack had been neutralised and their backs worn down by non-stop tackling as *"Bath took a firmer grip with pressure rugby which forced Nottingham into error...."* Ralston then slotted home two penalties, his second from 40 yards, and finally as *"Nottingham became increasingly desperate"* Bath prop Chris Lilley, to his great surprise (and everyone else's) found himself in the unlikely position of outside-half. But that was not all! Because Lilley (this time to his team-mates' astonishment) then calmly flighted a perfect diagonal kick that was pure John Horton over the Nottingham defence and into the box, and who should be there to seize the ball but David Trick! A try was his for the taking and Ralston, calmness personified, strode up to stroke the ball home for the conversion and a 3-12 victory. Oh, the sheer joy! The exhilaration! Twickenham lay ahead! And by extraordinary coincidence Bath would face Bristol!

With all thoughts now on Twickenham, the entire club (and city) had gone cup-crazy. Yet the inter-club programme was not over, and with players noticeably wary of injury, Bath cautiously won 22-19 against Llanelli but, Chilcott now ran out for his first game since suspension. He had continued hard training during his absence, looked in fine fettle, and everyone was just delighted to see him back! But, injury concerns for Richard Hill (among others) remained and team secretary David Lamb could only inform the media that Hill *"is now much happier and hopes to be playing over Easter."* Thank goodness then for the club's increasingly 'professional' medical and physio' staff (currently led by chartered physiotherapist Gareth George) who worked flat-out to get the 'A' team up and running for the final. No simple task as *"the games are much more competitive, and also simply because at this time of year the ground tends to be rather hard and unyielding if you hit it heavily"* Gareth George explained. Less of a problem was the clash of shirt colours between Bath and Bristol, a matter that was resolved by the simple toss of a coin at the Rugby Union. Bath won the call, hence were classed as the home side and therefore would wear their 'away' strip on the day! *"Say that again?"* one asks, doubtless bemused that a home team would be compelled to wear their 'away' colours. But, rules are rules as they say, and according to the custom of rugby union it was the home side 'who were required to change their normal strip should a colour-clash occur.' Bath anyway were happy to oblige and delighted to learn that they would be allocated use of the England 'home' dressing room. Nor were there objections raised regarding the sum of £3,375 guaranteed to both clubs from John Player as the finalists' share of the sponsor's £95,000 total for that season's cup competition. OK, in hindsight such figures seem a mere trifle compared to later sponsorship, but not then they didn't. Nor were there any qualms with the appointment of international referee Roger Quittenton to officiate the final. True, few referees are favourites with every team, and make no mistake Quittenton (of the London & Sussex society) was firm, indeed a little too firm for some peoples' liking. But he was unstintingly fair, and his eve-of-match comments to the Bath Chronicle were an insight into the character of the titanic struggle that lay ahead: *"I know what Bath-Bristol derbies can be like, but having controlled both clubs and knowing so many of their top players so well, I don't think there will be any problems."* Significant words, as events would reveal.

There only remained last-minute fitness tests prior to Bath announcing that they would be fielding their first-choice fifteen. Sadly, this determined that there would be no place for admired Irish international Ronnie Hakin, as the extra scrum power of Nigel Redmond was deemed critical in the expected set-piece phases against the street-wise Bristol pack. There was ironically one X factor however, not picked up by the press, namely that dominating 36-18 County Championship triumph inflicted by Gloucestershire (with a strong Bristol contingent) against a Somerset team fielding a virtual Bath team. Might not Bristol, as some suggested, be lulled into over-confidence? Maybe? It was John Stevens however whose prophetic pre-match analysis (Bath Chronicle) would be as close as any to where and how the game would be won when suggesting that the *"battle with Spurrell, Jon Hall and Paul Simpson in the loose probably holds the key."* Thus, come 28th April 1984 all the euphoria of reaching Twickenham was tempered with the realities of the mammoth task facing Bath. Bristol were current cup holders, a team for the big occasion, a club who in the public perception still overshadowed Bath. But, could the long-time underdogs now overcome that awesome and ultimate challenge asked of them at the conclusion of their Centenary year? This was the time for answers!

Bristol: *P. Cue, A,Morley, R. Knibbs, S. Hogg, J.F. Carr, S. Barnes, R. Harding, R. Doubleday, D.J. Palmer, A. Sheppard, N. Pomphrey, P. Stiff, P. Polledri, D. Chidgey, M.Rafter (capt.).Replacements: I. Duggan, J.Watson, L.Yandell, D. Hickey, K.Bogita.*

Bath: *C.R.Martin, D. Trick, J.A. Palmer, A. Rees, B. Trevaskis, J. Horton, R.Hill, G. Chilcott, R. Cunningham, M.R. Lee, N. Gaymond, N. Redman, R. Spurrrell (Capt.), J.P. Hall, P. Simpson. Replacements: A. Watkins, C. Stanley, C. Lilley, G. Bess, R. Hakin, P.*

Roger Spurrell and Bath's 1984 Cup Final team…. L to R (top) **D. Robson (coach), G. George (Physio), C. Stanley, R. Cunnigham, G.Bess, A. Watkins, P. Turner, N. Redman, N. Gaymond, J. Hall, R. Lee, C. Martin, C. Liley, A. Rees, R. Hakin, P. Simpson, J. Rowell (Coach).** (Front) **P. Pothecray (Medical), B. Trevaskis, J. Palmer, J. Horton, R. Spurrell (Capt.), R. Hill, D. Trick, G. Chilcott. (Twickenham 1984)**

Acknowledgements: Bath Chronicle

As John Stevens had predicted a key influence of this do-or-die battle was Bath's back-row of Spurrell, Jon Hall and Paul Simpson; another was the tactical mastery of out-half John Horton whose drop-goal within the opening five minutes would steady Bath nerves and show Bristol that this was going to be a long day. Both back divisions oozed class, and Trick's speed was a potential match-winner upon the firm, open Twickenham spaces. But risk-taking was for another day. For this game was above all about forward supremacy, and the dynamic first-half performance of that supreme Bath back-row dominated both ruck and maul, leading to Simpson's unstoppable charge for the line and the game's first try. The swirling Twickenham wind played its mischievous part too, seemingly unsettling John Palmer who failed with his first four opening-half penalty attempts, but who landed a touchline gem just prior to the interval. But with danger man Stuart Barnes notching an earlier penalty for Bristol it was obvious that the 10-3 half-time score was too close for Bath as yet to risk running the ball wide. Yet there was one second-half certainty, because sooner or later Bristol would be compelled to fight back. Pressure mounted. Bristol's back-division was fed the ball more frequently. The Bath

Redman (5) charges into Bath's pack against Bristol, inches from try-line.
Rees (12) awaits.
Acknowledgments Derek Carter

163

defence was now seriously tested. For the 21,000 crowd who could 'but stand and stare,' the unfolding drama was almost frightening in its intensity. But the Bath defence held firm save but once, when within 15 minutes of the re-start scrum-half Richard Harding darted through from close range for a try, Barnes converting. With the score poised on a knife-edge at 10-9 some 25 minutes of play remained, and during this torturous period the historic balance of power between Bath and Bristol literally hung in the balance. "*Not an inch was asked or given,*" wrote John Stevens, and although at times it seemed that Bristol might break through the Bath defence, "*they were ruthlessly scythed down by Bath's devasting tackling.*" But, in the final minute Bath's Barry Trevaskis, who had defended like 'Horatio on the bridge' throughout the match, felled England wing Alan Morley with a late tackle. It was a penalty, wide out on the right, and young Stuart Barnes would take it. The master kicker, whose five penalties and a conversion had proved decisive in Bristol's 21-18 semi-final win over Harlequins, who now steadied himself for the crucial kick. Twickenham fell silent. Barnes struck the ball. It went high, it went long but....maybe that curious Twickenham wind intervened as the kick veered off target. Quittenton's whistle blew. It would not be heard again that day.

Thousands of joyous Bath supporters now swarmed over the wide Twickenham spaces, glowing in pride as Roger Spurrell led his team wearily up the steep Twickenham steps to receive the Holy Grail of English rugby.....the John Player Special Cup. Oh, and how the much-loved Arnold Ridley (7th January 1896-12th March 1984) would have loved such a day! Jack Rowell described the victory as "*the greatest day in our history*." Referee Roger Quittenton spoke of "*one of the hardest matches I have ever had to referee, but there wasn't a boot or fist out of place. It could have gone either way, but I also thought Bath just had an edge and deserved to win.*" So, after all these long years of struggle to achieve a place among the elite of rugby, a once lowly Bath had reached the zenith of the English game. They had journeyed to Twickenham from a sleepy West Country city as yeoman. But they would depart as victorious gladiators! It was indeed their day of destiny, the day when Bath had confronted and finally overcame that once fearful 'ultimate challenge.'

Chapter 29. EXCALIBUR! (1984-6)

Having now achieved the prize that they so cherished, Bath could relax for a few summer months, enjoy their Canadian tour and bask in the glow of their supreme triumph. At long last a shadow had been lifted after endless years of Bristol domination and yet, one major obstacle remained....Gloucester! That said, as Bath prepared for season 1984-5 it was beyond doubt that they now possessed one of the best sides (perhaps 'the' best) in England, having attained a top-four place in the Anglo-Welsh Merit table for the previous seven seasons and winning 29 from 39 games in their recent glorious cup winning year. Yes, Bath were 'the' team to beat now. Yet despite all this success they would remain a 'family' club, where everyone seemed to know everyone, and where post-match both players and followers mingled in the clubhouse exchanging boisterous rugby banter. Meanwhile, the Combination continued to play its vital role. On the eve of Bath's September 1984 visit to Moseley for example, when Rob Cunningham, Greg Bess and Jimmy Deane were all side-lined through injury, only one viable possibility remained, namely Avonvale hooker David Russell whose Bath experience amounted to a single game in the Spartans. That one match 'had' to be enough however, as anxious selectors virtually dragged Russell out of bed (he was recovering from flu) for the Thursday evening 1st XV pre-match training session. And sure enough the boy did the Combination's reputation proud. Bath won 6-19 at the Reddings, adding to their 44-9 home win over Moseley in the previous season when another Combination player, namely Dean Padfield from Old Culverhaysians, proved yet again that rugby ability could be found right on Bath's own doorstep.

Furthermore, the senior side were further augmented by the ever-improving United XV. Devon wing Peter Drewitt for example, formerly of Exeter, could be relied upon for first team action whenever needed. It often was. A further acquisition was wing Martin Sparkes (younger brother of mid-1970's Bath back Andy), who admitted that when playing his first senior game on the wing he *"was paralysed with fear because everyone seemed to be running around at about a hundred miles an hour."* Fellow backs Pete Blackett and powerhouse Tony Gunner were others who proved they too could manage the pressure of 1st team rugby, while another demonstration of Bath's resources occurred on 22nd December when 'thanks' to a fixture hiccup the club found itself playing two first-team games (against Pontypool and Sale) on the same Saturday. Though entitled to withdraw from one of the encounters, Bath basically said *"Oh what the hell"* and just got on with it! The First XV travelled to 'Pool losing 18-10, while United (written off completely by forecasters) fell 7-25 at home to Sale, not a disgrace in the circumstances.

As for recent arrivals, perhaps none compared to a certain young three-quarter, selected for a Spartans side required to step up a level on a County day and play United's away fixture against the Swindon 1st XV. Spartans won! But that was not all, as Robbie Lye, now Spartans skipper, could not stop singing the praises of a certain newcomer who, he claimed, possessed quite remarkable talents. He could have added (perhaps he did) that

165

the youngster was maybe a 'mite too pleased with himself for some tastes.' Indeed, on one notable occasion in the following season the young protégé received some plain-talking from an established Bath and England winger, who warned the 'yearling' of the pitfalls of youthful over-confidence, advice incidentally from which the 'youngster' would be forever grateful. So began the rugby story of one Jeremy Guscott. It was at Bath's Ralph Allen School where Jeremy first touched a rugby ball, though not the only rugby-playing 'nursery' within a city that can boast of Monkton Combe where Vincent Coates learned his rugby skills, King Edward's where Geoff Frankcom's abilities were honed, Prior Park, alma mater of John Palmer, and Kingswood, almost certainly (1868) Bath's first rugby-playing school. In addition, the game has been played for decades at Beechen Cliff, Culverhay, St. Gregory's and Oldfield, each a priceless source of talent that has helped forge rugby football into a key part of Bath's sporting heritage. Meanwhile in early season Simon Halliday had resumed training following a specialist course at the RAF sports rehabilitation centre in Surrey, regaining a first team place by late October; and bolstering the club yet further was former Exeter University and Scotland B prop David Sole, and England U.23 No. 8 forward David Egerton. Previously, with the proximity of Bristol, Bath would have been lucky to capture one such player. Now both chose Bath.

But this luxury of top-class players (lock Redman was another example) could lead to selection headaches, none more sensitive than the request in December for John Palmer (an international since England's summer tour of South Africa) to play at outside-half at the express request of England selectors. And selected he 'was' in Bath's victories over Exeter and Harlequins. However, John Horton, indignant at a decision that had resulted from an outside influence, announced his retirement from both Bath and senior rugby. Supporters were horrified, albeit that the club insisted (Chronicle, 14th Dec. 1984) that Horton was merely rested and remained *"a very important part of our squad for our defence of the John Player Cup."* Not everyone, though sympathetic to the selectors' dilemma, were entirely convinced by this explanation.

Nigel Redman: hugely versatile lock for Bath and England.
Acknowledgements: Bath Past Players

To the relief of Bath, with whom in his own words Horton had experienced *"eleven wonderful years,"* the admired Lancastrian retracted his threat to retire. But such difficulties were/are sometimes unavoidable, and Bath were now attracting attention from even the government itself when on 17th November the Sports Minister Neil Macfarlane chose to attend the Bath v Coventry encounter. What he saw was a home 23-6 victory, and concluded thus: *"I think I have been watching the best side in England."* That opinion would now be tested as Bath prepared for an automatic third round encounter in late January, namely a home tie against the battlers from the Forest of Dean....Berry Hill; and though not everyone beyond the confines of Gloucestershire knew too much about this club, Bath 'did' know. Hence a pragmatic approach was adopted to hold the 'Foresters' at forward and then snap up chances when (hopefully) they arose. The tactics were spot-on, earning a 24-3 victory, with Bath running home 4 tries, plus a typically smart Horton drop goal and one Palmer penalty. For Berry Hill meanwhile, led by flanker and skipper Ian Seymour, there was a lone penalty from fullback Jeff Powell to savour. But these hardy 'foresters' 'were true to their reputation, and as John Stevens reported, the Gloucestershire Cup holders were never overawed, and produced a *"thoroughly disciplined and fiery display which denied Bath the chance of asserting complete command."*

Next cup opponents were Blackheath in February at home but, 'thanks' to severe weather any rugby during January was literally 'written off,' and the only game Bath could arrange was a Sunday friendly at distant Brixham on 16th February. For Bath this match was a desperately needed opportunity for game-practice, and thankfully the result was therefore largely immaterial. Just as well it was, because Brixham were now to produce 'the' shock of the season. They won! It is difficult to say how they won, because *"in every department of play, Bath were in another class to their gutsy Devon opponents...."* But, within ten minutes home wing Sean Irvine flighted home a huge drop goal from wide out, soon followed with his straightforward penalty bang in front of the posts. Late in the game, by which time Bath had exhausted virtually every tactic in the coaching manual, Irvine sent home another simple penalty prior to Bath's John Palmer scoring a perfectionist try and conversion. But it was too late; Brixham had clinched a win that was greeted with astonishment throughout the rugby heartlands of England. Yet Bath's strategic purpose of 'match-practice' had been achieved and it would now show when cup business presumed as normal against Blackheath. Indeed, despite the impressive performance of Blackheath's giant lock Doug Hursey, likewise half-backs Crispin Read and Nick Colyer, Bath held too many aces, and in reply to a lone Colyer penalty, Spurrell's men ran home 6 tries (2 converted) with Trevaskis scoring a hat-trick and John Palmer stroking home 3 penalties for a convincing 37-3 win, duly described by John Stevens (Bath Chronicle) as *"another thoroughly professional display...."* It was precisely this professionalism that Bath duly 'carried' to Sale in the quarter-finals. Their back-row of Spurrell, Hall and Simpson were simply too hot to handle, their defence in the backs could not be breached, while their pack produced *"a fearsome display of rucking and mauling....."* Moreover, though Sale full-back Graham Jennion banged over 5 penalties, Bath superiority was emphasised with two tries (Simpson and Trick), a drop-goal from Horton and four penalties, of which three were coolly executed by David Trick, now further enhancing his reputation as a goal-kicker.

Four clubs now remained in the Cup: London Welsh, Coventry, Bath and.....Gloucester! Oh.....the forbidding sound of that last name. However, if Bath were in truth the best side in England then they must now prove it, and prove it at Kingsholm. Small wonder

John Stevens predicted that this *"would not be for the faint hearted."* You can say that again! While on the eve of the clash Gloucester's acting captain Paul Taylor (in the absence of their England and RAF captain John Orwin) vowed that Gloucester would *"explode the myth that Bath are the best side in England,"* and with his side playing at home not many would have bet against him. Yet Bath held aces too, not least the 'never-say-die' fearlessness of skipper Roger Spurrell, now leading his forwards into hell and back (literally) amid the Kingsholm cauldron. Gloucester's Tim Smith clinched two tries and a penalty. Bath's Richard Hill plunged over for a try converted by John Palmer, thus adding to his penalty and then a vital Horton drop goal. Yet, not until three minutes into injury time when Gloucester full-back Tim Smith's last gasp penalty-attempt swung wide did Bath raise their arms in triumph, with the cheers of some hundreds of their travelling supporters in a 12,000 crowd saluting this supreme triumph. Boy was this one 'close,' with Bath just on the right side of an 11-12 result. While John Stevens summarised thus (Chronicle, 25th Mar. 1985): victory was in no small way due to *"an inspired defensive display, typified by Paul Simpson and John Hall, by the courage of Chris Martin and two match-saving tackles by Horton himself.*

John Horton:
Inspirational
outside– half.

London Welsh, whose 10-10 draw at Coventry had (under the 'away rule') ensured their place in the final, would be the opposition, and even now no club would underestimate the potential of this outpost of Welsh rugby-flair. Nonetheless, Bath were now a side transformed, thanks not least to their inspiring coaching triumvirate of Rowell, Robson and Hudson, nor forgetting Roger Spurrell, whose leadership at Twickenham against London Welsh would be his last game as captain. Always tenacious, he was not interested in coming second, and he didn't mind too much what opponents thought about his lack of diplomacy either. It has been reported (though never officially) that the Cornishman had been sought by the national selectors on the eve of England's January 1985 encounter against Romania, though contact could not be made. A pity, he would probably have played a 'stormer.' Meanwhile at Twickenham (27th Apr. 1985) accents both Welsh and West Country mingled among a 32,000 crowd; while a superstitious Bath, sensing that those white shirts against Bristol might just be their lucky colour chose to wear white shirts again; and as captains Roger Spurrell (Bath) and Clive Rees (London Welsh) led their respective teams on to Twickenham's immaculate surface one wondered: 'could Bath really win a back-to-back cup Double?

Bath: *C. Martin, D.Trick J. Palmer, S.Halliday, B. Trevaskis (J. Guscott 40 mins), J.Horton, R.Hill, G.Chilcott, G.Bess, R.Lee, N. Gaymond, N. Redman, R. Spurrell (capt.), J. Hall, J. Simpson.*

London Welsh: *M. Ebsworth, J. Hughes, R. Ackerman, D. Fouhy, C. Rees (Capt.), C. Price, M. Douglas, T. Jones, B. Light, B. Bradley, E. Lewis, J. Collins, S. Russell, M. Watkins, K. Bowring.* Referee: *R. Quittenton (London/Sussex Societies).*

Almost immediately the back-row of Spurrell, Jon Hall and Simpson stamped its authority as *"Bath swarmed forward, bristling with menace and purpose, and struck the vital psychological blows within 15 minutes...."* John Palmer struck the first of his four penalties. Trick then sped around his man for a try converted by Palmer, before scrum-half Hill fed Chilcott, whose subsequent try aroused a crescendo so loud that ear-defenders should have been compulsory, and within 30 minutes Bath were already 18 points clear. But it was not over yet. The Welsh, fielding potential match-winners in their Wales international trio of winger Clive Rees, centre Robert Ackerman and scrum-half Mark Douglas, and not forgetting giant 6ft 7in lock John Collins (Wales 'B' squad) never gave up. Yet their five successful penalties from Colyn Price were not enough to deny Bath's overall superiority and a clear 24-15 victory. It was, wrote John Stevens, *"another highly-professional Bath job...."* And it was this professionalism that few had previously ever associated with 'happy-go-lucky' Bath.

Jack Simpkins.... His two-year presidency witnessed two John Player triumphs.

Acknowledgements: Reg. Monk

On Sunday evening the team again toured the city in an open-top bus. **"***Cheers, clapping and car horns made a cacophony of sounds and amateur cameramen used all kinds of vantage points, from balconies in the Circus to trees, to get a good snap of their heroes;"* (Chronicle, Ian Abbott, 29th Apr. 1985). In Chapel Row the good clergy of Holy Trinity Church stepped outside to add their congratulations. Next stop the Pump Room to be received by the Mayor and Mayoress of Bath, namely Mr Tony and Mrs Muriel Rhymes, thence to a civil reception for the team, their wives and girlfriends. It was a joyous weekend, celebrating both a season of 30 victories (one draw and 8 defeats), and in addition a coveted back-to-back cup final triumph. Indeed, such was this achievement that it was no longer fanciful to suggest that Bath (yes Bath!) might even equal the three successive cup winning triumphs of Leicester from 1979-81, a thought that once would have seemed inconceivable.

So, how did others see the club, among them John Mason for example (then rugby correspondent, Daily Telegraph), who knew Bath well? Writing in the 1985 Bath v London Welsh cup final programme he noted that on visits to the Rec he had *"been struck that the club's relatively recent run of success nationwide has not altered any of them one scrap,* [adding that] *"There is an air of deprecating modesty, bordering on pessimism at times, running through the club."* Modesty? (true), Pessimism (er, maybe). What certainly had altered the landscape however were those respective cup campaign wins over Bristol (1984), then Gloucester (1985) when crucial psychological hurdles had been cleared. Bath no longer trailed in this West Country threesome, they led it!

Success is not always the easiest companion to live with however, and it is one thing to reach the top, but quite another staying there, where rivals want to bring you down a notch or two and not for one moment could Bath relax on their laurels during the following 1985-6 season. Little surprise therefore that Bath's coaching triumvirate (to steal a march on rivals) **visited Rugby League club Hull Kingston Rovers** in late November to make a first-hand study of Rugby League training techniques. Reportedly they were stunned by what they saw. Significant too, and that's putting it mildly, the RFU gave its (admittedly) guarded approval towards this unexpected perestroika with the League code; while John Stephens further commented (Chronicle, 25th Nov.1985) that rugby union *"has changed more in the past five years than in its entire history. It will probably never be quite the same again even when present evolution of the game is completed, which it isn't yet."* Moreover, to the amazement of English rugby it was a one-time middle-ranked Bath who now stood in the vanguard of these changes. Hardly surprisingly new recruits came thick and fast to the Rec, and with the arrival of young Bristol and England outside-half Stuart Barnes, the brilliant John Horton, whose influence had galvanised Bath into a team that could match any in the Land, switched to Bristol for one final season of senior rugby. But what a honeymoon for Barnes as Bath launched an Autumn offensive that included an astonishing 15-40 victory at Leicester, then Llanelli away (15-18), a cracker of a home win against Bristol (26-7), and finally a dazzling home 16-13 floodlit classic against Cardiff in late October watched by an estimated 10,000 attendance, a crowd so large the gates were locked for reasons of crowd safety. Another Bristolian now drawn to the Rec was full-back Phil Cue, a two-for-the-price-of-one full-back who in Bath's late-season 19-10 home win over Llanelli proved himself a first-rate cover for Barnes at No.10. England's Lancastrian winger Tony Swift then arrived from Swansea, likewise Pontypridd hooker Malcolm Roberts, while Cornish farmer Graham Dawe decided that he too would test his potential at the higher level. The reward? His later caps for England.

But could Bath really match Leicester and achieve that daunting Cup Treble? For sure there was no doubting the club's determination to take the bull by the horns, starting with a pre-season (Hudson-prepared) training programme of 'conditioning, endurance, muscular development and heart-lung efficiency.' An SAS-type training weekend had followed in Wales, so hardly surprising that Bath's launch into the new season had witnessed some 75% of their points coming in the final 20 minutes. *"It's their fitness,"* many were suggesting, although fitness coach Tom Hudson explained that there was more to fitness than people realised. *"Any athletics coach can get rugby players physically fit but that won't win them matches. It's about conditioning, psychologically and physiologically,"* he added. So, in theory at least all seemed set fair. But if only rugby, particularly cup rugby, was that simple! Indeed, with little more than a month prior to Bath's J.P. Cup opener at Orrell, an exasperated Jim Galley (speaking on behalf of himself and fellow selectors Brian Jenkins and Geoff Pillinger) would bemoan the increasing pressures upon the game. No longer was the County Championship the only obligation, as call-ups for players came from elsewhere, including the new Inter-Divisional championship. Welcomed however was the introduction of **a standardised John Smith sponsored National Merit Table**, albeit by late Autumn it was difficult to field anything approaching a Bath first-choice side, a crucial period explained Jim Galley when the *"first-class club season should be reaching a climax before the start of the John Player Cup in January,"* and there were bound to be 'those' international calls-ups.

It was this predicament that likely explained Bath's decidedly shaky performance in their opening J.P. Cup match at Orrell, where things did not go as expected up in Lancashire. The result was a 16-16 draw, both teams running home two tries (one converted) and two penalties apiece. But thankfully there was that 'away' ruling (introduced to off-set the significant advantage of a team drawn 'at home'), and it was with a sigh of relief that Bath departed homewards with their passport into the next round intact. The following round at Moseley presented no such problems, despite the need to cover the frost-hardened pitch with 1,300 straw bales as protection against overnight frost, so allowing a 6,000 crowd to watch a game otherwise likely to have been postponed. The Bath pack was simply awesome, laying the foundations for a 4-22 victory, and not least *"founded on another superb demonstration by Nigel Redman."* But, there was nonetheless undisguised anger regarding a facial injury to loose-head David Sole, now a full Scotland cap. In the 17th minute he was assisted from the field groggy, in genuine pain and with the ugliest fractured nose that one is likely to ever witness, one resulting from an opposing forward's elbow (a recent arrival at the Reddings) clashing into his face. The referee merely issued a 'mild' rebuke to the player responsible, yet awarded a penalty to Bath nonetheless, one that Barnes duly banged home.

Next it was London Welsh away, a challenge that concerned John Stevens not so much for possible on-field difficulties as the forward-orientated methods that Bath had employed in their previous cup rounds against Orrell and Moseley. *"What has happened to that almost entirely international back division...?"* asked the Chronicle correspondent. However, John Stevens simultaneously answered his own question, namely that sheer pressure was now taking its toll, and every cup opponent now regarded a game against Bath as a virtual cup final in its own right. Dare Bath take risks with a bit of fun-rugby thrown in to please the masses? "No way" was the answer. Risks were out; Pragmatism in! It was that simple. Moreover, the quarter-final at London Welsh was no different; and if it was any comfort to those criticising Bath's cautious approach, cup games elsewhere, especially in the later rounds, tended to be played no differently. Bath duly won 10-18, and who knows, if drawn at home in the semi-final, Bath might just choose to cut loose and bring those outstanding backs into action. Talking of backs, Simon Halliday's selection for his England debut in their 21-18 victory against Wales at

Twickenham (January 1986) was rich reward for his inspirational fight-back since serious injury two seasons previously. Meanwhile the semi-final pool of London Scottish, Wasps, Leicester and Bath again included a team and ground that Bath especially hoped to avoid. But this time it was not Gloucester, it was Leicester....away, the club who had already won 'the cup treble.' True, Bath in early season had swept the Tigers aside 15-40 at Welford Road, but that was then, this was now! It was no time for over-confidence therefore and in order to rest the 1st team for the forthcoming encounter, one week prior to the semi-final a near-reserve Bath XV were handed the baton against highly-rated Lancashire club Vale of Lune. Near-reserves indeed! Most, if not all, proved they could have played first-team rugby virtually anywhere. Typical of such players was prop Ian 'Taff' Davies, now returned from Gosforth; while wing Ian Abbott and scrum-half Steve Knight ran home tries in Bath's 16-4 home victory, and the back-row of Nick Riou, Kevin Withey and Nick Maslen was further evidence of Bath's wealth of back-row forwards. This proved significant, because in the semi-final, it would be the now rested back-row of Spurrell, Simpson and the ever-improving David Egerton that would be so dominant.

Yet though the semi-final was played amid a tension-filled atmosphere at Leicester, Bath by now seemed a team unfazed by pressure, for that is the only conclusion one could draw from their eventual 6-10 victory by way of one try and then two Stuart Barnes penalties against two Leicester penalties from Dusty Hare. The narrowness of the margin of victory nonetheless concealed the true scale of Bath's domination, a superiority described by John Stevens thus: Bath *"taught Leicester such a lesson in the art of pressure rugby in this pulsating semi-final that a final margin of the only try by centre Simon Halliday could be regarded as scant reward on the run of play."* While England international and Leicester skipper Les Cusworth humbly remarked thus: *"That pack of theirs is a fearful proposition and John Palmer has got his backs so well organised....it's difficult to see who's going to beat them."* That question would now be for Wasps to answer, (11-3 victors over London Scottish), and Bath were taking no chances against their rejuvenated London adversaries. Coached by former All Black Derek Arnold, they boasted a string of class players that included (assuming fitness) utility back Huw Davies, centre Richard Cardus, wings Mark Bailey and Simon Smith, full-back Nick Stringer and prop Paul Rendall, all (yes 'all') England players, and watched by a 24,500 crowd at Twickenham (26th April, 1986) this encounter promised much:

Bath: *C. Martin, D. Trick, J. Palmer (capt.), S. Halliday, A. Swift, S. Barnes, R. Hill, G. Chilcott, G. Dawe, R. Lee, J. Morrison, N. Redman, R. Spurrell, J. Hall, P. Simpson.*

Wasps: *N. Stringer, S. Smith, R .Cardus (capt.), R. Pellow, M. Bailey, G. Rees, S. Bates (P. Balcombe repl.), G. Holmes, A. Simmons, J. Probyn, J. Bonner. M. Pinnegar, K.* **Moss, M. Rigby. M. Rose.** Referee: **F. Howard (Liverpool Society).**

Ill-luck would rob Wasps of the services of England prop Paul Rendall, side-lined on the eve of the final with measles. But there were casualties within Bath ranks too, although the fact that Barnes had incurred a broken toe, and a John Palmer groin injury would limit both his running and kicking were handicaps carefully concealed. This was just as well, because within 25 minutes of play Bath trailed by 13-0 against rampant opponents, whose 18 years old Harrow Schoolboy Gary Rees (outside-half) launched his backs into a spate of masterful handling. It was a joy to watch, unless you were Bath, and hardly surprising therefore when backs Nick Stringer and Roger Pellow finished precision moves with stunning tries apiece (one converted), with Stringer slotting home a straightforward penalty. Indeed, such was the Wasps domination that many teams might have raised the white flag by half-time; but not Bath, the team for all occasions! Furthermore, it was at the stage when the Londoners surged into a 13-0 lead that a Wasps player (it is reliably reported) looked Spurrell in the eyes and said: "now you'll learn what it's like to lose." Of all the players to provoke, Spurrell is the last one on planet Earth to select for ridicule. Moreover, other Bath players were in earshot too. And coincidentally or not, it was now that the Bath fight-back commenced. Swift shot over for a blind-side try, followed by a successful penalty. Whether or not Wasps then sensed something was amiss when Trick, not Barnes or Palmer, strode up to take the penalty, was anyone's guess, but his kick just 'made it' over the cross-bar. And it was then that Bath really did turn on the power-play after the break.

Gradually the formidable Wasps pack was subdued, and as Bath tightened their grip and a vengeful Spurrell had stormed over for another try, scrum-half Hill flashed over for a third and war-horse Simpson crashed over for the fourth. Wing Trick meanwhile proceeded to play an invaluable role as deputy kicker, who with a penalty already under his belt then added three superbly struck conversions. And it was the last of these from near the touchline that would be boosted (literally so) by the assistance of a Twickenham steward known already to the England winger on his previous visits to Rugby HQ. Trick, gasping for a drink of water in the stadium's heat-trap was offered a flask by the kind-hearted steward, and the thankful recipient thus took a 'swig' from that same flask. But....water it wasn't! It was sherry, and there was no better way to revive 'one' David Trick. He duly sent the ball flying through the sticks and Bath were on their way to a 17-25 victory and a third successive Cup Final triumph. So, for another of those joyous Sunday evening open-bus tours through the streets of an adoring home city, nor forgetting the gathering in Chapel Row of the Holy Trinity congregation whose earnest prayers had again been answered; then onwards to the Pump Room reception by the Mayoress (Mrs Jan Hole). It was here that Bath captain John Palmer now candidly explained to the good lady that *"for the past two years, the Mayor has come into the changing room and seen us 'in all our glory' after the game. It was disappointing that it could not happen this year."* By all accounts, she took in good spirits too! And Bath? They had now achieved a third consecutive National Cup triumph, a record set by Leicester that many believed could never be equalled.... let alone surpassed.

Yet could Bath beat that remarkable record? That was the question! And for those who thought that Bath's star would shine but briefly, the club's recent Welsh recruit Mark

Roberts would remark at the conclusion of his short yet notable Rec career (1985-6) that *"nothing in [his] rugby career before or after compared to the intensity of the experience I had while playing for Bath;"* and it was an intoxicating experience for those devoted to the club and city to be a part of it all. But for how long could that star shine so brightly, notwithstanding the loneliness that sometimes befalls those leading the pack, a world where friends are few, where fierce rivals are many. While Clive Howard (his wing-three-quarter son Chris later captained Bath Youth) could not have guessed that when accepting the role of general secretary in 1982 he would handle the reins of a club destined for both national and international, acclaim. Yet this former Staffordshire county sprinter and wing for Newcastle-under-Lyme personified the ideal club official. With Bath now high-profile there was for this Building Society manager sometimes a near avalanche of letters filling his in-tray, be they from the RFU, from other clubs and from an ever-widening (home and international) fan-base. Additionally, there was increasing interest from the media. *"Sometimes I almost forget what my wife* [Ann] *and children look like,"* he was heard to reflect.

A contribution of another kind was demonstrated during Bath's 6-3 victory over Leicester in September when John Palmer collapsed at the feet of a Tigers surge near the Bath goal line. Lying motionless, his injury was initially thought to be serious, and among the reporters that day was the Guardian's David Frost, a witness to the resulting 17 minutes emergency action commendably marshalled by referee Laurie Prideaux. David Frost wrote thus: the *"care, skill and efficiency with which the Bath club dealt with this nasty accident was a lesson for all 1,500 clubs in the country. Bath had two GPs and an orthopaedic surgeon on the spot, and a stretcher was immediately available."* Meanwhile *"Palmer was fitted with a surgical collar. An ambulance was sent for and driven across the pitch to where Palmer was lying."* Palmer was then duly rushed to the RUH hospital. To everyone's relief it was learned on the following day that his injury was not serious. But the incident demonstrated the advances that Bath (and indeed many clubs) had made in the provision of expert back-up; and here Bath were indebted to their own Honorary Medical team led during this period by Dr Kevin Gruffydd Jones and fellow physicians, namely Doctors Simon Burrell, Robin While, Ian Grandison and Mess'rs Philip Bliss and Cledwyn Jones; while further invaluable assistance was provided by an honorary Physio team of Fiona Phillips, Rebecca Williams, Heather McKibbon, and now led by senior Physio Julie Bardner who had taken over this crucial role from Gareth George. And as injuries were unavoidable (not least at this level of rugby), 'crucial' is no exaggeration.

Apart from the John Palmer scare, the new season witnessed recent arrival Andy Robinson (former Loughborough Colleges) positively thrive during Bath's opening September blitzkrieg that included away wins at Pontypool (10-23), Moseley (0-36) and then Newport (6-33) where new skipper Richard Hill's side ran home no fewer than six tries (one by former England schoolboy international centre Ben Cundy) to record their biggest victory so far 'on' Welsh soil, and amongst a six thousand crowd was the

Guardian's Clem Thomas (25th Sep. 1986). He wrote thus of the West Countrymen's *"sheer strength of purpose and superb-balanced 15-man attacking rugby,"* adding significantly that no longer *"do Welsh teams hold any fears for them."* While in late September further recognition was emphasised with the appointment of Richard Hill as captain of England, an honour never previously accorded a Bath player; and followed up in the New Year with Graham Dawe's first of five England caps, notwithstanding that in the drama of England's 19-12 upset in Cardiff that season a free-for-all at forward (with sinners on both sides) did lead to a one match suspension for England lock Wade Dooley and (ahem!) Bath trio Richard Hill, Gareth Chilcott and the recently capped Dawe.

Meanwhile Bath's first cup opponents were Plymouth Albion on the Rec in January that secured a 32-10 home victory. There next followed the visit of the London Welsh, whom Bath had overcome 53-16 merely one month previously, whose once dazzling brilliance even now stirred the imagination and drawing a 6,000 crowd. But, 'the master and pupil role' was now reversed, and after eighty minutes of action Bath strode off the Rec as 30-4 victors over the masterful legends of yesteryear. Next the Rec played host to the England B team's 22-9 victory over France B on 20th February; an ideal opportunity for the watching England selectors to see Bath's Nigel Redman and in addition their non-stop human dynamo of a flanker Andy Robinson, two players whom Rec followers had already predicted were near certainties for future full-international call-ups. The following weekend quarter-finalists Moseley arrived to be greeted with a heavy pitch ill-suited to open, running rugby, so hardly surprising that they adopted the dour forward game at which Midland sides are adept. Furthermore, Bath were grateful indeed that visiting captain Ian Metcalfe only succeeded with one lone penalty from seven attempts, not sufficient to overhaul a drop-goal and penalty from Barnes and a Barnes converted penalty try. But the 12-3 win was uncomfortably close at times and a warning that Bath must not drop their guard for a single moment. Nor did they for their semi-final trip to Orrell in late March, where another swirling Pennine gale thwarted any serious attempts to attack outside the scrum and Richard Hill's team would instead concentrate their prime efforts through their pack, a tactic that would subsequently 'spell doom' to the Lancastrians. With an international front-row wall of David Sole, Graham Dawe and Gareth Chilcott, the opposition were pitilessly broken apart at set scrums. With the might of Jon Hall (*"world class"* in the words of John Stevens) and fellow back-row colleagues David Egerton and Andy Robinson, a total of six tries then followed, three of them push-overs. With total domination up-front Bath (who had struggled to get a 16-16 draw one season previously) now literally steamrollered towards an emphatic 7-31 victory. It was *"almost slaughter of the innocents,"* concluded John Stevens. And there was a further item for the archives: Bath had been compelled by the 'luck' of the draw to confront all their semi-final opponents on away territory and lived to tell the tale. So, for a fourth consecutive time Bath (on the 2nd May) would step out at neutral Twickenham, again to face Wasps, semi-final victors at home over Leicester.

These two clubs shared a healthy respect for each other; and Bath again thoroughly studied their 'brief', aware (inter alia) that with the exception of the as yet uncapped scrum-half Stephen Bates, their opponents could field an all-international back-division; while Wasps captain David Pegler (Chronicle, 1st May 1987) generously spoke thus of Bath: *"They are England's team of the 1980's and the prototype of what the next generation of successful clubs must be."* The likely outcome therefore? A narrow win…. for someone!

Bath: *C. Martin, A. Swift (J. Guscott, 55 mins), S.Halliday, J. Palmer, B. Trevaskis, S. Barnes, R. Hill (capt.), D. Sole, G. Dawe (G. Bess, 23 Mins), G. Chilcott, J. Morrison, N. Redman, J. Hall, A. Robinson, D. Egerton.*

Wasps: *H. Davies, S. Smith, K. Simms, R. Lozowski, M. Bailey, R. Andrew, S. Bates, P. Rendall, S. Simmons, J. Probyn, C. Pinnegar, J. Bonner, M. Rigby, M. Rose, D. Pegler (Capt.).* Referee: **F. Howard (Liverpool Society).**

It was this attempt for a fourth successive cup victory that would mentally test Bath like never before, and with barely ten minutes remaining it was rampant Wasps who led by a deserved margin of 12-4, with their back-row of Mark Rose, Mark Rigby and David Pegler masters of the field. By contrast Bath seemed overburdened by the sheer magnitude of their task. Save for a Nigel Redman try (a good one), Wasps had tightened their grip with a Rob Andrew drop-goal and a Huw Davies penalty, followed by a smartly taken try, again by the outstanding Huw Davies, Andrew converting. Had Bath now reached that fateful 'bridge too far' one wondered. But then, Stuart Barnes was presented with a penalty chance, and though from a difficult angle and 40 yards out it was bang on target. Suddenly, Bath were ignited into that fearsome force that all opponents dreaded. Ten minutes remained. Ten minutes that belonged to a Bath team that now extracted every ounce of physical and mental strength it possessed. First a Hill-Barnes dummy and a swift pass to Halliday saw the England centre shoot over for a try, Barnes converting. Now, Bath scented victory. Barnes received good ball and headed for the line. A ruck followed, Hill collected, fed Redman and the lock stormed over for his second try, Barnes converting. It was barely ten minutes of clinical destruction, but enough to put Bath 19-12 ahead. Referee Fred Howard's whistle was heard again. Game over! Game won! A fourth successive JP Cup triumph and Bath had achieved the near impossible!? Well, not quite!

True, the whistle blew to signal the Stuart Barnes conversion. But hundreds of fans (mistakenly believing that Fred Howard had signalled the end of the game) spilled on to the field in celebration. Referee Howard, who had intended to continue the game and ensure a full 40 minutes of play-time, was reportedly communicated by RFU secretary Dudley Wood to conclude the match 'there and then,' believing that it would be impossible to re-start the game. Although purely celebratory, the temporary chaotic scene (albeit calm soon followed) was hardly how Bath would have wished this momentous triumph to reach its climax; and the post-match party at the Rec that evening was noticeably subdued, likewise the Sunday celebrations around the city. 'Would the club,' one asked, 'be banned from the competition for the following year?' Would the media, until now so supportive, now turn their ire upon Bath? A worryingly few days followed.

The issue however was perhaps best put into perspective by Sunday Times rugby correspondent Stephen Jones (10th May 1987) who reminded readers that the main invasion occurred when the 'clock already showed seven minutes of injury time had passed.' Moreover, considering that the crowd on this occasion was a new record of 35,000 (at least two thirds thought to be Bath supporters) Stephen Jones added: *"How on earth is the game going to increase its following if it turns its nose at new followers? Every year, Bath's success attracts more people to the final and more people to rugby."* Indeed, his only criticism was that following their cup triumph Bath had put *"as much sweat and energy into apologising for themselves as they put in the cup run."* And such sentiments may well have influenced the RFU governing body. Indeed, save for the suggestion from some quarters that the Rugby League method of concluding matches with a klaxon-signal might be adopted, Bath were '*not*' reprimanded for those events at Twickenham that had briefly caused them such deep concern.

Instead, they were now free to savour that moment of triumph when these one-time journeymen from the West Country now raised rugby's own **Sword of Excalibur** to the Heavens, to achieve a feat unequalled in English rugby.

Chapter 30. A BOLT OF LIGHTNING. (1987-90)

As English rugby embarked upon season 1987-8 it no longer seemed implausible to wonder if Bath could extend their extraordinary cup-run to a 5th successive year. However, **a fully-standardized league competition sponsored by Courage** had now been launched with twelve clubs per division, promotion and relegation included, and Bath (not surprisingly) in Division One. But, this added yet further pressures and Bath's opening (Courage League) encounter at Leicester in September suggested as much with the Tigers, fine-tuned from their tour in New Zealand and Australia, looking razor-sharp for a 24-13 home win (8,000 watching) and *"holding Bath with surprising ease in tight forward exchanges and outplaying them in the loose...."* Furthermore, there were soon signs that the popularity of the Courage League could eclipse the once-revered County Championship. Indeed, when John Horton (36 years young and now player-coach of Combe Down) agreed to lead Somerset into their 1987-8 encounter against Gloucestershire, one could only reminisce how merely four years previously these two county rivals had contested the County final at Twickenham in front of thousands. So, as interest in the County game waned and with senior clubs now reluctant to release squad players to the counties, the task was left to junior clubs to make up the short-fall. Meanwhile, the Rec had welcomed promising St Ives lock/No.8 Martin Haag into the ranks; while ever improving lock Damien Cronin (ex Prior Park) won his first Scotland cap in a season that saw the introduction of a rule change allowing (within reason) a game to continue while an injured player was undergoing treatment on the pitch, a change that virtually killed off overnight the not unknown practice of the **'tactical injury'** that delayed a game at crucial periods.

Bath's opening K.O. cup campaign against Lichfield was not to be taken lightly however, since in recent seasons this supposedly junior club had seriously tested the reputations of both London Welsh and Harlequins. However, the Bath supporters' joyous post-match Twickenham pitch-invasion of the previous season had (to the club's astonishment) so concerned the local chief of police, that a large contingent of constabulary had been drafted in to first escort the Bath followers to the home ground, and secondly (though remaining in the background) to keep a watchful eye on events during the game. But trouble there was none, it was a cracker of a game, five thousand watched and Richard Hill's side ran home nine tries, winning 3-43 against plucky opponents, and in the words of at least one admiring home supporter proved they were simply *"the best team in Britain."* They would need to be. Their next cup opponents were Leicester.....away! Leicester, who would win the newly introduced Courage League, who in early September had subjected Bath to an emphatic 24-13 defeat, who held home advantage in front of some 11,000 home supporters in the 13,000 crowd, not surprisingly looked favourites to bring Bath's epic cup-run to an abrupt end. But.....after 80 minutes of compulsive action, where Bath's John Palmer had produced *"a near perfect display of tactical kicking,"* where Bath's pack had produced *"a display of awesome power and efficiency,"* and where full-back Phil Cue struck home two penalties, Palmer a drop-goal and David

Egerton a crucial try in answer to a Nick Youngs try converted by Dusty Hare, it was the West Countrymen who clinched a dramatic 6-13 fourth round cup triumph. An equally dramatic quarter-final encounter would follow at Moseley, an excellent team, yet following Bath's mighty achievement at Leicester it seemed that they too faced an uphill task when within 40 seconds Bath were awarded a penalty from 50 yards out. Phil Cue struck cleanly and Bath were 3 nil up!

But suddenly Moseley, fielding a pack huge in stature, chose this exact moment to show that they could hold, even dominate, the most feared opponents in English rugby. Their front row of Mark Linnett, Chris Barbor and Graham Smith, locks Al Recardo and Richard Denhardt, their tireless back-row of England's Nick Jeavons, S.Masters and Peter Shillingford would not give an inch to the Bath eight. Some 15 minutes of huge pressure followed and a shove deep inside Moseley's own hell-fire corner saw Shillingford crash over for a push-over try. Normally, when Bath fell behind in cup rugby there came that almost predictable moment when they decided that the niceties would end and the serious stuff begin. But on this day it never did begin. Kicking duties switched from Cue, to Guscott and finally to David Trick, but to no avail, albeit some attempts missed the target by barely an inch. Confusion then appeared to grip every Bath attempt to rectify an increasingly desperate situation. But nothing worked! Moseley meanwhile tackled and harried everything that moved. It wasn't pretty, as if they cared. It was however the perfect strategy on the day. For the Midlanders sensed, correctly so, that they had caught Bath at that key moment when four years of cup rugby had left them drained both physically and mentally. Bath were literally 'running on empty' as the minutes passed by, and with tensions on a knife-edge and the score on 4-3 the final whistle echoed over the Reddings with the score remaining at 4-3. The Moseley faithful erupted. For on that day a giant had fallen, for how long one could not say; and Bath supporters, some two thousand in number, did not stay long. Instead, they drove off into the night, deep, deep in their thoughts.

The Moseley defeat had potentially inflicted a deep psychological wound, one painfully suffered in the full glare of national publicity and no little 'schadenfreude.' Would Bath triumphs of recent seasons simply be a freakish accident of rugby history, echoing the thoughts of Alan Gibson's pre-match comments (1985 Twickenham match programme, Bath v London Welsh) as something: "*very pleasant to look back on: but a relief when it is all over?*" Or, could Bath recover and prove otherwise. But make no mistake, a West Country rugby city felt this defeat to its very bones, and dreaded the thought of a future of memories only, the glamour that had proved so intoxicating all gone. To face reality however was the answer to such concerns, for no club ever had or ever will win everything all of the time, and Bath's unprecedented achievements had taken an inevitable toll, and sooner or later there arrived that time for the inevitable fuel-stop. And over-reaction was the last thing that was needed. Instead for the first time in four years there was a golden opportunity for relaxation; and save for one ill-tempered 21-9 League victory against Harlequins, who ironically would later defeat Bristol to win that season's

JP Cup final, relaxation is exactly what the club got. David Egerton, Bath's 6ft 5in back-row forward won his first of five England caps against Ireland, while on the same day (23rd April) out-half general John Horton was invited to play one last match for Bath (his 379th) prior to his retirement from a game that he had graced for much of his now 37 years. The opponents were Bedford, the result was 35-7 to Bath, and not only did the maestro stroke home the conversion of former Plymouth Albion winger Steve Walklin's try, but in the closing minutes sent over his 125th Bath drop-goal to arouse a rapturous applause from a 3,000 strong worshipping home crowd.

Finally, Bath completed the season with Courage League action at Sale. Safe in 4th place in the new League competition, they travelled north without a care. It was jokes and banter all the way, and less seven of their internationals 'rested' for the forthcoming England tour to Australia, much would depend upon a number of Bath's less experienced personnel. Yet skipper Hill's side notched 8 tries (seven converted) and five scored by the young brilliant Guscott alone. Wings Barry Whitehead and Mark Westcott proved a revelation, Jon Bamsay looked a 'one-to-watch' half-back prospect and prop Steve Kipling, scrummaging powerfully, bulldozed over for his maiden senior club try. Sale, sadly already relegated (though not for long) played their part too, including a two-try burst from former Bath winger George Stanton. Most significantly however, it seemed that Bath had regained their 'touch' rather more quickly than their rivals would have hoped. And it was 'some' start to season 1988-9 under new skipper Stuart Barnes after (thankfully) an injury-free tour of Thailand, Malaysia and finally Holland, a journey that notched five straight wins including victory over French champions Toulon in Leiden, then continuing with Bath running riot at Pontypool with a 9-50 domestic campaign-opener that registered their 'now' biggest-ever win on Welsh soil. Shown live on BBC Wales, Peter Bills (The Times 5th September) wrote thus: "*Bath played such breath-taking rugby that many of the basic skills captured by the television cameras covering a club match live for the first time ought to become mandatory viewing for youngsters.*" Indeed, rampant Bath would remain unbeaten for 30 matches until mid-February, with some of rugby's finest among the vanquished. In fact, it barely mattered whether Bath played 'home or foreign,' as Courage League away opponents Harlequins (9-26), Rosslyn Park (6-19) and Moseley (0-38) would have testified, and likewise the defeated home Courage League opponents Gloucester (19-9) and Bristol (16-9). The two drawn games moreover were exhilarating to witness, namely the October 24-24 spectacle with visitors Stade Toulousain and the December 21-21 result at Newport with a virtual reserve side during a Divisional match weekend.

But cup rugby by contrast is unpredictable, and come the 3rd round (that stage of the competition when the senior clubs entered the fray) it was visitors Oxford RFC who in January would be the first to test Bath's cup resolve. Well, the result spoke much. "*Their support work is absolutely superb,*" Oxford skipper and flanker Roy Davies (formerly Sale) concluded after a 'virtuoso' performance yielding 16 tries (9 converted by Stuart Barnes), among them full-back Audley Lumsden and wing Tony Swift claiming four tries apiece, and fellow back Freddie Sagoe a hat-trick. Nonetheless to Oxford's delight and that of a generous 5,000 home crowd the visitors did get on the score-board, thanks to Andy Tiplady's penalty and a further Tiplady conversion of a full-back Steve Lazenby try. But the final result of 82-9 spelled out a warning, again voiced by Oxford's Roy Davies: *"I can't see anyone to touch them."* Next Hereford arrived, a hard, gutsy side who come half-time had *"played with such passionate commitment and tackled so well that they limited Bath to just one score."* Small wonder come the re-start Bath changed tactics, and with their superior fitness the ball was spread wide. Nine further tries resulted, the score closing at 48-0. But, with a guaranteed half-share of the Rec gate receipts (a standard practice in the National K.O. Cup), and hence some £2,000 in this case (Chronicle, 10th Feb. 1989), plus £1,800 from sponsors Pilkington for all 4th round losers, Hereford headed homewards with Bath skipper Barnes singing their praises for their tremendous first-half performance.

So far so good, but things were about to change. Yes, Bath were cruising through the Courage League like a demolition squad, but in drawing Bristol (last season's finalists) for the quarter-finals, Bath were now facing one of the big beasts. Again, on home territory, the match was an 8,500 sell-out; and not before time the RFU had recently instructed that from the quarter-finals onwards all **touch-judges must forthwith be chosen from a pool of neutral and qualified referees** with the authority to 'draw the referee's attention to any incidents of foul play.' It was a logical and welcomed change. It was furthermore a quarter-final that none watching would likely ever forget, not least as rain, sleet and snow just emptied onto the already saturated Rec. Not merely pools, but ponds of water accumulated virtually everywhere, and yet somehow two teams not only played on it, they played open running rugby on it. It was arguably a miracle no one drowned as players passed and held passes. They went for try scores and they got try scores. They tackled like demons, ran themselves to near exhaustion, and at the final whistle they virtually collapsed from their endeavours in a ferocious struggle played at a ferocious pace. Ironically, it was furthermore a game that Bristol had wished to play and Bath had not; yet after 80 minutes of drama it was the game that Bristol wished had not been played and Bath were delighted that it had.

Initially Bristol shook the hosts with a performance so commanding that by the time of their 4-12 half-time lead it seemed questionable whether or not Bath could close the gap in conditions so atrocious. The second half however saw a home side fight-back that would have broken through virtually any opposition in England, though the two Stuart Barnes penalties reducing the score to 10-12 were not sufficient to snatch the lead with the clock only three minutes from full-time. Then, despite a final desperate Bath surge at forward, one that reached the Bristol line, it was the Bristolians' pack that was awarded a life-saving put-in. A Bristol victory now seemed a certainty as Harding fed the set scrum. But…. those treacherous conditions played one last trick. The slippery ball spat out of the scrum at an awkward angle, and Bath scrum-half Richard Hill, as tigerish as ever, snatched at the ball, somehow held it, and shot over the line. Barnes failed to

181

convert. But no matter. It was now 14-12 to Bath, and too late for a Bristol reply. So ended a trial of strength played between two giants, and not forgetting one overriding message: 'Bath's recovery since that shock cup defeat at Moseley was just about the last thing English rugby wanted to hear.'

And there was another reason to gladden hearts around the Rec, not least the rise of Gareth Chilcott. Once known as something of a maverick, the Rec favourite who knew a thing or two about the front-row war zone had by now undergone a reputation-transformation. Known affectionately as 'Coochie' (or 'Oddjob,' as in James Bond's Goldfinger) he was now both role-model and hero. Indeed, following his power-performance in England's 11-nil home win over France in March (1989) he was hailed as '*the iron man of England!*' Selection for the British Lions summer tour would follow; and a former bad-boy of English rugby now found himself elevated to cult-figure status. Meanwhile for Chilcott and Bath another monster challenge loomed ahead, the spectre again of Gloucester in yet another semi-final at Kingsholm and a sell-out crowd of 10,500 watching. Not surprisingly the game followed the same pattern of every Gloucester v Bath clash since these two clubs had first met. Ferocious forward exchanges, bone-shaking tackling, heart-stopping tension….this confrontation had the lot. But though no side will fight harder than Gloucester when only one score down, Bath's re-born ability to absorb even the most frightening of pressure held off a late furious challenge to secure a 3-6 thriller. But their cup journey would get no easier, for soon enough it was learned that come Twickenham Bath would be facing Leicester!

Off-field too these were fast changing days and because of the wish of both the R.F.U. and the clubs to expand the game, financial back-up was vital. It was therefore significant for both Bath and the rugby game generally that in the New Year (Chronicle, 9th Jan. 1989) they **finalised a £150,000 sponsorship agreement** with the **South Western Electricity Board (SWEB)** for 'the biggest-ever such deal so far in club rugby.' Even Leicester's then current £100,000 brewery sponsorship deal was now surpassed. And significantly RFU secretary Dudley Wood congratulated Bath *"on the outstanding comprehensive nature of the whole scheme...."* essential moreover if Bath, in the words of secretary Clive Howard, were to realise plans to not only improve their facilities, but furthermore to assist the club to widen horizons into European rugby and hopefully to tour into the Southern hemisphere. In other words, Bath were not only thinking big, they too were now thinking global. Something, in fact 'someone' was also set to go global, namely Bath centre Jeremy Guscott, who *post Cup Final action* would be suddenly called up for England's away clash on 13th May against Romania, no less victors six months previously against Wales. Will Carling was injured, so selectors gambled on Guscott. Three dazzling debut tries in his Country's 58-3 win in Bucharest and the selectors had seen enough. The boy (sorry...the young man) was promptly selected to join Chilcott for the British Lions in Australia. There it was confirmed what many had long predicted....Guscott was world class! However, first came the 'small' matter of a Twickenham cup final on 29th April against Leicester, whose 15-12 home win the previous week had stalled somewhat Bath's unbeaten League record, though not as it happened their crowning as the season's Courage League champions.

On the eve of the final however, Bath (both team and officials), stayed overnight at a West End hotel; so no surprise that little 'change' remained, if any, of the £3,750 Pilkington sponsorship guaranteed to both finalists. But Bath thought it money well spent. Furthermore, though the huge gate receipts for the final (likewise the semi-final) were distributed by the RFU amongst the entire English rugby game, Bath's success had already led directly to that impressive SWEB sponsorship deal. As for their cup final team-sheet however, a neck injury would regrettably thwart the near-certain selection at full-back of England B international Audley Lumsden, although the hugely experienced John Palmer would prove invaluable on the day. And what a day! A world rugby 'club' record crowd of 59,300 and two of the best teams in England fighting for the crown:

Bath:). *J. Palmer, A. Swift, S. Halliday, J. Guscott, F. Sagoe, S. Barnes (capt), R. Hill, G. Chilcott, G. Dawe, R. Lee, J. Morrison, D. Cronin, J. Hall, A.Robinson, D. Egerton (P. Simpson 53 mins).*

Leicester: *W. Hare, B.Evans, P. Dodge (capt), I. Bates, R. Underwood, L.Cusworth, A. Kardooni, S. Redfern, T. Thacker, W. Richardson, M. Foulkes-Arnold, T.Smith, J. Wells, I. Smith, D. Richards. Referee:* **F.Howard (Liverpool Society).** Again, this was a clash of equals, both sides packed with internationals and impossible to predict a result. On fifteen minutes Halliday (perhaps the best centre in England) intercepted a Leicester pass into empty space near half-way, a lethal threat thwarted by Underwood (perhaps the fastest wing in England). England full-back Dusty Hare (playing his last senior game) then sent home two successful penalties, providing a 6-0 cushion for Leicester at half-time. But the Tigers were still far from dry land and come the re-start the Bath back-row of Jon Hall, Dave Egerton and the tearaway Andy Robinson (currently Whitbread Rugby World player of the year) now prowled the field like famished wolves, and it was The Guardian's Robert Armstrong who perhaps best described the stunning performance of Bath and Scotland lock Damien Cronin who *"drove with the kind of awesome momentum that scatters defenders like pigeons,"* and gradually the Bath eight took command, John Stevens writing: *"the physical strength and scrummaging techniques of the Bath pack was decisive;"* and never more so than a massive surge on 78 minutes that created a ruck 25 yards from the Leicester line on the left flank. Again, the still hungry back-row (Paul Simpson replacing the injured Egerton) shielded the ball to Hill who fed danger-man Barnes. The Bath skipper, with two second-half penalties already in his pocket, sensed instinctively that he could go for the 'kill,' and feinting a pass to Bath's power-wing Fred Sagoe instead cut inside two defenders to literally crash-dive over the line. It was 10-6. The conversion failed. But it didn't matter. Barely two minutes remained.....too late for a Tigers 'catch-up!' For the fifth time in six seasons Bath had triumphed in the Cup. Actually, they had won the cup (now Pilkington Cup) and Courage League Double. Once more it was the Sunday evening celebration-tour around the streets to acknowledge the adulation of a rugby-proud city. Onwards to the Pump Room, the mayor (Commander

183

John Malloy) awaiting to entertain the team to a civic reception, and an evening amid the splendour of the Abbey and the Roman Baths. Unforgettable!

Season 1989-90 followed, and after an epic era for Bath surely nothing could surpass the sheer scale of the achievements since that first Twickenham triumph of 1984. Well, something in fact did! But first Bath would again commence a new season in flamboyant style, concluding a September carnival of wins with victory over Romanian champions Steaua Bucharest. A good start, though the request by England selectors that in the interests of international preparations the 'senior-clubs should restrict their respective internationals' pre-Christmas club appearances to Courage League and Divisional matches only' included virtually half the current Bath first team. Two factors however softened this requirement. First, the quality of the United side was now so high (their home gates on occasions topped 1,000 spectators) that quality back-up for first team matches was readily available. Secondly, Bath's new five-year plan had widened the net to encourage the arrival of new talent that included a trio of Nigerian-born, but West Country educated players, namely prop and Oxford Blue Victor Ubogu, 'Dayo' Adebayo and Steve Ojomoh, a trio of whom much more would be seen. Nothing however diminished the appetite for continued K.O. Cup success, and with the senior clubs entering at the third-round stage, Bath were drawn against Harlequins, fortunately with a home tie adding a helping hand against opposition so potentially dangerous. But with conditions reminiscent of the epic Bath v Bristol quarter-final of the previous season the game predictably developed into a hard slog, the Quins fielding England's Paul Ackford and Richard Langhorn at lock, plus an all-international back-row of Mickey Skinner, Peter Winterbottom and Chris Butcher. Fortunately, Bath could match such class, not least locks Redman and Cronin who crashed over for the game's lone try converted by Barnes. Come the re-start (referee Ian Bullerwell having ordered a shirt-change at half-time) Barnes made a touchline penalty kick look easy, giving Bath a 9-0 margin, and for all their efforts the Quins could not gain those desperately needed catch-up points.

The next round brought Headingley down south, the heavy (mid-February) rainfall perhaps offering this tough Yorkshire side their best chance of a successful afternoon since they too were familiar with such conditions. Bath's reaction however to the early penalty by Headingley's Matthew Johnson then proved decisive, as almost immediately the home pack seized control, *"driving forward with awesome thoroughness."* Four tries resulted, with Hall powering over for a brace and Barnes slotting home three conversions and a penalty to put Bath clear at 25-3 within five minutes of the re-start. Thus, with the job effectively done the home side were content to preserve their comfortable lead. Tempers flared on occasions as conditions deteriorated yet further, but the route into the quarter-finals was now clear and that meant Richmond, with former Bath hooker Rob Cunningham among their coaching panel. Though potentially greater threats remained in a dangerously strong quarter-final pool (including Leicester and Gloucester) Bath were taking no chances, especially as one week previously Richmond had held visitors Bristol to a 21-21 draw. In the quarter-final however the gutsy Richmond, *"whose tackling and covering was of the highest order,"* had seemingly peaked one week too soon. For despite an early lead from out-half Martin Livesey's penalty, they could not constrain indefinitely Bath's mastery at forward that now established a platform for a six try haul and 3-35 victory.

Now the semi-final would entail a journey up to Moseley! True, in early season the Midlanders lost 27-9 in Courage League action on the Rec. But the Reddings was not the Rec, but a venue of recent painful memories. Hardly surprising therefore that Moseley skipper Bob Barr could not resist injecting a touch of mischief into the pre-match preparations. His words were few, but none missed the target: *"we are well aware that they [Bath] still remember vividly what happened the last time they came up here in the cup."* Yes, Bath 'did' remember. Nor did it calm the anxieties of their followers that the brilliant Guscott was inexplicably excluded from the Bath line-up. Yet watched by an estimated 9,000 crowd, Moseley's *"heavyweight pack was systematically dismantled by the ruthless efficiency of the Bath' eight,"* namely a front-row block of Chilcott, Dawe and Victor Ubogu, the line-out domination from Redman and Cronin, and the incessant marauding of back-row lions Andy Robinson, Simpson and Egerton. Three tries followed, the first a 30 yard sprint by wing Tony Swift followed by a Chilcott charge-down score, and finally Callard (so assured at full-back) swerving effortlessly home for a third. Barnes nailed all three conversions and added a penalty; while for the hosts there was little to savour apart from a Carl Arntzen penalty and a Chris Allen try. Job done, 'Painful memories' exorcized, and Bath now in the right frame of mind for another final. Just as well. Their Twickenham opponents were Gloucester, semi-final victors at Northampton. Who would bet on this one?

Perhaps (though only perhaps) Bath possessed the larger player-pool with places yet to be won so tight was the competition, demonstrated moreover with their April 6-25 win at Newport less ten regulars: Yet Gloucester too can put the fear of God into opponents, and when on the 5th May the following combatants stepped out at Twickenham (52,000 watching) the outcome was anyone's guess: **Bath: J. Callard, A. Swift, S. Halliday, J. Guscott, A. Adebayo, S. Barnes (capt.), R.Hill (S. Knight, 71 mins), V. Ugogu, G. Dawe, G. Chilcott, N. Redman, D. Cronin, A. Robinson, K. Withey, D.Egerton.**

Gloucester: T. Smith, D. Morgan, D. Caskie, R. Mogg, J. Breeze, M. Hamlin (capt.), M. Hannaford, M. Preedy, K. Dunn, R. Pascall, N. Scrivens, J. Brain, J. Gadd, I. Smith, M. Teague. Referee: **F. Howard (Liverpool Society).** What materialised however was an encounter described by the Sunday Times as *"probably the most remarkable club match ever played."* Two fearsome packs locked horns for forward domination, and two full-backs were tested to a barrage of 'bombs' booted high into the sky by half-backs Hill and Barnes (Bath) and Hamlin and Hannaford (Gloucester). Stalemate at first, but then fireworks after barely ten minutes when Bath flanker Kevin Withey seized loose line-out ball and ran blind-side, weaving and breaking grasping tackles for fully 50 yards to score in the left corner, Barnes calmly converting as if kicking a 'sitter' in front of the posts. Soon Barnes kicked home a long-range penalty with the same nonchalance, and Bath, had opened up a 9 points gap. Their pack matched the Gloucester eight, and supplied quality ball to their backs who positively thrived in perfect conditions. And now Bath really 'cut loose!' Guscott (fed by Halliday) then broke diagonally clean through, fed Swift whose return pass saw the British Lion streak inwards for try number two, Barnes coolly converting again. Next it was the turn of the assured Callard, who seizing ball some 30 yards out kicked ahead once, then twice and amid utter confusion in Gloucester ranks tore home for try number three. Soon Bath's lead extended to 25 points when on the verge of half-time, a wayward Gloucester pass dangerously near the Bath line was dramatically intercepted by Tony Swift. With an instinctive jink wrong-footing two opponents the Lancastrian-bullet now saw an entire field of open space in front of him. The winger struck.....like a bolt of lightning! Try!

It was stunning, and cometh the lightning, cometh the storm! Bath were now in complete command, and Gloucester were enduring the worst 80 minutes in their otherwise glorious history. Within two minutes into the second half Stuart Barnes extended the lead with another penalty. A temporary Bath 'breather' then followed that allowed Gloucester a well-executed Kevin Dunn try converted by Tim Smith. But Bath hit back and from the moment that Gloucester flanker John Gadd got marching orders it was carnival rugby all the way. Heat beat down upon a sun-drenched Twickenham reaching a reported 90 degrees out in the middle. Wisely when injuries delayed play, Bath, as ordered by their coaches, sheltered within the cooling shadows of the West stand. Not so Gloucester. Again, Bath played all the right cards. Next, Callard and Swift inter-passing launched the Lancastrian in for his second try. Graham Dawe then waltzed through for another, Barnes converting. It mattered not that in the final ten minutes Steve Knight effortlessly replaced scrum-half Richard Hill. Everything worked like clockwork. So, the deluge continued and Withey, with another break, fed Redman who crashed over for try number seven; while prop Victor Ubogu, not one who likes to be upstaged, then poached loose ball from careless Gloucester handling to charge home for number eight behind the posts. Fittingly Halliday (soon to leave Bath was invited to administer the 'coup de grâce,' his conversion bringing Gloucester's agony to an end....48-6!!

So ended the 1980's, the most remarkable decade for Bath since their formation in 1865. The national press, not surprisingly, heaped undiluted praise upon the performance, with both The Independent and The Sunday Express proclaiming that "It was slaughter in the sun." The Observer wrote of "*a thunderous occasion and a thunderous match played at breath-taking speed.*" The Mail on Sunday wrote of "*one of the most complete displays of 15-man rugby you could ever wish to see.*" While for those lost for words, perhaps it was necessary to rely upon the abstract to explain a result so dazzling as simply 'surreal.' Or in the words of the Sunday Mirror: Bath were now "*the uncrowned kings of club rugby.*" Uncrowned kings? Well no longer. For this day was their coronation!

The interception! The Bolt of Lightning ! In short Tony Swift,
Bath 48 v Gloucester 6, 1989-90, Twickenham Cup Final

Acknowledgements: Bath Chronicle

Chapter 31. TO PLAY WITH ONE HEARTBEAT. (1990-94)

During the summer of 1990 (Chronicle, 28th August 1990) John Stevens, the 'voice of Bath rugby,' retired from a profession (and vocation) that he had served for 37 years. During this period with the Bath Chronicle he had established himself as friend to an entire generation of Bath players, and indeed to countless readers, who followed his perceptive reports on the everyday life, setbacks and successes of a club that he loved. He spoke from the heart, and his 'word' would earn a respect and authority for which any sports writer would crave. But do not be lulled into assuming that JS (affectionately known as **'scoop'***) ever 'pulled his punches.' For he could (and frequently did) say things as he saw them. He was no mere home-side flatterer therefore. But all who knew him, and it seemed that most of the city did, always respected his thoughtful honesty.*

Come summer 1990, a new decade beckoned, and Bath departed to Australia in August for the most ambitious tour in their history so far. But in the background to this otherwise joyful time there lurked a shadow of discontent among a certain section of the club; for to the dismay of everyone coaches Dave Robson and Tom Hudson had unexpectedly resigned! The issue, so one was led to believe (Chronicle, 3rd Aug. 1990), concerned their dissatisfaction with the management committee, not merely regarding the fixture congestion at the outset of the forthcoming domestic season, but furthermore conflicting opinions as how to plan for the club's long-term future. Alarm was the immediate reaction throughout the club, where but three months previously Bath were basking in the glory of yet another dazzling Twickenham triumph. *"I think that Bath will go down-hill,"* Dave Robson (Chronicle, 3rd Sep. 1990) chillingly remarked. Furthermore, if this was not enough bad news, on the day of their departure to Australia eight Bath players (all with first-team experience) announced a mass exodus from the club, among them the outstanding Phil Cue, Barry Trevaskis and Ben Cundy; and soon to be followed by forward stalwarts Jon Morrison to Bristol and Twickenham hero Kevin Withey to Newport. In fairness to those departing, their best days were either over and/or better opportunities for regular first team rugby were available elsewhere. And Clifton, newly promoted to the National League Three and who over the years had provided a number of outstanding players to Bath, would now be among the beneficiaries of this exodus. Meanwhile, four seriously difficult matches between the 9th to 22nd August awaited Bath Down Under. While on their return a 'ludicrous' total of four top flight games were scheduled to be played within a mere eight days in the first week of September, a schedule that comprised just one of a number of reasons for the Robson/Hudson resignation.

But Australia is, well Australia! The opposition was top-ranking, and yet Bath (less those on tour with England in Argentina) proved marginally stronger at forward throughout. Enjoyment was another aim (and why not?), and as skipper Stuart Barnes explained: *"although winning was high on the agenda....developing fitness and team spirit for next month's domestic season [was] equally important."* The opener at Cairns (Northern

Queensland) against a star-studded international Barbarians team, a game hailed *"as one of the best ever seen on the ground"* climaxed with 24-27 Bath victory. The second against a Darling Downs Invitation XV was a 19-19 draw. Queensland followed, fielding some of Australia's finest, and a narrow 21-19 defeat for the tourists. Finally, Bath faced Australian club champions Randwick and Aussie legend Mark Ella. True to form, the out-half wizard duly climaxed a 60 yard handling movement with a try gem, and Bath less nine of their 1990 cup finalists fell 20-3, notwithstanding refereeing described (rightly or wrongly) as 'atrocious' by Bath team manager Richard Seaman. Nonetheless, in terms of sheer enjoyment, new friendships and rugby experience, the tour was deemed a success.

Moreover, on return the recent fears of upheaval would soon be dispelled when the touring Romania (victors over France four months previously and ironically now mentored by Dave Robson) were over-run 38-9 by a dominant Bath team, where an on-form Jon Bamsey blended impressively at centre with Oxford student Phil de Glanville. Three days later (the third match in five days) top French side Toulouse were over-run 44-6 in a win described by The Chronicle as *"an awesome performance."* Ten days onwards and Cardiff arrived on the Rec, only to return to Wales the worse for a 45-23 defeat; and if any more doubts remained as to whether or not Bath possessed the capacity to recover from those internal pre-season shocks then such misgivings would be dispelled

by their stunning Autumn Courage League form that returned six from six over some of England's best and climaxed with a 3-9 victory at Leicester! Heady stuff, with such outstanding results suggesting that Bath had resolved the early season coaching dilemma by applying an internal solution to an internal problem. So, relying on instinct Bath had lost no time in recruiting from their own home-produced resources. Thus, the experienced Simon Jones and John Palmer were appointed to Jack Rowell's coaching panel with Gareth Chilcott as player-coach, and any fears of a collapse were soon set aside.

However, another setback did occur when, having (as mentioned) defeated Leicester 3-9 away in the Courage League, Bath fell 0-12 one week later to Leicester on the Rec in the 3rd round of the Pilkington Cup, not an experience that Bath wished to remember, but where it was impossible not to remember the eye-

Jack Rowell ....a very great coach.

Acknowledgements: Reg. Monk

catching debut of young Leicester lock, one Martin Johnson, who a dozen years later would captain England to World Cup glory in Sydney. Meanwhile Bath swept cup disappointment aside and aimed for success in the increasingly high-profile Courage League, where a new cadre of players now joining their ranks would help them to do

precisely that. Cornwall lock forward recruit Andy Reed (Plymouth Albion), front-row new boys Chris Atkins and John Mallett, utility forwards Gareth Adams and Julian Olds would all prove themselves 'up to the mark,' so too a number of exciting backs, among them young Cornish scrum-half Ian Sanders, powerful wing Jim Fallon (formerly Richmond) and Laurie Heatherley, a typically tough New Zealand centre and probably the first Kiwi to play in a Bath first-team shirt.

Just days from Christmas (19th Dec. 1990) Bath played at Toulouse (early season losers on the Rec) who were celebrating 'their' Centenary, and Heatherley would now learn that French teams do not relish losing to English clubs on Gallic soil. Entente Cordiale this was not! Instead as the Bath Chronicle's new rugby correspondent Alan Pearey described events: it was "*a dreadful advertisement of rugby union.*" John Bamsey, playing centre, added that the match was "*like something out of the Mexican soccer League,*" while coach Jack Rowell needed only one word to summarise the encounter: "*scandalous!*" For the record an improvised Bath team (Christmas week not being the wisest time for the committee to dispatch a team across the Channel) would lose 23-6, though, as a gesture of seasonal goodwill skipper Nick Maslen and his Bath side diplomatically attended the post-match dinner (reportedly somewhat to the surprise of Toulouse). David Trick meanwhile could still capture headlines, and did so as only he could in a Bath v Wasps encounter in November described by Alan Pearey as "*a fabulous rugby spectacle,*" and where with the score poised at 26-26 the speed-machine was presented with a simple conversion attempt. Now Trick (no mean goal kicker) missed! In fact, his kick ended up in the West stand. Furthermore, his woeful attempt that would have clinched the result was received by an appreciative roar from the home crowd. What!? "Had the world gone mad?" Well no, because this was nothing less than the perfect climax to a Charity match held to raise trust funds for the family of 20 years old winger Raphael Tsagane (tragically killed in a road accident during Wasps 1990 Easter tour) and for the courageous young Stephen Roberts, who in the same previous season suffered a serious neck injury merely days prior to his 18th birthday while playing at forward for Bath Youth. The final result was thus irrelevant and Trick understood instinctively how the game should be concluded.

Yet, difficult challenges remained with a tranche of five late season crucial Courage League clashes, and as with Pilkington Cup defeat at home against Leicester in November, so now Bath suffered a 15-16 Courage League defeat at home against Wasps in March. But their essential self-belief remained and in the final run-in Bath got four from four with away victories at Nottingham and Gloucester, then Rosslyn Park at home and finally at Saracens away. Thus, the Courage League Championship was theirs! Indeed Bath, whom some in early season had predicted would go 'downhill,' would capture one more trophy when with a mere two coaching sessions under Simon Jones and Andy Robinson then duly won the Worthington Best Bitter National 7's tournament. Held on the Rec (previously at Richmond) and now in only its third year, a near 5,000 crowd roared home skipper Jon Callard's side to the final. London Irish were overcome first (28-6), next Rosslyn Park (16-8), followed by Sevens supremo's Harlequins (10-0) prior to a 24-10 final win over Leicester. And commenting upon the season's achievements head coach Jack Rowell spoke thus: *"Each year we try to improve the quality of the basics and move our game on,"* a modest explanation for a far from modest record of unparalleled success.

Andy Robinson was now appointed captain for season 1991-2, with Brian Ashton, former Orrell and England B scrum-half (now teaching at Kings Bruton) joining the coaching panel; while among the new intake of players Ben Clarke (No.8 from Saracens) ranked among the most formidable. Other arrivals too would waste no time in making an impression, as out-half Duncan Willet (England Students XV) demonstrated in the opening season 28-12 win over Pontypool. Likewise, Autumn wins over Richmond (10-9) and Plymouth Albion (34-3) revealed the exciting potential of, among others, prop John Mallett and backs Iestyn Lewis, Andrew Webber and Ian Palmer. A further indication of the sheer depth of talent was the selection of scrum-half Steve Knight, utility forward Mark Crane and flanker Nick Maslen (United skipper) for the South West Divisional side that season. As for 'supposed' forward reserves Colin Atkins and Pat McCoy, drafted in as late replacements for their Courage League debuts against Bristol in December on the Rec, neither would look remotely out of their depth in a winning forward team-effort described by the Chronicle as 'staggering.'

Meanwhile the second Rugby World Cup (RWC) commenced with England v New Zealand at Twickenham on 3rd October, Bath's Nigel Redman, Richard Hill, Jeremy Guscott and Jonathan Webb each playing a role during the course of England's progress. Sadly, Jon Hall had not recovered from injury, while the previous self-imposed international exile of the brilliant (but maverick) Stuart Barnes was judged by some commentators to have caused his exclusion from the final World Cup squad. England duly reached the final via wins over Italy (Bath's Webb and Guscott capturing 32 of the points in England's 36-6 victory), USA (37-9), France (a nail-biting 10-19 triumph in Paris) and a semi-final 6-9 win over Scotland in Edinburgh. Finally at Twickenham Australia sealed a 6-12 victory over Will Carling's England, with Bath's Jon Webb, Guscott and Richard Hill alongside him. *"You never forget the pain,"* Jeremy Guscott later reminisced.

Fortunately for Bath the rumoured post World Cup offers (reportedly Leeds and St. Helens among them) for the brilliant Guscott (employed anyway with British Gas) to 'go Rugby League' were declined, so too an offer from Australia rumoured to reach the millionaire level. However (Chronicle, 13th Dec. 1991) 'a one point deduction against Bath for fielding a non-registered player in a previous League game,' namely a 21-26 win at London Irish, left Bath skipper Robinson fuming at so costly (and unnecessary) an administrative lapse, since even a single point could cost Bath the League title if, as was highly likely, the championship race produced a tight finish. The team secretary honourably accepted responsibility (namely the failure to register Laurie Heatherley), though Bath appealed, submitting that the 'said' rule was designed to prevent players already League-tied with one club from switching to another in the same season. Heatherley by contrast had arrived at the club directly from New Zealand in the previous season and therefore was '**not**' already League-tied. In fairness the RFU accepted *"that the omission to register was inadvertent...."* But, point reductions had already been levied against other clubs in similar circumstances in the lower Courage Leagues, and with the necessity to ensure a uniformity of judgement, Bath's appeal failed.

Andy Robinson however, not fully reconciled by this outcome, would instead apply his considerable energies at winning if not the League, then that glamourous Pilkington Cup, where in November Bath would dispose of Nottingham with a 52-0 home victory, thanks not least to a ten try bonanza and a *"fusion of pace, power and sheer variety of moves....that would have destroyed any opposition."* Post-Christmas however the heat was really on with four opponents to face who really could block any hopes of a trophy. Yet, Leicester fell 37-6 before a crowd so threateningly large that not for the first time gates were shut prior to the kick-off, then Gloucester slipped up 29-9 on the Rec. Next followed 4th and 5th round Pilkington cup games at Northampton and Bristol respectively, where at Franklins Gardens Bath held their nerve to win 9-13, followed by a 5th round encounter at mega-rivals Bristol. As always it was eighty minutes of attrition, but a clash (literally a clash) where Bath triumphed 6-15 through a Phil de Glanville try converted by Jon Webb, two Barnes's penalties and one from Webb, as against Mark Tainton's two penalties for Bristol. Then followed the semi-final draw, and you guessed it: ....Gloucester v Bath at Kingsholm! It was win or bust thought skipper Robinson, predicting that with 'the' single point reduction around their necks, League front-runners Orrell and Northampton were now out of reach. Kingsholm K.O. Cup Tension followed, you could have cut it with a knife; and if you wanted to escape, forget it, because there was no escape with some 3,000 Bath supporters packed into a sell-out 12,000 crowd. Alan Pearey (Chronicle, 6th Apr. 1992) would report that *"never can the passion and fury of West Country cup rugby have been more in evidence than it was at Kingsholm on Saturday."* Critically it was the Bath backs who monopolized the open spaces, not least wings Jim Fallon (whose training, no kidding either, included one thousand press-ups nightly) and the ageless Tony Swift. Ah Swift! With the Cherry and Whites defending a narrow 18-15 lead into injury time he swept across from his opposite wing to take an inside pass from the powerful Fallon. Try! Barnes converted from wide out. Suddenly it was 18-21, and with Bath the away team and three tries clear, only a try could now save Gloucester, though Bath could have locked the game down with the clock racing towards end-time. Instead, they counter-attacked from the kick-off, whereupon an outrageous cross-field pass by Webb to Guscott was then fed to the accelerating Fallon. He blasted through two tackles for his second score and Barnes sweetly converted from wide. An 18-27 triumph. Again, elation for Bath....dejection for Gloucester.

One week later at Rosslyn Park there would be yet more celebration, and for reasons that would be as unexpected as they were welcome. It was the penultimate weekend of the Courage League, and Bath had achieved a comfortable 13-21 win at Roehampton when even before a post-match pint had been swallowed a roar arose among Bath players and supporters in and around the clubhouse. But why? Drama elsewhere, that's why, as sports results flashed across TV screens and radio, reporting that 'League front runners Orrell and Northampton had both fallen at the hands of Wasps and Nottingham respectively.' For Bath that meant one thing only; their final League match was just one week away against 4th placed Saracens.... at home! Win this one and the League was theirs. Game on! The fast improving Sarries were all aggression and in skipper and England centre John Buckton they gained a late consolation try to add to Ben Rudlings conversion and two long range penalties. But Bath at full strength save for the promising Iestyn Lewis at centre instead of the resting Gustcott *"sent them packing with such contemptuous ease that there was almost a sense of bathos about the proceedings."* Four tries were run home thanks to former Saracens No. 8 Ben Clarke (already a Rec favourite), then Fallon and two from 'the Master' himself....Stuart Barnes, whereupon the ever more prestigious Courage League was won for a third time. One week onwards an upbeat Bath would then face Harlequins (15-9 semi-final victors over Leicester) in the Pilkington Cup final with the satisfaction of one 'Major' already under their belts thanks to their 10 from 12 league wins, one draw (intriguingly 18-18 at Harlequins), and one defeat at Orrell, a venue reached by Dr Jon Webb after being rushed four hours up the motorway, having already performed surgery throughout the night.

Meanwhile the forthcoming Bath v Harlequins final would call for the superlatives once again, and described by Peter Jackson (Daily Mail) as *"the most momentous cup final of all."* It was furthermore the last occasion that Halliday (now with Quins) would be seen prior to his retirement, and the farewell appearance of England 'B' battering-ram Jim Fallon prior to his departure to Rugby League. And what a farewell as a capacity 53,000 crowd packed into a Twickenham now undergoing enlargement and where a classic would unfold, described by Alan Pearey (Chronicle, 4th May 1992) as *"rugby from another planet:"*

Bath: *J. Webb, T. Swift, P. de Glanville, J. Guscott, J. Fallon, S. Barnes, R. Hill, G. Chilcott, G. Dawe, V. Ubogu, M. Haag, N. Redman, A. Robinson (capt.), S. Ojomoh, B. Clarke.*

Harlequins: *D.Pears, D. Wedderburn, S. Halliday, W. Carling, E. Davis, P.Challinor, C. Luxton, M. Hobley, B. Moore, A. Mullins, N. Edwards, P. Ackford, P. Winterbottom (capt.), M. Russell, C. Sheasby.* Referee: **F. Howard, Liverpool Society,**

At times it seemed like a replay of Waterloo. It was that 'darn' close. While Bath coach Brian Ashton's previous claim at Kingsholm that: *"We've proved time and again that our mid-field is as good in defence as it is in attack,"* would be put through the ultimate test. At the interval Quins were deservedly 12-3 ahead, through two penalties from David Pears and a Peter Winterbottom try, while England lock Paul Ackford dominated the line-out. But, it was just their luck that their opponents were Bath, the club that possessed a plain 'bloody-minded' refusal to admit defeat even when it seemed to be staring them in the face. So, within minutes of the re-start Webb slotted home his second penalty that duly signalled a phase of massive Bath counter-pressure that would otherwise have broken a brick wall, but not the bone-shuddering Harlequins tackling. So, the tenacious struggle continued, until ten minutes from end-time when Ben Clarke, Dawe and Ojomoh at last broke a hole through the Quins defence. A pass to Guscott, a feed on to de Glanville and a try! Webb coolly converted. 12-12. Game On! Extra time! Guscott attempts a drop....just wide. Pears (Quins) attempts another, then two more, so does Quins Paul Challinor, each miss target. Barely sixty seconds remain, and it seemed that the rugby gods had decided that justice demanded (who could disagree) a drawn outcome and thus a shared trophy.

But upon that arena stood an impulsive genius who would dare to defy even the watching gods. A line-call for Bath. They shortened it. Redman jumps and feeds ball to that same rebellious talent known to one and all as Stuart Barnes. There, surrounded by exhausted cup heroes to a man, he calmly took aim, then sent a drop-kick of near 45 yards skimming (just) over the cross-bar. There was not even one second left of play, let alone sixty. And gallant

Stuart Barnes: sheer brilliance! The Drop-goal!!

Harlequins, so noble in defeat yet magnificent throughout, were thus in the words of Alan Pearey denied a successive cup triumph by "*a flash of unforgettable brilliance.*" But then that is genius for you, or putting it another way: 'that was Stuart Barnes.'

And skipper Andy Robinson? He had proved himself an outstanding leader, whose tenacious qualities had inspired his troops to win the League and Cup double with 28 wins, one draw and a mere 4 defeats; Oh, and in early season Bath had clinched their first ever win 'at' Cardiff (9-10). Bath thus entered season 1992-3 with an honours list of six Cup and three League Championships in a mere nine years, attracting unstinting praise. Coach Allen Foster (season 1991-2) in the aftermath of his Rugby RFC team's 32-0 home League defeat to Bath remarked that the West Countrymen were "*the most complete footballing side in English rugby.*" While (Chronicle, 5th Oct. 1992) Blackheath coach Kevin Short, having filmed for training purposes Bath's home 51-0 win against 'The Club,' spoke thus: "*We've come to the rugby university today.*" Bath's influence furthermore had reached far beyond home shores through the influence of former coach Dave Robson, whose five-year corporate rugby-plan for Namibia was already yielding benefits within this emerging rugby nation. So perhaps hardly surprising that this club that had risen from a small West Country city to the very pinnacle of the rugby game would now catch the attention of the Services. The 45 strong crew of minehunter HMS Brecon for instance not only honoured the club on occasions with their visits to the Rec, but had hosted the Bath club during shore visits at Newport and Gloucester. The somewhat larger warship, namely aircraft carrier HMS Ark Royal, paid a further huge compliment by adopting the club as their own.

But first, the 1992-3 season commenced with a tour of Italy where another recruit would reveal exciting potential, namely Llanelli born out-half Craig Raymond. Victories over Record Cucine Casale (15-62), whose President Vanni Maggiore had earlier exclaimed: "*All the town is dreaming of playing against English players*," then followed by a 15-18 win against Benetton Treviso. Albeit that perhaps few new lessons were learned on the field, others were learned off it. For starters, (Chronicle, 8th Sep. 1992) both Italian Division One clubs were sponsored (in Treviso's case by Benetton) and both imported prominent overseas players such as All Black Zinzan Brooke and Treviso's Australian wing David Campese. Hence, awash with money (Chronicle, 16th Sep. 1992) both clubs could (and reportedly did) pay top international players some pretty top salaries, whether for coaching or playing it was hard to say. Furthermore, by the 1990's this issue of money was fast becoming a hot topic of debate in the supposedly amateur world of rugby union in the British Isles; and to put it bluntly it was increasingly obvious that the definition of amateurism appeared to differ, depending upon whose language one was speaking and upon whose territory one was playing.

The launch of the 1992-3 domestic season meanwhile included **a set of new law changes,** over 40 in number, all introduced with the aim of creating a yet more open game. These included the raising of a try to five points, limiting a Mark to within the defendant's 22 line, banning the scrum-half from dummying to coax opponent's off-side and blood injuries to be treated immediately. There was general approval too for the allowance of a 'quick throw-in' anywhere between where the ball crossed into touch and the goal-line of that team throwing in but…only with the use of that same ball kicked into touch. And as Bath shot off the starting blocks for the Courage League with a winning haul of five from six, it suggested that such changes suited their style, revealed not least by the class of their Autumn victory at Bristol (31st October). This was the 200th game between these two rivals. But unlike the 3-3 drawn encounters in both the original derby in 1888 and later the 100th in 1936, the 200th game would be an 8-31 Bath rout, a score and performance that would have astonished their predecessors and a result that dwarfed their previous 'best' at Bristol, namely a 0-12 win in distant 1912. By season 1992-3 however the balance had changed, and as Alan Pearey wrote: "*….there can rarely have been a backs-performance quite so devastating as that dished up by the reigning League champions.*" Ominous news surely for second division side Waterloo, hosting Bath one week later in the 3rd round Pilkington Cup. But, if there are many reasons (not to mention excuses) for giant-killing upsets, the sensational defeat that the Lancastrians duly inflicted upon Bath is easily explained: 'Bath were quite awful.' In truth the hosts were little better. But they succeeded in dragging Bath down a level, a tactic that sometimes works and certainly did on this occasion. Half-back Paul Grayson proved to be the local hero, kicking home three penalties and sufficient to cancel out a Tony Swift try (a good one) plus a Jon Webb penalty. Yet that still made it 9-8 to the Northerners, a result arousing temporary horror when the news reached Bath.

One possible explanation for such upsets was the psychological factor that 'favourites' carry upon their shoulders when facing an 'underdog;' and Bath, for many decades a David amongst Goliaths, did not always feel comfortable when this position was reversed. Bob Jenkins (sports commentator, Bath Chronicle) later described such a phenomenon as the '*minnow syndrome.*' There was probably truth in this. But life as they say must go on, as indeed it did. Yes, the cup venture had hit the 'buffers' before it barely started in a Pilkington campaign that would see Leicester the eventual winners. But Bath, kicking themselves for a largely self-inflicted failure at Waterloo, now set about restoring their self-respect in League action. Moreover, with the Divisional Championship now underway and heavily reliant upon first-choice Bath players, it was an opportune time again for so-called reserves to show off their own prowess. And show it they did with a triple run of December victories at Nottingham (17-24), Richmond (22-38) and home to London Welsh (37-7).

Nor for the first-time other newcomers caught the eye, namely props Darren Crompton and Bristol recruit Dave Hilton, plus the discovery of 21 years old South African Mike Catt, whose home senior debut in Bath's January 47-5 non-League win over London Irish revealed his remarkable maturity. Now with a British passport (his mother was English) and recently domiciled in the city since leaving Stroud, selectors and supporters alike soon predicted that a special talent was now in their midst. He could play literally anywhere in the backs (save perhaps scrum-half) and one decade later the young man from Eastern Province would play a critical role in England's triumphant World Cup winning side. And irony of ironies, save for a delay in responding to Catt's initial enquiries to Gloucester, he might 'never' have joined the Rec, but instead gone 40 miles up the motorway to (yes, you've guessed it) Kingsholm instead. In October prop Victor Ubogu won his first England cap in their 26-13 win against Canada (held as it happened at Wembley); while at Twickenham (November 1992) Ben Clarke made his debut in England's 33-16 victory come South Africa's return from the international political wilderness, with Phil de Glanville winning his first cap too as replacement. This was followed up when in December the hugely talented Audley Lumsden won his Oxford Blue at Twickenham. And that was not all, because both flanker Julian Olds and hooker Hugh Butler (now playing for the British Club of Bangkok) were called up for Thailand! Er….how come? Well Thailand, bless 'em, were (pardon the pun) a bit short of tall players. So as Major Anan Boonsupa (TRU) explained (Chronicle, 10th Nov. 1992): Thailand decided to select "*from an excellent batch of ex-pat ruggerites in the country*" for the forthcoming Asia championships. Despite a somewhat bumpy ride, the Thai lads got a tidy 55-10 win over Malaysia, though no one got close to eventual winners Japan.

Meanwhile, throughout rugby football important developments were emerging from the side-lines, not least at Bath where numerous supporters were now aware of the need to update the infrastructure of the club; and the committee decision in the previous season to oppose the appointment of a full-time club administrator was, many believed, an opportunity missed. *"I think the club should be managed professionally,"* stated businessman Malcolm Pearce (Chronicle, 28th Sep. 1992), and while seeking no change to rugby union's amateur status, other changes were now vital, he argued. Such views were widely supported by the membership, some of whom pointed to the revival of a previously-struggling Northampton. There, staring down at the abyss, a near mutiny by their supporters had led to a complete re-organisation of the management, plus the appointment of a full-time paid coach and a Birmingham firm assigned to organise the commercial aspects of the club.

Concerns, though not so dramatic, culminated (Chronicle, 25th Nov. 1992) with an EGM at the Rec. Conducted under the chairmanship of professor Cyril Tomkins, the agenda included (inter alia) the issue of plans to widen and improve both the commercial management at the club and the proposal for an increased role for players at the committee level. But in contrast to the aforementioned events at Northampton, this meeting did not produce the drama that many supporters (and not least the media) were anticipating, due partly to certain positive decisions already taken. First, a business group at Bath University was currently making a full study of the club's management structure, with a report and recommendations to follow in due course. Secondly, in addition to the cumbersome 30 strong management committee, an executive committee of seven members was now established, one designed to meet on a fortnightly basis, and on a daily basis if circumstances demanded. Third, the construction of a futuristic stand on the Rec had now received the 'go-ahead.' Significantly, an agenda item calling for the resignation of the present committee was blocked anyway by rule 7.3 of the club constitution, a rule that 'only' permitted such drastic an action if taken at a full AGM. So, with the leading item on the agenda now side-lined, there followed in the concluding words of club chairman John Gaynor *"a full and frank exchange of views."* But, it was hardly an outcome for headlines, and not a single vote was taken throughout the proceedings. However, the meeting drew some five hundred members, so many that closed-circuit TV was installed to ensure the overspill could watch the events from adjoining rooms in the clubhouse. But while many opinions addressed to the committee on the need for management improvements were 'heated' to say the least, it was quite obvious that the membership, though advocating changes, desired no de-stabilising 'shock and awe' tactics; and that while they wished for improvements, these they sought from within the established structure of the club. That then was the message of the night!

Another message was delivered come the New Year. First in February England 'A' led by Jon Hall and including the human dynamo Steve Ojomoh swept aside Italy 'A' to the tune of 59-0 on the Rec, 8,000 watching. Later there followed a result so extraordinary that one would have been forgiven for thinking it was a hoax, Bath winning 79-3 against

Swansea, reigning Welsh champions, the biggest defeat in their proud history. And with young scrum-half Jamie Knight (brother of Steve) making his 1st team debut since his serious injury incurred when playing for England Colts against France in 1989, and lock Sean O'Leary (ex Wasps) prominent in a highly mobile home pack, Bath's night of total rugby produced a result that belonged to the realms of fantasy. One week later (13th Mar. 1993) and Wasps would 'engage' (for want of a better word) in Courage League action on the Rec, and this time no one was kidding. This high-profile game drew a capacity crowd, many attempting to gate-crash, others arriving too close to kick-off. Forget scrummages on the field, there were scrummages off it (with two people fainting in the scramble to get into the ground). Wisely the game was delayed for five minutes. But this caused yet more dressing-room tension; and when finally unleashed at kick-off, two totally hyped-up teams went into (literally 'into') each other like 'bats out of hell.' Within ten minutes so 'hot' did things get among the two packs that referee David Matthews (Liverpool Soc.y) was compelled to read the Riot Act: *"next bit of trouble and someone goes off!"* It made not a scrap of difference, and then…Guscott tackled Fran Clough hard but fair, and then…he tapped Clough with his boot stupidly but light-footed, and then….Clough (not without reason) rushed at Guscott who ducked to avoid contact. The crowd in the West stand, under whose noses the episode occurred and whose Bath-partisanship by now could have given Kingsholm a run for its money, only added to the pressure as first the referee consulted with his touch-judge and then dismissed…. a despairing Clough. To the Wasps (again not without reason) it was an utter injustice pure and simple. Yet the referee's action may well have saved the game from descending into utter chaos. Mercifully things calmed down somewhat, but mistakes (there were 36 penalties) littered the next 65 minutes of rugby with Bath finally winning 22-11. Though Wasps would have doubtless disagreed, there may have been some truth in the Bath post-match verdict that *"Wasps set out to intimidate and got their just desserts."* Be that as it may, Rob Andrew sent home two penalties (one from within his own half) and Phil Hopley ran home a try. While for Bath Guscott scored his 90th try for the club (Webb converting), Webb kicked 4 penalties, and Barnes a drop goal.

Yet it was hardly surprising that come the inauguration of the National Cup in 1972, followed later by the standardised Leagues, would add high-octane competitive spirits among crowds and participants alike. Yet it was nothing new in rugby union. Indeed, though perhaps long forgotten, pre-First World War days of the Somerset cup were but one example of passions breaking through the safety barrier, providing headaches for referees trying to control things. Yet though since 1888 the ultimate sanction of an outright dismissal had been available, referees were often reluctant to use so total a punishment. A simple rule-change would have solved the problem however, namely a short, sharp 10 minutes shock into a 'sin-bin.' It could have proved useful in the Bath v Wasps game and its time had surely come. And come it did, though not fully implemented until season 1998-9. Soon though the squad for the British Lions tour of New Zealand was announced. Rob Andrew of Wasps was among the names. Included too was Damian Cronin (formerly Bath, now London Scottish) and Bath's Stuart Barnes, Jeremy Guscott, Andy Reed and Ben Clarke. Bath and Wasps now were 'neck and neck' at the top of the Courage table and tensions were likewise mounting at the bottom, as four clubs were due to be relegated come the conclusion of season 1992-3, with Division 1 reduced to a mere ten clubs. *Meanwhile a game of a quite different character between a Bath XV and a President's XV would be held on 4th April on the Rec in memory of former Welsh lock Mark Jones. Mark, 6ft 5in, was not a first-choice lock at Bath, but 'boy' could he not play a 'mean' game when his 22 senior call-ups did come. After four seasons from 1984-88 he departed to Swansea, then Clifton, for more regular senior rugby. But, in Autumn 1992 he would lose a long fight against serious illness. So, Bath remembered Mark, and did so in a manner befitting so pleasing a person to know.*

With one League match remaining, the Courage title hinged upon the respective fortunes of Wasps at home to Bristol and Bath away to Saracens. It was here that the majestic Jonathan Webb would play his final game. With challengers Wasps winning narrowly 7-6 at home to Bristol, Bath were given a hell of a fight by the already relegated Saracens. Nonetheless, Robinson's men squeezed home 13-19, thanks not least to Callard's two tries, so gaining compensation for early Pilkington Cup defeat at Waterloo but now, thanks to 27 victories from 32 played, winning a fourth League title.

Nor did the following 1993-4 campaign under the captaincy of Jon Hall (Guscott's rating as the best player he ever knew) lack for challenges. Commencing at friendly Garryowen, where, watched by a 4,000 Irish crowd bitterly disappointed by Jeremy Guscott's late withdrawal through injury, six tries (four converted) ensured a comfortable 8-38 away Bath victory. But sterner challenges awaited, though with an early season return of five from five over Bristol, Northampton, Orrell, Gloucester and Wasps respectively it seemed likely that Bath would be among the chasers for honours in the Courage League. Yet no club could ignore the ever-increasing toll of injuries at this higher level of rugby, a problem only too evident during Bath's ferocious 10-18 win at Bristol in September. Often thirty-one persons (not thirty) were seen on the field owing to the almost constant need for Bath's assistant physio Heather McKibbin to treat an endless stream of casualties on the pitch. And that was just the Bath list of walking wounded. Furthermore, with the club's four recent British Lions (Barnes, Andy Reed, Guscott and Ben Clarke) all nursing troubling injuries originating from the recent New Zealand tour, head physio Julie Bardner (Chronicle, 23rd Oct. 1993) now entered the debate with some no-nonsense comments. It was the Lions she was most concerned about, players whom she argued *"had about a ten-month playing season with not enough time to recover at the end of it"* and *"the human body is just not designed to cope with the punishment these players are expected to go through."* Referring then to the rigours of training and the demands of League, divisional, cup ties and internationals she rightly emphasised: *"Ideally it would be great if they did not have to play every week."* Ideally it would. But try telling that to a mustard keen rugby player, especially if a first team place is up for grabs. So it was no small tribute to the medics that on 30th October (1993) no fewer than eleven fit Bath players at Redruth were selected for the South West XV against the touring New Zealand All Blacks, namely **Jon Callard, Phil de Glanville, Audley Lumsden, Mike Catt, and at forward Chris Clark, Graham Dawe, Victor Ubogu, Nigel Redman, Andy Robinson, Jon Hall (captain) and Ben Clarke.**

Knowing only too well the value of home support, Graham Dawe (a Cornwall county player) was requested on the eve of the match to appear on Cornwall TV so as to implore the faithful to fill Redruth to capacity. The message hit home. Fifteen thousand crammed the terraces to witness a game that would stir Cornish hearts: with passion and sheer guts! Above all there stood the mighty presence of skipper Jon Hall; small wonder he regained his England place against Scotland in February. His fellow forwards were not far behind, among them Chris Clark, recent loose-head arrival at Bath; who not surprisingly would win his Oxford Blue in December. Attrition took its toll though, and De Glanville's eye injury, one requiring fifteen stitches, was described as a shocker and allegedly not acquired purely by accident. The Kiwis, at virtual Test strength won by a narrow 15-19 margin with a Jamie Joseph try and five Matthew Cooper penalties against Paul Hull's drop goal and Callard's four penalties.

At the Rec, with fitness now in the hands of Ged Roddy, Director of Sports Development, Bath University, five starters (Callard, de Glanville, Ubogu, Redman and Ben Clarke) and three replacements (Barnes, Dawe and Jon Hall) were selected for England against New Zealand in November. No Guscott however, side-lined alas by injury. But de Glanville's faultless defensive qualities were to prove invaluable, likewise the maturity of Redman ('man of the match' claimed All Blacks coach Laurie Mains), and so too the four debut international penalties of Jon Callard that bettered J. Wilson's trio for the tourists, and earned the new Rec favourite instant Twickenham adulation. These, added to the Rob Andrews drop goal, gained England a treasured (and rare) 15-9 victory over New Zealand who, one week previously had defeated Scotland 51-15.

League action followed with victory in December at Harlequins (12-14), where local and national hero Gareth Chilcott would bid farewell to senior rugby, next a home win over London Irish, shortly followed by a 24-11 Pilkington Cup victory over Wasps. So far, so good, likewise the perfectly cordial after-match atmosphere that had followed the Quins match; a curious fact in view of allegations (first by Harlequins, then London Irish) that followed, accusing Bath (inter alia) of eye-gauging and biting. But rightfully granted the freedom to put their side of the story (Chronicle, 13th Dec. 1993), Bath secretary John Quin, skipper Jon Hall and chairman John Gaynor scrutinised the match video sent down from the Harlequins. Their opinion concluded as follows, as *"a result of our investigation....no evidence of any misbehaviour by a Bath player which can be adjudged a deliberate act was observed."* With that response the matter was subsequently laid to rest by both parties. No sooner had this issue subsided however than another appeared to take its place (Chronicle, 20th Dec. 1993) when Bath found themselves facing allegations by Bristol of attempting to lure players (two in particular) to the Rec. True or otherwise, it was a fact well known for decades that Bath and Bristol (nor forgetting Clifton) had operated a 'revolving-door' policy regarding the movement of players between clubs, and doing so without anyone batting an eye-lid. Moreover, when Simon Jones (Bath chairman of selectors) responded by stating that *"if someone tells us a player is interested we check..."* he was merely stating the 'blindingly' obvious. Or as Steve Bale had put it equally bluntly (The Independent, 10th Jan. 1989) *"nobody much loves a winner, as Bath have found in their long years of success."* Indeed so, and perhaps significantly no use was made by Harlequins or London Irish of the 'citing' procedure (already introduced) that permitted watching officials to raise a foul-play issue within the following twelve hours.

Despite added excitement, the arrival of the National Leagues and the Cup, meant that the days of playing rugby solely for the fun of it were fading and senior clubs knew that the consequences of relegation meant falling attendances and less sponsorship. Allegations of foul play (true or otherwise) were therefore one possible symptom of the jitters now affecting the game. Even the Combination expressed concerns about Bath's recently formed U.21 team monopolising available young talent. It was fair comment, threatening not least the historic bond between Bath and the Combination. However, when in late season Bath U.21's convincingly overcame the touring Netherland's U.21's by 46-3, few guessed that they would play no further part in the club's future beyond the following season, when Bath decided to channel players from 18 years onwards directly into the Spartans (or higher), and simultaneously to develop the potential of the newly-formed Bath 'Emerging Players.' Furthermore, it would previously have been unthinkable that the electrifying Anglo-Welsh encounters could be another casualty of a changing rugby world. But now with clubs frequently fielding half-strength teams for non-League fixtures the glamour of those Anglo-Welsh fixtures was sadly diminished. If the clubs fielded full strength sides *"we could fill any ground in the country,"* Neath team manager John Williams had remarked on witnessing his side fall 13-27 at home to Bath (both teams under-strength) in Autumn 1990. Bath's Jack Rowell concurred, adding that *"there should be an Anglo-Welsh League and after that you've got to bring the French in as well because that's how big the game is."* But there was no Anglo-Welsh League; and while many on both sides of Offa's *Dyke* mourned this sudden decline, it was perhaps too late.

Come season 1993-4, the RAF's utility back Ed Rayner (winning an Oxford Blue in December) arrived on the Rec and Steve Ojomoh won his first England cap at Twickenham against Ireland. As the season progressed moreover it seemed that Bath might be in the race for another League and Cup double, but they'd have to ride their luck for so demanding a challenge. But there was nothing lucky about the 5th round January cup tie against Bristol, where Bath created just enough space to run home tries from Ojomoh and Catt, Barnes converting both, and their highly disciplined defence that limited Bristol to Mark Tainton's three penalties proved sufficient to ensure a home 14-9 victory. Touchingly, on this same occasion there was a one minute's silence by the 7,500 crowd in memory of former player, club official and Bath devotee Jack Arnold, who had sadly passed away soon after the Bath v Bristol League match two weeks previously. Meanwhile the quarter-final at Saracens watched by Andrew Baldock (Chronicle, 28th Feb. 1994) revealed the same discipline as applied against Bristol, and Bath, *"largely efficient, if rarely flamboyant....briskly went about their business,"* leading to tries from de Glanville, and a scorcher from Adebayo that showed *"what wonderful magic Bath can conjure when it all clicks."* And despite Andy Tuningly's two conversions for Sarries, Callard's two conversions and three penalties would put clear water between the teams and a 6-23 Bath win.

But, the semi-final against Harlequins away, a televised game, was to be the stuff of nervous breakdowns. First, it was the Quins who were literally swept aside in a 25 minute blitz that left the hosts trailing 0-19 as first Swift, then Barnes and next Callard all sped over for searing tries. Bath looked unstoppable. But looks can be deceiving, and now Harlequins moved up a gear to show some of their own tricks. They had plenty of them. First came a Paul Challinor penalty, then a Martin Pepper try and next a penalty try. But that was not all, because further massive 'Quin's pressure led to a Justyn Cassell try followed by Challinor adding a drop-goal to his two conversions. And as 'end-time' approached the Harlequins looked good for a 25-19 semi-final victory. Just one problem....a team called Bath with several minutes remaining on the clock; and as if taunting the Quins in the final seconds of the 1992 cup final was not torture enough, mischievous Fate returned to play one more trick upon 8,000 emotionally drained spectators. So, it just 'had' to happen: Catt broke through to pass on to Callard who passed to Swift and ominously for Harlequins, the try line was already within his sights and range. Two broken tackles en route and he was over the line near the posts. Callard steps forward and calmly sends over conversion number three. That made it 25-26 to Bath. Touché.

"We never lie down and die..." said Jon Hall, Bath having performed yet another of their Houdini escapes from the jaws of defeat but, could they overcome Leicester, their co-finalists at Twickenham? Three weeks onwards the Harlequins were faced in the League, and Jon Hall's side needed only a draw to win their 5th Courage championship outright with the luxury of a game to spare. So hardly surprising that Bath scorned playing it safe, unleashing all their fire-power from the 'off.' Four tries resulted in a 32-13 home win and cause for spontaneous celebration. That made it 30 wins from 37 played, skipper Jon Hall proudly receiving the Courage trophy from RFU president Ian Beer, formerly of England and appropriately: both Harlequins and Bath. With a two-week respite until Twickenham and the probable Twickenham XV rested, the final season's Courage League match (against London Irish) was captained by Bath forward Nick Maslen, who took a virtual United team to Sunbury with Kevin Yates, Tim Beddow, Darren Crompton and Eric Peters among the forwards. Irish, admittedly demoralised since losing their struggle against relegation, were nonetheless strong opponents. However, emphasizing Bath's strength in depth an admittedly close 31-32 away win was achieved, with three

tries (one from wing Mark Woodman) and a 17 points contribution from the boot of out-half Ed Rayner.

Rayner and hooker Tim Beddow were duly selected among the replacements for the Pilkington cup final (7th May) against a Dean Richards-led Leicester; with Twickenham filled to its recently enlarged 68,000 all-seater capacity (a new world-club record):

Bath: *J. Callard, A. Swift, P. de Glanville, M. Catt, A. Adebayo, S. Barnes, R. Hill, D. Hilton, G. Dawe, V. Ubogu, N. Redman, A. Reed, A. Robinson (S. Ojomoh 48), J.Hall (capt.), B.* Clarke.

Leicester: W. Kilford, T. Underwood, S. Potter, L. Boyle, R. Underwood, J. Harris, A Kardooni, G. Rowntree, R. Cockerill, D. Garforth, M. Johnson, M. Poole, J. Wells, N. Back, D. Richards (capt.). Referee: **E. Morrison (Bristol/RFU).**

Two of England's finest? Well yes…. but Leicester's tactics were puzzling and Andrew Baldock (Chronicle, 9th May. 1994) concurred accordingly: the *"Tigers seemed hell-bent on intimidation, and it was to everybody's detriment."* True, and it was probably to everyone's surprise, with two power-packs and two quality back divisions promising something special. Yet there was no passion to be seen…no drama, and former Harlequins and England lock Paul Ackford, (Sunday Telegraph, 8th May) wrote: *"Passes were dropped, tackles missed and there was an undercurrent of tension, but the match never exploded into life."* Indeed, Twickenham remained a try-free zone until ten minutes after the break when Barnes fed de Glanville who, aware that Swift was drifting into space far out on the right, kicked over the Leicester cover and into the Lancastrian's path. Rory Underwood slipped and Swift shot for the line…his 152nd try for Bath. With five minutes remaining scrum-half Hill fed Callard who reached deep into Tigers territory and floated a pass that reached the hands of Mike Catt…try number two, with Callard converting beautifully to add to his three penalties. By contrast Leicester were simply not themselves, and although packed to the gunwales with class, they kept their powder dry, save for three Jez Harris penalties. Oh, such a waste of their undoubted talents.

However, Bath were not complaining about their 21-9 victory, despite abandoning their previous 'lucky' white shirts for the standard colours of blue, white and black. They had won their eighth knock-out cup trophy, their third League and Cup Double, and they just kept winning when it mattered. Again, Paul Ackford wrote: *"It is impossible to do justice to their achievements."* And then with the mind of the soothsayer he pondered thus: perhaps Bath *"should turn professional and take on Wigan at Rugby League. Now that would be a real contest."* It most certainly would!

Naturally, in the real world a club would be delighted to win one Major in a season, let alone two. But to win three Majors would be deemed just ridiculous. Well, Bath did win three! Because following their Pilkington cup triumph a 7's team under Jon Callard embarked for Twickenham one week later to have a go at the Middlesex (Save & Prosper) Sevens, the top 7's competition in Britain and one that Bath had never won. Their chances looked hardly promising, with one hour (yes, 'one 'hour') of pre-tournament training. Indeed, in their 1st round opener against London Scottish when 21-0 up at the interval, an Exiles recovery left Bath clinging on for dear life to scrape through on 28-26. But they recovered to deal with Loughborough Students (24-0), and then left Saracens trailing 19-0. **In the final Eric Peters, Gareth Adams, Martin Haag, Audley Lumsden, Ian Sanders, Jon Callard (capt.) and Ed Rayner** found Orrell sterner stuff. But despite tries from Naylor and another from Wynn converted by Paul Johnson, Bath as so often held one card too many. Tries from Rayner, Lumsden and Callard, plus Callard's two conversions were sufficient to seal a 19-12 triumph. The 'Double' for season 1993-4? No…**the Treble!**

However, on the news of his appointment as new England rugby manager, there would now be a future without Jack Rowell. Hartlepool born, later an Oxford graduate and a John Player winning coach at Gosforth (later Newcastle Falcons), his leadership at Bath had proved simply inspirational. Shortly before his farewell following the Courage League decider against Harlequins he had spoken thus (Chronicle, 25th Apr. 1994): *"We have built a Rolls Royce, one that is a lot easier to drive than it is to build. I have sought to make the players strong…mentally, physically and technically…and to play with one heartbeat."* 'To play with one heartbeat?' Ah yes, just five words of pure rugby poetry that would inspire any team, anytime, anywhere.

Chapter 32. THE BURIAL OF THE HATCHET. (1994-96)

All seemed normal throughout much of the 1994-5 rugby season. Bath remained 'the' team to beat; nor did a single side beat them until March at Cardiff. Their new breath-taking South Stand was open for business. Talent continued to arrive from all corners of the British Isles, including Scotland scrum-half Andy Nicol and Ireland winger Simon Geoghegan, whose *"dashing 70-yard solo try brought the loudest, longest ovation"* plus the instant devotion of the Rec in Bath's October 22-11 League victory over Harlequins. *"Pure box office material"* added the Chronicle's Andrew Baldock of the Irish flyer. Too true it was!

Not surprisingly the national media went into 'hyper-active frenzy' (the Sun included) on learning of Jeremy Guscott's recovery from long-term injury and his return to League action at West Hartlepool on the 15th October. Indeed, by all accounts the hosts couldn't remember if such a response had ever happened before. They would remember however the mad rush for tickets (their press officer receiving *"more ticket demands in one day than he normally does in a season"*) and they could hardly forget the outcome either, because West Hartlepool narrowly missed creating another national sensation, just failing (18-22) to topple Bath. Meanwhile young ex Clifton College flanker Ed Pearce stole half the show and former Harlequin Richard Butland (backs) stole the other half in Bath's Autumn 33-26 win over Oxford University; with both players joined in November by fullback Phil Belgian, wing David Timmington, scrum-half Phil Harvey and locks Craig Gillies and Tim Maguire in Bath's 65-7 win over Loughborough Students, a non-League encounter producing a non-stop galaxy of handling. Another performance, that of young Llandovery scrum-half Marcus Olsen, then stole the show in Bath's knife-edged 9-10 League win at Bristol in January.

Meanwhile one could hardly keep pace with the Bath players called-up for international duties: **Ed Pearce, centre Ben Stafford, scrum-half Phil Harvey, full-back Phil Belgian, lock Craig Gillies and Andrew Blyth, George Truelove, Fraser Waters, Roy Winters and Trevor Woodman** (say all that in one breath), each selected for the season's England Colts squad. Later prop **Kevin Yates, Martin Haag, Gareth Adams, Darren Crompton and Jon Sleightholme** were chosen for the England A tour to Australia and Fiji; while in late March further requests arrived for yet more seniors, namely **Jon Callard, Mike Catt, Ben Clarke, Graham Dawe, Phil de Glanville, Jeremy Guscott, John Mallet, Steve Ojomoh and Victor Ubogu**, all nine selected for England's 1995 World Cup party to South Africa. Scottish selectors then called up Glasgow born **Eric Peters** (back-row) and prop **David Hilton** for their January debuts against Canada. Phew! Yet there remained the serious domestic business of Cup rugby, and having already disposed of 4th round opponents London Scottish by 31-6 at home in December, Bath travelled north for 5th round January action at Orrell, whom it was wise not to underestimate. And Bath knew it. They knew it when 16-6 down at half-time, and but for a masterful line-out display by Martin Haag they might still have known it 40 minutes later. They held their nerve however, as they so often did in such situations, fighting back to earn an admittedly narrow 19-25 win. Next, visitors Northampton arrived for the quarter-finals, a famous club though not enjoying one of their better seasons and in difficulties virtually from the kick-off. Bath went clear with two tries (worth five points since season 1992-3), both converted by Callard, plus his four penalties, and cruising to a 26-6 victory and onwards to the semi-finals.

Ah those semi-finals, where Bath were always drawn away? And no change this time either with a difficult hurdle at Harlequins to clear. Actually, Bath made things look simple, or in the words of Andrew Baldock (the Chronicle): "*Saturday was one of those wonderful Bath occasions-great rugby in great weather with great supporters roaring their heads off.*" Or to be precise it was a 13-31 triumph with tries by de Glanville and two from Swift, two Callard conversions plus his three penalties, and a Catt drop goal, as against tries from Staples and Challinor and a Staples penalty. But Bath's chances of overcoming co-finalists Wasps seemed somewhat less simple, for so inept was their 13-18 defeat at home to Sale on the final Saturday of the Courage League that Andrew Baldock (Chronicle) wrote: "*On this evidence, Wasps can sleep easily and afford to let Bath have the nightmares:*" nightmares hardly eased by the absence of the injured Jon Hall (like Swift due to retire after Twickenham) to play in the final.

More drama however, this time at a national level, would now unfold. Because below the surface of the rugby game tensions were stirring, and had been for some considerable time. When feelings then erupted into 'open space,' as they shortly would, the previously unchallenged control imposed by the RFU since its formation in 1871 would evaporate virtually over-night. The cause of the unrest was the RFU's stringent policy regarding amateurism, and since the mid-1980's voices had been raised within the game (and media) asking for at least some flexibility on this matter. Admittedly the governing body didn't actually shoot the messenger. They just ignored him instead. But the fact was that considerable sums of money were now pouring into a rugby success story, and as a direct result commercial interests, the media, administrators and the advertising industry were among those benefiting financially, save for one notable exception....the players! But the refusal to at least consider the possibility that an advertising deal, for example, between a sports kit producer and players was deemed off-limits. Off-limits or not, in 1982 the Welsh RFU (Bath Chronicle, 14th Dec. 1982) stated that "*it was saddening to learn*" that certain former Welsh internationals had on occasions received payment for wearing sponsored rugby boots. It was further reported "*that there are other companies involved;*" and rumour during this era (it is stressed 'rumour only') suggested that such arrangements extended to other Home international players, and to at least one entire international team. Ironically such a ban was arguably a restraint of trade and thus *prima facie* illegal. Heaven help the player however if known to have broken the rigid interpretation of amateurism as imposed by the RFU! Such attitudes for example that had led to the ban on Tremayne Rodd (former Scotland international) for freelance rugby journalism, Dave Alred for playing US pro' football and would ban 1994 Cambridge

Blue out-half Adrian Spencer for previous appearances in Rugby League (as an amateur!) were attitudes that had not changed.

But beyond the confines of Twickenham something had changed....and many senior players (nor lacking wider support either) had just about 'had' enough. It was their efforts after all that had led rugby union to new heights of popularity, and not forgetting either that international games could by this stage generate some £1.5 million a match. Le Monde for instance featured an article about the Bath club prior to the England v France match in February, and the Chronicle, (9th Feb. 1995) reported that '**Bath rugby shirts**' were among the top sellers in Japan, Africa and the US.' Indeed, at an 'emergency meeting of the Courage League first division clubs' (20th April) Bath chairman Richard Mawditt spoke for many when stating: "*We, as first division clubs, are fed up being dictated to, even ignored. We want to have a clear place in the structure and a better form of communication within the RFU.*" Moreover, the governing body now faced open defiance from some quarters, and since sporting prowess has never hindered employment prospects, it was significant that at least one major London club made no apologies for admitting that jobs could be arranged without difficulty for their leading players if so required. Such a practice was '*not*' confined to London clubs either!

Meanwhile Leicester had established a trust fund in 1993, with the purpose of 'generating cash for their players;' and (Chronicle, 7th Apr. 1995) Bath, under the guidance of businessman Malcolm Pearce, launched a similar project, namely their own limited company (Bath Players Initiative) geared to 'market off-field activities' both for the benefit of the players and a chosen charity. In effect the two clubs were introducing a format for part-time professionalism, and if the RFU had at least considered the advantages of such a scheme, then huge difficulties ahead might well have been avoided. But seemingly the gloves were 'off!' The RFU would not compromise, and comments by England captain Will Carling broadcast on a TV Channel 4 documentary ('The State of the Union') two days before the Cup final would see to that. His views seemed perfectly rational, among them the comment that "*....everybody seems to do very well out of rugby except the players.*" Few, it seemed, would disagree!

Carling's comments however included a somewhat disrespectful (though undeniable comical) reference to the senior members of the RFU, whom he described (in West Country vernacular at least) as a 'bunch of 57 old turnips.' It was spoken in jest really, as anyone with a modicum of humour would normally brush aside ....but not the RFU! Thus, from the East India Club, St James's Square (no less!) a statement was drafted by the RFU president Dennis Easby and his executive committee, and duly announced on the morning of the Twickenham showpiece as follows: "*it has been decided with regret that Will Carling's captaincy of the England team will be terminated forthwith and an announcement concerning his replacement will be made shortly. In the light of the views Will Carling has recently expressed regarding administrators, it is considered inappropriate for him to continue to represent as the England captain, the Rugby Football Union and, indeed, English sport.*" Significantly, not all members of the RFU committee agreed with this statement, among them the Army representative Lt. Colonel Graham Lilley, a former Bedford, Army and Barbarians flanker. *"Way over the top,"* he remarked. You could say that again. And the timing of the RFU statement that coincided with the rugby Cup Final itself and England preparing for the World Cup two weeks hence was catastrophic, as the hierarchy would realise at the exact moment (6th May 1995) when the two finalists stepped on to the Twickenham turf as follows:

Bath: *J. Callard, A. Swift, P. de Glanville, J. Guscott, A. Adebayo, R. Butland, I. Sanders, K. Yates, G. Adams, V. Ubogu (J. Mallet 73min), M. Haag, N. Redman, A. Robinson, S. Ojomoh, B. Clarke.*

Wasps: *J. Ufton, P. Hopley, D. Hopley, G. Childs, N. Greenstock, R. Andrew, S. Bates, D. Molloy, K. Dunn, I. Dunstan, M. Greenwood, N. Hadley, L. Dallaglio, M. White, D. Ryan.* Referee: *J. Pearson (Durham/RFU).*

As was customary the finalists would be introduced to an invited dignitary who, just happened to be Dennis Easby. Suffice to say the introduction-formalities were strained, and the chants of *"Carling, Carling"* echoing around a packed Twickenham suddenly ceased. Instead booing now greeted the RFU president and the message was unmistakable. Bob Jenkins (sports editor, Bath Chronicle, 11th May 1995) subsequently 'hit the nail' when writing that the trouble with the blazers is *"that they think English rugby belongs to them."* Well at Twickenham on 6th May the RFU had learned something else....it didn't!

But what a final! Seven tries (five from Bath), non-stop attack, bone-shaking tackling....it was two of England's best showing English rugby at its best; and the off-field drama was forgotten for the next eighty minutes of blistering action. Though Wasps were rated by most forecasters as pre-match favourites, Paul Ackford (Sunday Telegraph, 7th May) had later concluded that: *"the professional critics must learn never to write off the West Country champions;"* appropriate advice as events showed. During the opening 40 minutes half-backs Sanders and Butland grew steadily in confidence and the whole Bath team responded accordingly. There was furthermore the presence of lock forward Martin Haag. Perfectly capable of playing No.8 or lock at the highest level, his colleagues had long predicted that he would play for England one day. Indeed he would, and on this sunny day he demonstrated exactly why. He was everywhere. His two tries (the first within five minutes) were confirmation of that. Ben Clarke then galloped over for a third before Sanders and Callard set up Tony Swift for the fourth. Ah Swift, the perfect name for a perfect winger. The maestro turns inside, then accelerates round three defenders trying to catch him. No chance. He's over....try number 161 for his Bath collection, alas his last for the club. Engulfed by his team-mates, you could almost feel the emotion that swept through the ranks of his adoring followers. 'Farewell Swifty,' a Bath great.

When on 65 minutes Callard rounded off a Butland-Guscott created overlap for a try to add to his four conversions it seemed that it was all over; well not quite. Wasps, though losing 16-36 were a class act too. Rob Andrew's four penalties (Callard notched a brace for Bath) warned of gifting him goal opportunities within his huge kicking range. Meanwhile prop Paddy Dunstan and Damien Hopley at centre finished off tenacious pressure with individual tries to emphasise that no team can ever drop its guard against these London guys. There was furthermore the threat of the Wasps back-row of England international Dean Ryan, White, and a certain Laurence Dallaglio destined for World Cup greatness in 2003. But this was Twickenham, almost a second home now for Bath with their ninth Cup triumph in twelve seasons. Nor could one overlook the performance of Phil de Glanville, shouldered with the leadership just days prior to the final. The captaincy for the following season was thus his for the taking, and the club he was now destined to lead had completed a season of 34 games, winning 25 with 4 draws and a mere 5 defeats. And now at the culmination of arguably the most dramatic year in rugby history, Bath and coach Brian Ashton could hopefully 'take a breather.' They certainly deserved one.

Before the season closed down completely however one engagement remained, namely the annual club dinner. Invariably a jolly affair, the guest of honour at the Pavilion on 10th May just happened to be the president of the RFU himself, Dennis Easby. By now Carling had been reinstated as England captain, not least because all other nominations to replace him had announced that they would refuse to accept the captaincy in such circumstances. Moreover, the England squad had politely requested that the RFU re-think its actions and so too the national press and rugby fraternity in general. Not surprisingly there was a somewhat uneasy atmosphere prior to the after-dinner speeches, and a subdued groan was audible as the RFU president rose to speak. However, if some had come to mock, soon enough they had reason not to. Dennis Easby, who by his own admission to the press was *resigned to the fact that I will be the most unpopular man in British sport,"* was nonetheless a man of charm, grace, no little contrition and....humour. He sat down to warm, prolonged applause. As Stephen Jones (Sunday Times, 7th Jan, 1996) later reported: *"He and his wife were also brave enough to travel everywhere with the team during the world cup. Even the hardened 'professionals' in the team paid tribute to him for not hiding."* There was irony in all this, for since changes regarding amateurism in rugby union were now inevitable, Dennis Easby suddenly seemed an ideal candidate to lead the game through the stormy waters ahead. How come therefore that the RFU had remained so remote from the changing mood within the sport, and so reluctant to contemplate at least some form of compromise on this issue? Instead, an omnipotent dynasty no longer ruled by Divine Right, and as so often following revolutions (for a revolution this was) no one had the slightest idea who would now lead the new Order. Yes....the King is dead! Long live the King! But which King? No one had a clue.

The action on (and off!) the field would continue into the following 1995-6 season, not least for a Bath club that in Autumn League action not only routed Bristol 52-19 at home to secure the biggest winning margin since these rivals first met in 1888, but then effectively surpassed this feat in March with their stunning 5-43 victory....away! And such was the value attached to 1ˢᵗ team representation in Bath colours that young prop Neil McCarthy gained selection for England U.21's against Ireland in November after only three senior outings. Another one to watch was 18 years old William Gay (son of former Bath and England No.8 David Gay), winning selection that season for England Schoolboys at lock against Japan. Meanwhile the stupendous form of Andy Robinson led to his international recall for England against South Africa at Twickenham in November, albeit England fell 14-24; and come January Bath's former Wakefield wing Jon Sleightholme received news of his call-up for England, this time against France in Paris.

But it would be impossible to ignore the ramifications that commenced from September 1995 when the International Rugby Board (IRB) had suddenly announced that the union game was now professional. Soon enough this decision would dominate an otherwise stupendous season at Bath and lead directly towards two hugely significant events for the club. First there would be the occasion of a life-changer of a club meeting. Secondly, Bath would be called upon to uphold the prestige of the entire rugby union game against arguably the most formidable rugby League club in the world….**Wigan.** But this sudden change was a step into the Unknown, and though professionalism had been accepted in principle, its application was a different matter altogether. Indeed, apart from the fact that players could now be contracted for international matches (likewise fees for international referees and touch judges) there was no immediate blue-print for the wider club professionalised game.

Meanwhile two recently formed groups, namely the EFDR (English First Division Rugby) and EPRUC Ltd (English Professional Rugby Union Clubs) were fast losing patience with the new chairman of the RFU executive, Cliff Brittle, who they argued was stalling efforts to establish a professional format. Indeed, there would be suggestions of a 'breakaway' by a group of senior clubs if their own plans were shelved by the RFU. The counties furthermore, who formed a powerful voting group, did not always see eye to eye with the senior clubs, and according to Bath secretary John Quin, *"….their actions may ultimately force the first division clubs to go their own way."*

Among the first shocks resulted from the Autumn announcement that England international Rob Andrew had accepted an appointment as rugby director at renamed Newcastle Gosforth (later 'Falcons') for a reported signing-on fee (Chronicle, 20ᵗʰ Oct. 1995) of £750,000! This figure dwarfed the £40,000 annual fee recently offered to the 21 members of England's elite international squad, and the rumour that other top players would soon head to Newcastle (some did) quickly aroused fears among rivals that their star players might depart in a new regime of *cheque-book* rugby. Such fears were justified. First, any chances of establishing a part-time professional game, one which a number of first-class clubs could probably have financed, were thrown out of the proverbial window. Secondly, despite the admirable achievements of Gosforth in the 1970's, they were hardly a club that attracted the attendances that could sustain such a massive financial outlay. But they didn't have to! Their financial clout was provided from elsewhere, in Newcastle Gosforth's case the backing of North East businessman Sir John Hall, Newcastle United F.C. chairman and multi-millionaire. Thus, it was immediately realised that money alone could literally buy a whole team of rugby stars, akin in fact to cheque-book football at clubs such as Sir John Hall's Newcastle United and so change rugby union out of all recognition. And when Sir John Hall was quoted as saying: "*I am not investing in a professional sport to have it run by amateurs,*" he wasn't joking. Just as well he wasn't, because the game would soon realise that the professionals weren't always much good at running it either.

Fortunately, Bath chairman **(Professor) Richard Mawditt**, Secretary and Registrar of Bath University, was adamant that the club must not be left defenceless against cheque-book raiders now strongly rumoured to be hovering over the Rec. Nor would he countenance any thoughts of a 'professional club breakaway' from the RFU. But he insisted "*Bath have to maintain our place into the 21st century;*" in other words there was no alternative but to swim with the tide and adopt professionalism. This proposal was duly placed before the members for approval, or otherwise, on the evening of 11th March 1996 at the Pavilion. The membership (they were present in their hundreds) were requested to vote on the proposals accordingly, and arguments both for and against the motion were invited from the 'floor' during the course of the meeting. It was soon apparent from the 'floor' that the proposals would meet with overall approval, and the crucial vote was taken: 806 in favour, six against and eight abstentions. It was a clear acceptance by the membership that Bath simply must bite the bullet of professionalism, even if they didn't like the taste. In short it was realism versus romanticism, and realism won. The decision not only made media headlines, it even attracted interest across the Atlantic, so widespread in fact that club PR officer Ken Johnstone received an 'approach from a Wall Street agency concerning the possibility of a share issue.' Thus the technicalities of the vote (Chronicle, Neville Smith, 12th March 1996) would lead to the: *establishment (and transfer of assets) to a trust company; for the existing trustees to be members of the council of the trust company; and for the dissolving of the Club and forming a limited company, namely Bath Football Club Ltd.* Painful though such changes were to many members, they were absolutely necessary in the circumstances. The predators meanwhile (no doubt drooling at the prospects of a dawn raid on a Bath squad that included 17 full internationals) would have to look elsewhere for spoils.

Notwithstanding the off-field drama that was dominating so much of the season, matters on-field were reaching a climax too and Bath, lest it be forgotten, were not only among the front-runners in the League, they had already reached the semi-finals of the Pilkington Cup. Getting there however was not plain sailing and the pre-Christmas 4th round challenge of Division Two Northampton on the Rec required overcoming atrocious conditions and opponents who looked dead-certs for promotion. But Bath, now so street-wise, overcame the handicaps for a hard-earned 12-3 victory, with Callard's lethal boot winning the kicking dual with his four penalties against Paul Grayson's lone reply for the Saints. Meanwhile the next stop was away at lowly Division Two

Wakefield. Lowly!? This hard team of Yorkshiremen came within 60 seconds of causing the biggest cup upset in English rugby since, well…. Bath's 9-8 defeat at Waterloo in season 1992-3. It was home skipper Mike Jackson who Bath could blame for the damage, his four penalties keeping his gutsy side ahead (if only by a hairs-breadth) from Callard's two penalties and a Guscott try. But just when it seemed that Wakefield were home and dry, recycled ball was spun out by Sanders to half-back partner Richard Butland and close enough for a 'go' at the line. The pair chose to attack on the narrow side with less defensive cover yet just enough space for Butland to do the damage. Try! Wakefield's faithful, cheering themselves hoarse throughout, were silenced. One minute 'ago' it was 12-11 to the Yorkshiremen. Now it was 12-16 to those pesky southerners. Bath….they sure knew how to make themselves unpopular.

One week later, Bath let rip against Wasps with a 36-12 home League victory, followed by their 12-19 quarter-final Cup win at Bristol. That left four teams in a final pool that included Bath and Gloucester. Naturally it just 'had' to be the Kingsholm boys who were drawn against Bath. But, this time there was one consolation, it was a home tie. That the respective coaches were Bath's Jon Hall and Gloucester's ex Bath legend Richard Hill (who knew all the secrets of the Rec) added spice to the impending challenge. Yet Home advantage did help, so too the immaculate kicking of Callard. He would coolly (Oh, so coolly) send five penalties sailing through the uprights, the first within two minutes of the start. He converted from wide out the spectacular solo try of wing Ade Adebayo that sent Bath 19-3 ahead minutes into the second half, at which point it seemed that Gloucester could be heading for a thoroughly uncomfortable afternoon. But never relax against the Cherry and Whites. A Martin Kimber drop goal had given Gloucester at least a fighting chance. While a real gem of a try from scrum-half Scott Benton converted by Mark Mapletoft suggested that the visitors were getting a little too close for comfort. But the fact that they were kept at arm's length was due to Bath's defensive capabilities. It was 19-10, and despite a typical Gloucester fight-back 19-10 it remained. Bath it seemed were by now virtually impregnable against all-comers, save for the possible challenge of Leicester. Ah the Tigers, again Bath's cup final opponents.

The Courage League would be settled in April with a draw on the Rec against Sale. But this was hardly your average drawn game. It concluded on 38-38, with Bath (totally dominant in the first half, yet run ragged in the second) fighting for dear life to squeeze home for a League Champions triumph by a single point over…. Leicester! And Leicester it would be once again on 4th May at Twickenham in glorious sunshine and a 75,000 crowd (another new world club record):

Bath: *J. Callard, A. Lumsden, P. de Glanville (capt.), A.Adebayo, J.Sleightholme, M. Catt, A. Nicol, D. Hilton, G. Dawe, J. Mallett, M. Haag, N. Redman, S. Ojomoh, A. Robinson, W. Peters.*

Leicester: *J. Liley, S. Hackney, S. Potter, R. Robinson, R. Underwood, R.Malone, A. Kardooni, G. Rowntree, R. Cockerill, D. Garforth, M.Johnson, M. Poole, J. Wells, N. Back, D. Richards (capt.).* Referee: **S.** *Lander (Liverpool).*

Teams of this calibre will hopefully produce vintage rugby…. 'hopefully' that is. Instead, the Tigers (winning the lion's share of possession) *"chose to grind Bath into the Twickenham turf."* And, they seemed to have it in the bag when barely five minutes remaining on the clock Matt Poole stole Bath line-out ball and crashed over for a second try, adding that to out-half Niall Malone's in the opening minutes (John Liley converting), plus a Liley penalty. Bath, replying with two Callard penalties and a Mike Catt drop goal were trailing 15-9, and if Liley had converted this second Tigers try then Leicester would surely have put the result beyond doubt. Yet now, with Leicester's hands all but on the trophy it was Bath who suddenly went on the rampage. *"Throwing themselves at Leicester in a concerted charge,* (Dick Tugwell, Bath Chronicle) *they swarmed into the Tiger's 22 following a determined run by centre Adebayo and proceeded to run a series of penalties, before referee Lander became weary of Leicester's persistent offending and blew for a crucial penalty try."* Law 26, clause 2(d) thus kicked in, so allowing for either a penalty or penalty try for persistent infringement of the laws. That gifted Callard a sitter bang in front of the posts and the seven priceless points that would clinch the cup. He couldn't miss surely? Nor did he. Thus Bath, masters of the great escape, had triumphed again for a 16-15 victory! Leicester meanwhile looked devastated.

It was Bath's tenth Cup triumph. Not only that, it was their fifth Cup and League double, and as John Mason (D. Telegraph) exclaimed: *"Given different reasons, the record beggars belief."* Leicester too found it hard to believe. But sport, like Nature, can be cruel, and so anguished was their young (and brilliant) flanker Neil Back that on the final whistle his emotions got the better of him. He pushed aside referee Steve Lander, a potentially dreadful lapse from which he apologised in person, and would later regain his good name with quite stunning displays for England. For Bath, for whom winning by a photo finish was now the norm (some might call it 'sadism'), one further test remained. Because in December the gauntlet had been thrown down to play Wigan, one game under League rules in the North and one under Union rules at Twickenham. And Bath accepted without a second thought. However, it was a high-risk undertaking, with nothing less than the reputation of the Union code at stake, moreover against Wigan, regarded as arguably the best Rugby League club on the planet. Fortunately, some 'inside' information was available in the person of Gary French who, hailing from the North had previous Rugby League experience. In fact, apart from the World War Two era he was the first known League recruit to play Union for Bath. A hooker, he had gained his Bath 1st team baptism in the final Courage match against Sale and was willing to bet that Bath would win under the Union code rules. But under League rules against Wigan (Chronicle, 4th May 1996) it was a different matter. *"They are the best there is,"* he said. *"It will be very difficult to hold them in a game where it is much easier to score tries."* And he warned: *"You simply must not miss a tackle...."*

Gary French wasn't kidding, and on the evening of 8th May Wigan, full-time professionals, would unleash a stunning 82-6 display of non-stop handling at Maine Road, Manchester, running home 16 tries as against one by Bath. *"They were just fabulous...."* said Jon Callard, the scorer of Bath's lone try on the night. *"One minute we thought we had them going nowhere and the next they just took off again."* But the masters from the North were not finished yet. Next, they swept down to London at the weekend, seizing the Middlesex Sevens title with their 38-15 victory over Wasps in the final. Wasps captain Laurence Dallaglio (Chronicle, 13th May 1996) marvelled at what he saw. *"Their sheer power, fitness, lines of running and support play were awesome,"* then adding: *"For the sake of all of rugby union Bath must beat Wigan."* So, with the pride of Rugby Union at stake the two contestants stepped out upon a sun-drenched Twickenham on 25th May as follows:

Bath: *J. Callard, A. Lumsden, P. de Glanville (capt.), Adebayo (J. Ewens 57m), J. Sleightholme (R. Butland 73), Catt, I. Sanders, K.Yates, G. Dawe (G.French 74), V. Ubogu (N. McCarthy 46) M. Haag, N. Redman, A. Robinson, E. Pearce. S. Ojomoh.*

Wigan: *K.Radlinski (Smyth 75m), J. Robinson, H. Paul, G.Connelly, M.Offiah, J.Lydon (Cassidy 41), C.Murdock, T.O'Connor, M. Hall, N.Cowie, G. West (Tallec 50), A.Farrell (capt.), S.Tatupu, V.Tugamala, S.Quinnell.* **Referee:** *B. Campsall (Yorks/RFU panel).*

The likes of Jason Robinson, Henry Paul (both set to join Bath), Martin Offiah, Joe Lydon, Andy Farrell (later Union player and coach of Saracens and England), Scott Quinnell and Va'iga Tugamala were enough to cause heart-attacks just by reading their names on the team-sheet. Yet this time it was Union rules, not League. And it would show. Indeed, come the 50th minute Bath had already surged into a 39-0 lead, and their front row of Yates, Dawe and Ubogu had lifted the Wigan front trio out of the scrum so often that many among the 40,000 crowd perhaps wondered if Bath themselves could reach 80 points or more. But in the last quarter the fitness factor stepped in, and the pro's of Wigan's began to make their mark. It led to three tries, all gems, that would narrow the gap; though not enough to overtake Bath's seven (six of them real scorchers), plus their deserved penalty try when Wigan had killed the ball while being steam-rolled backwards at a five-yard scrum. The seven try tally and a Callard penalty ensured a 44-19 victory and.... the restoration of Union pride and self-belief. It was truly an historic day, not least for Bath's former League hooker Gary French who replaced Graham Dawe late on, and for 18 years old Colston schoolboy Joe Ewens (England U.19 captain) introduced as replacement wing on 57 minutes. Ian Sanders too was in confident mode, appearing totally underwhelmed (as did the entire Bath team) by the occasion; hence the push-over try and the six touch-downs from Ade Adebayo (a double), Sleightholme, Catt, de Glanville and the dynamic Sanders. What an occasion! Majestic Wigan, humble in victory then noble in defeat, proved themselves the supreme ambassadors of their code. Scrum-half Craig Murdock, scorer of two superb tries (the fearsome Tuigamala crashed through for their third) spoke thus (Chronicle, 27 May 1996): *"The pace of the game was phenomenal. All credit to Bath for winning and for the way they played."* Thus, on a glorious May day at rugby HQ the two codes had at long last 'drawn a line' under the disputes of the past. The game really could move forwards, and watching from the stands was Wigan's injured half-back legend Shaun Edwards. His post-match verdict said it all: *"That was the finest game of rugby union I have ever seen."* And so it was that Bath and Wigan had closed the book on one hundred years of divide since the Great Schism, and simultaneously had opened the first pages of a new chapter of harmony between the two codes.

Sleightholme hands off Jason Robinson. Bath 44 v Wigan 19 at Twickenham 1996
Acknowledgements: Bob Ascott.

Chapter 33. TRIUMPH amid The MAELSTROM (1996-2000)

Season 1996-7 would see British rugby sailing into unchartered waters, duly summarised by Mick Cleary and Norman Harris (Observer, 16th Feb. 1997) thus: *"when the green light was given 18 months ago, clubs were forced to go from quaint, parochial amateur outfits to lean, vigorous and slick businesses in a matter of a few weeks...."* Well, some were not exactly parochial amateurs, but few if any were prepared for the shock-waves ahead. At Bath the priority was to ring-fence the club's talented player-pool, some of whom were *"understandably tempted by a flood of staggering contract offers from other clubs"* (Dick Tugwell, Chronicle, 29th Aug. 1996). Ben Clarke accepted a reported £500,000 deal to join Richmond, with club-mates Darren Crompton, Chris Clark and Adam Vander joining him. That the club did not lose other stars was due, not least, to their Director of Rugby Jon Hall and the crucial intervention of businessman Andrew Brownsword who, recognising the huge importance of Bath rugby to the city, provided a £2.5 million financial safety-net that would ensure vital stability during this period of upheaval. Hence Hall could not only keep the majority of a talented squad, but furthermore strengthen it, including rugby league recruits Christian Tyrer (Widnes), former Wales and British Lions flanker Richard Webster (Salford) and backs Henry Paul and Jason Robinson (Wigan). Their brilliance was witnessed in Bath's 87-15 win over Swansea in September. Henry Paul impressed, *"scoring two magical tries,"* and Jason Robinson's first of two was typically finished off with *"a jink inside, a flash of instant acceleration and he was in the clear, ghosting in by the posts to a huge roar of acclaim."*

Yet beneath the surface there was no little chaos resulting from the introduction of professionalism. England had initially been threatened with exclusion from the Five-Nations owing to a pre-season separate TV deal with Sky; a September England training session was abandoned owing to a boycott by the entire squad, and a continued threat by the English Professional Rugby Union Clubs (EPRUC) to breakaway was not resolved until late Autumn, a schism (Chronicle, 4th Oct. 1996) that potentially might have excluded every player in Divisions 1 and 2 from England selection. Meanwhile financial problems were already afflicting numbers of clubs, including Llanelli, reportedly facing bankruptcy. Thankfully, Bath's first professional Courage League season ran smoothly enough and included a 76-7 home win against Bristol that saw Charlie Harrison at scrum-half and Jason Robinson at full-back in a performance that was to *"leave a Rec crowd spellbound."* Others shone too, including wing Mike Horne and utility back Matt Perry (son of former Bath favourite Brendan Perry) now showing remarkable promise. In addition, the season would see Bath (de Glanville in his second year of his captaincy) take their first steps into European competition (the Heineken European Cup) with an emphatic 55-26 Pool A victory over Edinburgh, next a 19-6 defeat at Pontypridd, then a 25-16 victory over Dax. With Treviso then swept aside 27-50 it was off to the quarter-final at Cardiff, the Welshmen winning 22-19 in a nail biter, and doubtless to the Welsh club's relief, Bath's kicking-ace Callard was surprisingly omitted from the Bath line-up.

And to think a fortnight later Callard notched five penalties and three conversions in Bath's 36-17 win over touring (Western) Samoa.

Bath nonetheless were no more sheltered from the 'storm' than anyone else, and it was now reported that head coach Brian Ashton was concerned as to his exact role within the club's re-organisation. To the dismay of many, he resigned in January, and issued (7th Jan. 1997) the following statement: *"I leave Bath taking some wonderful memories with me. It was a privilege working alongside so many talented players."* And significantly Ireland nominated Ashton as advisory coach to the Irish national squad within a week of his departure. Two weeks later **Andrew Brownsword** appointed himself as Bath chairman, so taking a hands-on role in the club. Former player Tony Swift was then nominated as chief executive and this strengthening at the top was to prove timely. Because Bath, out of Europe, would shortly be out of the Pilkington Cup when come the 6th round against Leicester they lost 39-28.... at home. The reaction was immediate. Andy Robinson was confirmed as head coach. Nigel Redman was accorded responsibility for the forwards, while Dave Robson re-joined in a youth development and recruitment capacity. In addition, the task of overall manager was handed to former Leicester and England centre Clive Woodward, recent coach at London Irish. No one realised then, but the Woodward-Robinson link would later prove to be one of profound importance. Alas, there would be no place for the great Jon Hall, whose fate (likewise that of others elsewhere) was to have stepped into a pivotal role as Director of Rugby at this most uncertain time in rugby history. In less demanding days there would have been time to 'grow' into such a role. No longer....time was now of the essence! Indeed, between April 1996 and May 1997 the departures of Tony Russ (Leicester), Paul Turner (Sale), Barrie Corless (Moseley), Peter Williams (Orrell), Mark Ring (West Hartlepool), Dick Best (Harlequins) and Jon Hall (Bath) were testament to that. As Peter Jackson wrote (D. Mail, 14th May 1997): when it comes to the sacking business *"the game has taken less than one season of full-blown professionalism to become every bit as ruthless as soccer...."*

Disruption or not, the team produced some of their most deadly home form with later demolition-jobs against the likes of Gloucester (71-21) and Leicester (47-9), form that secured the runners-up slot in the Courage League, qualification for Europe, plus the selection of eight current Bath players, namely **Adebayo, Catt, de Glanville, Sleightholme, Ojomoh, Mallett and the uncapped Martin Haag and Kevin Yates** for the forthcoming England tour of Argentina, Haag and Yates winning their debut caps in England's 20-46 win over the hosts in May 1997. So, Bath had survived the first full year of professional rugby union largely unscathed. However, pre-season (Chronicle, 21st Aug. 1997) it was announced that '**Jack Rowell** had resigned as coach of the National team,' and a deeply moved Phil de Glanville spoke thus: *"He [Rowell] has had a wonderful career as England coach....."* Indeed so. Meawhile Bath, with three international captains in their ranks, namely de Glanville (England), Dan Lyle (USA), and Andy Nicol (Scotland and now Bath skipper) faced challenges for the Big Three: the

Premiership (League), the National Cup, and the Heineken European Cup, and it was during the latter that nerves would be tested to breaking point. So, it was fortunate that added to the player-pool was Ieuan Evans, a classic Llanelli and Wales wing who in early League action *"conjured up two brilliant tries....as Bath clinched a decisive 47-31 victory over Allied Dunbar Premiership One rivals Richmond..."* Then in November two outstanding 20-year olds, namely hooker **Andy Long** (formerly Bournemouth RFC) and **Matt Perry** at full-back, made their England debuts against Australia at Twickenham (result: 15-15). In United's earlier 71-17 win over Moseley, recently signed Zimbabwe international No.10 Kennedy Tsimba's try hat-trick revealed the exciting rugby potential of the African Nations, while teenage back Iain Balshaw added 26 points from two tries and eight conversions and centre Mike Tindall demonstrated sufficient power to collapse a brick wall. Come March tight-head prop **Chris Horsman**, struck by illness so severe it had threatened his entire rugby career, was selected within weeks of recovery for England U.21's v Scotland.

With European action in Autumn, Bath took their reputation to fortress Pontypridd, and as Victor Ubogu remarked: *"....they don't lose that many games here."* Well, on this occasion they did, and with tries from Ubogu, Butland, and a conversion and three penalties from Callard (who else), Bath clinched a critical 15-21 away win, followed by a 17-31 success at Borders side Hawick. But....next opponents were formidable reigning Heineken champions Brive on the Rec, with coach Andy Robinson's exhortations that to win they simply must " ***dominate the French side up front."*** They did just that! And with Nigel Redman omnipotent throughout and *"superb tries from Matt Perry and Mike Catt;"* plus 17 priceless points from Callard's boot, it was an inches-close 27-25 victory. The return visit of Hawick seemed far less demanding, except it wasn't. Indeed, tries from Bryan Redpath, Michael Dodds and Tony Stanger, plus two penalties and conversion from Craig Chalmers came close to spoiling the party save for Callard's five penalties, a conversion, his try and the Eric Peters try for a 27-23 win. While in the return at Brive the party was indeed spoiled, the holders gaining La Revanche with a 29-12 victory. And yet, 'if' Bath could clinch their home leg against Pontypridd in Pool C, plus 'if' the other results went right, a quarter-final was theirs. Moreover, when Callard (now Woodward's replacement as club player-coach) notched five penalties, Catt added a drop goal and Dan Lyle a try, as against a Neil Jenkins penalty and a conversion of Gareth Wyatt's try for Pontypridd**,** a quarter-final followed in November against Cardiff, thankfully at home, yet still tough as hell.

And hell it proved to be, though Bath clinched a 32-21 win thanks to some outstanding performances. Callard notched five penalties and a conversion, punishing a Cardiff side frequently pulled up by French referee Didier Mene for offside. Cardiff however, upset by the numerous penalties against them and the disallowing of a 'possible' Craig Morgan try, saw things differently. Their angst moreover spread to Cardiff followers (Chronicle, 10th Nov. 1997), and not only did the referee at the final whistle find *"himself surrounded by a group of visiting supporters as he tried to leave the field....,"* (Bath's Richard

Webster, Callard and Ieuan Evans intervening to calm matters), he was later provided with a police escort to his car. Elsewhere the English contingent were falling like flies, with Harlequins, Wasps and Leicester all ousted by French opposition. That left Toulouse (inaugural Heineken winners in 1996), Brive, and Bath (at home) to face Pau. The try count was one apiece from Ubogu and Pau's Philipp Barnat-Salles. The penalty-count favoured Bath with Callard's five and David Aucagne's three. The play-pattern was attacking French flair versus Bath's stone-wall defence, not forgetting piercing running from Matt Perry. Defence triumphed for a 20-14 Bath win that concluded with skipper Andy Nicol leading his elated team on a joyous lap of honour.

Now for the final against Brive at neutral Bordeaux where all questions would be answered on 31st January 1998 as the two sides stepped out onto the magnificent Stade Lescure as follows: **Bath: *J.Callard, I.Evans, P.de Glanville, J. Guscott, A. Adebayo, M. Catt, A.Nicol, D.Hilton, M.Regan (F.Mendez 77), V.Ubogu, N. Redman, M. Haag, N. Thomas (R. Earnshaw 71), R. Webster, D. Lyle.***

Brive: *Penaud, J.Carrat, Lamaison, Venditti, S.Carrat (Viars), Arbizu, Carbonneau, Casadei, Travers, Crespy (Laperne 49), Alegret, Manhes, van der Linden, Magne, Duboisset (Sonnes 70).* Referee: ***J. Fleming, (Scotland)*** .

Heineken Cup Final 1998. Richard Webster blocks Brive forward drive. Other Bath players (L to R) Ubogu, Hilton, Lyle, Nicol.

Acknowledgements: Bob Ascott.

Those watching included a reported 35 million on TV and an estimated 6,500 Bath supporters amongst a packed stadium, and for long periods Brive led. As Steve Hill wrote (Chronicle, 2nd Feb. 1998): Brive (ahead 15-6 at the interval) *"....dominated the first half to such an extent that victory for the French side seemed a formality."* Later....Bath countered with a potential game-changer when 22 metres from the Brive line Dan Lyle fed Nicol, who launched the deadly Guscott into open space. Unselfishly he lined up Callard for the run-in....and a try and conversion by the fullback brought Bath within two points of Brive at 15-13. This was countered by an Alain Penaud drop goal to lift Brive to 18-13, only for Callard to flight home two penalties in reply, leaving **Bath tenuously 18-19 ahead** at normal full-time. Home and dry? Not on your life! Five minutes of extra-time remained and don't even talk about 'pressure!' Lamaison (already successful with five penalties) spliced another. Then came out-half Lissandro Arbizu's chance to settle things with a simple drop-goal attempt. Nerves got to him too. His kick veered wide; and just when tensions reached breaking point the final whistle sounded. Jubilation! On Sunday evening the team bus chauffeured skipper Andy Nicol and his returning heroes through the Bath streets in scenes *"hardly ever seen before in the city."* In Victoria Park alone an estimated two thousand crowd had braved a cold winter's night to acclaim the victors with rapturous cheers and applause. And in a season that included early exit from the National K.O. Cup, but a creditable 3rd place in the Allied Dunbar Premiership (nor forgetting a £2 million sponsorship deal with Blackthorn Cider for three years) Bath were now crowned 1997-8 **Kings of Europe.**

But the Maelstrom was taking its toll and Bristol, of all people, dropped out of the top flight, a warning that literally no one was safe now! And though Bath 'appeared' to be on dry land, confusion abounded elsewhere, including Wales where a rescue package of a reported £1.2 million had been loaned by the Welsh RFU to save seven leading clubs from financial collapse and legendary Llanelli, found themselves in the words of chairman Ron Jones (D. Mail, 11th Dec. 1997) struggling in a *"rugby environment which is so uncertain that nothing surprises us anymore."* The earthquakes hit England too, and by March 1999 Richmond had already cost their benefactor Ashley Levett a staggering £8 million to bankroll. He withdrew his support and the club's fate was ejection from the Premiership per the rules of English First Division Rugby Ltd, namely that a club in administration *'automatically forfeits its right to membership of the elite.'* Since the Premiership (Peter Jackson, D. Mail, 13th May 1999) was already reportedly £30 million in debt, the finances of top flight English club rugby could not sustain any further losses without the possible collapse of the entire pro' game in England. Happily, Richmond and likewise others, though dropping from the top flight, did not disappear, and would be among those competing in the Championship (one below the Premiership) in the seasons ahead, among them: Bedford, Nottingham, Coventry, L. Scottish and *'Richmond.'* Yet professionalism 'could' have been introduced in managed stages, and as Blackheath chairman Frank McCarthy commented ruefully (D. Mail, 12th Apr. 1998): *"We should have taken two years over professionalism and done it properly. Instead, we tried to do the whole thing in about two weeks and made a mess."* And Bath, under new skipper Richard Webster would be denied the chance to defend their Heineken crown, because 'English First Division Rugby' had withdrawn their members from the 1998-9 competition due to a dispute over both the commercial income and control of the European tournament. A positive change however was the 1998-9 introduction of the ten-minute **'sin-bin' rule** now available to Allied Dunbar Premiership referees and coincidentally the season when de Glanville would be the first Bath player to wear a No. 13 shirt (since the early 1950's) following a League decision to now harmonise shirt numbers. Lucky 13? Well, not when Bath's Cup hopes ended with 25-22 defeat at Newcastle Falcons. Yet, expectations rose with the arrival, among others, of All Black half-back Jon Preston and Irish international centre Kevin Maggs. But this was no guarantee of a top six League place for Euro' entry the following season, a task that looked distinctly shaky until Bath clinched a 'must' 14-33 win at Saracens. Moreover, other results went 'right' and a 76-13 victory over London Scottish for 6th (Allied Dunbar) 1998-9 League position secured the last ticket for Europe.

Now, season 1999-2000 brought the curtain down on a century of Rugby Union that had undergone dramatic changes in a mere four years since commencing professionalism in 1996-7, and despite the absence of Guscott, Matt Perry and de Glanville on Autumn World Cup duty for England, Bath shot off the starting-blocks under new skipper Jon Callard with a sparkling September 10-30 win at Harlequins and standout performances from Welsh flanker Gavin Thomas, Irish prop Clem Boyd and Australian centre Shaun Berne. But, in the Heineken European Cup Bath found themselves in another 'Group from Hell.' However, the unexpected happened with Bath losing 25-32 against Toulouse at home, yet winning 14-19 in France with five goals from All Black Jon Preston, and prop Jon Mallett producing a massive front-row performance. So, with Bath and Toulouse level, victories away (15-56) and then home (41-0) against Padova, plus a 20-9 home win over Swansea would probably have put Bath into the last eight, but for an earlier 10-9 defeat at Swansea. Nor was it any comfort to lose 13-6 at Gloucester in the opening National (now Tetley's Bitter) K.O. Cup. Nonetheless, post-Christmas a string of victories followed (leading to the league runners-up spot) that included a nine try and 16-64 blitz at London Irish that inspired Stuart Collier (Chronicle, 13th Mar. 2000) to write thus: *"....rarely in the professional era had the team appeared to believe so firmly in their collective ability."* Backs Mike Tindall and Iain Balshaw duly commenced England careers in the inaugural 'Six Nations' against Ireland at Twickenham (5th February 2000), with Kevin Maggs playing for Ireland. While Bath flankers Angus Gardiner and Gavin Thomas represented England and Wales respectively in the 'A' international on the Rec in March, (rslt: home win 14-9). Alas, the admired Victor Ubogu would now call it a day, his regrets shared by the departing 6ft 10in former giant Wallaby lock Warwick Waugh from a city that he had in his own words: *"fallen in love with."*

Chapter 34. THE FATEFUL HOUR. (2000-03)

Come the opening season of the 21st century and the Rugby Game's trauma of the past five years Ben Clarke was now captain, with Jon Callard stepping into the role vacated by Andy Robinson's call-up to the England coaching staff, and backs Tom Voyce, Stuart Bellinger and prop forward David Barnes among the new arrivals. But despite a trio of wins kick-starting the now Zurich sponsored Premiership season of 2000-01, defeats, a home 21-33 fall to Saracens for instance, spelt 'caution.' Heineken Cup hopes too were mixed, with an opening 26-13 home win over Castres in October, followed by defeats at Newport and Munster. Castres were then overcome 19-32 in France and Munster were convincingly defeated 38-10 at home; but second chances rarely happen in European

Jerry Guscott England v Tonga 15/10/1999
Jeremy Guscott scores and Mike Catt supports

Acknowledgements: Bob Ascott

competition, and the ground lost by those earlier upsets could not be recovered. The National Cup K.O. ('Tetley's Bitter') was proving no more successful, with Bath falling at first attempt with an 18-24 home defeat against, wait for it….Gloucester! While rubbing salt into wounds was a 16-9 defeat in December, namely Bristol's first victory against their arch rivals for thirteen long years; and where Bath's promising Sam Cox (19 years) was presented with the hardest task in rugby, namely stepping into the shoes of the retiring Jeremy Guscott. Meanwhile the season would not pass without Bath's international contingent finding themselves locked in a dispute described by England manager Clive Woodward as *"one the saddest days in the history of English rugby union."* The issue involved a disagreement with the RFU over players' match fees, and the entire England squad simply withdrew their services until their demand was met. They sought (Chronicle, 22nd Nov. 2000) a match guarantee fee-ratio of 70 per cent up front and a win bonus of 30 per cent, as opposed to the RFU's offer of an alternative 60/40 per cent ratio. The RFU, perhaps chastened by the experience of the mid-1990's schism, duly agreed with the demands. However, it was Bath's pre-Christmas 56-20 home win over London Irish that would inspire the self-belief that led directly to a sparkling second half of the season, revealing again a capacity to leap from darkness into daylight in the space of a single week.

The surge put the club amongst the pack chasing the Zurich Premiership title, with Tigers looking favourites. Or so it seemed, save for an unexpected announcement duly reported by the Chronicle's Owen Houlihan (8th Feb. 2001) as follows: *the winners of the Zurich **play-offs** will be crowned English champions, **rather than the side that tops the Premiership table**.*" It was furthermore planned that the League's top 'eight' finishers would be involved in these play-offs, so raising the outside possibility (though highly unlikely) that the team in 8th position could win the play-offs, and with it the Championship title, plus 'the' Heineken place thrown in for good measure. The plan was quickly withdrawn, though not the 'play-off' concept itself. Indeed, the play-offs did commence as first stated, but as a competition separate from the Premiership, and Bath, assisted by former Wigan 'great' Ellery Hanley as temporary defensive coach reached the final after a 31-36 semi-final victory at Wasps. Nonetheless, with Leicester already crowned League champions few among Twickenham's 33,500 attendance (13th May) would begrudge the Tigers their 22-10 victory on final-day at Twickenham.

However, a 3rd Zurick Premiership place ensured qualification for next season's Heineken, while scrum-half Gareth Cooper won his debut cap for Wales against Italy, likewise lock Steve Borthwick winning his debut cap in England's impressive home 48-19 success over France and come April Mike Catt, Iain Balshaw and Matt Perry gained selection for the Lions tour of Australia. Tom Voyce, Mark Regan and Andy Long were selected for the England 2001 summer tour of Canada and USA, along with Bath back Ollie Barkley (19 years), a virtual newcomer to senior rugby, who won his first cap on the same tour. In addition, the respective international debuts of Andy Lloyd (lock/back row) and Gavin Thomas (back-row) for Wales on the Welsh summer tour of 2001 raised Bath hopes for the following 2001-2 season. However, by the end of September three League defeats, including a nightmare 48-9 drubbing at Leicester, raised serious questions, despite an Autumn run of Heineken success at Biarritz (6-14), then at home to Swansea (38-9), followed by a competent home and away double over Edinburgh that offered some encouragement for new captain Dan Lyle and coach Jon Callard.

There was relief too for traditionalists regarding the issue of 'name-change' in line with a then current trend that led to, for example, Sale 'Sharks,' and Newcastle 'Falcons.' The idea was even put to the popular vote. But despite (or perhaps 'because of') nominations that included Bath Dragons, the Bullets, and not forgetting the Wreckers (Oh No!) the response was somewhat muted. Even the Romans, the smart-money favourite, failed to gain sufficient support. So once again this idea 'hit the buffers.' 'Bath' it was and 'Bath' it b…..y well would stay! Yet of the events (on and off the field) during the first half of the season, none were to be more poignant than the heart-felt respect shown prior to the Bath v Saracens match on Saturday 15th September following the 'nightmare' of New York, 9/11. A hushed silence fell over the Rec during the one minute's silence, an especially painful experience for Bath and US Eagles captain Dan Lyle, whose father (fortunately not among the twin tower victims) headed the New York Military Academy. Perhaps with thoughts elsewhere, Bath didn't win that day, and by the half-way stage of the season it was painfully obvious that their erratic League form plus a 12-20 home defeat to London Irish in their opening shot at the National K.O. Cup (now Powergen-sponsored) was ringing alarm-bells. Nor were pressures eased when in January Bath, preparing for a crucial Heineken quarter-final against Llanelli (losing 10-27) were handed a £5,000 fine (suspended) for retaining six players otherwise required for an England training session. Coach Jon Callard was adamant that 'England Rugby Ltd' (the club/RFU organ administering England's international affairs) had granted permission for the player-retention. But, whoever 'waved through' the request could not (or 'would' not) be identified when requested by Bath to do so.

Yet it was League form that increasingly aroused fears of the appalling consequences of relegation, and not making matters easier was the departure of head coach Jon Callard in March, handing over the reins to assistant coach Michael Foley, the former Wallaby hooker perhaps mindful of the words of England scrum-half Matt Dawson following Northampton's recent 11-29 win at Bath (Chronicle, 28th Mar. 2002): *"No team in the country apart from Leicester perhaps can really afford to lose players of the calibre of Mike Catt, Matt Perry, Kevin Maggs, Gareth Cooper and Andy Williams to long-term injuries in a league as competitive as the Premiership."* In fact Leeds, not Bath, lay at the foot of the table, Bath one place above, and then quite unexpectedly both clubs were granted their stay of execution; since Rotherham, National League Division One champions had failed to complete the *RFU's* '85' stringent criteria' required for promotion. The club protested vehemently. But the RFU and English Rugby Ltd refused to budge an inch. Nonetheless, it was now obvious that no club was safe from relegation, any more than the Titanic was unsinkable, and Bath for long nigh-on unbeatable had endured a frightening experience. Soon, things would be downright terrifying!

Indeed, come season 2002-3 there was no respite for Bath. True, the arrivals of French prop Alessio Galasso, Welsh international hooker Jonathan Humphries, back row men Adam Vander (England 'A') and Andy Beattie, plus backs Alex Crocket (England U.21), ex Bristol scrum-half Ross Blake and Australian U.21 half-back Chris Malone from Exeter, would strengthen the squad, and not for the first time Bath would excel in at least one competition, in this case the **Parker Pen Challenge Cup**, a home and away event for those clubs in the top European Leagues, but who failed to qualify for the Heineken. However, another problem was the 8,250 crowd-capacity limit of the Rec. Ticket demands frequently exceeded ticket availability, while Premier Rugby had now stipulated that a minimum capacity of 10,000 must be reached by the end of season 2003-4. Furthermore, a Court action resulting from a local group's opposition to further Rec development had recently ruled that 'supervision of the Rec should now pass to a charitable trust,' and it seemed impossible to predict when this issue might be resolved. Yet there were brighter moments too, not least when in February alongside club-mate Gareth Cooper, Jon Humphreys of Bath captained Wales against England in Cardiff, in fact a win for Clive Woodward's ever-improving English side, and the League debut in March of Samoan international back Elvis (yes, 'Elvis') Seveali'i, who against Saracens this former Wellington Lions winger sure had 'em all kinda shook up' (as the Chronicle's Mike Tremlett put it) with a chip-and-chaser for an 80 metre try that aroused rapturous applause around the Rec in a desperately needed 30-9 win that lifted the club off the foot of the table. But brighter moments apart, there were further quandaries, not least outside the scrum. In the 29-16 defeat at Kingsholm for example, Bath fielded an entire international back-line, yet failed even once to cross the Gloucester line, a shortfall that led Brian Smith to comment ruefully (Chronicle, 11th Feb. 2003) that Bath have *"got a star-studded international back division on paper. The trouble is the game isn't played on paper, it's played on grass."* Nicely put. Moreover, while progress in the European (Parker Pen) Challenge Cup would normally have generated considerable excitement and Grewcock's side had overcome Gran Parma (Italy), Bridgend and then Montauban (France) to reach the semi-finals against Saracens, Bath's League form was literally set to nose-dive. Indeed, come late April when Bath reached the Challenge Cup final itself, they looked the likely contenders for the 'drop,' barring one other club…. Bristol!

How Fate has long played games with these two rivals, and when in the penultimate weekend of the 2002-3 League programme Bristol ironically faced Bath (and winning 30-20) before some 21,000 at Ashton Gate, it seemed the dice had already fallen in their favour, since even if Bath then won by a landslide against Newcastle Falcons, it would come to nought if Bristol won at London Irish. For Bath, their destiny no longer in their own hands, all else was now irrelevant. Their Powergen K.O. Cup venture had ended in 29-30 quarter-final defeat at home to Northampton. So what! They had reached the European Challenge Cup final itself. So what! Survival in the Premiership….that it is now what mattered. Nothing else! As for a suggested merger between the two rivals, centre Mike Tindall (Chronicle, 9th May 2003) spoke thus: *"I love [Bath] too much to want the merger with Bristol to go ahead."* And on 10th May there came the fateful hour, a terrifying task duly summarised by the Chronicle's Mike Tremlett as *"the most important game in the club's entire 138-year old history."* That was no exaggeration, and Jack Rowell (club director of rugby) had already warned (Chronicle, 9th Dec. 2002) that *"the team which goes down, unless it keeps its players, could go into oblivion."* Such were the awesome responsibilities now thrust upon Danny Grewcock's team that saw action that day. The match, under Cheltenham referee Chris White, started badly for Bath, their nerves tested from two Jonny Wilkinson penalties. But some confidence returned with Fullback Balshaw's try under the posts and Barkley's conversion. Wilkinson then replied with a 40 metre penalty to reclaim a 7-9 Falcons lead, only for Bath to respond when hooker Jon Humphries fired the starting pistol on a handling move that reached Tindall, then Balshaw, then Voyce's try wide-out, then Barclay's next conversion and Bath now 14-9 ahead. Half-time and news from Reading: '*Irish were leading 24-13!* Now the heat was on Bristol. But within the opening minutes of the re-start a bullet-like 40 metre drop-goal by Wilkinson reduced the Bath lead to 14-12, Yet Bath were the better side for scoring tries, and on 50 minutes they struck again. Falcons 'messed-up' in their 22, Tindall pounced on stray ball and Bath were in no mood to waste chances like this one. The pack stormed forward and a fired-up Nathan Thomas made it try number three, again wide-out, though Barkley made the conversion look easy. Meanwhile further Bath pressure led to the inevitable penalty, Barkley duly collecting the three points and Bath were now 24-12 ahead going into the home straight. Job done? No! For Bath's Premiership survival (and quite possibly their entire future in senior rugby) depended on another encounter. Apprehensively, and fully aware of its implications, the Rec crowd held its collective breath. Then….a voice on the tannoy interrupted the stillness and the sound of sheer relief could have lifted the roof off the West stand. Irish had won 41-21! Bath 'had' survived. Countless prayers answered.

Mike Tindall. Wasps v Bath 07/02/1999
Powerful running Bath and England centre

Acknowledgements: Bob Ascott

If Bath had lost then perhaps the defeat would have formed the epilogue of their otherwise remarkable story. Their early struggles, their almost innocent early attempts to emulate their mighty neighbours at Bristol, their tentative steps towards first-class rugby status, and finally their stunning domination of English (nay British) club rugby in the latter two decades of the 20th century….an extraordinary tale that would perhaps have passed into memory. Yet it was now a relegated Bristol who might face just such a fate, a mighty rugby family from whom Bath had learned so much that was so good.

On Sunday 25th May 2003 there remained one more engagement, namely the Parker Pen Challenge Cup final against Wasps at the Madejski stadium, Reading; and it would be the following two line-ups watched by 18,000, that took the field that day: **Bath:** *Matt Perry, Ian Balshaw, Elvis Seveali'i (Mike Catt, 56mins), Kevin Maggs, Mike Tindall, Olly Barkley, Gareth Cooper, David Barnes, Jonathon Humphries (Lee Mears, 52), John Mallett (Matt Stevens, 54), Andy Beattie, Danny Grewcock (capt.), Gavin Thomas (James Scaysbrook, 43), Nathan Thomas, Dan Lyle (Gareth Delve, 61).*

 Wasps: *Mark Van Guisbergen, Josh Lewsey, Fraser Waters, Stuart Abbott (Ayoola Erinle, 64), John Rudd (Kenny Logan, 31), Alex King, Martyn Wood, Craig Dowd, Phil Greening (Trevor Leota, 61), Will Green, Simon Shaw, Richard Birkett, Joe Worsley, Paul Volley (Peter Schrivenor 64), Lawrence Dallaglio (capt., Mark Lock 64).* Referee: *Nigel Williams (Wales).*

If already relegated, the experience would have been almost unbearable for the Rec faithful, where a rampant Wasps won the try count six to four, thanks to first-half scores from Josh Lewsey, Fraser Waters and Phil Greening, then followed by another three for Martyn Wood (soon to join Bath), Kenny Logan and finally Trevor Leota, all six converted by No.10 Alex King plus his brace of penalties for an absolute field-day with the boot. For Bath, one could only gasp at the two huge 50 metre plus penalties from out-half Olly Barkley, whose own try and conversion were followed by further tries from Scaysbrook, and ironically, after skipper Grewcock's late dismissal there followed two more from Tindall and then Balshaw's own try and conversion to end the day with Bath the worse for a 48-30 defeat. And yet, though Bath had missed-out on the Challenge Cup, they had already overcome the one challenge that really did matter, the battle (for battle it was) for survival in the Premiership.

Chapter 35. WALKING A TIGHT-ROPE (2003-10)

Six key players were unavailable at the start of season 2003-4 owing to World Cup call-ups in Australia for Ireland's Kevin Maggs, Scotland's Simon Danielle, and club captain Danny Grewcock, Iain Balshaw, Mike Catt and Mike Tindall (all England), presenting headaches for Bath coaches John Connelly, Michael Foley and director of rugby Jack Rowell. Thus, short-term replacements were called-up with Chris Malone from Bristol, Robbie Kidd (Otago Highlanders) and Springbok Wylie Human (Blue Bulls) among them. Joining too was Springbok Robbie Fleck (Western Province) who (Chronicle, 3rd Nov. 2003) spoke thus: *"I've been very impressed with the set-up here at Bath....the whole professionalism of the club, the managers, the coaches and the players, has been unbelievable."* And as if to prove his point Bath, led by acting skipper Jon Humphreys were, by late October, leading the Premiership with six from six straight wins. Only four months previously they were fighting for their 'dear' lives. By mid-October eyes were now on Australia and the World Cup, with a Martin Johnson-led England edging closer to achieving their own dreams with Jonny Wilkinson (assisted by former Bath goal-kick specialist Dave Alred) causing nightmares among opponents. Come Sydney (22nd Nov. 2003) his Bath colleagues would duly play their role in England's 17-20 epic World Cup final triumph over Australia; come January a proud Bath city would duly honour Messrs Catt, Balshaw, Tindall and Grewcock (England's World Cup squad all now MBEs) and England's assistant coach Andy Robinson (now an OBE) the freedom of Bath. At club level meanwhile it was not all 'plain sailing,' with Bath falling 21-10 in their quarter-final Powergen quarter-final National K.O. defeat at a struggling Tykes, though the Parker Pen (European) Challenge Cup promised better things, Bath sweeping through to a 29-15 win over Montferrand, only for the Frenchmen's home 38-22 win sending them to the final instead, though they too would fall 28-27 to Harlequins.

But Bath's objective for the following season was now to gain a top six Zurich League position and thus a place in the Heineken Cup. Indeed, come their last game and a 42-13 home win against Gloucester they topped the table. Time for the champagne? Well no....because in the previous 2002-3 season **the 'play-offs' had formerly been introduced,** whereby the team topping the table at the completion of the regular season would play the winner of a play-off between teams two and three for the Premiership final, so resulting with Wasps beating Gloucester to face Bath in the final at Twickenham. Wasps meanwhile had already won the Heineken Cup 27-20 over Toulouse, and if Bath had hoped that they had escaped the danger of pre-final injuries then they had thought wrong, because literally minutes prior to kick-off Matt Perry twisted his ankle in the team warm-up and Catt, passed fit only that morning, was rushed into the fullback vacancy to join the teams now stepping onto the field as follows:

Bath Rugby: M. Catt, A. Higgins, R. Fleck, K. Tindall (Ollie Barkley 76min), A. Crockett, C. Malone, M.Wood (H.Marten 80m), D. Barnes, J. Humphreys (capt. Lee Mears 55m), D. Bell (M. Stevens 48m), S.Borthwick, D. Grewcock (R. Fidler 80m), A. Beattie, M. Lipman (J. Scaysbrook 80m), Zach Fiaunati.

Wasps: M.Van Gisbergen, Josh Lewsey, F. Waters (M. Denny 79m), S. Abbott, T. Voyce, Alex King, R. Howley, T. Payne, T.Leota (B.Gotting 53m), Will Green, S. Shaw. R. Birkett, J. Worsley, P. Volley, L. Dallalio (capt.). *Referee: Chris White.*

Two evenly matched packs battled for supremacy with Bath narrowly 3-0 ahead at the interval thanks to Chris Malone's penalty on seven minutes. Soon after the re-start a 35 yard drop-goal by Wasps's Alex King levelled matters, and in a game described by Mike Tremlett (Bath Chronicle) as an *"an 80-minute pitched battle played at Test match levels of intensity"* it seemed that just one more score could settle matters when Borthwick's line-out feed to Malone saw the half-back flight a 30 yard drop-goal for a 6-3 Bath lead. But, on 65 minutes former Rec favourite Tom Voyce held on to a loose pass inside the danger zone, immediately sending Abbot away for a try, fullback Mark Van Gisbergen converting and putting Wasps 10-6 ahead and the trophy into their hands. Deep disappointment aside, Bath were a team transformed. Their six players called-up for World Cup duty emphasised the quality within the squad. While prop Matt Stevens (South African born of English parentage) and flanker Michael Lipman would win their first caps against New Zealand on England's summer tour of Australasia. Now the task was to maintain this momentum.

It was South Africa that Bath chose for their 2004-5 pre-season training venue, and despite losing 29-23 against Natal Sharks, former Springbok half-back and Sharks coach Kevin Putt predicted 'that Bath would again emerge as one of the top teams in the Zurich Premiership in the forthcoming season.' Indeed, by March under the captaincy of Jon Humphreys and coaches John Connelly and Michael Foley they had already reached a top-four League place and seemed a good bet for the National (Powergen) Cup. But there would be little escape from the ceaseless pressures facing clubs in the Premiership where: *"The demands on squads these days are incredibly tough but the play still keeps getting better and better"* spoke Falcons director of rugby Rob Andrew (Chronicle, 23rd Sep. 2004). Too true, because when the Premiership commenced in mid-August 1997 the reported cumulative attendance for that weekend totalled 28,370. For the first weekend of season 2004-5 that figure had jumped to a reported 82,358. Small wonder then that the hierarchy now stipulated that grounds must plan for a minimum capacity of ten thousand as another condition of Premiership entry. Quality back-up players were now an essential at this level as Bath skipper Jon Humphreys well knew, literally singing the praises for the likes of locks James Hudson and Rob Fidler, flanker James Scaysbrook and utility back Alex Crockett, all deputising so ably during the absence of players either injured or on international duties.

The development of young academy talent was another priority, its value highlighted when the likes of back Kieran Lewitt played an absolute 'blinder' and scoring a try-stunner in Bath's late September 10-18 win at Harlequins. While in March 19 years old centres Tom Cheeseman (already attracting attention from Welsh selectors) and Ryan Davis (England U.21captain) played like accomplished veterans in the 18-10 victory over Worcester. Others attracting attention included Nick Abendanon, Chris Brooker and

Mike Myerscough, each appearing in late season for England in the inaugural U.19 World Cup, hosted by the eventual winners South Africa. Yet another talent was England U.19's wing Ian Davey (he could run a10.9 seconds 100 metres) and would *"show his electric pace out wide when he was given the opportunity in Bath's home EDF Cup match against Ospreys"* (Chronicle, 9 Oct. 2006). By now the arms of the Premiership reached across the globe, and reflected at Bath with the arrival of backs Joe Maddock (NZ), and South African Frickie Welsh (Blue Bulls) whose first impressions of English rugby were startling: *"The pace was very quick at times, but not that much quicker than back at home...."* 'Not that much quicker than back home in South Africa!? Crickey....that's some compliment Frickie.' Yet though Bath were progressing onwards in the Powergen all-English Cup, Heineken hopes vanished in January with Leinster's 23-27 win on the Rec. The National Powergen Cup was still 'on' though and come the 6th round Bath struck with a 33-7 win over Harlequins and hooker Lee Mears displaying the class that led coach Connolly to predict that *"England might start taking a serious look at him."* Next, a 23-24 win at Sale was followed by a semi-final test of nerves at Gloucester for a 19-24 Bath victory thanks to a late try by Andy Williams, now returned to the Rec as a Welsh scrum-half cap, and proving himself a top-rate winger (that's Wales for you). So, Twickenham next, against fellow Cup finalists Leeds Tykes, while individual Bath honours saw prop Duncan Bell gain his debut cap in England's win over Italy and Danny Grewcock, Matt Stevens and Mike Tindall all selected for the forthcoming British & Irish Lions tour of New Zealand, though injury forced a desperately unlucky Tindall to withdraw. Worse still, salary cap restraints compelled Bath to sell this awesome player to rivals Gloucester (Ah!) come the following season.

But, with eight places and 18 points clear of Leeds it was no surprise that Bath were reportedly 1/4 favourites to win at Twickenham (Chronicle, 15th Apr. 2005), albeit coach John Connolly had stressed caution, since the Leeds *"record in the last month has been outstanding"* with recent wins over Leicester, Gloucester and Harlequins, and Jon Callard (now joint coach at Tykes with Phil Davies) knowing Bath inside-out. Well, 80 minutes of game-time at Twickenham on 16th April before 57,000 spectators would prove just how far Leeds had or had not improved:

Bath: *Matt Perry, Frikkie Welsh, Andrew Higgins, Olly Barkley, Joe Maddock (Brendan Daniel, 59 mins), Chris Malone, Nick Walshe (Martyn Wood, 66), Matt Stevens, Lee Mears, Duncan Bell, Rob Fidler, Danny Grewcock (capt.) Geraint Lewis, James Scaysbrook, Zach Feaunati.*

Leeds Tykes: *Ian Balshaw (capt, Diego Albanese, 3 mins), Andre Snyman, Phil Christophers (Craig McMullen, 26 mins), Chris Bell, Tom Biggs, Gordon Ross, Alan Dickens, Mike Shelley, Mark Regan (Rob Rawlinson,73), Gavin Kerr (Matt Holt, 60), Stuart Hooper, Tom Palmer, Scott Morgan, Richard Parks (Dan Hyde 60), Alix Popham (Jon Dunbar, 69 mins). Referee: David Pearson (RFU).*

Did those 1/4 odds backfire? Were Bath over-confident? Maybe, because things began to go badly wrong from that moment in the first half when Tykes and Scottish international out-half Gordon Ross (replying to a Malone penalty for Bath) sent over two Leeds penalties to gain a 6-3 lead, and from then onwards it would be Bath playing 'catch-up.' The narrow 6-3 margin would then increase thanks to a touch of sheer class, again by courtesy of Ross, when his astute chip ahead presented a gift for Chris Bell to score bang under the posts. The underdogs were now13-3 ahead. Two further Malone penalties narrowed the margin but, the Tykes were then presented with a chance on a plate when the normally immaculate Malone risked a 50:50 pass that dropped straight into the hands of South African wing Andre Snyman. He was now staring into 70 metres of open space and a try under the posts was his for the taking. He took it! And this would be the turning point psychologically. The Leeds tactics did not change one iota and frankly nor did they need to, despite Bath securing some '85% of the possession and over 65% of territorial advantage.' Meanwhile an increasingly anxious Bath discovered that their repeated attacks were far too predictable. It would be 12-20 with Malone's fourth penalty, and 12-20 it would stay. There was no change of game-plan, and the simple option of the high kick over the Tykes defence, a tactic that might just have yielded dividends, was ignored. No complaints though, as this was a match won fair and square by a gutsy team of underdogs, and this despite the injury loss of their skipper Balshaw on three minutes (lock Hooper taking command). To rub salt into wounds Leeds visited the Rec for the final League game of the season, ensuring a safe 8th Premiership place by their 6-10 win against a Bath club reaching 4th. But, for a now relegated Harlequins their own immediate future looked bleak, and proof that merely one off-season could threaten a Premiership club to rugby's version of La Guillotine. True, cups and trophies looked just great on the sideboard. But these were now simply 'extras.' Relegation was now the number one threat; avoiding it the number one priority.

Come the 2005-6 season under new captain Steve Borthwick there was another change to the play-off format, plus a few more tricky off-field issues, one of which was soon resolved after the season commenced, and involved an attempt by the RFU to 'central-contract' England's elite players, thus making them subject first and foremost to the requests of Twickenham as opposed to their parent Premiership clubs. The attempt failed owing to intensely strong opposition from both Premier Rugby and Premiership clubs, an alliance proving to be unbreakable. The Chronicle's Mike Tremlett moreover (14th Oct. 2005) did not doubt the outcome if such a policy was implemented, stating that central contracts would: *end the most competitive club league in world rugby.* Competitive it certainly was, and throughout season 2005-6 Bath found it a struggle to escape from the lower half of the now Guinness-sponsored Premiership. Fortunately, a handful of vital victories proved sufficient to ensure safety, including a double over Gloucester, and a January 28-16 success against Wasps inspired by French international wing David Bory and a debut try from centre Eliota Fuimaono (alongside fellow Samoan international forward Jonny Fa'amatuainu). Next, minus Matt Stevens, Borthwick,

Grewcock, Lee Mears (all on England duty) and flanker Gareth Delve winning his debut cap for Wales, Bath faced a hugely improved Saracens, and with Zimbabwean hooker Pieter Dixon (formerly Western Stormers), lock Peter Short, and fullback Joe Maddock, Bath's makeshift side calmed relegation jitters with a critical 29-34 win.

This was followed by the welcome return in January of Brian Ashton, removing the headache of seeking a replacement head coach due to John Connolly's appointment as Australia's national coach and Michael Foley as assistant. The availability of Ashton (coincidentally managing the National Junior Academy at Bath University) was a godsend; and among his priorities was the retention of key players whose contracts were due for renewal. Borthwick was reportedly among Leicester's most wanted, and Saracens it was rumoured could hardly wait to clinch Olly Barkley's signature. Regarding inwards recruitment an impressive list included Samoans Fa'amatuainu and Fuimaono, Auckland scrum-half Billy Fulton, likewise Tongan international prop Taufa'ao Filise, all 6ft 4in and 19st 5lbs of his Pacific power ready to be unleashed. On-field, an inconsistent League season was compensated with progress in the Heineken and Powergen Cups. The latter, formerly accommodating every club in English club rugby (those wonderful days!) was now re-formed as an Anglo-Welsh competition, limited to the twelve Premiership clubs, plus the four Welsh teams of Newport Gwent Dragons, Cardiff Blues, Llanelli and Ospreys (Swansea-Neath). Yes, potentially exciting action lay ahead with the welcome renewal of Anglo-Welsh rugby and where Bath duly swept into the semi-finals only for visitors Llanelli to spoil the Rec party with a 26-27 victory prior to 'their' own cup-final defeat to Wasps, now closing in on Bath's reputation as Cup winning kings.

With sufficient points from the first Heineken Cup stage against Leinster, Bourgoin and Glasgow Warriors, Bath then faced a quarter-final challenge at Leicester, a tie so electrifying that it was switched to Leicester City's Walker Stadium, where a capacity 32,500 crowd witnessed a magnificent 12-15 Bath triumph. The glamour of a semi-final win at Biarritz now beckoned and yet….there remained a yet bigger challenge: for despite a seemingly comfortable margin of eleven points in mid-April separating Bath from a Leeds side struggling at the base of the Premiership, Brian Ashton, assessing the Bath v Bristol league game one week prior to the Heineken semi-final, stressed the absolute priority of top-flight survival: *"this [the Premiership match] is more important in the long term than next week [at Biarritz]….we want to be here in the Premiership next season. It's fantastic to be in a Heineken Cup semi-final but that's next week not this week."* Ashton's words put things into sharp perspective, as the subsequent 31-16 victory over Bristol not only lifted Bath to Premiership safety, but softened the blow in the following week when losing 18-9 in France. At the conclusion of the Guinness Premiership campaign meanwhile Bath finished in a crucially safe 9th position, while there had been a veritable scramble for a top four play-off slot, with Sale top, followed by Leicester, London Irish and Wasps respectively; and now under a further revised format the 1st placed side played at home against the 4th, and the 2nd at home against the 3rd. Come 'the' final, Sale then defeated Leicester to win the Championship. But, the

2005-6 season did not pass without another warning from former international Rob Andrew (Chronicle, 30th Jan. 2006) who again spoke of *"the suffocating fear of Premiership relegation, but somebody is going to go through the trap door in May."* That somebody would be Leeds, and the huge outlay in effort and cost required to climb back into the Premiership were just two of the harsh realities that contributed to that aforementioned *'suffocating fear'*. Quite simply, the clubs were walking a tight-rope!

Season 2006-7 was another roller-coaster, with hopes for stability hardly helped with the departure of Brian Ashton with his call-up to the England coaching staff during the close-season. Rated by Mike Tremlett as *"the northern hemisphere's top attacking coach"* the club were left frantically searching for a replacement who 'just might' be out of contract. 'Out of the blue' two newcomers were recruited to assist forwards coach Mark Bakewell, of whom the first was former Castleford rugby League star Brad Davis as defence coach, and fellow Australian Steve Meehan, whose experience as backs-coach at Stade Francais had attracted the attention of the Bath management. Nor could one doubt their heavy responsibilities as they stepped into a Premiership described by fellow Australian Shaun Berne (returning to Bath colours after a five year absence) thus: there *"isn't a domestic League in world rugby which makes the comparable demands on players or, for that matter coaches,"* (Chronicle, 2nd Sep. 2006). Indeed, the pair had barely unpacked their bags before Bath demonstrated the full repertoire of their numerous contradictions. First, with defeats at Bristol, then home to Ospreys and finally a 30-12 fall at Gloucester, the club would wave goodbye to further participation in the now EDF Energy-sponsored Anglo-Welsh Cup by December. But, by mid-April, having scattered opponents aside with (in most cases) nonchalant ease, Bath would storm into the final of the European Challenge Cup, while another highlight was the arrival of ex Leeds Rhinos and Great Britain back Chev Walker. His baptism in Bath's November 20-14 win against Newcastle Falcons revealed the 24 years old Walker looking equally comfortable in the Union game. Playing wing (he preferred centre), his presence was 'felt' across the park. His defence was sound, and when the ball reached his hands it was a case of 'watch-out, sparks could fly.' Furthermore, his summary of his first Union outing was humbling from one so gifted: *"I felt vulnerable at times but it was a great comfort to have somebody like Matt Perry out there to keep me right."*

But head coach Meehan suffered no illusions about the challenges in the Premiership, and not making things easier during this period was Bath's reputation for spilling penalties. Injuries too were a headache and on occasions just one player can make the difference, as shown when Matt Stevens (side-lined for eleven months) re-joined the front-row in Bath's January home League match against Quins. The 24 years old tight-head *"lifted Bath's forward-play on to a different plane;"* producing a four try 31-23 win ranking among Bath's best performances of the season. Equally good were Bath's performances in the 2006-7 European Challenge Cup. First it was 14-21 at Montpellier, followed by a 42-17 win at home. Next Connacht fell 21-19 in Bath, and then 24-36 in Ireland, followed by a Harlequins side defeated 18-24 at the Stoop, and 20-14 at home.

And then…. there was to be one of those days when Bath 'go slightly barmy.' It was the Challenge Cup quarter-final against Bristol and at half-time Bath trooped off the park the wrong side of a 10-12 score-line. Forty minutes of pulsating action later they strode off that same park with a 51-12 victory under their belts, an 8 to 2 try count in their favour that included a trio from rising star Nick Abendanon, soon to be a full international on England's summer tour of South Africa. Saracens, now on full alert in the semi-finals and playing on home soil, provided a serious obstacle; though not serious enough to prevent Bath inching home in a 30-31 nail-biter that opened the gateway to a final between Bath and French side Clermont on 19th May at the Stoop.

The financial reward from a successful campaign in, for example, the European Challenge Cup (formerly Parker Pen Challenge Cup), partly assists in financing a Premiership club, and the Bath figures for the previous season of 2005-6 (Chronicle, 30th Jan. 2007) referring to profits of £283,000 suggested that fiscally all was well. But figures can be deceptive, and as chief executive Bob Calleja remarked, they were only *"superficially encouraging."* Indeed, the total was partly *"achieved because [of] a good run in the Heineken Cup and [because of] compensation from the RFU for releasing Brian Ashton from his coaching contract."* Furthermore, *"the total wage bill [inclusive of non-playing staff] amounted to £2,2 million."* Yes, a lot of money. In conclusion the report emphasised that the club were *"still very much relying on the decision over the development of the Rec."*

Ah, **the Rec** (Chronicle 9th Nov. 2006), was subject to a covenant made in April 1922 between the trustees of the estate and the Bath and County Recreation Ground Trust: that the *"Corporation* (among other conditions) *will not use The Recreation Ground otherwise than as an open space and will not show preference to or in favour of any particular game or sport, club, body or organisation."* Well, Bath RFC had never departed from this principal, having for decades shared the Rec with cricket, hockey, lacrosse, tennis and indeed other sporting/leisure activities. Admittedly, a more contested issue was the fact that the 1922 document also *"excludes all building of any kind;"* and it was this condition that opponents argued would block any plans for enlarged stands and facilities. However, years before the 1922 document had been issued, there existed the original West stand (later replaced) and the cricket club pavilion. Significantly no one associated with the 1922 document (be it drafters or signatories) had raised any objections to these buildings. But then why should they? Because neither of the buildings, nor those that followed, were built 'on' the Rec, but around its perimeter, and hence it could be claimed that they were not infringing upon either the wording, or of equal significance, the intentions of the conveyance. Meanwhile a campaign to 'Keep Bath Rugby at the Rec' had been launched 'big time' by the Bath Chronicle in its editorial column of 16th Sep. 2006, emphasising that *"forcing Bath Rugby off the Rec would be akin to pebble-dashing the Royal Crescent,"* adding that the *"club is responsible for bringing a huge amount of money into the local economy and is at the heart of the community of Bath."* The arguments, for and against, then went into overdrive. It was 'touching' therefore that in addition to the huge wall of local support, it was the views of many from far beyond the city who also felt something 'special' about this unique ground. Joanne Owers from Hertfordshire was but one of many distant visitors and spoke thus: *"It is 130 miles each way and I come to every home game….I don't miss one."* Media big-names likewise joined the chorus. The Rec *"is a beautiful and historic location and is in such a unique setting….it personifies Bath,"* commented former England hooker and by now TV/Radio rugby pundit Brian Moore. While by mid-November the Penny Brinton led Supporters Club petition (assisted by Helen Grace) had already reached the 20,000 signature mark for the 'Keep' campaign. Local businessmen and tourist chiefs piled in too, Robin Bischert of Bath Tourism Plus declaring that *"The Rec is iconic. Very few cities have such an accessible stadium – it attracts people to the city rather like The Coliseum."* And….Bath Rugby chairman **Andrew Brownsword** (Chronicle, 12th Jan. 2007) spoke thus: *"keeping rugby at the Rec was vital,"* he said, *"and I think Bath rugby is the beating heart of this fantastic city."* Bath chief executive Bob Calleja added that a survey stated that regular Rec attendances of some 10,500 (Chronicle, 4th Apr. 2006) saw *"retail outlets improve turnover by 20% on match days."* That left the decision in the hands of the Charity Commission, whose permission was granted come June 2013, though even then hurdles remained.

In the League Bath reached a safe 8th position, though a victory in the European Challenge Cup final against Clermont Auvergne would certainly change the complexion of an otherwise moderate 2006-7 Premiership campaign; and come 19th May at the Stoop it was left to the following **Bath** side to provide just that change: *Nick Abendanon, Joe Maddock, Eliota Fuimaono, Olly Barkley, David Bory (Tom Cheeseman, 50min), Shaun Berne (Chris Malone, 60min), Nick Walshe (Andy Williams, 61min), David Barnes, Lee Mears (Pieter Dixon 72min), Matt Stevens, Steve Borthwick (capt.), Danny Grewcock, Andy Beattie (Peter Short, 62min), Michael Lipman, Zak Feaunati (James Scaysbrook 61min).*

Clermont Auvergne: *Anthony Floch, Aurelien Rougerie, Grant Esterhuizen (Seremaia Baikenuku, 59min), Tony Marsh, Julien Malzieu, Brock James, Pierre Mignoni, Laurent Emmanuelli, Mario Ledesma (Brice Miguel, 64min), Martin Szelco (Goderzi Shvelidze, 62min), Jamie Cudmore, Thibaud Privat (Loic Jacquet, 44min), Michel Dieude (Gonzalo Longo, 45min), Sam Broomhall, Elvis Vermuelen.* Referee: *Nigel Owen (Wales).*

Loyalties aside, this was one of those days when there could be no complaints about the outcome, Clermont's three tries to one in their 16-22 victory emphasised that. And despite 6-3 ahead at the interval through two Olly Barkley penalties to one by Clermont's Australian half-back Brock James, Clermont had looked a team with 'that' something extra in the tank. Come the second half it showed. First Clermont wing Julien Malsieu's pace took him over, James converting. Next, clean ball found Tony Marsh for a try. Next, James chipped over the Bath defence and with bounce going kindly scored under the posts, and Clermont were now in command! Though trailing 6-23, Bath did re-organised and threw caution aside. Joe Maddock smashed through four tackles to land a try beneath the posts, Barkley converting. Next a driving maul led Bath to believe that Peter Short had touched down, but the 'TMO' ruled otherwise. A long range 40 metres penalty by Barkley then sent pulses racing amongst the 10,134 mostly Bath supporting crowd. But again 'Non,' as Clermont's lead proved to be out of range, sending the French side homewards clutching the European Challenge Cup, while for Bath it was now four attempts in five years that a trophy had slipped through their fingers at the final hurdle of a major competition. It was almost becoming a habit. Yet it could have been worse, and with the relegation of Northampton (of all people), Bath had again secured 'the' foremost objective....survival in the Premiership.

Butch James: Bath's Springbok outside half: none better at unlocking defences.

Acknowledgments Bob Ascott

Come 2007-8 Alex Crockett was appointed acting captain during the World Cup absence of Steve Borthwick, Matt Stevens, Lee Mears, Olly Barkley (all England) and Samoan Eliota Fuimaono, while newcomers Matt Banahan (wing), lock Mike Myerscough and back-rower Chris Goodman joined the Rec stable, so too Michael Claassens from Free State Cheetahs and out-half Butch James from Natal Sharks, a genuine world-class Springboks half-back pairing. Added too were the acquisitions of New Zealander Daniel Browne (Back-row) from Northampton, lock Martin Purdy (Wasps), Lorne Ward (Harlequins), Neil Clarke (Launceston), scrum-half Mike Baxter (Pertemps Bees) and powerhouse prop Paulica Ion from Steaua Bucuresti of Romania. The additional Rugby League experience of defence coach Brad Davis would add additional ideas and input, with the former Castleford Tiger impressed by the 'response of the squad and their eagerness to learn.' The key Rugby League lessons to impart, he explained, included the importance of 'discipline in the defence line, the ability to double up in the tackle, and gang-tackle ball-carriers so as to limit the ground they make and the danger they pose.' While some teams apply a drift, rush or scramble defence, Davis emphasised that 'the smart team can play all three as and when required.' He concluded (Chronicle, 3rd Sep. 2007): *"The target is always to defend high as a team, to win the ball back in your opponent's half and harness the most dangerous form of possession – turnover ball – to launch attacks from the shortest range possible."*

Pre-season included a 'leadership & team-building' training camp in Wales and come the starting pistol for Guinness Premiership action coach Meehan (Chronicle, 3rd Sep. 2007) put his 'neck on the line,' backing his team for a top four play-off slot in the

Premiership. Indeed, by late October's 20-14 victory over Leicester it was a joy to witness a rejuvenated Bath that oozed confidence, had notched six wins from seven, and were neck-and-neck with Gloucester at the top of the Premiership. By contrast, England's initial defence of the Webb Ellis trophy included a walloping nil-36 defeat by South Africa, but then hitting form when defeating quarter-finalists Australia, followed by a superb semi-final victory over hosts France, before facing South Africa (again) in the October final. No repeat humiliation here, though still a 15-6 victory to South Africa. On the home front Bath efforts were now focused on the Guinness Championship, the EDF Energy Anglo-Welsh Cup and the European Challenge Cup. But, with opening round home defeat against Sale and then at Cardiff, Bath would end their EDF cup campaign almost as soon as it had started. The European Challenge Cup however would be a different story from the moment when French side Auch were overcome 6-28 in November, and so perfectly did Claassens blend with James as to inspire the watching Mike Tremlett to report that the one hundred-odd travelling Bath supporters had perhaps witnessed *"the birth of a midfield partnership which provides the creativity that Bath supporters have yearned for since the glory days."* From that moment (home and away) Bath swept aside Auch, Italian side Overmach Parma, French opponents Albi, then overcoming Leeds (now Leeds Carnegie) 57-5 in the quarter-finals, to reach a semi-final clash against Sale in April.

Preparing players for this intensity of rugby however is partly dependent upon an off-field task-force (medical, fitness) working non-stop throughout the year, nor forgetting the Academy, managed during this period by former Camborne player Frank Butler and guided by player-recommendations from, among others, junior rugby coaches, school-teachers and contacts throughout the South West. A carefully prepared short-list of nominated players is then closely watched by members of the Academy staff, and if judged to possess the necessary potential, duly invited to spend a number of weeks involved in full-time summer training at the club. When completed, the players (their parents consulted too) decide whether or not to join, including those continuing academic studies alongside their rugby development; and the value of this source of recruitment can be judged by the fact that in some seasons as many as 45% of the Bath senior squad has consisted of an impressive (past or current) Academy-produced players. Meehan's prophecy meanwhile of a top four League position 'was' achieved with Bath gaining 3rd place and so drawn at 2nd placed Wasps, and 4th placed Leicester drawn away at top-table Gloucester. Bath's progress was halted at Wasps, while 4th placed Leicester defeated 1st placed Gloucester for a final at Twickenham against Wasps. Wasps won, their 4th Premiership title in the previous seven seasons, though ironically yet to top the regular season table. But, as one door shut for Bath, another had opened, their convincing 36-14 semi-final home win against Sale securing a place in the final of the European Challenge Cup.

A departure meanwhile at the top level of the game was that of local boy **Tony Spreadbury,** an international referee with, until season 2007-8, 41 matches to his credit, his experience including both amateur and professional eras of the game. Described by Phil Winstanley (Premier rugby's manager) as *"one of the most charismatic referees in world rugby,"* Spreadbury now announced his retirement from the international arena. Friendly, many were the times when Tony gathered along the terraces among the faithful to watch the mid-week games and exchange rugby banter. But, on the field it was always 'Mr Spreadbury Sir', and with eyes like a hawk it was only rarely that a misdemeanour would ever escape the shrill sound of Mr Spreadbury's whistle.

Come Sunday, 25th May, 2008 at Kingsholm, (16,106 watching) Bath looked to be favourites in the European Challenge Cup final, their opponents Worcester finishing a lowly 10th in the regular League season to that of 3rd placed Bath. But, during the previous five seasons Bath had come off worse in four major finals, leaving no room for complacency: **Bath Rugby:** *N. Abendanon (T. Cheeseman 78m), J. Maddock, Alex Crockett, Olly Barkley (S. Berne 70m), M. Banahan, Butch James, M. Claassens (N. Walsh 78m), D. Flatman (D. Bell 61m), Lee Mears (Pieter Dixon 70m), M. Stevens, S. Borthwick (capt.), D. Grewcock, J. Faamatuainu, M.Lipman (Peter Short) 68m), D. Browne (Zak Feaunati 70m).*

Worcester Warriors: *T. Deport, M. Garvey. D.Rasmussen (Rico Gear 71m), S. Tuitupou, M. Benjamin, Shane Drahm (J. Carlisle 78m), Matt Powell (Ryan Powell 65m), Tony Windo (Matt Mullan 52m), Aleki Lutui, Tevita Taumoepeau (C.Horsman 56m), G.Rawlinson, C.Gillies (W. Bowley 68m), Drew Hickey (Netani Talei 44m), P. Sanderson (capt.), Kai Horstmann.* Referee: *Christophe Berdos (France).*

This time however Bath did not under-rate these Cup opponents one iota and Bath Skipper Steve Borthwick (five steals against) dominated those crucial line-outs. Gradually the Bath pack (including a brave Michael Lipman with 17 stitches in his mouth) established an overall command at forward. So, despite two Shane Drahm penalties for Warriors, Bath struck a critical psychological blow with tries from flanker Jonny Faamatuainu and fullback Nick Abendanon for a 15-6 interval lead. This pressure continued throughout the second period, and despite Drahm's dependable boot sending over a third Worcester penalty and their No. 15 Thinus Delport darting over for a last gasp try converted by replacement out-half Joe Carlisle, Bath were just that bit sharper. Nor was Barkley's name off the score-sheet (it rarely was) as he duly struck home with two penalties, plus a conversion, with Butch James adding another. That made it 24-16 on the final whistle, so ending a ten-year drought since winning a 'Major.' Admittedly it was not 'the' top European trophy. But it was mighty gratifying to win some shining 'silver' again.

Bath Front Row 2006: Duncan Bell, Lee Mears, David Flatman.

Acknowledgments Bob Ascott

As for Steve Meehan, his success would have come as no surprise to Juan Martin Hernandez (*El Magico*) of Stade Francais. Universally acclaimed as inspirational in Argentina's outstanding 3rd place in the recent World Cup, he had during the competition spoken briefly to the Chronicle's Mike Tremlett. Meehan, he said, was *"a coach with the golden touch."* El Magico had spoken!

And now with renewed confidence a Michael Lipman-led Bath stormed into season 2008-9, all guns blazing, with a scorching run of Guinness Premiership victories (briefly interrupted by Gloucester and Harlequins) in an otherwise unbeaten surge that reached late December; this with a squad further strengthened with the acquisitions of Australian lock Justin Harrison from Ulster, former Leicester scrum-half Scott Bemand, and lock Stuart Hooper (Leeds and England Saxons) whom many Rec followers remembered for his outstanding performance for the Tykes in their 2005 Powergen Cup final triumph against Bath. But, come October in the early phase of the Heineken Cup some 1,500 travelling Rec supporters experienced one of those heart-stop moments when with barely two minutes remaining at Toulouse the brilliant Abendanon added a second try to that of Claassens, putting Bath 15-16 ahead; and if possession had then been secured cleanly from the kick-off, Bath probably needed only to boot the ball into the streets to win a remarkable away victory. Instead, a ruck ensued, followed by a penalty-gift (wide out) to the French. Ominously No. 10 David Skrela, who had already kicked five penalties, sent over his sixth and Toulouse snatched an 18-16 victory in the last seconds. Yet with wins home and away against Newport Gwent Dragons, Glasgow and a 3-3 home draw with Toulouse in January, Bath had clocked sufficient points to reach the quarter-final and an April date at Leicester. Watched by near 27,000 at Leicester City's Walker Stadium, Bath again won the try count by 2 to 1 thanks to Shaun Berne and Joe Maddock. But this time it was Sam Vesty banging home five penalties as against Bath's two that would put the score at 15 apiece, and with a minute left Julien Dupuy dummied through from close range for a try-gem and a 20-15 Leicester victory. Agony again, for supporters and not forgetting the club treasurer, since big competitions attract big sponsors, big attendances and TV revenue, essential in financing a Premiership club. Yet, there was Bath's earlier capture (August 2008) of New Zealander Shontayne Hape from Bradford Bulls. Hape, fourteen Rugby League internationals to his credit, nonetheless modestly insisted that he remained merely a student of the Union game, stating: "*I'm having to learn a lot of new things here....things like releasing the ball after the tackle, clearing out at the break-down, and the way we have to line up much deeper in the back-line in attack and defence are all new to me.*" But Hape would prove himself a quick learner, as revealed during Bath's March 45-8 win over Bristol. The Chronicle was impressed: "*[Hape] convinced the Rec that he was the real deal in union,*" adding that "*the rapturous applause he received when substituted with a quarter of the game to go said it all.*"

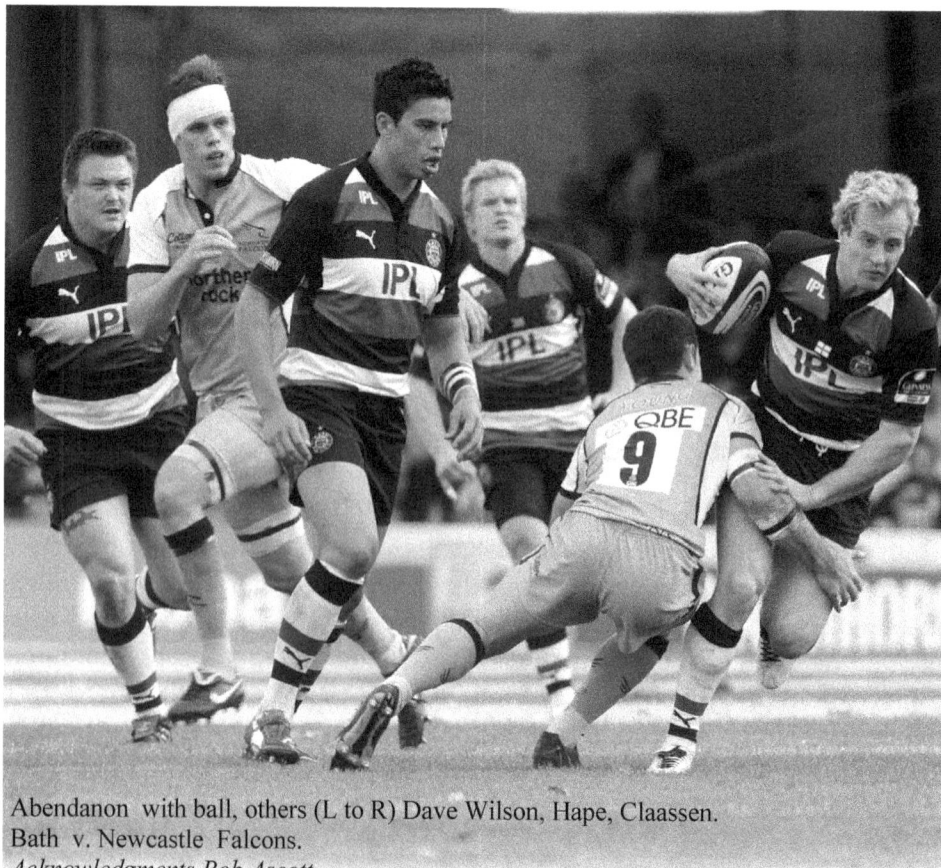

Abendanon with ball, others (L to R) Dave Wilson, Hape, Claassen.
Bath v. Newcastle Falcons.
Acknowledgments Bob Ascott

Later, come Bath's 36-25 win over Falcons it was the turn of Rob Hawkins (appropriately on his 50th club appearance, and a hooker of unusual speed) to win the plaudits as the Chronicle's Star Man, and whose *"athleticism and power in the loose has been magnificent, not only against Newcastle but ever since he stepped up into the starting XV following Pieter Dixon's knee injury."* Finally, not least thanks to the seven spot-on goals from out-half Ryan Davis, Bath's 33-18 win over Saracens would lift them to a commendable 4th League position, thus the play-offs, though between them and the final stood the small matter of Leicester away; and on the day the best team won 24-10. The Tigers would be celebrating again when winning the Championship final, while Bristol (still not their true selves) would drop from the top flight.

For the following 2009-10 campaign Michael Claassens was appointed captain, alongside a group of selected 'elders:' namely Danny Grewcock, Joe Maddock, David Flatman and Stuart Hooper, nor forgetting the experienced David Barnes, then chairman of the Professional Rugby Players Association (PRA) and who had recently accepted an invitation to join the RFU's 'Image of The Game Task Group.' Another acquisition was Nick Blofeld, recruited as chief executive and whose experience included his management of Epsom, the modernization of its facilities, nor forgetting his service with the Gurkhas and previous captaincy of the Combined Services rugby team. Coaching remained in the capable hands of Steve Meehan, Brad Davies, kicking coach Rowley Williams, and former Bath player Martin Haag as forwards coach. In addition to Ben Skirving (ex Saracens, England) in the playing-squad there would be recently-capped prop David Wilson (England & Newcastle Falcons), Fiji half-back Nicky Little, and Australians Matt Carraro (backs) and loose-forward Julian Salvi. Early season optimism however would be short-lived, and it didn't help that Bath's Guinness Premiership commenced at fortress Kingsholm with a 24-5 defeat. Come December, by which stage Bath had won just one League game from ten, alarms bells were ringing, not least after a home nil-16 rain-soaked horror-show at the hands of London Irish in late November. What could go wrong did go wrong and hordes of despairing Bath supporters headed off early to their home-fires in near despair.

But, what a difference even a single victory can make; especially one at the expense of Gloucester who in late December were decisively beaten 28-8 on the Rec. Oh Salvation! This one victory was the rocket-booster for what proved to be a mid-season recovery. Prominent too was the collective back-row performance of Julian Salvi, recently arrived Springbok No.8 Luke Watson and Andy Beattie, their drive *"emasculating Gloucester's attacking ambitions,"* as opposing skipper Gareth Delve generously conceded post-match. And though the surge of confidence from this single victory against the 'auld' enemy would not necessarily be understood by those not acquainted with this ancient rivalry, the home supporters knew instinctively the force of its almost spiritual effect. Suddenly the clouds lifted, and there was a sense that the worst might be over. And, waiting in the wings was a batch of 'young guns' only recently tested (and found good) at first team level, namely centre Ben Williams, lock Scott Hobson, flankers Guy Mercer and Josh Ovens, plus props Nathan Catt and Mark Lilley (son of former Bath favourite Graham Lilley). Nor was coach Brad Davis kidding when warning his starters: *'watch out you guys, these youngsters are after your places.'*

Confidence returned overnight, and a Bath team who had notched merely one League win pre-Christmas, would lose merely one League game post-Christmas; and in a near unstoppable surge towards the play-offs the realisation that Bath had re-discovered their true selves was emphatically shown in their 22-35 revenge at London Irish in February. Next Barkley, back to his best on his return in Bath's 37-13 win over Worcester, demonstrated what straight running down the middle can do to a back division; while Butch James showed again his 'uncanny ability to unlock defences.' More encouraging news then followed with confirmation that Leicester's fearless England flanker Lewis Moody and highly versatile back Sam Vesty would arrive for the following season, so too Scotland No.8 Simon Taylor from Stade Francais. Such was this recovery that the 35-19 televised victory on St. George's Day against Wasps at Twickenham not only drew a 60,208 attendance, but saw Bath closing in on the play-offs. Here, with forward superiority secured by the interval, half-backs Claassens and Butch James galvanized the backs into overdrive with a try hat-trick from Joe

Andrew Brownsword (right) hands over to Bruce Craig (left) in front of Farleigh House, Bath Rugby's Headquarters.

Acknowledgments: Bath Chronicle 15th April 2010

Maddock, another from Barkley who then duly added three conversions and three penalties to the score-sheet. Prior to the kick-off British troops abseiled into Twickenham complete with flags of St. George swirling alongside them; Land of Hope and Glory was played (and sang!); and there was one further gesture shown, one reaching back to January when a young girl of 12 years had stepped on to the Rec alongside skipper Michael Claassens as the Bath team mascot. Later the squad, frequently involved in community work, had arranged a chauffeur-driven car to drive her and her family to Twickenham for the 6-Nations match against Wales. There, it was VIP treatment and a meeting no less with Jonny Wilkinson and Steve Borthwick. But the lovely young girl (Chronicle, 6th May. 2010) was far from well, and but days prior to the game against Wasps she lost her brave struggle against leukaemia. So it was that as Bath stepped on to the Twickenham turf, skipper Michael Claassens and his entire team wore white armbands in her memory. Yes, it was 'that' sort of day. The final League game against Leeds Carnegie then saw Bath sweep home to a 39-3 win to gain a 4th play-off place against Leicester, the Tigers 15-6 winners and then climaxing their season as Champions. Though no silver, a mid-season transformation had lifted Bath into the play-offs; while in April a new owner, **Bruce Craig,** had taken over the reins at the club. *"For me [he* *said] buying Bath wasn't a monetary thing – it was about a passion,"* and the former half-back with Racing Metro (later founding a multi-million pound pharmaceutical distribution company in France), would establish a rugby HQ at nearby **Farleigh Hungerford** in a mansion straight out of the pages of Downton Abbey. To Andrew Brownsword meanwhile the club thus owed an enormous sense of gratitude for his 14 years guardianship of Bath Rugby, likewise to Bruce Craig for accepting so demanding a mission. Thus, in this season of contrasts the club had come through a tortuous test to emerge the stronger for it. And now there was genuine optimism that *"the winter of Bath's discontent"* was transformed by the sheer scale and suddenness of that transformation.

Chapter 36. SO NEARLY THE DREAM ANNIVERSARY (2010-2015).

Come season 2010-11 Bath closed-in on their 150th anniversary, a club that by the late 1980's and with the then top four Cup Majors under its belt, sat upon the throne of English rugby. But now, under Luke Watson's captaincy, could Bath again win a top 'Major?' The Rec capacity was increased to 12,300, new players had arrived, and it was 'some' list: winger Jacques Boussuge (French 7's international), John van der Giessen, Argentinian power-house lock Ignacio Fernandez Lobbe, Scotland 'A' scrum-half Mark McMillan (Glasgow Warriors), hooker Ross Batty and former Scottish and British Lion Simon Taylor (Stade Francais), all now among back-row prospects Josh Ovens and Guy Mercer; while Lewis Moody would skipper England (Hape in the backs) to a 35-18 home win over Australia; nor forgetting two more promising Bath arrivals, namely wing Tom Biggs and Australian centre Matt Carraro. Nonetheless, the Premiership is always full of traps for the unwary. Indeed, by January Bath lurked worryingly close to the foot of the table, floundering in a hopeless position in the Heineken, while despite some encouraging performances they fell one win short of a semi-final place in the LV Cup. True, the 'LV' is not as challenging as the Heineken but, it provided a window of opportunity for those players needing (and deserving) game-time, including promising scrum-half Chris Cook, utility back Jack Cuthbert who played a 'cracker' in Bath's 29-18 November win over Cardiff, and then full-back Nick Scott in Bath's splendid 12-26 victory at Leicester in February.

Olly Barkley, a first-choice starter naturally, had by now thanks to his telescopic kicking accuracy reached an 81% success rate with the boot. Yet, it was at Gloucester that grim misfortune struck during a 34-22 away upset when a freak injury resulting from a collision with team-mate Butch James saw Barkley collapse with a double leg-fracture. Medics from 'both' teams rushed to his side. A mask was placed over his head and nitrous oxide administered. A splint was applied to his leg and throughout this period Kingsholm watched in hushed silence. Respectful and sympathetic applause then accompanied the player when stretchered from the field, and the televised encounter revealed an admirable generosity of spirit among those Kingsholm faithful. Alas, it was already known that Luke Watson and Butch James would soon be leaving the Rec come the season's conclusion. Both were South Africa bound to join Eastern Province Kings (Port Elizabeth) and Golden Lions respectively. Both too would depart with treasured memories, expressed by Luke Watson thus: leaving Bath is *"the most difficult decision I've ever had to make,"* and Butch James: *"I have made great friends....and have been amazed by the Bath supporters...."* Again, in a season of surprises Lions coach Sir Ian McGeechen (former Scotland international) had arrived as performance-director, and within ten weeks was appointed 'director of rugby and Number One in the chain of command,' followed by the end of season departure of Steve Meehan. Few though would forget the excitement that Meehan had injected into Bath's style of play during his four seasons at the Rec, and albeit that only once during his tenure was 'silver' (the European Challenge Cup, May 2008) brought home, the Meehan era would be one to remember.

Looking into the future meanwhile, there was anticipation at the prospects of Gloucester's (6ft 7in) England lock Dave Attwood's arrival for the following season, along with Springbok flanker Francois Louw from Cape Town club Stormers and former Leicester and England centre Dan Hipkiss.

The season would again be one of contrasts (nothing unusual about that) with disappointing defeats yet sparkling victories and where Bath saved perhaps their best for another St. George's Day televised epic at Twickenham. This was a virtuoso performance, winning 10-43 against Wasps (38,000 watching), with Tom Biggs over for a try hat-trick, a Banahan double and another from Carraro, all master-minded by half-back Sam Vesty's immaculate performance and his five conversions and a penalty. Yet, back in January Bath had dropped to 4th from the Premiership base. At the conclusion of the season however they had recovered to within one victory short of the play-offs. No surprises though for those who knew Bath's sometimes erratic form, summed up with simple perfection when Sam Vesty assessed the strengths from the weaknesses at his new club (Chronicle, 12th May 2011): *"when things go well we're an awesome side and we're so difficult to defend. We just need to be a bit more consistent and win those tight games...."* You can say that again Sam!

Season 2011-12 would now be Stuart Hooper's turn at the helm, though initially hampered by six players on World Cup duties, namely England captain Moody, Banahan, Lee Mears, Davy Wilson, plus Francois Louw (S.A.) and newcomers Anthony Perenise (Samoa), nor forgetting No.10 Stephen Donald rushed late into the Kiwi side and whose critical penalty ensured their 8-7 World Cup final triumph over France. But, filling the gaps there now arrived another tranche of newcomers, including Ryan Caldwell (lock, Ulster), Carl Fearns (back-row, Sale), prop Charlie Beech (Wasps), and the thrilling potential of St. Helens Rugby League utility back Kyle Eastmond. Talk about competition for places! But, talk about injuries too, because in March Lewis Moody (a man without fear) was forced into retirement from active rugby. Was an admiring Tom Bradshaw just joking when writing thus? [The] *"tale of his injuries, operations and comebacks will doubtless form a textbook for first year medical students;"* or was he being serious? Bath meanwhile would have to be content with 8th place at the culmination of the regular season; while only a home 16-13 win over Montpellier (where Stephen Donald's exquisite 'over-arm-miss-pass' opened the Red Sea for Olly Woodburn to glide through for a gem of a try) lit up an otherwise depressing Heineken campaign that included a 52-27 hammering at Leinster. But again.... The club was safe from the drop!

Spirits were temporally lifted moreover during an LV Cup campaign that reached the semi-final stage, and revealed a new seam of promising academy talent that included Will Skuse (back-row), Will Tanner (hooker), Will Spencer (lock) and backs Richard Lane and outside-half Heathcote. But it was defeats, and two in particular, that would impact on the club like few others had for years past. The first was the home LV Cup semi-final defeat to Leicester in March that followed Bath's otherwise impressive form against previous opponents, including recent cup wins over Northampton (46-16) and

Exeter (3-31) respectively. But for the semi-final against Leicester (not at full strength), home advantage was squandered, the line-out at times was a scramble, and scrums, free kicks and penalties (plus a 16-17 win) were gifted to Leicester as if it was Christmas. The second defeat, again at home, occurred in March with a 6-26 league crash to Northampton. As Tom Bradshaw reported (Chronicle): 'against Tigers, Bath fumbled a crucial line-out from their own throw-in near their own line that led to the Leicester try; while the line-out against Northampton was in disarray.' Despair is not too strong a word to describe feelings felt around the terraces, emotions furthermore expressed forcefully with the vitriol and online messages (not forgetting alarm) that followed these two setbacks.

The ramifications were by no means finished yet. Sir Ian McGeechan was set to depart anyway, while forwards-coach Martin Haag, graciously accepting that he should accept some responsibility, would be departing too. True, if Bath had won the LV Cup things may have ended differently, though one cannot be certain. What was certain however was that the club *'did'* act quickly? Former Springboks assistant-coach Gary Gold was appointed head coach, along with former England defence coach Mike Ford, plus Toby Booth and Neal Hatley from London Irish, with Brad Davis remaining as the lynchpin. There was now an urgency to 'tighten-up' on Bath errors in set-piece play, to improve line-out performance and win the close-result games, and as former England international hooker Brian Moore had earlier stated (Chronicle, 15th Dec. 2011): *"the Bath team he played against used to strike terror into opposition hearts. That fear factor is no longer there."*

'To regain self-belief:' this numbered among the key objectives for **season 2012-13,** and though Bath did not lack for class, they seemed to lack the confidence to fulfil it. Hence in the hunt for yet more experience, some interesting names now appeared at Farleigh House, including England hooker Rob Webber (Wasps), Wales prop Paul James (Ospreys) and lock Dominic Day (Scarlets,). Less known initially were flanker Nick Koster (Western Province), Argentinian international wing Horacio Agulla and the Army Fijian flyer Samesa Rokoduguni. And with this trio running home tries like they were going out of fashion they were soon the talk along the terraces. Talent? It was coming out of the woodwork, not least the awesome potential of Kyle Eastmond, whose brilliance was shown in Bath's early season 30-23 win over Wasps with his mesmerising 25 yards run through a human barrier of five (some say six) defenders for a try that was the nearest thing to rugby-perfection. And the march to the Amlin Cup (now European Challenge Cup) quarter-finals and the LV Cup semi-finals provided excitement, though still no silver for the trophy cupboard. Furthermore, while it was an emotional day when in September Olly Barkley (thankfully returned to fitness) banged 16 points over the cross-bar in the 31-10 win over Sale prior to his departure to Racing Metro, a long-striding utility back by the name of Ollie Devoto, one year out of Bryanston School, would thankfully step right up to 1st team action during the same season. Two other players would depart however, namely hooker Lee Mears with 42 England caps during his 16 devoted years at Bath, and the more recent arrival Dan Hipkiss, both heeding medical advice to retire from the game or risk possible further consequences as a result. Saracens now announced that their plan to play on their synthetic surface at their new Allianz Park home in Barnet would commence in the New Year. 'Plastic fantastic' claimed Chris Roy (D. Mail), with a prediction that other clubs would likely follow. But,

Bath v. Stade Français. Jonny Fa'amatuainu with ball. Dave Wilson, (left) Stuart Hooper (right).

Acknowledgements: Bob Ascott

apart from Falcons there was no immediate stampede, with some critics arguing that hard surfaces caused injuries and some players simply refusing to play on them. Come the New Year an injury side-lined Bath scrum-half Claassens, and Munster No.9 Peter Stringer was rushed over as cover. Peter who!?....since few recalled this Irish international now in his mid-thirties. But, when sent into LV debut action in late January against Exeter (Bath winning 16-6) he became an 'instant hero.' Next, hopes were raised high again with Gloucester routed 5-32 at fortress Kingsholm, though 31-23 defeat at Harlequins then closed the door to any further LV final plans. Likewise, Stade Francais then brought Amlin Challenge Cup quarter-final ambitions to an abrupt end with their 20-36 win on the Rec, albeit they too would fall 34-13 to Leinster in the final. Hooper's team however achieved a comfortable 7th position in the final League table, nor forgetting Bath's individual talents clearly recognised by the inclusion for England's summer tour to Uruguay and Argentina of Dave Attwood, Dave Wilson, Rob Webber, and also with Kyle Eastmond celebrating his first cap (against Argentina) with a breath-taking try.

Naturally, there was no chance of Bath ambitions for more silver disappearing, their pre-season preparations commencing with a week-long attendance at the specialist **Spala Olympic Training Centre in Poland**, followed by their 2013-14 League campaign starting-off with a 0-21 win at Newcastle Falcons. Furthermore, another draft of talent arrived: George Ford, Micky Young (both Leicester), Matt Garvey, England three-quarter Jonathan Joseph, David Sisi, Anthony Watson (all London Irish), Alafoti Fa'osiliva (Bristol), Gavin Henson (L.Welsh), Leroy Houston (Colomiers) and Juan Pablo Orlandi (Racing Metro) all numbered among the 'new boys on the block' with Bath holding a top-four Premiership slot by January. Only the unexpected mid-season departure of popular coach Gary Gold clouded the horizon.

Not surprisingly perhaps Bath were cutting a swathe through LV and Amlin Cup opponents like a dreadnought; and in a season of outstanding individual performances perhaps one player especially stood out…. No.10 George Ford. The 20 years old duly enchanted the Rec with sublime running, astute kicking, glorious tries and a master play-maker. He was an England cap (against Wales and Italy) come the Six Nations. Included among outstanding league encounters meanwhile was the knife-edged winning double over Gloucester; though the 15-13 home win was later tarnished by the violent 17-18 Bath victory in April where Gloucester (having two men sent-off, another two sin-binned) finished with eleven men standing, and Bath (no angels themselves on the day) having three of their own sin-binned during a match described by Lee Nolan, Mail on Sunday, as "*a day of shame at Kingsholm.*" Yet the game is not necessarily more violent than in amateur days. On the contrary, a new generation of professional referees were (are) stricter, possessing both the yellow and red cards, and even the most ill-disciplined players would think twice before arguing with their decisions. Rugby, is arguably the better for such changes.

Furthermore, one match alone (as at Kingsholm) does not define a season, one that saw Bath close in on a top-four Premiership place and possibly two cup finals. Indeed, it was a highly polished LV Cup quarter-final win at Leicester that included three conversions and three penalties from Chronicle Star Man Gavin Henson, that clinched a 17-35 passport into the LV semi-finals at home against Exeter. Since Bath had already defeated the Chiefs three times that season they were favourites to 'up' that to four, especially when within the first minute an interception and pass to Agulla and then a quick-fire off-load to Leroy Houston for a try saw Bath off to a flyer. But Bath, equipped to win this match on paper, lost it on the field. Exeter played things sensibly, Bath played as if it was a 7's tournament. Thus, the underdogs, who had never beaten Bath since the introduction of professionalism won 19-22 and triumphed again 15-8 in the final against Northampton. Foolhardy Bath could hardly complain. But, in an unstoppable run in the Amlin Challenge Cup where, among others, lock Will Spencer and again winger Richard Lane excelled, Bath faced semi-final action at Wasps, a tough hurdle, but one they cleared 18-24, having survived a nerve-racking final five minutes less a sin-binned three-quarter. Meanwhile, a top four Premiership place now hinged on a minimum of at least one victory against either Harlequins or Northampton, with the Saints confronted first in May. These two were evenly matched with a try apiece from Ford (a beauty) and Elliott, and likewise a conversion and four penalties apiece from Ford and Myler but, the possible (nay probable) difference was the early injury to hooker Rob Webber, and then 'as luck would have it' another injury to sub' hooker Ross Batty. With Hooper's plea for uncontested scrums rejected, prop Nathan Catt nobly volunteered to accept the role on 55 minutes, but advantage now swung Northampton's way. Even so, Bath commendably held out for a 19-19 draw, though this necessitated 'absolute' victory at Harlequins for the top-fours. They got close, 19-16 close, but that left them outside the loop in fifth position.

Yet the Amlin Challenge Cup final against Northampton at Cardiff Arms Park (Friday, 23rd May) offered another chance of glory, one decided by the following two teams: **Bath:** *N. Abendanon, Semesa Rokoduguni, J. Joseph, O. Devoto, A. Watson, G. Ford, M. Young, P. James, T. Dunn. D. Wilson, S. Hooper (capt.), D. Attwood, C. Fearns, F. Louw, L. Housten, Replacements: P. Stringer, G.Mercer, N. Catt, A. Perenise, G. Henson, H.Agulla, E.Guinazu, D.Day.*

Northampton: *B. Foden, K. Pisi, G, Pisi (Wilson), L.Burrell (Stephenson), G. North, S. Myler, L. Dickson (Fotuali'i), Corbisiero (Waller), Haywood, Mercey (Denman), Manoa (Day), Lawes, Clark (Dowson), Wood (capt.), Dickinson.* Although Bath's local-born young hooker Tom Dunn produced a 'massive' performance, George Ford was however awaiting surgery on a damaged shoulder, possibly explaining his three penalty strikes that strayed off target. Yet, he sent home a conversion for Anthony Watson's glorious try from 60 yards out, and a further trio of penalties. But, Saints won the try count through Dowson and Foden, and the precision-kicking of Myler reaped a conversion and six penalties for a 30-16 Amlin Cup final victory. Again, no trophy for Bath, though hints they were heading in the right direction.

Yet that relegation issue remained, with no less an authority than Sir Ian McGeechan (S.Telegraph, 4th May 2014) suggesting (inter alia) that the **Premiership be increased** to 14 clubs, so allowing *"coaches and players the opportunity for competition....but also to develop the game and tactically push it forwards, because there could be that openness in the play that the fear of relegation often shuts out."* In the Chronicle meanwhile **(21st Aug. 2014)** Super League champions **Wigan** (Warriors) honoured Bath with their presence at Farleigh House for two days of cross-code training and an exchange of ideas. The Northern giants were much impressed. Shane Wane (Warriors head-coach) stated that *"it's been a great benefit coming down here, so if [Wigan] can return the favour and do anything for Bath in the North West we'd gladly do it. Bath's a fantastic club and the facilities are second to none.* Praise indeed! Two weeks later Bath head coach Mike Ford spoke thus of his squad: 'they are chomping at the bit to get the new Aviva Premiership season under way.' He wasn't wrong! In September Bath launched their 2014/15 season with a 20-29 victory at powerful Sale. In mid September they went 'bananas,' running home five tries to defeat Leicester 45-0! *"Quite stunning,"* wrote Steve James

(S.Telegraph, 21st Sep.). "*Very rarely in the Aviva Premiership will you see a performance that screams a message as loudly as that issued by Bath here. They are the real deal.*" But, then came a sharp warning against any complacency, losing 37-10 at Glasgow Warriors (18th Oct. 2014) for Bath's opener in the European Rugby Champions Cup (successor of the Heineken), and one week later falling 19-21 to four-times European Champions Toulouse. That was an emphatic reality-check, since no club 'had ever qualified from a pool in Europe's top competition having lost their opening two matches.' Admittedly Bath's reputation was partly salvaged thanks to their win-double over Montpellier but, awaiting them next were Toulouse….this time in France! So, over the Channel to suffer humiliation? No….there to scatter all predictions to the four winds and triumph 18-35! New skills-coach Darren Edwards must have now decided that Bath was his kind of club. Chris Foy (D. Mail, 19th Jan. 2015) duly wrote of the "*demolition of one of Europe's superpowers [as] a result to rank with the finest achieved by Premiership teams in Continental combat,*" adding that "*this was a stand-alone performance of stunning quality and magnitude.*" Daniel Evans (Chronicle, 22nd Jan. 2015) spoke in awe of, among others, Jonathan Joseph's brilliance, and although George

Matt Banahan with ball (L to R) Fa'osiliva, Tom Dunn, Devoto (on ground), Henson, Wacokecoke, Chris Cook.
Bath v. Scarlets, September 2014

Acknowledgements: Bob Ascott

Ford could kick goals all afternoon, the victory was built around four dazzling tries. Banahan clinched the first. Chris Cook then casually took an interception (merci beaucoup) and with 60 metres of space ahead bolted off for number two. Joseph swept home for number three, and so outstanding were Bath that on 26 minutes they were already 7-22 ahead, with their travelling supporters probably needing tranquillizers, so euphoric was the atmosphere.

There was however the 'small' matter of the bonus point. No problem! On 71 minutes the magical Joseph ran on to his own grubber-kick and weaved his way through desperate defenders to switch-pass with sub-hooker Ross Batty. He found Francois Louw in support, the flanker swallow-diving over for try number four. C'est magnifique! Albeit Toulouse were ever-dangerous with lock Yoann Maestri and wing Huget clinching home tries, while Toby Flood was spot-on with the boot, this only added to the impact of Bath's remarkable achievement; and if results elsewhere went in their favour and Glasgow could then be subdued (if!) then a path into the quarter-finals was 'on the cards,' a prospect that previously had seemed impossible. However, someone 'up there' must have supported Bath too, because Montpellier, whom Bath had already trounced twice, would then beat Toulouse. That left one obstacle between Hooper's side and the quarter-finals....Glasgow Warriors.

Jonathan Joseph with ball, other (L to R) Thomas, Louw, Garvey.
Bath v Wasps 10/01/2015

Acknowledgements: Bob Ascott

Warriors were 'some' side, though they now found themselves facing a Bath pack both powerful, confident, on its own home ground, roared-on by its own home supporters, and winning things up front. *"A rumbling maul and massive pack-effort prompted referee James Lacey to award two [converted] penalty tries"* (Daniel Evans, Chronicle, 29th Jan. 2015), and with two penalties from Ford, Bath got home 20-15 against highly capable opponents who themselves ran home tries from Dunbar and Vernon, one converted, and a Russell penalty. The quarter-finals now beckoned across the Irish Sea, where in Dublin (4th Apr.) against Leinster this particular European journey would end, nor did it help that Bath's poor discipline conceded no fewer than 18 turnovers, and in addition 12 penalties, six of which went flying through the sticks thanks to Ian Madigan's deadly accuracy. Yet despite Leinster looking totally dominant throughout the first-half, notwithstanding a mesmeric Bath try from Ford, the home side (D. Mail, 5th Apr) were later *"hanging on for dear life as wave after wave of Bath attacks threatened to deliver one of the great European comebacks."* In fact, with Hooper's converted try bringing the score to 18-15, Bath closed to within 15 metres of the Leinster's line for one last attempt for possible victory. But, *"Garvey was harshly penalised by [referee] Garcia with seconds on the clock"* (Sam Peters, Daily Mail), and to the huge relief of most amongst a near 44,000 crowd the whistle sounded for full-time.

Other gates remained open moreover, and though LV Cup hopes would end with a10-13 defeat to Ospreys, this too had opened opportunities for 'young guns,' as exemplified by the debuts of Rory Jennings (out-half), Will Homer (scrum-half) and prop Max Lahiff in a highly creditable January 21-23 win at Harlequins. One week later and full-back Tom Homer (brother of Will) was given his league debut at Saracens almost before he had time to unpack his bags. A proven goal-kicker (he had a 50 metre range) he banged home four from four; albeit Bath fell 34-24, a set-back as competition now intensified for a top four league place. Defeat or not, Saracens had graciously permitted a pre-match minute's silence in memory of four lives lost (one, a four year old girl) in a nationally reported recent road accident-tragedy in Bath. Come October meanwhile the Chronicle had previously 'spoken' of the imminent arrival from Australia of Sam Burgess (Sydney **Rabbitos),** Rugby League's then current World Player of the Year, and **(28th November)** he duly came off the bench to rapturous applause on 63 minutes, playing full-back during Bath's 25-6 win over Harlequins. Burgess, 6ft 5in and 18 stone of speed and power, and whose tackle probably breached the Geneva Convention, was an all-rounder and able to play back-row forward or in the backs. Nonetheless, even for the best switch-coders, adapting to their respective new code can sometimes take time. *"Could he gain England rugby Union caps."* Time would tell.

Meanwhile the stampede for a top-four place was intensifying, and not until a 26-27 win at Harlequins in May was a play-off place assured, and 'boy, was it close.' Bath had not won a 'league' game at Quins since 2004, and as coach Mike Ford later stated (Chronicle, 14th May, 2015) *"the Premiership's brutal and if you don't play well, or you don't prepare well, you can get beaten by anybody."* Well thankfully Bath did play well. Tries came from Louw, Aguilla and Chronicle star man Leroy Houston, while Banahan's second half 40 metre dash and try-saving tackle on centre George Lowe prevented an otherwise certain try. George Ford (showing nerves of steel) then struck home a 40 metre penalty from a tricky angle to edge Bath one point ahead six minutes from time, and Harlequins's soon to depart winger Ugo Monye ran home two tries on an emotional night that commenced with a minute's silence to mark the 70th Anniversary of VE Day. It was a night to remember. Thanks moreover to other critical results then going right, Bath at 2nd place were now assured of a home semi-final. And the opposition: Leicester!

Yet it is doubtful if any Bath follower (however optimistic) would have dared dream of the carnival that would now lead to a remarkable victory on 23rd May before a capacity

Rec crowd of 13,350. Sam Peters (D. Mail, 24th May) then wrote of a Bath team that *"turned scraps into five-star fare….that should not only excite their own fans, but all supporters of English rugby;"* adding that *"the way Bath are playing will surely fill [England coach Lancaster] with joy."* The stars were many, actually the entire Bath team, and as Daniel Evans (Chronicle, 28th May 2015) wrote: Bath *"had less ball and less territory, but once they got a sniff of the line they were deadly, seven tries deadly."* Of these Banahan stormed over for the first-ever semi-final hat-trick, with Eastmond, Stringer, Ford and Watson weaving their way over for the other four. It was rugby pageantry, a 47-10 victory, and on the final whistle an outburst of sheer joy engulfed the Rec. The home players walked around this famous ground milking the applause, many holding in strong arms their proud, adoring young children who smiled and laughed as only children can. Yes, Bath were heading to Twickenham for their first Premiership final since 2004. They would face…. Saracens!

A glorious sun-drenched day, an official 80,891 attendance, tension (Oh lots of tension) and a rugby cup-final thrown-in for good measure, that was the rugby gala at Twickenham on Saturday, 30th May 2015:

Bath: *Watson (Devoto 8), Rokoduguni, Joseph, Eastmond, Banahan, Ford, Stringer (Cook 67), James (Auterac 48), Batty (Webber 47), Wilson (Thomas 49), Hooper, capt. (Day 55), Attwood (Garvey 59) Burgess, Louw, Houston (Fearns 61).*

Saracens: *Goode, Strettle (Barritt 66/Hodgson 70), Taylor, Barritt (Ashton 61 blood), Wyles, Farrell, Wigglesworth (De Kock 56), M.Vunipola (Barrington 77), George (Brits 53), Du Plessis (Figallo 49), Kruis, Hargreaves, capt, (Wray 32), Itoye (Hamiton 67), Burger, B.Vunipola.* Referee: **Wayne Barnes.**

In October Bath had beaten Saracens 21-11 at home. In February Sarries had beaten Bath 34-24 at Allianz Park. On paper it looked 50:50, though on the field their strategies were different. Sarries were calculating pragmatists. Bath, during this season especially, were cavaliers personified. So, it was a near certainty that this would be a clash of styles. It was! It would also be a clash resulting from a high tackle from Owen Farrell on Bath fullback Watson (from which he would not return) in the early minutes. The excellent Ollie Devoto (primarily a centre) stepped into Watson's shoes, but Bath's cohesion was now disrupted, and it showed. Farrell meanwhile had escaped a red card, probably correctly, but a yellow too (Hmm?). He had scored an opening try on seven minutes with some press-box reporters believing he should have been sitting on the bench, and later won nomination as 'man of the match.' His was a good day. But in perfect conditions Bath would not only lose too many turn-overs and come off worse in set-piece play, they sought to compensate by playing risk-rugby, so gifting further tries to hooker Jamie George and winger Chris Wyles respectively. So far Bath had only a Ford penalty to offer some hope of catch-up, but even that was neutralised when Wilson (unjustly it is submitted) was penalised for an alleged late-tackle. Farrell couldn't miss in front of the posts, and on the break Saracens were already 3-25 ahead. Things were not looking good.

As Daniel Evans wrote (Chronicle, 4th June 2015): *"Bath's attacking prowess - a mightily impressive sight this season - relies heavily on precision. The passing, handling and timing of their options need to be spot-on for what can be a majestic machine when it functions."* But street-wise Sarries had prepared their brief well. They predicted the tactics of their opponents, and the majestic machine didn't function; and though Bath would show glimpses of their attacking abilities in the second-half with a Kyle Eastmond run finished off with a try from Joseph, and Ford succeeding with a conversion and three penalties, this was 'not' their day, though one will never be sure of the effect of Watson's early injury. The honours instead belonged to Saracens with their three-try tally, two conversions and three penalties for a 16-28 Aviva Premiership final victory.

For Bath's huge loyal following among the 80,000 plus crowd that day, let us ponder however the post-match words of Daniel Evans (Chronicle): *"Sometimes, you have to lose to taste victory. Sometimes, you have to show chinks of weakness to strengthen your armour. Despite the heartbreak at Twickenham, Bath's exciting and talented squad have exceeded expectations this season and produced some memories that will last for years. Next season they will be shooting for the stars, both at home and in Europe."* Nicely put, with attacking rugby produced by the most adventurous Bath squad for a decade, and nor forgetting those risks they sometimes took. Yet that was all part of the joy of watching them, and their followers (probably numerous neutrals too) loved them for it. For their 150th Centenary, well…. it was so nearly the Dream finale.

Chapter 37. **THE ENIGMA. (2015-2020)**

Despite 'that' result at Twickenham, season 2014-15 had nonetheless been a pageantry. A bright future was promised it seemed and yet, some shocks lay ahead. Of these the first involved Bath's Rugby League cross-coder Sam Burgess during England's opening-round Twickenham encounter in the 2015 World Cup against Wales when, inexplicably (with Burgess playing a dominant role at centre) he was replaced by head coach Stuart Lancaster in the 2nd half with England comfortably leading 22-12. Almost immediately England (as the press generally agreed) looked unsettled, and seizing the initiative Wales duly clinched a 25-28 victory. Next, losing a must-win game against Australia and then despite beating Uruguay, hosts England now fell out of their own World Cup without even reaching round 2. Oh, for what might have been if Burgess had not been replaced and England had advanced into the latter stages? But instead, on 6th November a further shock came with headlines announcing his return to Sydney Rabbitos, news that not only stunned Bath, but the entire rugby game, and with no little sadness. "If true then so sorry 2c Sam Burgess go," stated Jonny Wilkinson (D. Mail, 6 Nov. 2015), just one of many commiserations. And later Steve James (S. Telegraph, 22nd May 2016) suggested that among the probable reasons for his Bath departure was *"where best to play him....blindside flanker or centre,"* positions already held by Carl Fearns (who subsequently moved to Lyon) and centres Eastmond and Joseph respectfully. Thus four class players vying for three positions, and as the saying goes: "last in....first out." That meant Burgess, and yes it 'was' sad. Next, come the evening visit of Saracens (1st Apr. 2016) another shock echoed into the night with the Rec crowd's howl of despair at the red-card dismissal of Anthony Watson for a mid-air tackle (some thought collision) on Sarries fullback Alex Goode, both players vying to catch a Watson kick-ahead. Watson's own unpunished injury at the Twickenham final last season rankled a still unforgiving Rec crowd and from the moment of his red card the Rec atmosphere got seriously 'unfriendly.' Home No.9 Chris Cook then got a yellow for a trip takle (no arguments there), though that was not the case when later home wing Rokoduguni, kicking ahead, was block-tackled less the ball by Alex Goode. A red? No. A yellow? No. Then a scrum, surely? No, nothing. And 'Boy' did that not 'light the fuse! Allow then Brendon Mitchell (BBC Sport, 1st Apr. 2016) to add his view of the events now unfolding: "Referee Garmen's officiating, particularly around the scrum, led to an increasingly hostile atmosphere at the Rec" and (BBC Radio 5 Live's Sonja McLaughlan) added: [it] "even prompted a [home] supporter to enter the referee's room and confront the officials after the match." The game meanwhile, watched by perhaps the most hostile Rec crowd in Bath's history, closed at 10-30 to Saracens who, subsequently 'walked it' to the top of the Premiership, staying there. By contrast Bath, the carefree cavaliers of the previous season finished 9th, and when within two weeks of the season's conclusion head coach Mike Ford was informed by club chairman Bruce Craig that his time at the Rec, spanning four years, was over, one wondered if things could get any worse? Actually, Bath's season concluded with a tonic 38-27 win under skipper Stuart Hooper over 4th placed Leicester. But then, *that's Bath for you*!

Yet, there could hardly have been a better start to 2016/17 than a 14-18 win at Northampton (ending a 16 year fruitless wait at Franklins), lifting spirits at the Rec, not least for flanker and new captain Guy Mercer (Bath born and bred) and the coaching team at Farleigh HQ of Darren Edwards, Toby Booth, Tabai Matson and director of rugby Todd Blackadder. Ah, Todd Blackadder, a former All Blacks captain, coach of Canterbury Crusaders and ex Scotland forward's coach had prepared his new brief well, studying every Bath game of the previous season. He spoke thus: "….the people here are just fantastic and the players are really open….if you get the culture right and get the players feeling comfortable and relaxed in this environment, that's when the best learning takes place" (Chronicle, 1st Sep. 2016), adding: "the best teams in the world have internationals at 8, 9 and 10….and we've got that here. Too right, with the likes of No. 10's Rhys Priestland and George Ford (both world-class said Blackadder), No.9 Kahn Fotuali'i and then Taulupe Faletau at 8. With an impressive 8 wins from 9 kick-starting the new season, including a 10-13 win at Exeter, Bath's early form put them right among front runners. Discipline too was transformed from the worst in the Premiership (22 yellows against in 2015-16) to the best, with the team gaining a top-six Premiership place from 9th previously, nor forgetting reaching the European Challenge Cup semi-final, albeit losing narrowly 28-25 at Stade Francais. And all this despite a depilating injury crisis that required George Ford and Matt Garvey to be drafted in as co-captains. Great tries (plenty of 'em), including hooker Ross Batty's unreal 70m effort against Cardiff Blues (European Challenge Cup) and in the quarter-final of same competition the tackle-busting try-clinching run of Samesa Rokoduguni against Brive (top choice of the Chronicle's Daniel Evans). Emerging Talent? Yes plenty: including forwards Nick Auterac, Tom Dunn, Tom Ellis, Nathan Catt, Kane Palma-Newport, Beno Obano (a massively strong loosehead) and the irrepressible Zach Mercer. And two more: the aforementioned Wales No. 8 Taulupe Faletau from Newport Gwent Dragons (among "the outstanding talents of the Northern-Hemishphere" wrote Daniel Evans (Chronicle (1st Sep. 2016); nor forgetting 6ft 9ins lock Luke Charteris, Cornish born, Wales international and not surprisingly a line-out specialist.

Another boost came early with the surprise, albeit brief, September return of the ever smiling No. 8 Leroy Houston answering an injury-crisis call-up, first bagging a brace in the 37-22 win over Worcester and then?.....his call-up start for Australia v Argentina (at Twickenham!!), **Bath's first Australian international!** Another highlight was **THE CLASH**, a Bath home match v Leicester (8th Apr. 2017), held at Twickenham with 61,000 plus watching. The atmosphere was electric, though not until 12 minutes from time did Bath manage catch-up from a 13-21 deficit. Then Watson struck with his try-brace (adding to Joseph's first), rounding off a devasting break by Faletau, and next 'the' climax with lightening offloads along the backs and Watson's second touch-down, with Ford converting both, so securing Bath a 27-21 win and sending their supporters crazy, those same supporters of whom Blackadder remarked: "I thought it was a great crowd….I really believed they carried us over the line in that last ten minutes." (**Bath**: **Tries**: Joseph, Watson 2, **Cons**: Ford 3, **Pens**: Ford 2. *Leicester*: **Tries**: O'Conner, Veainu, **Cons**: Burns, **Pens**: Burns 3,). This win and later the 44-20 ('bragging rights') victory over Gloucester with Faletau smashing over for a hat-trick lifted Bath to finish 5th in the Aviva Premiership. Coincidentally, Ford (Bath) and Freddie Burns (Leicester), respective No.10's at Twickenham, would switch clubs at the culmination of the season, while Adam Hastings (Bath's emerging No.10, and son of the legendary Gavin) would join Glasgow Warriors, there gaining his first Scotland caps. Player of the season? Well, that's a close-call. But joint skipper Matt Garvey and the Chronicle's Daniel Evans (11th May 2017) couldn't be far out with their choice of No. 9 Kahn Fotuali'i, a seriously good feeder and superb all-rounder! Oh, and with Matt Garvey adding a nice touch with his warm praise for two 'unsung' heroes, namely kit man **Steve Middleton** and team manager **Sophie Bennett**. *Meanwhile earlier in the season The Chronicle (22 Dec, 2016) had reported as follows: 'a scheme set out by the Charity Commission in 2013 has been clarified to determine how the famous piece of ground [the Rec] can be managed by the Recreation Ground Trust. This decision from the First Tier Tribunal – Charity, confirms that as absolute owner the Trust can "sell, lease, license or otherwise dispose of all or any part of the Rec as it works to achieve its charitable objectives." 'The club expressed their delight at this decision.'* (However, delight or not, the Rec issue has been on-going for at least a decade, so 'best-advice' probably remains at: "**watch this space**.).

When Bath shot off the 2017-18 starting-blocks under skipper Matt Garvey with a league win at Leicester, their first at Welford Road since 2003 (centre Max Clark superb), followed by a home 31-21 thriller over Saracens (wing Rokodugini superb), a top four place seemed possible. And notwithstanding a continuing injury list that included highly rated Bath born prop Kane Palma-Newport (achilles' tendon) new talent stepped into the breach: Levi Douglas (lock/bk row), Josh Bayliss (bk.row), Darren Atkins (full-back), Will Vaughan (prop), and Max Green (scrum-half). Yet, despite impressive wins, including a December European Champions Cup victory against Toulon (26-21), there were 'careless' defeats. Bath dropped their guard and a comfortable lead at home against Falcons to lose 32-33, while with a home win against Gloucester begging, they conceded a late penalty from which their grateful visitors grabbed a last-minute try, winning 21-22. Then, having previously won 13-18 away at Scarlets, Bath were outplayed 17-35 at home, unable to gain even the precious bonus point that would have taken them into the European Championship Cup knock-out stages. However, Bath could also shine, their 25-46 win at Worcester for example where the thunderous try of lock James Phillips blasting through four tackles on a 25 metre try-scoring charge was a wondrous sight. By contrast the Anglo-Welsh final against Exeter (30th Mar. 2018) was a different story. The 11-28 defeat explains that.

However, in this season of inconsistency one April victory stood out, and that against hot-favourites Gloucester at Kingsholm, who faced a Bath side with four successive demoralising defeats behind them. But forget any form-guide when these two collide on a rugby field, and when the contest was over Bath had triumphed 20-43 from six tries from six players: first hooker Tom Dunn within 72 seconds, followed by Rhys Priestland, then former Wales wing Aled Brew, and a stunning 60 metre evasive run from No. 15 Tom Homer putting Bath 13-26 ahead at the break. But ruthless Bath were not finished yet, adding further run-ins from wing Cooper Vuna (what a hand-off!) and New Zealander James Wilson on injury-cover loan from Bedford. Of 34 years vintage this utility back played like a teenager. Yes, Gloucester too ran home tries, good ones, from Slater and Woodward. Nonetheless, this decisive win was both psychological and strategic, as this bonus point win was to prove critical in elevating Bath into the top six in the final table, overtaking Gloucester who finished 7th, and Todd Blackadder (Charlie Morgan, Sun' Telegraph, 29 Apr. 2018) was spot-on when adding that this traditional derby was "bigger than Texas." Too right! Bristling with confidence, Bath then romped home 63-19 against London Irish, another vital league result in their season's final game, where wing Matt Banahan (ironically Gloucester bound) played his last game for Bath after twelve seasons on the Rec…. plus a century of tries tucked into his pocket for good measure. A club legend, he was lifted shoulder high by his team-mates come the final whistle.

Season 2018-19 (Matt Garvey Skipper) offered something new, namely **Katie Warriner** (previously working with Team GB at Olympic Games level and England Sevens rugby) and now joining the club to 'work with coaches and players developing strategies and skill-sets to cope with the *mind-related* areas of high-performance sport.' And this too would be a season not without its contradictions: a 20-22 Autumn home upset against Toulouse (European Champions Cup), a January League defeat at Worcester with Bath ahead 3-19 at the break, only to lose 21-19 after 14 minutes of extra time, down to 11 men in the latter stages, and the worst for one red and 3 yellows against. While the plus side included the Freddie Burns inspired 14-24 December victory at Wasps, the No.10 scoring 19 points including a try-gem, and lifting Bath straight into the top six. Two newcomers meanwhile were introduced to the Rec, namely top-rated wing Joe Cokanasiga from London Irish, and Ruaridh (Rory) Mconnochie from Tenterden, Kent, whose zenith in 15's rugby was Nuneaton (Midlands Premier, National Three). But Sevens was a different story for this former sports/exercise Gloucestershire University student. Indeed, he was a World Series player by 2015 and a member of the 2016 GB Olympic silver medal rugby 7's team. Come 2018 Bath then introduced this 26 year old, 6ft 3in wing into Premiership rugby and Chris Foy (D. Mail, 20th May 2019) summarizes his first season thus: [he] "made a stunning impact in his debut pro season," so stunning in fact he would gain his first England cap (against Italy, September, 2019) and his second against the USA in the 2019 Rugby World Cup, Japan. But this was a season part predictable, part fascinating. Newcastle, struggling again, were battling against the drop. But so too were Leicester of all people! Meanwhile, though Saracens (would-be champions) and Exeter clearly had the league top-places wrapped up by Christmas, come the last day of the season no less than four clubs (among them Bath) were battling it out for one remaining top four slot. Northampton clinched it. But Bath, thanks to prop Jacques van Rooyan's late try (Priestland converting), won 31-32 at Leicester to secure a 6th place entry into the European Champions Cup. The win was a deserved and fitting farewell for much admired departing Director of Rugby Todd Blackadder.

Filling Todd Blackadder's shoes for season 2019-20 was **Stuart Hooper**, alongside new skipper Charlie Ewels, and they, Premiership rugby (indeed sport generally) would now face a truly unprecedented crisis: *Corona-virus/Covid-19!* Indeed, the January 2020 decision to relegate Saracens (five-times Premiership Champions) for breaches of the salary cap could almost be described as a minor issue! What could not be so described was the impact upon rugby that came with the following **RFU announcement (D. Mail, 17 Mar. 2020):** *"Rugby's total shutdown was confirmed last night as the Premiership, European cups and all community games were suspended….until the weekend of April 24-26 at the earliest."* Some hope! Premiership rugby did **not resume until 15th August**, and even then spectators (though thankfully not T.V.) were excluded. So not surprisingly financial problems arose. Indeed, the Chronicle (2nd Apr. 2020) explained that in normal circumstances Premiership clubs earned 'between £300,000 and £500,000 on matchdays,' thus now inflicting a revenue loss that, along with other factors necessitated (inter alia) salary reductions. Reports then followed concerning adverse 'player reaction,' with Bath, among others, targeted, suggesting that 'Bath stars were in revolt over pay cuts.' "They were 'not," as club captain Ewels strongly emphasised (Chronicle, 2nd Apr. 2020).

However, rather ironically one less hurdle now faced English rugby's Premiership 12 clubs, which unlike the Pro 14 clubs are required ('unfairly so,' many would doubtless say) to play league matches concurrently with internationals. But this factor was now temporarily set aside, **as the Six Nations were lifted into Autumn 2020,** so leaving the road clear for a continuation of **the 2019/2020** Premiership unhindered by international call-ups, which in Bath's case (D. Mail, 21 Jan. 2020) would have involved probable selection for coach Eddie Jones's England squad of: Will Stuart, Tom Dunn, Charlie Ewels, Sam Underhill, Jonathan Joseph and Anthony Watson (plus Taulupe Falatau for Wales). Later, Beno Obano and Tom de Glanville would be added. **Relegation too was suspended** (likewise for season 2020/21). Meanwhile, come **the August 2019/2020** re-start and now with powerful lock **Josh McNally** from London Irish, utility back **Cameron Redpath** (later Scotland) from Sale, and **Ben Spencer** (Saracens) among the newcomers, Bath hit top gear. Wins over London Irish 34-7, then 16-38 at Leicester where No.10 **Josh Matevesi** (Cornish Born Fiji international) sold an outrageous dummy to launch Tom De Glanville over the white-wash, featured among early highlights. Next, Northampton fell 3-18 at Franklins, though Bath then slipped up 23-27 at home to Wasps. But back on track again it was: 'Bath thrill crowd' ((3,500 approx.)) in English rugby's first **spectator *'test'* crowd** game (at Harlequins), winning 27-41 in the process. Oh, and what a sight to witness **Lewis Boyce's** interception try 30 yards out. A prop, he left defenders for dead. "Not that Bath just rely upon grunt work" added Daniel Scholfield (Sun' Tel, 6th Sep. 2020) in this televised encounter. 'Their backs combine invention and precision, marshalled brilliantly by half-backs Ben Spencer and Rhys Priestland, with Rory McConnochie showing his poaching instincts with a brace, No. 8 Josh Bayliss a tour de force at blindside and Elliot Stooke thumping everything that moved.' The win, a thriller, lifted Bath to fifth on 50 pts, tailing Wasps on 51.

Exeter had already reached the finishing post on 68 pts, while following were four clubs scrambling for three remaining Top Four places. Four games remained with Bath winning 40-15 over Worcester, 22-37 at powerful Sale and then when trailing Gloucester 20-3 with tries from Chris Harris and Banahan, and the accurate boot of Twelvetrees, Bath looked out of it. But looks can be deceiving, and with 20 minutes remaining they struck back, always the sign of a good side. Hooker Tom Dunn scored twice as Bath had now "become an unstoppable force" (Chris Foy, D. Mail, 23rd Sep. 2020). Jinking Anthony Watson then inspired another surge, finished off by prop Lewis Boyce. With Rhys Preistland's immaculate kicking and flanker Underhill outstanding as always, wing Joe Cokanasiga then stormed down the left, his inside pass leaving Ben Spencer to touch down for a thumping 31-21 bonus point win. "That was box- office" exclaimed Stuart Hooper. And yet, there now came another twist to the covid-19 tale, one that originated back in August when 'all' clubs had *signed up to an agreement that they would forfeit a match if suffering significant numbers of Covid-19 tests."* But albeit just such an outbreak (16 cases) now happened at Sale prior to their final round league match with Worcester, Premiership Rugby, contrary to its own original stipulation, postponed the game to the following Wednesday. Disapproval followed throughout the Premiership, with comments including (inter alia) '*claims of goalposts being moved; serious concerns for the integrity of the Premiership; Sale will have distinct advantage in knowing what result they need to qualify.*'

Bath however had drawn 17-17 in a mighty struggle at Saracens, their 2 points no guarantee of a semi-final place if Sale overcame Worcester, though the conundrum was then concluded when a further eight Sale players and staff failed Covid-19 tests, so opening the gate for Bath to reach their first Premiership semi-final for five years. But, as 4th in the Top Four play-offs, they would play at 1st placed Exeter (destined to win both the Gallagher Premiership and European Champions Cup). And, albeit Bath looked to be in with a chance during the first half, the game is about two halves, and there can be no argument about Exeter's 35-6 win based upon five tries (Luke Cowan-Dickie, Stuart Hogg, Olly Devoto and a brace from Jonny Hill) against two penalties from Rhys Priestland, a score line that alone writes the script. And yet, despite the mountain of difficulties during **this virus affected 2019/20 rugby season**, there were great tries, great games…. and great moments to remember! For life (not least sport) as they say, **must** go on and…. that is exactly what happened!

Meanwhile, at the season's conclusion loose-head prop **Nathan Catt** would retire from a Bath club he had served for a dozen years. He rose from the Academy to the England

U.20's Grand Slam winners 2008, England Saxons 2009, and then the England training squad 2018, and his poignant words of farewell (Chronicle 5th Nov. 2020) spoke for generations of Bath players AND, his club's almost spiritual bond with its parent city: "The city is phenomenal," he says, "the players of past and present. It's all been a fantastic journey. I can't thank Bath Rugby enough for giving me this opportunity to experience so many great memories (adding): to the supporters I just want to say a huge thank you for backing me on my journey, you have been nothing short of amazing." Fine words Nathan!

Yet, is there perhaps just one single word that could define this West Country rugby family, who in theory should never have got near the likes of Bristol and those top Welsh sides. Yet they did! They won four successive Twickenham Cup Finals in the 1980's. In theory (that word again), no club could achieve such a feat. But they did! In January 1998 Bath became the first British club to win the top European Cup (Heineken). So much for theory then….for this was all fact, breath-taking in its scale. True, they couldn't hold such dominance forever, who could? Even so, they have rarely been seriously troubled in the Premiership, and post 2015/16 (a difficult and unhappy season) they have not failed to gain a place in European Rugby's Premiership Cup competition. So, what might be that elusive 'word' that describes a club from a genteel Georgian city to then suddenly storm through the ranks on the inside lane and seize that treasured crown of English rugby? It's not an easy choice, how could it be. But maybe one word does fit the description we seek. For Bath have always been an 'Enigma!' And, their history suggests that it is an Enigma that they are likely to remain.

REVIEW of 2020/21.

Update: *the RFU scrapped* **relegation** *for season* **2020/21**; **February 20/21 Cameron Redpath** *and* **Beno Obano** *gain their respective debut Scotland and England caps (6 Nations, Twickenham), Scotland win 6-11;* **March 2021:** *it was announced that Bath winger* **Will Muir** *(former England 7's player of the Year) was named in GB 7's pre-Olympic training squad;* **4th March 2021:** *confirmed (Chronicle) that* **'Rhys Priestland** *had now surpassed the then all-time Premiership goal-kicking record when kicking* **29** *consecutive goal-kicks in Bath's 22-23 win at Northampton; South Africans* **Tian Schoeman** *(backs),* **Juan Schoeman** *(f.row),* **Jacques du Toit** *(f.row) already first-teamers;* **25th March 2021:** *it was announced that former England No.10* **Danny Cipriani** *would be joining Bath for the following season; so too (later announced) Scotland cap* **D'Arcy Rae** *(f.row) and South African* **Johannes Jonker** *(f.row);* **1ˢᵗ May 2021: European Challenge Cup semi-final,** *Bath lose 10-19 to Montpellier on Rec;*

Tom Doughty *(f.row) advances from Academy to first senior team debut.* **Girvan Dempsey** *(attack/backs coach) departs at end of 2020/21 season with* **David Williams** *(Sharks, Super Rugby) to replace him. Season* **2020/21: Bath finish 7ᵗʰ in Premiership**, *(final match beating Northampton 30-24 at home, 3000 'test' crowd watching) to qualify for next season's* **European rugby's Premier Cup competition**, **now open to top eight clubs.** *Zach Mercer (bk.row) now departs for Montpelier.*

Bath Rugby 2020/21 Club Award winners: *Top try scorer:* **Tom Dunn** *and* **Will Muir.** *Try of Season:* **Will Muir** *v Worcester. Academy player of Season:* **Orlando Bailey.** *Breakthrough Player of Season:* **Will Muir.** *Best forward:* **Josh McNally.** *Best Back:* **Ben Spencer.** *Supporters' Player of Season:* **Zach Mercer.** *Players' Player of Season:* **Miles Reid.**

At conclusion of 2020/21 season nine Bath players called-up for Eddie Jones's England training Squad: *locks* **Josh McNally** & **Charlie Ewels**, **Joe Cokanasiga** *(wing),* **Sam Underhill** *(bk row),* **Ben Spencer** *(No.9),* **Beno Obano** *(f.row),* **Tom de Glanville** *(f.bk),* **Max Ojomoh** *(centre),* **Miles Reid** *(bk row).* **Also, Josh Bayliss** *(bk.row) "set to be involved during summer with* **Scotland." Also, Anthony Watson** *(wing/f.back) & Wales No.8* **Taulupe Faletau** *called-up for* **British and Irish Lions.** *(4/July/2021) Bath players* **Josh McNally** *(debut England cap),* **Charlie Ewels, Sam Underhill** *(one try)* **and Cokanasiga** *(2 tries) play for* **England v USA,** *rslt: England win 43-29.*

Footnote: *It was reported* **(club website, 26/05/21)** *that 'Bath Rugby* **launches women's team** *with aim to meet Premier 15s criteria in next licence cycle.'*

Chronicle/June/2021): *it was reported that University of Bath graduates* **Deborah Fleming** *and* **Natasha Hunt** *named in Team GB women's 7's squad for Tokyo Olympic Games.*

RUGBY BOOK – BATH CHRONOLOGY.

1823: at **Rugby School** a pupil (**William Webb Ellis**) reportedly runs with a football, contrary to the rules as played at that time. **In 1841** the practice of 'running with the ball' was formally adopted by Rugby School.

1843: Guys Hospital rugby club are founded, and are now generally recognised as the first ever rugby club to be formed in England.

1858: Blackheath (The Club) are founded and claim to be the first 'open' club ever formed. However, **Liverpool RFC** (later Liverpool St. Helens) argue that their formation on **19th December 1857** establishes their claim as the first 'open' club in rugby football.

Marlborough v Clifton College on 20th November **1864** is probably first ever inter-schools match in England. Marlborough win by one drop goal.

(Note: Merchiston Castle (Edinburgh) v The High School, 13th February 1858, probably the first inter-school match in British Isles (see book: The Edinburgh Academical Football Club Centenary History). Meanwhile Edinburgh Academy v Merchiston Castle (11th December 1858) commenced fixtures, probably the oldest continuously played inter-schools match anywhere in the British Isles.

1865: Bath are founded (by a "few gentlemen of the city"). Their first venue was the spacious **North Parade ground,** now home of the Bath Cricket Club, at rent of two shillings and sixpence (a half-crown) per game. As was the norm in this era, they were called Bath Football Club.

1868/9: "a form of rugby" is played for first time at **Kingswood School,** almost certainly the first school in Bath to adopt rugby football.

1871: on 26th January 1871 the **Rugby Football Union (RFU) founded** at the Pall Mall Restaurant, No.1 Cockspur Street, London (near Trafalgar Square). A committee subsequently agrees a definite national set of 'laws' for the game of Rugby Football.

On 27 March 1871 the **first ever international match** is played at Raeburn Place, Edinburgh, Scotland winning against England by one goal and one try against one try, and teams consisting of 20 players each.

1871: Keene's Bath Journal reports on *"an interesting match that was played on the North Parade ground."* The result was Bath (4 rouges) versus Bedminster of Bristol (one goal, 7 rouges and one try). The Bedminster goal was kicked by **W.G. Grace** (Gloucestershire and England cricket legend).

1872: Francis D'Aguila, Royal Engineers and Bath player is capped at forward for England against Scotland, as Bath's first international. His brother **J.D'Aguila** was to captain both Bath (1882-84) and on occasions Somerset. **Clifton** are formed in same season during which time they beat Bath twice.

1873: Gloucester Football Club was founded. By the 1900's they had developed into one of the most formidable rugby teams in England.

1875/6: Somerset commence county matches; though the **Somerset** Rugby Football Union was not formed until 1882.

1877: England v Ireland (5th February at the Oval, London) are first international teams to play with sides **reduced to fifteen players** (England win by 2 goals and two tries to nil).

1878-80: Major **Francis D'Aguila** (Bath & England) is decorated for service in the **Afghan War** of 1878-80.

1879: first **Calcutta Cup** match played, then as always between England and Scotland (result was drawn). Cup donated by Calcutta Rugby Club, India (membership then mainly of 3rd Buffs regiment) who elected to gift a cup to the RFU (made from melted down rupees from club bank account).

1882: the **Somerset Rugby Union** is formed at a meeting held at the Clarence Hotel in Bridgwater. Somerset immediately became the parent county of the Bath club. In this first season Herbert Fuller of Bath is among those selected to play for the county.

1882: Bath's **Herbert Fuller** (he also played for Clifton) wins his first cap for England, against Scotland. A forward he wins 6 caps. He had already captained Bath from 1874-6.

1882: Rule interpretation still causing some difficulties in the rugby game. Bath's match at Devizes abandoned (when Bath, so it is reported, were ahead) owing to an outbreak of heated argument as to differing interpretations of the rules by the two teams. It was never concluded as to whose interpretation was actually correct.

1883: the **Home Nations Championship** commenced between England, Wales, Scotland and Ireland, becoming the **5 Nations** in **1910** when France joined, then the **6 Nations** when Italy joined in **2000.**

1885: *referees now commenced the use of whistles and touch-judges the use of sticks (later flags).*

1888: Bristol Football Club was founded.

1888 (27th October): Bath played Bristol on the Kensington Meadows, Bath. It seems very likely from reliable records that this was the **first ever game** between the two clubs. The result was a draw (3 minors each). Bath played with **four threequarters** for the first time in their history in this inaugural match (according to the match programme for the 100th Bath v Bristol match, 29 Feb.1936).

The Bath Centenary 1865-1965 booklet records that the first Bath match played at Bristol witnessed **Francis White** of Bath scoring *"the winning try at Bristol **minus his shorts**, the remains of which were still in the hands of the Bristol fullback when White* *ran round to ground the ball behind the posts. The applause lasted until the goal kick was taken."*

1888/9 season saw the arrival of the **New Zealand Maoris**, the first ever Dominion side to tour England. Bath's **Frank Soane and C.J.B. Moneypenny** selected for Somerset side which loses 4-17 against the tourists.

1890-91: three sandwich men were now engaged to 'walk' the main streets on match-days to **advertise** Bath home matches.

1891-92: during this season Frank Soane and C.J.B. Moneypenny became the first Bath players to represent the **Barbarians** (founded in 1890).

1893: Frank **Soane** wins first cap for England, against Scotland. A forward, he wins total of 4 caps.

1894: in 1894 Bath make the crucial decision to move from nearby **Henrietta Park** to The Pulteney Meadows **(The Rec).** The **Bath v Exeter** game (06.Oct.1894) which Bath won is reportedly Bath's first ever inter-club match on The Rec. After almost thirty 'nomadic' years, Bath now possessed a permanent rugby home. On 24th December 1894 **Bath played the Barbarians** for the first time, losing 0-14 (on The Rec). The clubs then faced each other in 1896, the result being a 13-13 draw (2 goals and 1 try apiece). They were to play again in 1897, the Barbarians winning 3-8.

1895-96: it was decided to award **Bath caps** to players who during a season had played at least 10 matches for the 1st team.

Insurance was now paid to injured players, on condition of a medical certificate being obtained. One case was awarded £5 (good money then) for a near six week absence through injury; while ten shillings was awarded to another case in which a player missed work for a week.

Various venues have been utilised as a club-house/HQ by Bath, including the adoption of the **Angel Hotel** in Westgate Street in 1895 (where 'smokers, get-togethers etc were also held), while a room at No. 4 Bath Street was likewise hired at a weekly two shillings and sixpence rent for the club secretary and treasurer. At the turn of the century the club had moved to the **Crown Hotel,** Old Orchard Street, where they remained until 1914. A move was then made to the **Old Red House** (New Bond Street), which would remain as favoured HQ until 1954 and the opening of **the Club House** on the Rec.

In November **1896** the club decided that **teas** would be paid for at the **club's expense** for visiting teams playing beyond a ten mile radius of Bath. This would apply to all three teams.

Training: the Riding School, Montpelier, Julian Road was **rented** for training nights on Tuesdays and Fridays.

The GWR, the Midland Railway and the Somerset & Dorset Railway declined to allow reduced **Cheap Return Tickets** for Bath's away games.

1896: Herbert Fuller (Bath & England) (2 Jan. 1896) died in Streatham by way of a cerebral tumour. Admired by many, his loss was deeply felt. A Cambridge Blue who would represent the university on the Rugby Union for many years, he was laid to rest at Lansdown Cemetery.

Frank D'Aguila, Bath's first international and later a major with the Royal Engineers, died in July 1896.

1897: it was decided to ensure that a bottle of **best brandy** was always available on the Rec, but for *"use in case of accident or illness, for players only."*

1899: after much negotiation, Bath and **Walcot RFC** agree that Walcot be permitted to play at the Kensington Meadows at rent of £3 p.a., plus the release to Bath of two Walcot players if so requested on a Friday night by Bath.

Devon win the **County Championship** (by a goal) against previous season holders Northumberland at Newcastle. The first Western County side to win the Championship, their victory set in motion a West Country domination of the Championship for the next twenty-three years.

1900: Portsmouth vice-captain **George Trerise** was **fatally injured** on The Rec (16th April). Bath were mortified, but Portsmouth captain Mr Edmonds wrote saying that the game had been *"more free from rough or unfair play than any game he had ever played."*

1901: J.B.S. D'Aguila died. One of two sons of Francis D'Aguila (Bath & England), J.B.S himself was a highly popular player for both Bath and Somerset.

1901: The **Bath & District Rugby Combination** is established.

1902: Flood-Lights on Bath training nights were introduced. This innovation was thanks to the support of Mr Hine (local ironmonger and committee man). He arranged a set of oil lamps to be positioned around the ground on training nights. No fee for their use was required. The first recorded floodlit rugby match was played in 1878 - **Broughton v Swinton** – far earlier than is often realised.

1904-05: the **Bath Schools Rugby Union** is founded. During this era (and beyond) clubs would sometimes request a **guarantee** so as to cover travel costs (etc.).

1904: J.G. Milton, while still a pupil at Bedford School, is selected as a forward for England against Wales on 9th January 1904 (venue: Leicester), match drawn at 14-14.

1905-06: on 21st October 1905 the Bath threequarters **James Timmins** (captain) and **R. Meister** play for Somerset against the New Zealand tourists, the visitors making their first ever visit to the British Isles (result: Somerset 0, New Zealand 23). Venue: Taunton, crowd estimated at near 9000.

1905-6: Bath win a **mere seven games**, leading some commentators to wonder if the club could survive in its present form. A slow, but steady recovery would follow however.

1906-07: Bath's threequarter **R.Meister** plays for Somerset against touring "South Africans" (result: Somerset 0, South Africans 14). Venue: Taunton.

1907- 08: Bath play their first ever game against **Harlequins,** losing 49-8 at The Quins (19th October 1907). Later that season (21st March 1908) Bath overcome Harlequins by 9-8 at home, following a **two week ban** against Bath for crowd trouble on the Rec during a Somerset Cup game against Weston-super-Mare.

Bath host Racing Club de France on the Rec (**1st Nov, 1907**), their first overseas opponents. The result was a 6-6 draw.

1908-09: Bath threequarters **J. Timmins** and **R. Ascott** both play for Somerset against touring Australians (result: Somerset 0, Australians 8). Venue: Taunton.

1909: Bath's **Tom White** switches codes, joining professional club Oldham of the Northern Union (later **The Rugby League**). Joining him in the professional code by 1912 were Bath's **Tom West** (Rochdale Hornets), **R. Ascott** and **Riley West** (both Hull Kingston Rovers) and **J. Robinson.**

1910: Bath initially wore shirts of blue, later blue & black hoops were the **club colours** until 1906-7 when white shirts were adopted. Then **in season 1909-1910** the present colours of '**blue, white and black**' hoops were adopted, and duly described in that order. Also: *international matches commence at **Twickenham** from January 1910 with the England v Wales encounter (although Harlequins had played club matches on the pitch in the previous season).*

Bath Chronicle (13th Jan. 1912) confirms that a *"**Bath Club cap** is given to a player who puts in ten 1ST XV matches in one season."*

1912: on 3rd October in Bath, Somerset play the South African tourists on The Rec, (result: Somerset 3, South Africa 24). Included in Somerset team were Bath players **Vincent and Norman Coates** (backs), **F. Hill** (scrum-half) and **W.F. Warde** (forwards).

1912-13 season: Bath wing **Vincent Coates** played in all five England internationals, including match against South Africa. His six tries in one season was an England record, ironically surpassed in following season by fellow England wing C.N. Lowe (Blackheath) who scored eight.

1913-14: Taunton Albion (initially named Rowbarton Albion on their formation in 1901) would cease to play again after season 1913-14. The club merged into the **Taunton club** in the post 1914-18 era.

1914 (on 1st September) Bath (Britain now at war with Germany since 4th August) send telegram to Leicester, stating that the Bath club (with much reluctance) would have to withdraw from their forthcoming match at the Tigers in view of the worsening situation.

Every club in the Country was doing likewise. Official club rugby would now effectively cease for the duration of the war. **Anzac Forces** use Rec at various stages of War as required.

Plymouth Albion are formed (circa 1915) with an amalgamation of Devonport Albion and Plymouth RFC. **Devonport Services** had commenced recorded matches in 1904. **1914-18:** at various stages during the 1914-18 conflict the Rec is **requisitioned by the Armed Forces.**

1919: in mid-February of 1919 the RAF (prior to April 1918 the Royal Flying Corps) vacated the Rec. It was now available for rugby again. Barely days later (22nd February 1919) Bath play their **first post-war club** game against a Bristol XV, **winning 8-3.**

1919: Bath hold their **Golden Jubilee Dinner** (postponed during 1914/15 because of the War) on 26th August 1919. On 27th December Bath host Welsh opponents Cross-Keys. Bath back **Clifford Walwin** suffers **fatal injury** from accidental collision with an opponent.

1920-1 season: **Bath Rugby Supporters Club** formed. Dedicated work is given to (inter alia) helping Junior clubs by way of aid and players-insurance cover, plus organising trips to International games which reportedly were so successful that **some tourist agencies copied them.**

1921 (September): **Bristol** depart from their County cricket ground venue and commence playing at the **Memorial ground**. Bath play their first game at this new venue on 28 Jan. 1922. It was a home win for Bristol by **8-3.** By coincidence, on the Rec (22 Feb. 1919) Bath had previously won the two clubs' first post-war game. Again, this was a home win by **8-3** for Bath.

1922 (13 April): Bath play French club **Stade Bordelais** on the Rec (13 Apr.1922), Bath winning 11-3. In same year Bridgwater merged with Bridgwater Albion; the combined club choosing to retain the name of **Bridgwater Albion.** Also, in season **1921-2** Bath attain **new club record of 25 victories.**

1922-3: Bath's **26 wins** is new club record, but only if an '*exhibition*' game at **Blundell's School** is accepted as an official 1st team match.

1925 (13 Apr): S.G.U. Considine plays wing for England against France (Paris), England winning 11-13. During the game the Bath genius was injured and would never play serious rugby again. (Circa 1925) a Bath supporter gifts the so-called **Rag Doll** to all future winners of Bath v Llanelli rugby matches.

Season **1925-6**: **Diamond Jubilee year**, and the club's first **England Trial** (19th December 1925) held on Rec, 8,000 reportedly attending. In Autumn 1925 the club's new **North stand** (seated) was opened. Bath unexpectedly experience a loss of form, with **only seven wins gained**, exactly the same total attained twenty years previously in 1905-6. But a rapid recovery achieved in following season.

1931-2: on 21st Mar. 1931 Bath forwards **Crichton-Miller (Scotland)** and **G.G.Gregory (England)** opposed each other at Murrayfield, Scotland winning 28-19. George Haydon sets **new Bath club try-record of 29 tries.**

1932 (2 Jan): Bath centre **R.A. Gerrard** wins his **first cap for England** in their encounter against South Africa at Twickenham. Rslt: England 0, South Africa 7. Bath's new **West Stand** (replacing the original) was opened at start of season **1932-3** (6 Sep 1932)).

1934: Bath's **R.A. Gerrard** played in the winning Barbarians team in the **Twickenham Sevens tournament.**

1934: in the close season of 1934 the **Bath Ex-schools XV** is established for young players between 14-16 years.

1935 (16 Mar): a controversial try awarded to visitors Blackheath (who won 8-13) leads to a post-match **demonstration** by small vociferous group of angered Bath supporters.

1935: The **Bath Colts XV** (16-18 years) is established. **By 1980** it would be re-organised as the **Bath Youth XV.**

1936 (4 Jan): England defeat New Zealand by 13-0. Bath's **R.A. Gerrard** plays key defensive role in England backs.

1936 (29 Feb): the **100th official match** between Bath and Bristol. It resulted in a 3-3 draw on the Rec, the same score as that made in the inaugural game played in 1888 on Bath's Kensington Meadows.

1937 (20 March): a controversial late try by Bath (who won 4-14) at Torquay Athletic led to a **post-match demonstration** by angry home supporters. Much to the regret of many, future fixtures between the clubs were cancelled by Bath as a result, though later restored in post-World War Two era.

1938-39: Bath gain their **first ever away win at Gloucester** (3-5) on 19 Nov. 1938; Bath then clinch the Double with their return home win (6-5) on 18 Feb. 1939.

1939-40: as a result of the escalation of the war, Bath's opening match against Llanelli on 9th September 1939 is cancelled. Official rugby ceases. Nonetheless rugby (and professional soccer) continue on a regional format among many clubs in the British Isles. Bath now play as the **Bath & Admiralty RFC** (formed in Sep.1939) throughout duration of war.

1944: 9th December, Bath win at Bridgwater and field **rugby league** scrum-half **S. Morgan** of Hull Kinston Rovers.

1945 (08 Sep): post-war official rugby commences once more, and Bath host Llanelli (who win 0-16), six years less one day since their previous game cancelled at outset of World War Two. Owing to war effort, rugby kit now depended upon availability of government 'clothing coupons,' and Bath are restricted to white shirts only, blue shorts and red socks. Not until season 1948-9 would Bath return to wearing shirts of blue, white and black.

1946-7: Bath's **Ian Lumsden** now playing for **Scotland** at outside-half. With a club policy change announced in October 1946 Bath chose to **abandon shirt No.13.** Change not fully implemented until season 1951-2 with shirts numbered from 1-16 and omitting No. 13 (see too: **Ch. 20).**

1948: Bath gain their **first ever away win in Wales** against Llanelli (0-3) on 2 Oct.1948; Bath then clinch the Double against the 'Sospans' with their return home win (6-0) in late December1948. In opening week of February 1949 Bath win 3-5 at powerful Newbridge to record **their 2ⁿᵈ ever win in Wales.**

1951: Bath's 3-9 away win at Moseley on 21ˢᵗ April 1951 set **a new club record** of 27 wins in a season, beating the previous record of 26 wins gained by the Vowles 1922-3 side.

1951: the **Bath old Players Association** is formed, later re-named **Bath Past Players** in June 2005.

1952: against South Africa at Twickenham in January 1952 **Alec Lewis** plays his **first international** for England at the age of 31 years. Result: England lose 3-8.

1952-3: famed Oxford Blue **John MacGregor Kendall-Carpenter** joined Bath and during season of 1952-3 both he and Alec Lewis were playing for England.

1954: a **new club house** was opened on 6ᵗʰ March 1954 following Bath's 16-6 win over great rivals Bristol. This was their first ever club house on the Rec.

1954: another **West Stand** (replacing the stand destroyed in the War) is officially opened on 2ⁿᵈ October 1954 seating 1100 plus spectators.

1954: in late April Bath head for France in their **first-ever overseas tour**. They return with a triumphant victory 'treble' under their belts.

1957: Bath's Old Sulian out-side half **Brian Weston** wins **Blue for Oxford.**

1959: fixtures between **Bath and Torquay,** withdrawn since March 1937 owing to post-match demonstration at Torquay, restored on 4ᵗʰ April 1959, Bath winning 11-12 away.

1961: in January Bath wing-forward **Laurie Rimmer** gains the first of 5 caps when **selected for England** against South Africa at Twickenham (England losing 0-5). In February Bath prop **Pete Parfitt** is chosen as a reserve for England against Ireland.

1961: at Twickenham (December) Bath centre **Geoff Frankcom** and Bath fullback **Ian Balding** simultaneously win **Blues for Cambridge** in the narrow win over Oxford, Frankcom clinching the winning try.

1962: Bath's first experience of playing under **floodlights** occurred at Stradey Park on Friday evening, 19th January 1962, Llanelli winning 16-3.

1965: in January 1965 Bath centre **Geoff Frankcom** gains the first of his 4 caps for England. Bath invited for their first-ever appearance in the Twickenham **Middlesex 'sevens' classic,** and are beaten 13-0 by Rosslyn Park in first round.

1965-6: Bath celebrate their **Centenary season.**

1967: on 18th November 1967 the Bath home win over Devonport Services is televised on BBC 2's Rugby Special, the clubs **first televised game.** At Twickenham (December 1967) Bath's **James (Jamie) Monahan** (former Kingswood School pupil) wins his Cambridge Blue at prop. The light Blues achieve a narrow victory.

1968: in January Bath's **David Gay** (19 years) wins his first England cap at No.8 against Wales at Twickenham (11-11 draw).

1968-9: Bath set a **new club record of 29 victories** in a season.

1971: Bath wing **Peter Glover** re-called for England in 1971 Home Championship, and in September both **Mike Hannell** (prop) and wing **Peter Glover** are selected for England's three match tour to Japan. In season **1971-2** ex Bath fullback **David Dolman** (cousin of former club wing John Dolman) was appointed the club's **first official coach**.

In season **1971-2** the RFU launch the **National Knock-out Cup** for English clubs, Gloucester winning inaugural final at Twickenham against Moseley 17-6. **Try** increased to **4 points**.

1972: in January Bath's **Mike Beese** (although with Liverpool at this time) wins his first cap for England at centre against Wales at Twickenham (England losing 3-12).

1974-5: at Twickenham (December) Bath's **Jim Waterman** wins his **Oxford Blue** playing full-back. Light Blues win a narrow victory. On Boxing Day Bath introduce **floodlights on the Rec** in their win over Clifton, soon followed when hosting the Royal Navy in early January.

1975-6: Bath set a **new club record of 31 wins** in a season (32 if Somerset Cup final incl.).

1976-77 season: RFU now permits **sponsorship** (namely by John Player) in National KO Cup; Bath's home game with Bristol then sponsored by stockbrokers Godfrey, Derby & Co (March 1977), see Ch. 26.

1979-80: Bath set a **new club record of 37 wins** in a season.

1981: at Twickenham (December) Bath's **Derek Wyatt** wins his **Oxford Blue**. **Simon Halliday** and **Tony Brooks**, two fellow Oxford Blues (playing alongside Wyatt) joined Bath one week later. Cambridge won.

1982-3: Bath set a **new club record of 38 wins** in a season. **Barry Trevaskis** sets new club record of **32 tries. 1983:** Dublin (March) Bath wing **David Trick** wins the first of his two England caps (Ireland winning 25-15).

1983-4: in November 1983 Bath flanker **Paul Simpson** wins his first **England cap** in the 15-9 victory against New Zealand at Twickenham. In same season Bath flanker **Jon Hall** wins his first **England cap** against Scotland at Murrayfield (Feb. 1984).

1984: on 28th April Bath win the **John Player Special Knock-out Cup final** for the first time in their history, defeating Bristol by 10-9 at Twickenham. Bath scrum-half **Richard Hill** wins his first **cap on the England** summer tour of South Africa, likewise Bath utility back **John Palmer.**

1984-5: Bath's **Gareth Chilcott** (prop) and **Nigel Redman** (lock) win their first **England caps** against Australia at Twickenham (Nov.1984). Bath fullback **Chris Martin** wins his first **England cap** at Twickenham against France (Feb. 1985).

1985: on 27th April Bath (fielding 9 England internationals) again win the **John Player Special Cup final** for the second successive year, overcoming London Welsh 24-15 at Twickenham.

1986: Bath centre **Simon Halliday** wins his first **England cap** (January 1986) against Wales at Twickenham; **David Sole** wins his first **cap for Scotland** v France in same 5 Nations Home Championship; on 26th April 1986 Bath win a third successive **John Player Special Cup final**, overcoming Wasps 25-17 at Twickenham.

1986-7: **Richard Hill** is appointed **England captain** for the 1986-7 season's Home Championship, Bath's first international captain; **Graham Dawe** (hooker) wins his first **England cap v Ireland** (February 1987); meanwhile Bath win an unprecedented fourth successive **(John Player Special) Cup final**, winning 19-12 at Twickenham against Wasps.

1988: in January 1988 Bath lock **Damian Cronin** wins his first **cap for Scotland** against Ireland, while in April Bath back-row forward **David Egerton** wins his first **England cap** against Ireland in the Dublin Millennium match. Bath's unprecedented run of four successive cup final victories ends with 4-3 quarter-final **defeat at Moseley** (27th February 1988). Flanker **Andy Robinson** wins first **England cap** in victory against Australia at Twickenham (5th November 1988).

1987-8 would see the commencement of a **fully standardised English Rugby Union league** with **the inaugural season of the Courage League.**

1989: in May, **Jeremy Guscott** scores try hat-trick on his **England debut** in victory against Romania in Bucharest. Guscott, Andy Robinson and Gareth Chilcott all selected for **British Lions** on summer tour of Australia. Bath win their first league and cup **Double** by winning the **Courage League** for the first time and the **Pilkington Cup** (previously John Player Special Cup) with their 10-6 win over Leicester at Twickenham.

1990: Bath win the **Pilkington Cup** by defeating Gloucester 48-6 at Twickenham.

1990-1: Bath win the **Courage League**, and complete their season by winning their first

Worthington Bitter National sevens tournament.

1991-2: backs **Jon Webb, Jeremy Guscott, Richard Hill** and forward **Nigel Redman** all selected for England's **World Cup** squad, each playing during the tournament. Bath win **the Double**, winning the **Courage League**, and the **Pilkington Cup** with a 15-12 victory against Harlequins at Twickenham.

1992-3: The **200th game** between Bath and Bristol is won 8-31 by Bath at the Memorial Ground (31st October 1992). Prop **Victor Ubogu** wins first **England cap** in win against Canada (October 1992); in November back-row forward **Ben Clarke** and centre **Phil de Glanville** win first **caps in England's** win against South Africa: in December utility back **Audley Lumsden** wins his **Oxford Blue**. In the Home Championships lock **Andy Reed** wins his first **Scotland cap** in their defeat by England at Twickenham (March 1993). Bath win the **Courage League**. **A try** increased to **5 points**.

1993-4: in November 1993 **Jon Callard** wins his first **England cap** at Twickenham, England winning 15-9 against New Zealand. In December at Twickenham, Bath's **Chris Clark** (prop) and utility back **Ed Rayner** win **Blues for Oxford.** In February 1994 **Steve Ojomoh** wins his first **cap for England** against Ireland. In March 1994 **Mike Catt** wins his first **England cap** against Wales at Twickenham.

By winning the **Courage League** Bath won **the League/Cup Double** for the third time, and the **National knock-out cup for the 8th time** with their 21-9 **Pilkington Cup** victory over Leicester. One week later Bath won the **Middlesex (Save & Prosper) Sevens** at Twickenham for the first time in their history, so winning three Majors in one season.

1994-5: nine Bath players are selected for the **1995 England World Cup** party to South Africa, namely Jon Callard, Mike Catt, Ben Clarke, Graham Dawe, Phil de Glanville, Jeremy Guscott, John Mallett, Steve Ojomoh and Victor Ubogu; prop **John Mallett** winning his first **England cap** against Western Samoa. Bath win the **Pilkington cup**, their **ninth Cup Final** success in 12 years (May 1995).

1995-6: in January 1996 wing **Jon Sleightholme** wins first **England cap** against France in Paris. On 4th May 1996 Bath, having already won the **Courage League**, win their **tenth Cup Final (Pilkington)** and their **fifth Cup and League Double**. Later in May 1996 Rugby League side **Wigan** win 82-6 against Bath under RL rules at Maine Road, Manchester. In late May **Bath** defeat Wigan 44-19 under Union rules at Twickenham, and a century of divide between the two codes ends.

Season **1996-7:** rugby union commences a **newly professionalised** Courage League.

In November 1996 **Ade Adebayo** wins his first **England cap** against Italy at Twickenham. In December 1996 **Nathan Thomas** (flanker) wins first **cap for Wales** against South Africa. In May 1997 **Martin Haag** and **Kevin Yates** win debut caps in England's victory in Argentina.

1997-8: in summer 1997 **Jeremy Guscott** (joined later by **Mike Catt**) played on the

British & Irish Lions tour of S. Africa. In November 1997 Bath's **Matt Perry** (f.back) and **Andy Long** (hooker) make their **debuts for England** v Australia (15-15) at Twickenham. On 31st January 1998 Bath defeat Brive 18-19 at Bordeaux to win the **(Heineken) European Cup**, the first British club to do so. Season 1997-8 would see the **Allied Dunbar Premiership** succeed the Courage League.

The '**Sin-bin**' option was adopted for Allied Dunbar Premiership One and Two from season **1998-9**. Also, in Bath's first league match of 1998-9 de Glanville wore **No 13 shirt,** the first time the club had worn this number since early 1950's. It proved lucky 13, Bath winning 36-27 over Wasps.

1999-2000: having fluctuated between 10 and 14 clubs at the top level since the advent of a standardised league in 1987, the **Premiership** is now set at 12 clubs. **Guscott, Matt Perry and de Glanville** play for England during the Autumn **World Cup** of 1999, England losing to S. Africa in the quarter-finals. In the **inaugural Six Nations** Championship at Twickenham (5th February 2000) **Mike Tyndall** at centre scores try on **debut for England** in 50-18 win against Ireland and **Iain Balshaw** makes **England debut** as sub for Bath fullback Matt Perry in same match.

2000-1: debut for Wales of Bath scrum-half **Gareth Cooper** against Italy in April 2001; later back row forwards **Andy Lloyd** and **Gavin Thomas** both **debut for Wales** on their summer tour to Japan, Lloyd scoring try in Welsh victory. In summer 2001 **Iain Balshaw, Matt Perry, Mike Catt** and Bath new-boy **Danny Grewcock** selected for Lions tour of Australia. Also in summer 2001 Bath backs **Tom Voyce** and **Ollie Barkley** win debut **caps for England** against USA in their Country's tour of North America, Barkley having yet to play a full game in senior club rugby. In Season 2000-1 the **Zurich Premiership** succeeded Allied Dunbar, and **bonus points** introduced to matches.

2002-3: hooker **Jon Humphreys,** already a Welsh cap when arriving at Bath, **captained Wales** against a winning England side in Cardiff (February 2003); scrum-half and Bath club colleague **Gareth Cooper** also playing. On 25th May 2003 Bath play Wasps in the **Parker Pen Challenge Cup final**, losing 48-30 at the Madejski stadium, Reading. Bath wing **Simon Danielli** wins **debut cap for Scotland** v Italy (Aug. 2003) in World Cup warm-up match. In season 2002-3 a **new PLAY- OFF system** was introduced **to decide the Premiership champions.**

2003-4: Kevin Maggs (Ireland), **Simon Danielle** (Scotland) **and Danny Grewcock, Iain Balshaw, Mike Tindall and Mike Catt** (all England) played for their respective Countries in the 2003 Autumn **World Cup** in Australia. Despite top side of the 2003-4 Zurich Premiership regular league table Bath would fall 10-6 to Wasps in the **Play-off final** at Twickenham. Meanwhile **Michael Lipman** and **Matt Stevens** win their **debut caps** on England's 2004 summer tour of Australasia.

2004-5: in March 2005 **Duncan Bell** wins debut **England cap** in the 6 Nations win over Italy at Twickenham. **Danny Grewcock, Matt Stevens** and **Mike Tindall** win selection for the British & Irish Lions tour of New Zealand, although Tindall later withdraws for injury/fitness reasons. At Twickenham (April 2005) Bath lose 20-12 to Leeds Tykes in the **Powergen National Cup final.**

2005-6: in November 2005 **Lee Mears** (hooker) wins **debut cap** in England's win over Manu Samoa at Twickenham. In February 2006 **Gareth Delve** (back-row) wins debut **cap for Wales** against Scotland at Cardiff. Season 2005-6 would see the **Guinness Premiership** succeed the Zurich Premiership, with an **alteration** to the Premiership **play-off format. The RFU National Cup competition** (launched in 1972) was now limited to the 12 Premiership clubs, plus the four regional Welsh sides, in an **Anglo-Welsh Cup competition.** The **European (formerly Parker Pen) Challenge Cup** would next be known (for sponsorship reasons) as **the Amlin Challenge Cup.**

2006-7: In early season Leeds Rhinos and Great Britain centre **Chev Walker** switched codes to join Bath. In post-Christmas league encounter at Ashton Gate (Bristol City FC), Bristol defeat Bath 16-6 and **crowd of 21,203** attend. Bath unable to reach beyond the first Pool stage of the now re-named **EDF Energy Anglo-Welsh Cup**, but reach the final of the **European Challenge Cup**, losing 16-22 to Clermont Auvergne. Against South Africa (summer tour 2007) **Nick Abendanon** wins debut **cap for England**.

2008: The Bath foursome of **Lee Mears, Michael Lipman, Matt Stevens,** and **Steve Borthwick (**who led England against Italy in Rome) all feature for England in the Six Nations of 2008. All four players, plus **Olly Barkley,** selected for the summer England touring side to New Zealand, **Borthwick as captain.** In May Bath win the **2007-8 European Challenge Cup** 24-16 against Worcester Warriors.

In season **2008-9** the **Aviva Premiership** succeeds the Guinness Premiership.

2009-10: **Matt Banahan** wins first **cap for England** in victory against Argentina (in Manchester), June 2009. EDF Energy Cup is **re-named the LV Cup** (Liverpool & Victoria insurance group) owing to sponsorship change.

2010-11: in June 2010 **Shontayne Hape** (ex Kiwi Rugby League international) wins debut **England rugby Union cap** on tour match in Australia. The **National Division One is renamed as the Championship**; but a play-off format included to determine promotion to the Premiership. In April 2010 **Bath** announce move to new headquarters at **Farleigh House** (Farleigh Hungerford) with state of the art training facilities.

2011-12: Bath's season begins less four players picked by England for the **2011 World Cup** held by (and won by) New Zealand: **Lewis Moody** (capt.), **Matt Banahan, Lee Mears** and **Davey Wilson.**

2012-13: in January 2013 Bath out-half **Tom Heathcote** wins **debut cap for Scotland** against Tonga at Murrayfield. In second half of 2012-13 season Saracens commence Premiership rugby on their innovative 'synthetic surface' at their new Allianz Park ground. Bath's **Rob Webber, Davey Wilson, Dave Attwood** and **Kyle Eastmond**

selected for England's 2013 summer tour of Argentina and Uruguay, Eastmond scoring brilliant try on debut in England's win over Argentina.

2014: Bath out-side half **George Ford** wins debut cap for England in post-Christmas Six Nations win over Wales (Twickenham). Bath win the **Premiership 'A League' title** of 2014. In the **2014-15 Autumn internationals** Bath backs **Samesa Rokoduguni,** and also **Anthony Watson** win their **debut caps** against New Zealand at Twickenham (NZ win 21-24). While Bath forwards **Dave Attwood, David Wilson, Henry Thomas, Rob Webber** and **backs Kyle Eastmond, George Ford, Jonathan Joseph and Anthony Watson,** also appear for England at various stages of the Autumn Internationals and the 2015 Six Nations Championship; likewise prop **Paul James for Wales.**

2015: Sam Burgess made his **England Saxons** debut in their 18-9 win over Ireland Wolfhounds in Cork in late January. Meanwhile under head coach **Jon Callard** (former Bath & England) Bath lock **Charlie Ewels** captained England to win **the U-20's Six Nations Championship** with a 24-11 win over France at Brighton's Amex stadium, 12,600 watching. Bath outside-half **Rory Jennings** scored 14 points with 'the boot.'

In Cremona, Italy, Bath's **Charlie Ewels (capt,) Rory Jennings (out-half), Max Clark (centre) and Will Homer (scrum-half)** all play in England's U-20.s **World Championship final** in June against New Zealand, the Kiwis winning 21-16.

Nick Abendanon (recently moved from Bath to Clermont Auvergne) now voted **'European Player of the Year.'**

At conclusion of **2014-2015** regular-season Bath achieve 2nd place and so reach **semi-finals** at home against Leicester, winning 47-10.

30th May 2015 Bath lose 16-28 against Saracens in the **AVIVA Premiership Final** at Twickenham (over 80,000 attendance).

31st July 2015: Bath's appeal at the Royal Courts of Justice had been upheld, the decision 'seemingly' allowing expansion of the Rec and its facilities.

At conclusion of season ***2015-16*** *old friends (and rivals) Bristol) win promotion back to the Premiership.*

August 2015: the following Bath players are chosen for the **England World Cup Squad**: **Rob Webber** (hooker), **David Wilson** (prop), and backs **Anthony Watson, George Ford, Jonathan Joseph** and **Sam Burgess**. Also: **Dominic Day** (lock, **Wales**), **Paul James** (prop, **Wales**), **Alafoti Fa'osiliva** (flanker, **Samoa**), **Francois Louw** (back-row, **S. Africa**), and **Horacio Agulla** (wing, **Argentina**). While **during Bath's 150th Anniversary season of 2015-16 Ollie Devoto** also added to England squad, in 6 Nations), hence twelve Bath players involved in World Cup and/or 6 Nations duty. This was a great honour, but simultaneously proved a 'drain' on player-resources that partly explained the club's final disappointing 9th League position.

Sep 2016: No.8 **Leroy Housten** returns from Australia to cover a Bath injury crisis and in first game against Worcester scores 2 tries in Bath win, then gains **debut cap for Australia v Argentina** prior to a return to Super Rugby as **Bath's first Australian international.** At conclusion of **2016-17 season** Bath's **Taulupe Faletau** (No.8) plus backs Jonathan Joseph and Anthony Watson selected for British & Irish Lions tour to New Zealand. **8th Apr 2017** Bath choose to stage their home match v Leicester **at Twickenham** winning 27-21, 60,000 plus watching.

In **summer 2018** Welsh legend **Jamie Roberts** (centre) joins Bath, joining Stormers come summer 2020. At conclusion of **2017-18 season** flank forward **Zach Mercer** and lock **Elliott Stooke** play for England v Barbarians at Twickenham (non-cap match), and **Mercer** wins first Test cap **(November 2018)** in England's 12-11 win v South Africa. Also, in **November 2018**, Bath wing **Joe Cokanasiga** wins debut cap in England's win v Japan (Twickenham), and scores try.

May 2019: scrum-half **Chris Cooke** selected for England 7s squad for final leg of HSBC World Rugby Sevens Series in Paris. **1st June 2019** at Twickenham Bath's **Beno Obano, Tom Dunn, Elliott Stooke, Tom Ellis** play for England v Barbarians, & **Francois Louw** played for the Barbarians (rslt: England win 51-43).

Aug 2019: Joe Cokanasiga, Ruaridh (Rory) McConnochie, Anthony Watson, Jonathan Joseph, and **Sam Underhill** are selected for England's World Cup squad for the **(20th Sep, to 2nd Nov, 2019)** World Cup in Japan. All make appearances. **6th Sep, 2019: Rory McConnochie** had won first England cap v Italy. **Feb 2020: Will Stuart** (prop) wins first England cap v France (Paris). **31st Oct 2020: Tom Dunn** (hooker) wins first England cap against Italy.

9th Sep 2021 (Bath Chronicle): Kevin & Pat Lawrence awarded the **Stone King Award** by the **Bath Supporters' Club Committee** 'in going the extra mile for fans with Kevin most recently serving as chairman. Award presented by **Tracy Smith,** (head of family/mediation) saying "Kevin and Pat have put in countless hours on behalf of BRSC and it is lovely to see them recognised in this way."

Footnote:

11th Feb. 2021: *The Bath Chronicle reported that former Bath player DAVID EGERTON had passed away at the age of 59 as a result of Covid 19. Winning 7 England caps, a dynamic No.8, and hugely popular, seasons 1988/89 to 1993/1994 rank among his finest. Bath Rugby paid their tribute as follows: "We are all deeply shocked and incredibly sad to learn that club legend, Dave Egerton, has passed away. A wonderful gentleman and talented player, taken from us far too soon. Our thoughts and love go out to his family and friends."*

RUGBY BOOK – BIBLIOGRAPHY

- A Goodly Heritage. A History of Monkton Combe School, by A.F. Lace (printed for Monkton Combe School by Sir Isaac Pitman and Sons Ltd. Bath 1968).
- A History of Clifton College 1860-1934, by O.F. Christie, published by J. W .Arrowsmith, Quay St, Bristol.
- A History of Marlborough College (1843-1893), by A.G. Bradley, A.C. Champneys and J.W. Baines, printed by Hazell, Watson & Viney, Ltd, London and Aylesbury. Later revised and continued by J.R. Taylor, H.C. Brentnall and G.C. Turner (1923); ALSO first surviving Marlborough RFC logbook with report of 'first Marlborough v Clifton College match.'
- American Olympic R.F. Team v Blackheath, April 1924, match programme; USA win rugby football Olympic Gold, Paris, Minnesota Museum of Rugby.
- Barnstaple RFC, archives (see: the Michael Hughes profile of Mike Blackmore, 10 Jan. 2008).
- Bath Central Lending & Reference Library archives of Bath Chronicle (and related journals), The Podium, Northgate Street, Bath, BA1 5AN.
- Bath Chronicle (The) *incorporated with Bath Weekly Argus*, and sister papers Bath & Wilts Chronicle (& Herald), Bath Weekly Chronicle, Bath Football Herald: with reports from (inter alia) 'Football Talk,' 'Play up' and "The Mascot."
- Bath Football Club 1865-1965, Centenary booklet (printed by The Mendip Press Ltd), Bath.
- Bath Football club (R.F.U.), official Year Book Season 1993-1994 (Triple Triumph). Published and edited by Ken Johnstone; produced and printed by Francomb Printers Ltd.
- Bath RFC Minutes – Club committee meetings (1944-5, 1945-6).
- Bath RFC Past Players archives; archivist Geoff Pillinger.
- Bath Records Office (The), The Guildhall, Bath; for details of (inter alia): Bath College Register 1878-1908 (Richard Clay & Sons, Bread Street Hill, London and Bungay, Suffolk).
- Bath RFC club archives/records (various).
- Bath Competitive College & Hermitage School records.
- Bedford School magazine 'The Ousel' (1896-1904), Ref: J.G.Milton.
- Bristol RFC archives; Mark Hoskins (archivist).
- Boys Own (The), 1907-8 edition.
- Bystander (The) 15 February 1928.
- Cardiff Rugby Club, history and statistics 1876-1975, by D.E. Davies.
- Cheltenham College (archives).
- Clifton College (archives), and Sri Lanka 2004, Rugby & Netball tour (magazine).

- Complete who's who of England Rugby Union Internationals (The); Raymond Maule, Breedon Books Sport. I   SBN: 1-873626.10X.
- Daily Mail (The), article by Robert Lacey (King George V), 29 July 2004.
- Edinburgh Academy (archives).
- Edinburgh Academicals Football Club Centenary History (The), printed by Pillans and Wilson   Ltd, Edinburgh and Glasgow.
- Eton College (archives).
- For College, Club and Country' (A History of Clifton Rugby Football Club), by Patrick Casey & Richard I. Hale, MX Publishing Ltd, 335 Princes Park Manor, Royal Drive, London N11 3GX.
- Georgian Summer, by David Gadd, Moonraker Press, 26 St. Margarets street, Bradford-on-Avon, Wiltshire. SBN. 239.00167.2
- Gladiators of a Roman City, by Harry W. Barstow.
- Keene's Bath Journal. `
- Guys, King's & St. Thomas' Hospitals RFC, 'a brief history.'
- History of Kingswood School (The), by Three Old Boys (Charles H. Kelly, 2, Castle st., City Rd   and 26 Paternoster Row, E.C. 1898.
- Kingswood School, Bath, archives.
- Langholm RFC, 1871- 1971 (Centenary book).
- Marlborough College (archives).
- Match programmes of: Bath, Bristol, Gloucester, Leicester, & (various).
- Matthew Bloxam's Letter, "The Meteor," Rugby at Bigside/William Webb Ellis.".
- 'Men of a Stout Countenance' (autobiography of R.A. Gerrard, by D. Crichton-Miller) – dp publications, Abertillery, Gwent, UK.
- Merchiston Castle School, see 'The Merchiston Register.'
- Minnesota Museum of rugby, USA.
- Monktonian (The), first issue, Lent term 1879, 1897-1904, and Monkton Combe School (archives).
- Official England Rugby Miscellany (The), by Stuart Farmer, Vision Sports Publishing, 2 Coombe Gardens, London, SW20 0QU.
- One Hundred Years at Raeburn Place 1854-1954 (A short history of the Edinburgh Academy's playing field), printed by T. and A. Constable Ltd., Hopetoun Street, Printers to the
- University of Edinburgh.
- One hundred years of Scarlet (Llanelli RFC history).
- Picture Post (magazine), 7 December 1946, 'the life of a rugby club,'
- Rugby Football at Cheltenham College 1844-1944; by E.Scott Skirving, 1945; (Cheltenham, Darters bookshop).
- Rugby School (archives).

- RULES of the Wiveliscombe (Rugby) Football Club, 1872.
- Seventy years of Somerset rugby 1875 – 1945 (HY. Bryant & Sons, printers, High Street, Wellington, Somerset).
- Sunday Times Magazine 7 January 1996; Will's tough ruck, Stephen Jones,
- Torquay Athletic RFC archives.
- Torquay press, 'Football Herald' (of Herald Express), see match report: Torquay v Bath (20th March 1937).
- Triple Triumph, Official Year Book, season 1993/4; produced and printed by Francomb Printers Ltd, England.
- Walcot Old Boys Centenary 1882-1982, ISBN 0950959206 (WOB 100 MFG 1983).
- World Rugby Museum, Twickenham: www.rfu.com/museum (Tel:020 8892 88

Bath Football Club 1st XV Records

Season	Played	Won	Lost	Drawn	Points For	Points Against
1895-1896	33	11	14	8	180	207
1896-1897	35	20	12	3	235	233
1897-1898	36	13	19	4	186	268
1898-1899	34	16	15	3	177	163
1899-1900	29	12	14	3	127	201
1900-1901	33	17	15	1	235	179
1901-1902	30	8	17	5	147	260
1902-1903	33	15	16	2	209	211
1903-1904	31	9	19	3	158	258
1904-1905	39	21	15	3	401	285
1905-1906	33	7	24	2	151	210
1906-1907	29	12	15	2	150	199
1907-1908	32	9	20	3	196	319
1908-1909	35	18	15	2	312	216
1909-1910	36	15	12	9	237	198
1910-1911	35	16	16	3	264	203
1911-1912	32	20	11	1	332	263
1912-1913	34	21	12	1	376	195
1913-1914	35	22	12	1	334	228
1914-1918				War Years		
1918-1919	11	6	5	0	111	64
1919-1920	39	20	15	4	458	273
1920-1921	38	21	14	3	462	220
1921-1922	40	25	9	6	413	157
1922-1923	45	26	16	3	380	233
1923-1924	40	18	18	4	310	283
1924-1925	37	22	13	2	389	321
1925-1926	35	7	27	1	167	246
1926-1927	35	21	13	1	330	296
1927-1928	39	22	14	3	325	309
1928-1929	41	17	22	2	396	359
1929-1930	37	19	15	3	388	265
1930-1931	37	22	12	3	452	250
1931-1932	38	25	12	1	418	280
1932-1933	38	24	13	1	356	247
1933-1934	36	20	16	0	330	353
1934-1935	40	20	19	1	330	302
1935-1936	34	13	18	3	239	288
1936-1937	34	18	13	3	314	242
1937-1938	34	13	20	1	173	312
1938-1939	35	9	20	6	161	315
1939-1945				War Years		
1945-1946	36	16	19	1	367	423
1946-1947	32	18	10	4	274	20
1947-1948	37	15	20	2	274	278
1948-1949	40	19	16	5	346	326
1949-1950	39	15	21	3	267	355
1950-1951	41	27	10	4	324	277
1951-1952	39	21	15	3	314	249

Bath Football Club 1st XV Records

Season	Played	Won	Lost	Drawn	Points For	Points Against
1952-1953	40	19	15	6	359	291
1953-1954	40	20	16	4	331	293
1954-1955	42	25	15	2	403	296
1955-1956	38	17	18	3	289	334
1956-1957	39	15	19	5	315	320
1957-1958	42	11	27	4	282	371
1958-1959	39	12	19	8	290	398
1959-1960	41	16	20	5	364	364
1960-1961	44	21	21	2	418	437
1961-1962	43	20	20	3	470	409
1962-1963	39	14	24	1	324	409
1963-1964	45	20	22	3	342	377
1964-1965	46	15	28	3	563	688
1965-1966	48	19	28	1	479	483
1966-1967	48	27	20	1	628	466
1967-1968	43	24	14	5	540	368
1968-1969	44	24	17	3	645	521
1969-1970	43	29	13	1	710	480
1970-1971	41	26	13	2	660	478
1971-1972	50	23	27	0	745	817
1972-1973	49	24	23	2	875	723
1973-1974	55	26	28	1	823	693
1974-1975	46	28	17	1	619	539
1975-1976	50	31	18	1	850	634
1976-1977	46	26	18	2	749	659
1977-1978	49	28	20	1	984	754
1978-1979	44	31	10	3	853	440
1979-1980	48	37	10	1	962	557
1980-1981	50	30	18	2	819	549
1981-1982	49	29	19	1	801	719
1982-1983	50	38	9	3	1278	555
1983-1984	39	29	10	0	870	468
1984-1985	39	30	8	1	923	400
1985-1986	43	33	7	3	1055	507
1986-1987	44	36	7	1	1167	519
1987-1988	44	28	12	4	1098	549
1988-1989	44	36	6	2	1262	521
1989-1990	41	35	5	1	1166	379
1990-1991	34	29	4	1	984	392
1991-1992	33	28	4	1	774	363
1992-1993	32	27	5	0	1112	321
1993-1994	37	30	7	0	891	499
1994-1995	34	25	5	4	839	474
1995-1996	34	26	7	1	1005	562

PRESIDENTS: The known role of Honour:

1882 - 1883	Maj. Gen. C. Fitzroy Mundy		
1883 - 1884	R. B. Bagnall-Wild	1973 - 1975	G.S. Brown
1884- 1885		1975 - 1977	H.L. Bradford
1885 - 1886	Col. Chandler	1977 - 1979	C.H.G. Beazer
1886 - 1888		1979 - 1981	W.J.F Arnold
1888 - 1898	Sir Robert Blaine	1981 - 1983	G.S. Brown
1900 - 1926	Captain F.W. Forester	1983 - 1985	H.J.F Simpkins
1926 - 1927	A. J. Stuart Gould	1985 - 1987	J.W.P. Roberts
1927 - 1938	J. H. Colmer	1987 - 1989	N.P. Halse
1938 - 1946	Dr R. Scott Reid	1989 - 1991	A.O. Lewis
1946 - 1950	Captain S.L. Amor OBE	1991 - 1993	L.A. Hughes
1950 - 1952	A. Ridley OBE	1993 - 1995	G.W. Hancock
1952 - 1954	Sir James Pitman	1995 - 1997	B. Perry
1954 - 1956	Major L. D. Wardle	1997 - 1999	A.J. Meek
1956 - 1958	B. C. Barber	1999 - 2001	R. A. Berry
1958 - 1960	Dr R. Scott Reid	2001 - 2003	P.G. Hall
1960 - 1962	W.S. Bascombe	2003 - 2005	J. Barber
1962 - 1964	C.H.G Beazer	2005 - 2007	P. Bliss
1964 - 1966	B.C .Barber	2007 - 2009	J Rowell
1966 - 1967	H. J. Crane	2009 - 2011	A Gay
1967 - 1969	J.F. Bevan-Jones	2011 - 2013	D Trick
1969 - 1971	D.M. Smith	2013 - 2015	M. C. Beese
1971 - 1973	Mrs Molly Gerrard	2015 – 2019	D. Trick
		2019 – 2020	J. Hall

Captains 1st XV

1874-1876	H. G. Fuller	1947-1948	T.W. Hicks
1877-1878	J. Petgrave	1948-1949	A.W. Todd
1881-1882	E. Digby	1949-1950	L.S. Harter
1882-1883	H.S. Jacobs	1950-1952	A.O. Lewis
1883-1884	A.K. Cunninghame	1952-1955	J.W.P. Roberts
1887-1890	W.A. Walker	1955-1956	J.McG. Kendall Carpenter
1890-1898	F. Soane	1956-1958	J.W.P. Roberts
1898-1899	F. Derrick	1958-1959	G.F. Drewett
1899-1900	Norman Biggs	1959-1960	J. Jacobson
1900-1902	G. Ruddick	1960-1961	A.H. Meek
1902-1903	F. J. Cashnella	1961-1962	R. Farnham
1903-1906	T.B. Timmins	1962-1963	L.I. Rimmer
1906-1907	R. Meister	1963-1965	K.P. Andrews
1907-1908	T. West	1965-1966	G.F. Margretts
1908-1910	A. Ford	1966-1969	P,Sibley
1910-1911	A. Hatherill	1969-1970	T.Martland/P. Heindorff
1911-1913	Norman Coates	1970-1971	P.Heindorff
1913-1915	P.P. Hope	1971-1972	R. Walkey
	WAR YEARS	1972-1974	Phil Hall
1918-1922	P.P. Hope	1974-1975	Chris Perry
1922-1924	H. Vowles	1975-1976	J. Waterman
1924-1925	S.G.U. Considine	1976-1977	J. Horton
1925-1927	W.J. Gibbs	1977-1978	J. Waterman
1927-1928	I.J. Pitman	1978-1979	M.Beese
1928-1929	W.H. Sheppard	1979-1980	J. Horton
1929-1931	I.J.M. Spence	1980-1981	R. Lye
1931-1933	M.V. Shaw	1981-1982	Damien Murphy/R. Spurrell
1933-1934	B.C. Barber	1982-1985	R. Spurrell
1934-1936	R.A. Gerrard	1985-1986	J. Palmer
1936-1937	N.W. Matthews	1986-1988	Richard Hill
1937-1938	R.A. Gerrard	1988-1991	S. Barnes
1938-1939	K.J. Foss	1091-1993	Andy Robinson
	WAR YEARS	1993-1995	Jon Hall
1945-1946	A. Higgins	1995-1996	P. de Glanville
1946-1947	I.J.M. Lumsden		

Captains 1st XV since Club turned Professional

1996-1997	Philip de Glanville
1997-1998	Andy Nicol
1998-1999	Richard Webster
1999-2000	Jon Callard
2000-2001	Ben Clarke
2001-2002	Dan Lyle
2002-2004	Danny Grewcock
2004-2005	Jon Humphreys
2005-2008	Steve Borthwick
2008-2009	Michael Lipman
2009-2010	Michael Claassens
2910-2011	Luke Watson
2011-2012	Stuart Hooper
212-2013	Stuart Hooper
2013-2014	Stuart Hooper
2014-2015	Stuart Hooper
2015-2016	Stuart Hooper
2016-2017	Guy Mercer, *(joint captains George Ford/Matt Garvey, injury cover)*
2017-2018	Matt Garvey
2018-2019	Matt Garvey
2019-2020	Charlie Ewels

1913-1914 Features:- Early Season Ruminations - Tedium of Railway Travel - Functions of a Trainer - Dangers of Rugby - Northern Union - Association Jealousy - v Llanelly - Spirit of the Game - Review.

Date	Opponents	Venue	Result	For	Against
13/9/1913	Leicester	A	L	5	19
20/9	Penylan	H	W	18	5
27/9	Bridgwater	H	W	29	3
4/10	Exeter	H	W	9	0
11/10	Devonport Albion	A	L	6	15
18/10	Bristol	A	L	0	5
25/10	Bridgwater	A	L	0	6
1/11	Wellington	H	W	33	0
8/11	Llanelly	A	L	8	15
22/11	Abertillery	H	W	10	5
29/11	Gloucester	A	L	0	19
6/12	Pontypool	A	L	0	11
13/12	Machen	H	W	15	7
20/12	Cheltenham	H	W	6	3
26/12	Crumlin	H	W	3	0
27/12	Penylan	H	W	6	3
3/1/1914	Clifton	H	W	16	3
10/1	Old Edwardians	A	W	11	6
17/1	Gloucester Regiment	H	W	22	13
31/1	Bristol	H	W	9	0
7/2	Penylan	H	W	6	3
14/2	Pontypool	H	L	0	5
21/2	Penarth	H	W	9	8
28/2	Coventry	A	L	3	14
5/3	Middlesex Hospital	H	W	9	3
7/3	Clifton	A	W	15	0
14/3	Devonport Albion	H	D	3	3
21/3	Exeter	A	L	6	9
28/3	Llanelly	H	W	5	0
4/4	Bridgwater Albion	H	W	6	3
11/4	Cheltenham	A	W	8	3
13/4	Coventry	H	W	41	10
14/4	Leicester	H	W	14	3
18/4	Gloucester	H	L	3	10
25/4	Penarth	A	L	0	16
				334	228
	Played 35 Won 22 Lost 12				
	Drawn 1				
	P.P.Hope (Capt)				

1922-1923 Features:- Rugger Night - County rift - Ground improvements - Supporters' Programme - Stoop's tips - Church Service - Lucky Programme - Down a Mine - A Bit of a Do - Makeshift side - County Champs - Honorarium.

Date	Opponents	Venue	Result	For	Against
2/9/1922	LEICESTER	A	L	8	16
9/9	NEWTON ABBOT	H	W	15	6
10/9	GLOUCESTER	A	L	5	17
23/9	UNITED SERVICES	H	W	9	4
30/9	PLYMOUTH ALBION	A	L	0	3
2/10	CAMBORNE	A	W	18	0
7/10	ABERAVON	H	W	18	0
11/10	BLUNDELL'S SCHOOL	A	W	17	0
14/10	MOSELEY	A	W	19	3
21/10	EXMOUTH	H	W	14	3
28/10	BRIDGWATER	A	L	0	3
4/11	STROUD	H	W	10	3
11/11	LLANELLY	A	L	9	10
18/11	LONDON WELSH	H	W	20	0
25/11	OLD EDWARDIANS	H	W	8	0
2/12	CROSS KEYS	H	W	4	3
9/12	LONDON WELSH	A	W	7	0
16/12	EXMOUTH	A	L	8	11
23/12	OLD BLUES	H	W	6	3
26/12	MOUNTAIN ASH	H	D	0	0
27/12	GLOUCESTER	H	W	9	6
30/12	PLYMOUTH ALBION	H	W	13	0
6/1/1923	STROUD	A	W	22	0
11/1	CLIFTON	A	L	3	9
13/1	DEVONPORT SERVICES	H	W	5	4
20/1	BRISTOL	H	L	8	10
27/1	MOUNTAIN ASH	A	L	3	13
3/2	BRIDGWATER	H	D	3	3
10/2	NEWPORT	H	L	0	4
17/2	BRISTOL	A	L	0	11
24/2	R.A.F.	H	W	6	0
28/2	OXFORD UNIVERSITY	A	W	9	0
3/3	NEWTON ABBOT	A	D	3	3
10/3	PONTYPOOL	H	W	4	0
15/3	BRISTOL UNIVERSITY	H	W	12	0
17/3	LLANELLY	H	L	3	7
19/3	ABERAVON	A	L	3	26
24/3	CROSSKEYS	A	L	3	19
31/3	ST. THOMAS HOSPITAL	H	W	22	0
2/4	PONTYMINSTER	H	W	13	0
4/4	LEICESTER	H	W	17	3
7/4	BLACKHEATH	H	W	13	10
11/4	BRISTOL	A	L	0	3
14/4	MOSELEY	H	W	8	0
21/4	PONTYPOOL	A	L	3	17
	Played 45 Won 26 Lost 16 Drawn 3			380	233
	H. Vowles (Captain)				

AGM 19/6/1922
T J Gandy and J T Piper elected as Life Members.
Proposed - that the Bath Football Club affiliate with Somerset County Rugby Union.
Amendment that it was not desirable. After much discussion the original motion was not carried and meeting agreed to hold another General Meeting to discuss affiliation and draw up rules.

1931-32 Features:- New Jerseys - New Law - Physical Training - Hot exchanges v Bridgend - Agreed Bath City on Rec 5/5/1931 - "Springbok" - Gerrard - Cashnella - A wonderful Day - v Leicester - F Soane Dcd.

Date	Opponents	Venue	Result	For	Against
5/9/1931	LEICESTER	A	L	0	6
12/9	SWANSEA	H	L	5	8
19/9	UNITED SERVICES	A	W	10	3
24/9	CLIFTON	A	W	21	5
3/10	ST. BARTS HOSPITAL	H	W	18	8
10/10	BRIDGEND	H	W	16	15
17/10	BRISTOL	A	W	13	11
24/10	LONDON WELSH	H	W	9	8
31/10	HARLEQUINS	A	L	0	19
7/11	OLD PAULINES	H	W	32	3
14/11	NEATH	H	L	3	4
21/11	LLANELLY	A	L	0	16
28/11	EXETER	H	W	10	3
12/12	RICHMOND	H	W	13	6
19/12	ST. MARY'S HOSPITAL	H	L	14	16
26/12	OLD BLUES	H	W	15	11
28/12	PONTYPOOL	H	W	5	3
2/1/1932	DEVONPORT SERVICES	H	W	16	0
9/1	NEATH	A	L	3	6
16/1	GLOUCESTER	A	L	3	8
23/1	CAMBORNE	H	W	14	0
30/1	PLYMOUTH ALBION	A	L	0	15
6/2	LLANELLY	H	W	5	3
13/2	LONDON WELSH	A	W	21	7
20/2	NORTHAMPTON	A	W	18	5
27/2	EXETER	A	D	6	6
5/3	BRISTOL	H	W	11	6
10/3	NEWPORT	A	L	0	16
12/3	PLYMOUTH ALBION	H	W	14	3
19/3	DEVONPORT SERVICES	A	W	16	8
26/3	NORTHAMPTON	H	W	14	6
28/3	OLD MERCHANT TAYLORS	H	W	9	3
29/3	LEICESTER	H	W	11	9
2/4	UNITED SERVICES	H	W	29	16
9/4	CAMBORNE	A	L	8	9
11/4	NEWTON ABBOT	A	L	0	6
16/4	LONDON IRISH	H	W	28	0
19/4	GLOUCESTER	H	W	8	3
	Played 38 Won 25 Lost 12 Drawn 1			**418**	**280**
	M V Shaw (Captain)				

1944-1945

Date	Opponents	Venue	Result	For	Against
7/10/44	R.A.F.	H	W	16	0
14/10 *	R.A.A.F.	H	L	5	24
21/10	BRISTOL	H	L	3	8
28/10	B.A.C.	H	W	8	0
4/11	R.A.F.	H	D	5	5
11/11 **	R.N.A.S.	H	W	20	0
25/11	PARACHUTE REGIMENT	H	L	6	8
2/12	R.A.F. LYNHAM	H	W	29	3
9/12 #	BRIDGWATER	A	L	16	6
16/12	ROTOL	H	W	9	8
23/12	CARDIFF	A	L	3	12
13/1/45	R.A.F. XV	H	W	38	0
20/1	R.A.F. XV	H	W	37	3
3/2	ST. MARY'S HOSPITAL	H	W	15	13
10/2	R.A.F. COLERNE	H	W	20	0
17/2	CARDIFF	H	L	0	13
24/2	OXFORD UNIVERSITY GREYHOUNDS	H	W	16	3
3/3	R.A.F. ST. ATHAN	H	W	6	3
10/3	R.A.F. MELKSHAM	H	W	33	0
17/3	BRIDGWATER	H	W	10	0
24/3	BRISTOL	A	L	6	9
31/3 +	NUNEATON	H	L	0	3
2/4 ***	LEICESTER BARBARIANS	H	W	5	3
				306	124
	Played 23 Won 15 Lost 7 Drawn 1				
	Flt. Lieut. D D Evans (Capt.)				

*Best team of the War at the Rec.

"Bath entertained to dinner afterwards. A rare courtesy in these austerity days."

** Royal Naval Air Service – side never had 15 men on field at any time!

+ Peter Brown (Pre war Bath hooker) home on leave from Middle East – left the field with a cut eye and went to surgery of Club President – Dr. Scott Reid for 4 stitches. He did not return to the field. In later life, P H Brown was to undertake intensive research, write and produce the 1865-1965 Club booklet.

***2000 spectators.

July 1945 Lance-Corporal L. Phillips reported missing in Normandy.

1966-67 Features:- Bill Carling - Players arranging own games - Jeremy Spencer - Centenary Book - The Sibley Touch - Two Sets of Brothers - A Ripping Time.

Date	Opponents	Venue	Result	For	Against
1/9/1966	ZUMMERZET BABAAS	H	W	25	8
3/9	LLANELLI	A	L	0	14
5/9	BROUGHTON PARK	H	L	3	6
10/9	LEICESTER	A	W	14	8
15/9	WESTON-SUPER-MARE	H	W	13	6
17/9	EBBW VALE	A	L	8	24
22/9	CLIFTON	A	W	19	3
24/9	ST. MARY'S HOSPITAL	H	W	15	13
29/9	BRIDGWATER	A	W	21	6
1/10	ABERAVON	H	L	11	18
8/10	NEWBRIDGE	A	D	16	16
15/10	BRISTOL	A	L	3	6
22/10	DEVONPORT SERVICES	H	W	24	8
29/10	BRIDGEND	A	L	0	21
5/11	NEATH	H	L	5	19
12/11	SARACENS	H	W	6	0
19/11	PONTYPOOL	A	W	3	0
26/11	UNITED SERVICES	H	W	14	0
3/12	LONDON SCOTTISH	A	L	9	10
10/12	GLOUCESTER	H	L	11	16
17/12	LONDON IRISH	H	W	14	6
24/12	RUGBY	H	W	17	6
26/12	OLD BLUES	H	W	30	3
31/12	NORTHAMPTON	A	L	6	11
14/1	LONDON WELSH	H	L	13	20
19/1	R.A.F.	H	W	6	5
21/1	METROPOLITAN POLICE	H	L	18	21
28/1	ST. MARY'S HOSPITAL	A	W	20	0
4/2	ROSSLYN PARK	A	W	8	6
11/2	GLOUCESTER	A	W	19	14
18/2	CHELTENHAM	A	W	9	6
25/2	WASPS	H	L	0	3
1/3	LEICESTER	A	L	3	11
4/3	BRISTOL	H	L	6	24
18/3	MOSELEY	A	L	9	19
23/3	HARLEQUINS	H	L	5	13
25/3	LIVERPOOL	H	W	11	6
27/3	OLD MERCHANT TAYLORS	H	W	25	0
28/3	SHEFFIELD	H	W	14	9
¼	SALE	A	W	16	3
4/4	LLANELLI	H	W	11	3
6/4	STROUD	H	W	24	3
8/4	EXETER	H	W	14	3
11/4	WESTON-SUPER-MARE	A	W	11	5
14/4	COMBINED SERVICES XV	A	W	52	3
15/4	WEST GERMANY	A	L	5	9
16/4	VICTORIA CL.	A	W	9	3
22/4	COVENTRY	A	L	3	32
27/4	TAUNTON	H	W	24	8
29/4	BEDFORD	A	L	6	9
	Played 50 Won 29 Lost 20 Drawn 1			**628**	**466**
	P Sibley (Captain) P.R Hall (Vice Captain)				

LAWS:- International Board proposed standard numbering of players.

1979-80 Features:- v Pontypool - California Tour -v Moseley - 'Tricky' -A Faultless Bastion – van der Loos - President's Room - v Quins - What a Shocker! - Exit Cup - Horton's Silky Skills - Trick at his Best - SW Sevens - Kendall-Carpenter honoured - Burgeoning talent.

Date	Opponents	Venue	Result	For	Against
1/9/1979	PONTYPOOL	H	W	16	9
5/9	NEWPORT	A	W	6	3
8/9	LEICESTER	A	W	10	9
15/9	MOSELEY	H	W	22	11
18/9	SEAHAWKS (SAN JOSE, CALIFORNIA)	H	W	58	0
22/9	LLANELLI	A	L	6	14
25/9	CLIFTON	A	W	33	13
29/9	NEATH	H	D	22	22
3/10	SOUTH WALES POLICE	A	W	13	4
5/10	ABERAVON	A	L	15	17
20/10	BRISTOL	H	W	38	17
27/10	ST. MARY'S HOSPITAL	A	W	28	6
31/10	CHELTENHAM	A	W	16	9
3/11	HARLEQUINS	A	W	41	17
10/11	NEWBRIDGE	H	W	21	16
17/11	COVENTRY	A	W	3	0
24/11	UNITED SERVICES (PORTSMOUTH)	A	W	29	12
1/12	LONDON SCOTTISH	H	W	36	7
10/12	GLOUCESTER	A	L	3	10
15/12	HARLEQUINS	H	W	27	10
22/12	PLYMOUTH ALBION	H	W	16	12
26/12	CLIFTON	H	W	15	4
1/1/1980	CARDIFF	A	L	4	16
5/1	LEICESTER	H	L	12	22
9/1	ROYAL NAVY	H	W	22	10
12/1	LONDON WELSH	A	L	7	37
19/1	METROPOLITAN POLICE	A	W	20	12
26/1	MARLOW	H	W	30	6
½	ROSSLYN PARK	H	L	9	10
6/2	R.A.F.	H	W	21	0
9/2	CHELTENHAM (On Civil Service Ground)	H	W	25	10
15/2	BRIDGEND	H	W	22	10
23/2	LIVERPOOL (2nd Round John Player Cup)	A	W	19	12
28/2	EXETER UNIVERSITY	H	W	27	0
8/3	LONDON IRISH (Quarter Final of John Player Cup)	H	L	3	6
14/3	NUNEATON	A	W	6	3
17/3	EBBW VALE	H	W	24	6
22/3	RICHMOND	A	W	27	15
26/3	GLOUCESTER	H	W	24	9
29/3	EXETER	A	W	19	4
¾	GLAMORGAN WANDERERS	H	W	28	15
5/4	BRISTOL	A	L	6	44
7/4	WILMSLOW	H	W	46	7
12/4	BIRKENHEAD PARK	A	W	22	3
16/4	NEWPORT	H	W	17	7
19/4	LLANELLI	H	W	13	6
26/4	BEDFORD	H	W	22	16
30/4	PONTYPRIDD	A	L	3	49
	Played 48 Won 37 Lost 10 Drawn 1			**962**	**557**
	J P Horton (Captain)				

MANCOM 19/7/1979
John Horton endorsed the acceptance of Roger Spurrell as a playing member of the Club.

1982-83

Date	Opponents	Venue	Result	For	Against
1/9/1982	CHELTENHAM	H	W	38	11
4/9	PONTYPOOL	A	L	16	37
11/9	LEICESTER	H	W	24	15
18/9	MOSELEY	A	L	11	13
22/9	NEWPORT	A	W	12	3
25/9	LLANELLI	A	L	10	15
29/9	HAVANT	H	W	21	9
2/10	ABERAVON	H	W	17	16
6/10	WYVERN 1st Round of Somerset K.O. Cup	A	W	76	3
9/10	LIVERPOOL	A	L	4	12
16/10	BRISTOL	A	L	4	6
23/10	UNITED SERVICES	A	L	16	18
30/10	NEATH	A	L	21	22
3/11	Bath XV v MARLOW (Not in statistics 16-10)	H	W		
6/11	HARLEQUINS	A	W	21	7
10/11	CLIFTON	A	W	20	6
15/11	NEWBRIDGE	H	L	3	12
20/11	COVENTRY	H	W	19	15
1/12	SOUTH WALES POLICE	H	W	28	0
4/12	LONDON SCOTTISH	A	W	21	9
11/12	GLOUCESTER	H	W	21	12
12/12	FROME Somerset Cup	H	W	46	6
18/12	HARLEQUINS	H	D	13	13
27/12	CLIFTON	H	W	53	4
1/1/1983	LEICESTER	A	L	9	21
8/1	LONDON WELSH	H	W	16	11
15/1	METROPOLITAN POLICE	A	W	34	15
19/1	ROYAL NAVY	H	W	27	13
22/1	EXETER	H	W	74	3
29/1	NORTHAMPTON	A	W	19	16
2/2	R.A.F.	H	W	43	4
5/2	ROSSLYN PARK	H	W	35	12
9/2	WESTON-S-MARE (Quarter Final Somerset Cup)	H	W	43	7
12/2	GLOUCESTER	A	D	7	7
26/2	FYLDE	H	W	31	12
2/3	CHELTENHAM	A	W	31	9
5/3	GORDANO (Semi Final Somerset Cup)	A	W	10	6
7/3	PONTYPRIDD	H	W	19	6
12/3	SWANSEA	H	W	30	14
15/3	EBBW VALE	A	W	7	3
23/3	EXETER UNIVERSITY	H	D	6	6
26/3	RICHMOND	H	W	32	18
2/4	BRISTOL	H	W	21	16
4/4	NEW BRIGHTON	H	W	53	10
9/4	NEWPORT	H	W	13	7
12/4	PLYMOUTH	A	W	30	3
16/4	LLANELLI	H	W	31	28
20/4	MAESTEG	H	W	45	10
23/4	CARDIFF	H	W	28	9
27/4	OLD REDCLIFFIANS **Somerset K.O. Cup Final**	W-SM	W	39	10
30/4	BEDFORD	A	W	30	15
	Played 50 Won 38 Lost 9 Drawn 3 R Spurrell Captain)			1278	555

ABOUT the AUTHOR:

Harry W. Barstow first witnessed the extraordinary landscape of Bath one Spring evening in the late 1960's. It was love at first sight. Shortly afterwards he joined Bath and was soon aware that the city and Bath RFC (later Bath Rugby) are almost one and the same thing.

A winger, he played County rugby for Hampshire, also for the Army against the Royal Navy and the RAF at Twickenham and played near twenty games in a first team shirt for Bath during the late 1960's and early 1970's. In the late 1970's he played in Germany for Hannover (Victoria). Rugby has always been a special part of his life, its friendship, its culture, its uniqueness.

Following a career in the Army (Infantry), later followed by Teacher Training at St. Luke's College, Exeter, he later read Law at the University of the West of England. Teaching Law (mainly at the City of Bath College of Further Education) would then follow.

A former Hon. Historian of the club in the late pre-Professional era, 'Bath the Enigma,' (now with this 2nd edition), has been for the author a labour of love, both for the club, its wonderful supporters and its unique parent city.

Milton Keynes UK
Ingram Content Group UK Ltd.
UKHW031825071223
433949UK00010B/213

9 781787 059382